1998

Pocket Planner
& Ephemeris

Printed in the United States of America
Typography property of Llewellyn Worldwide, Ltd.

ISBN: 1-56718-936-9

**Cover design and illustration by Anne Marie Garrison
Designed by Susan Van Sant
Edited by Roxanna Rejali**

A special thanks to Leslie Nielsen for astrological proofreading.

Set in Eastern and Pacific Standard Times. Ephemeris and aspect data generated
by Matrix Software, Big Rapids, Michigan 49307. Re-use is prohibited.

Published by
LLEWELLYN PUBLICATIONS
P.O. Box 64383 Dept. 936-9
St. Paul, MN 55164-0383, U.S.A.

Table of Contents

Mercury Retrograde

DATE	EST	PST		DATE	EST	PST
Mercury Retrograde 3/27	2:37 pm	11:37 am	—	Mercury Direct 4/20	2:28 am	4/19 11:28 pm
Mercury Retrograde 7/30	9:23 pm	6:23 pm	—	Mercury Direct 8/23	5:30 pm	2:30 pm
Mercury Retrograde 11/21	6:40 am	3:40 am	—	Mercury Direct 12/11	1:24 am	12/10 10:24 pm

Moon Void-of-Course

Times are listed in Eastern Standard Time in this table only. All other information in the *Pocket Planner* is listed in both Eastern Standard Time and Pacific Standard Time. Refer to "Time Zone Conversions" on page 11 for changing to other time zones.

Last Aspect		Moon Enters New Sign			Last Aspect		Moon Enters New Sign			Last Aspect		Moon Enters New Sign		
Date	Time	Date	Sign	Time	Date	Time	Date	Sign	Time	Date	Time	Date	Sign	Time
JANUARY					**FEBRUARY**					**MARCH**				
1	4:08 pm	2	♓	4:56 am	2	3:46 pm	2	♉	4:25 pm	1	8:57 pm	2	♉	12:01 am
4	6:09 am	4	♈	7:44 am	4	12:08 am	4	♊	8:09 pm	4	1:45 am	4	♊	2:15 am
6	9:25 am	6	♉	10:53 am	6	2:58 am	7	♋	1:58 am	6	12:09 am	6	♋	7:27 am
8	1:22 pm	8	♊	2:42 pm	8	12:28 pm	9	♌	9:57 am	7	6:33 pm	8	♌	3:46 pm
10	3:45 pm	10	♋	7:43 pm	11	5:23 am	11	♍	8:10 pm	10	5:06 am	11	♍	2:36 am
13	1:37 am	13	♌	2:45 am	13	11:21 am	14	♎	8:18 am	12	11:35 pm	13	♎	2:59 pm
15	3:23 am	15	♍	12:31 pm	16	5:15 pm	16	♏	9:14 pm	15	7:04 am	16	♏	3:51 am
17	11:54 pm	18	♎	12:45 am	19	5:26 am	19	♐	8:56 am	18	11:45 am	18	♐	3:56 pm
20	12:57 pm	20	♏	1:35 pm	21	1:08 am	21	♑	5:30 pm	20	7:29 am	21	♑	1:43 am
23	12:00 am	23	♐	12:26 am	23	12:01 pm	23	♒	10:10 pm	22	3:29 pm	23	♒	8:02 am
25	3:27 am	25	♑	7:40 am	25	3:41 am	25	♓	11:42 pm	24	7:51 pm	25	♓	10:43 am
27	11:22 am	27	♒	11:27 am	27	6:25 pm	27	♈	11:42 pm	26	6:03 am	27	♈	10:49 am
29	10:54 am	29	♓	1:09 pm						28	8:59 pm	29	♉	10:07 am
31	9:06 am	31	♈	2:21 pm						31	12:30 am	31	♊	10:38 am

Moon Void-of-Course (cont.)

APRIL

Last Aspect Date	Time	Moon Enters New Sign Date Sign	Time
2	7:23 am	2 ♋	2:10 pm
4	9:35 am	4 ♌	9:36 pm
6	11:41 pm	7 ♍	8:26 am
8	2:30 pm	9 ♎	9:05 pm
12	9:15 am	12 ♏	9:55 am
13	6:10 pm	14 ♐	9:52 pm
17	2:33 am	17 ♑	8:05 am
19	2:53 pm	19 ♒	3:42 pm
21	10:32 am	21 ♓	8:07 pm
23	2:35 am	23 ♈	9:31 pm
25	1:06 pm	25 ♉	9:09 pm
27	9:47 am	27 ♊	8:56 pm
29	3:21 pm	29 ♋	10:57 pm

MAY

Last Aspect Date	Time	Moon Enters New Sign Date Sign	Time
2	1:38 am	2 ♌	4:49 am
4	6:49 am	4 ♍	2:47 pm
6	8:11 am	7 ♎	3:19 am
9	9:19 am	9 ♏	4:10 pm
11	11:06 am	12 ♐	3:48 am
14	12:43 pm	14 ♑	1:40 pm
16	4:54 pm	16 ♒	9:31 pm
18	11:36 pm	19 ♓	3:04 am
21	2:45 am	21 ♈	6:06 am
23	4:13 am	23 ♉	7:06 am
24	9:15 pm	25 ♊	7:25 am
27	6:43 am	27 ♋	8:58 am
29	1:09 pm	29 ♌	1:38 pm
31	9:24 pm	31 ♍	10:21 pm

JUNE

Last Aspect Date	Time	Moon Enters New Sign Date Sign	Time
3	12:08 am	3 ♎	10:17 am
5	10:29 pm	5 ♏	11:06 pm
8	2:01 am	8 ♐	10:35 am
10	12:08 pm	10 ♑	7:51 pm
12	8:04 pm	13 ♒	3:03 am
14	9:39 pm	15 ♓	8:32 am
17	6:34 am	17 ♈	12:23 pm
19	11:48 am	19 ♉	2:47 pm
21	11:24 am	21 ♊	4:26 pm
23	1:46 pm	23 ♋	6:39 pm
25	6:11 pm	25 ♌	11:04 pm
27	8:05 pm	28 ♍	6:55 am
30	5:58 pm	30 ♎	6:06 pm

JULY

Last Aspect Date	Time	Moon Enters New Sign Date Sign	Time
3	2:35 am	3 ♏	6:46 am
5	2:09 pm	5 ♐	6:24 pm
7	11:34 pm	8 ♑	3:28 am
10	6:15 am	10 ♒	9:52 am
11	10:48 pm	12 ♓	2:22 pm
14	2:25 pm	14 ♈	5:45 pm
16	2:51 pm	16 ♉	8:34 pm
18	8:01 pm	18 ♊	11:18 pm
20	11:20 pm	21 ♋	2:43 am
23	4:14 am	23 ♌	7:49 am
25	9:57 am	25 ♍	3:34 pm
27	10:03 pm	28 ♎	2:15 am
30	11:13 am	30 ♏	2:45 pm

AUGUST

Last Aspect Date	Time	Moon Enters New Sign Date Sign	Time
1	11:02 pm	2 ♐	2:48 am
4	7:45 am	4 ♑	12:18 pm
6	1:59 pm	6 ♒	6:31 pm
8	1:47 pm	8 ♓	10:04 pm
10	7:25 pm	11 ♈	12:11 am
13	1:53 am	13 ♉	2:05 am
14	11:18 pm	15 ♊	4:46 am
17	2:56 am	17 ♋	8:56 am
19	1:48 pm	19 ♌	3:01 pm
21	9:04 pm	21 ♍	11:22 pm
24	9:58 am	24 ♎	10:02 am
26	10:14 pm	26 ♏	10:25 pm
29	10:38 am	29 ♐	10:55 am
31	11:57 am	31 ♑	9:23 pm

SEPTEMBER

Last Aspect Date	Time	Moon Enters New Sign Date Sign	Time
3	3:56 am	3 ♒	4:21 am
5	4:56 am	5 ♓	7:48 am
7	8:23 am	7 ♈	8:53 am
9	8:43 am	9 ♉	9:17 am
11	10:03 am	11 ♊	10:41 am
13	2:47 am	13 ♋	2:20 pm
15	7:59 am	15 ♌	8:48 pm
17	5:57 pm	18 ♍	5:51 am
20	3:57 pm	20 ♎	4:57 pm
23	4:18 am	23 ♏	5:22 am
25	4:59 pm	25 ♐	6:05 pm
27	10:42 pm	28 ♑	5:31 am
30	1:27 pm	30 ♒	1:54 pm

OCTOBER

Last Aspect Date	Time	Moon Enters New Sign Date Sign	Time
2	1:28 pm	2 ♓	6:24 pm
4	6:35 pm	4 ♈	7:32 pm
6	6:26 pm	6 ♉	6:58 pm
8	5:44 pm	8 ♊	6:44 pm
10	5:36 pm	10 ♋	8:48 pm
13	1:17 am	13 ♌	2:25 am
14	6:54 pm	15 ♍	11:32 am
17	9:50 pm	17 ♎	11:02 pm
20	10:25 am	20 ♏	11:37 am
22	11:07 pm	23 ♐	12:17 am
24	1:58 pm	25 ♑	12:05 pm
27	9:24 pm	27 ♒	9:45 pm
30	3:20 am	30 ♓	3:58 am

NOVEMBER

Last Aspect Date	Time	Moon Enters New Sign Date Sign	Time
1	5:59 am	1 ♈	6:27 am
3	5:28 am	3 ♉	6:12 am
5	4:29 am	5 ♊	5:11 am
7	4:01 am	7 ♋	5:39 am
9	8:52 am	9 ♌	9:33 am
11	3:06 pm	11 ♍	5:38 pm
14	4:22 am	14 ♎	4:58 am
16	5:11 pm	16 ♏	5:42 pm
19	5:49 am	19 ♐	6:13 am
21	1:52 pm	21 ♑	5:46 pm
24	3:33 am	24 ♒	3:43 am
26	7:10 am	26 ♓	11:14 am
27	7:56 pm	28 ♈	3:34 pm
30	12:53 pm	30 ♉	4:52 pm

DECEMBER

Last Aspect Date	Time	Moon Enters New Sign Date Sign	Time
1	10:43 pm	2 ♊	4:30 pm
4	12:08 pm	4 ♋	4:28 pm
6	2:09 pm	6 ♌	6:56 pm
8	8:02 pm	9 ♍	1:22 am
11	11:31 am	11 ♎	11:44 am
13	6:11 pm	14 ♏	12:17 am
15	4:33 pm	16 ♐	12:47 pm
18	5:50 pm	18 ♑	11:55 pm
21	3:18 pm	21 ♒	9:17 am
23	10:56 am	23 ♓	4:45 pm
25	6:23 am	25 ♈	10:04 pm
27	7:42 pm	28 ♉	1:05 am
29	2:22 pm	30 ♊	2:22 am
31	9:58 pm	1/1 ♋	3:16 am

Planetary Stations for 1998

Planet	Retrograde Periods
☿	11/21–12/11, 03/27–04/20, 07/30–08/23
♀	12/26–02/05
♂	
♃	07/19–11/12, 10/10–1/16
⋄	01/25–05/10
✷	12/19–3/23
⚹	
♃	07/17–11/13
♄	08/15–12/29
♅	05/17–10/18, 03/01–07/11
♆	05/04–10/11
♇	03/10–08/15

How to Use the *Pocket Planner*

by Noel Tyl

On a daily basis, the Moon is all-important; it's the leader of the planetary band. But the Moon takes a break every so often and leaves the stage. The "v/c" void-of-course symbol to the right of the Moon symbol says that the music stops until the Moon returns, when the Moon "enters" the concert hall and rejoins the band.

Don't initiate new projects when the Moon is void-of-course: for example, on January 4 (see page 13) between 6:09 am (EST) and 7:44 am. That's no hardship on a Sunday. When a longer v/c period occurs during business hours, as on Thursday, January 29, just before lunch and lasting through the afternoon EST, it's strategically important: It's best not to schedule new presentations or major purchases at that time. Appointments may be changed at the last minute if made *during* that time period or *for* that period.

Bonus: If you have a big argument during the v/c period, chances are nothing much will come of it either! Neither "No" nor "Yes" endures out of v/c periods, and that goes for contract signings, too. Sales people can increase efficiency by staying low-profile during v/c periods. Test it yourself!

The last major aspect the Moon makes before entering the v/c period is critical. It flavors any high-profile project set up during the preceding time period, from the previous "enters" (ingress) time.

When the Moon's last aspect time is followed by a triangle or an asterisk (trine or sextile aspect), the music will probably end well out of the preceding period. Any other symbol is a warning, especially if the planet following it is Mars, Saturn, Uranus, Neptune, or Pluto.

Knowing this, you can look at two- or three-day intervals as generally favorable or unfavorable to initiate things, like buying a car, applying for a job, asking for a raise, or having surgery (note the part of the body ruled by the Moon's sign).

Put this knowledge together with a sharp eye for Mercury ℞ (retrograde, see March 27 on page 37). This notation shows the beginning of a three-week period when Mercury leaves the band and goes out with the Moon! Things don't work out easily. This period is like an emphasized v/c Moon period, until "D" (Direct, on April 20 on page 44) says, "Do Continue!"

When a *planet* makes an ingress, its symbolism is given new music to play in terms of the new sign. But remember that the planets need a director, and using the *Pocket Planner*, you can lead the band yourself!

Symbol Key

Planets:	☉ Sun	⚳ Ceres	♄ Saturn
	☽ Moon	⚴ Pallas	⚷ Chiron
	☿ Mercury	⚵ Juno	♅ Uranus
	♀ Venus	⚶ Vesta	♆ Neptune
	♂ Mars	♃ Jupiter	♇ Pluto
Signs:	♈ Aries	♌ Leo	♐ Sagittarius
	♉ Taurus	♍ Virgo	♑ Capricorn
	♊ Gemini	♎ Libra	♒ Aquarius
	♋ Cancer	♏ Scorpio	♓ Pisces
Aspects:	☌ Conjunction	□ Square	☍ Opposition
	⚺ Semisextile	△ Trine	
	⚹ Sextile	⚻ Quincunx	
Motion:	℞ Retrograde	D Direct	

Both Eastern Standard Time (to the left in **bold typeface**) and Pacific Standard Time (to the right in medium typeface) are listed in the datebook. Adjustments have not been made for Daylight Saving Time. You need to add one hour to the time given if your locale uses Daylight Saving Time. On days when an event or aspect occurs only for one time zone and not the other, it is indicated next to the appropriate column and then repeated on the next day for the other time zone. The ephemeris is shown for midnight, Greenwich Mean Time.

Things Ruled by the Planets

To check aspects for the activity you have in mind, find the planet that rules it. Activities have been put into three categories—look at all three for a full picture.

Sun — **Occupations**: Advertising, all positions of managerial and executive authority, positions related to organizational ability, acting, banking, finance, government, jewelry, law, public relations. **Hobbies**: Community work, civic action, volunteer services, exercise, outdoor sports. **Activities**: Advertising, buying, selling, speculating, short trips, meeting people, anything involving groups or showmanship, putting up exhibits, running fairs and raffles, growing crops, health matters.

Moon — **Occupations**: Caterer, domestic science, home economics, nursing, fishing, navigator, sailor. **Hobbies**: Collecting stamps, antique furniture, anything to do

with the sea and sailing. **Activities:** Any small change in routine, asking favors, borrowing or lending money, household activities, such as baking, canning, cooking, washing, ironing, cleaning, taking care of small children.

Mercury — **Occupations:** Accountant, ambassador, bookkeeper, broker, clerk, critic, craftsman, disc jockey, editor, journalist, inspector, lecturer, librarian, linguist, medical technician, scientist, secretary, student, teacher, writer. **Hobbies:** Writing stories, watching TV, anything dealing with communication and the mass media. **Activities:** Bargaining, bookkeeping, dealing with literary agents, publishing, filing, hiring employees, learning languages, literary work, placing ads, preparing accounts, studying, telephoning, visiting friends.

Venus — **Occupations:** Architect, artist, beautician, chiropractor, dancer, designer, domestic work, entertainer, fashion marketing, musician, painter, poet. **Hobbies:** Embroidery, making clothes, music, painting, sculpture, sewing, landscape gardening. **Activities:** Amusement, beauty care, courtship, dating, decorating homes, designing, getting together with friends, household improvements, planning parties, shopping.

Mars — **Occupations:** Barber, butcher, carpenter, chemist, construction worker, dentist, metal worker, surgeon, soldier. **Hobbies:** Anything that involves work with tools or machinery such as repairing cars, gardening, grafting, household improvements, woodworking. **Activities:** Good for all business matters, mechanical affairs, buying or selling animals, dealing with contractors, hunting, studying.

Jupiter — **Occupations:** Counselor, doctor, educator, guardian, horse-trainer, hunter, jockey, judge, lawyer, legislator, merchant, minister, pharmacist, psychologist, public analyst. **Hobbies:** Social clubs, travel. **Activities:** Charity, education, or science, correspondence courses, self-improvement, reading, researching, studying.

Saturn — **Occupations:** Agronomist, builder, civil servant, excavator, farm worker, magistrate, mathematician, miner, osteopath, plumber, politician, real estate agent, repair person, shoemaker, printer. **Hobbies:** Dealing with public matters, farming or working with the soil, papermaking. **Activities:** Anything involving family ties or legal matters such as wills and estates, taking care of debts, dealing with lawyers, financing, joint money matters, real estate, relations with older people.

Uranus — **Occupations:** Aeronautics adviser, aerospace technician, broadcaster, electrician, government official, inventor, lecturer, radiologist, computers. **Hobbies:** Electronics, experimenting with ESP, novel ideas, the occult, studying, computer programming. **Activities:** Air travel, all partnerships, changes and adjustment, civil rights, new contacts, new ideas, new rules, patenting inventions, progress, social action, starting journeys.

Neptune — Occupations: Chain store manager, character actor, chemist, diplomat, photographer, psychiatrist, secret agent, wine merchant, working with religious institutions, the shipping business and the sea. **Hobbies:** Acting, pets, photography, music, movies. **Activities:** Advertising, dealing with psychological upsets, health foods and resorts, large social affairs, nightclubs, psychic healing, travel by water, restaurants, visits, welfare, working with institutions.

Pluto — Occupations: Acrobatics, athletic manager, field of atomic energy, research breakthroughs, speculation, sports, stockbroker. **Hobbies:** Any purely personal endeavor, working with children. **Activities:** Anything dealing with energy and enthusiasm, skill and alertness, personal relationships, original thought.

Planetary Business Guide

Collections: Try to make collections on days when your Sun is well aspected. Avoid days when Mars or Saturn are aspected. If possible, the Moon should be in a Cardinal sign: Aries, Cancer, Libra, or Capricorn. It is more difficult to collect when the Moon is in Taurus or Scorpio.

Employment, Promotion: Choose a day when your Sun is favorably aspected or the Moon is in your 10th house. Good aspects of Venus or Jupiter to your 10th house are beneficial.

Loans: Moon in the First and Second Quarters favors the lender, in the Third and Fourth it favors the borrower. Good aspects of Jupiter or Venus to the Moon are favorable to both, as is Moon in Leo, Sagittarius, Aquarius, or Pisces.

New Ventures: Things usually get off to a better start during the increase of the Moon. If there is impatience, anxiety, or deadlock, it can often be broken at the Full Moon. Agreements can be reached then.

Partnerships: Agreements and partnerships should be made on a day that is favorable to both parties. Mars, Neptune, Pluto, and Saturn should not be square or opposite the Moon. It is best to make an agreement or partnership when the Moon is in a Mutable sign, especially Gemini or Virgo. The other signs are not favorable with the possible exception of Leo or Capricorn. Begin partnerships when the Moon is increasing in light, as this is a favorable time for starting new ventures.

Public Relations: The Moon rules the public, so this must be well aspected, particularly by the Sun, Mercury, Uranus, or Neptune.

Selling: In general, selling is favored by good aspects of Venus, Jupiter, or Mercury to the Moon. Afflictions of Saturn retard. If you know the planetary ruler of your product, try to get this well aspected by Venus, Jupiter, or the Moon. Your product will be more highly valued then.

Signing Important Papers: Sign contracts or agreements when the Moon is increasing in a fruitful sign. Avoid days when Mars, Saturn, Neptune, or Pluto are afflicting the Moon. Don't sign anything if your Sun is badly afflicted.

Planetary Associations

Sun: Authority figures, favors, advancement, health, success, display, drama, promotion, fun, matters related to Leo and the 5th house.

Moon: Short trips, women, children, the public, domestic concerns, emotions, fluids, matters related to Cancer and the 4th house.

Mercury: Communications, correspondence, phone calls, computers, messages, education, students, travel, merchants, editing, writing, advertising, signing contracts, siblings, neighbors, kin, matters related to Gemini, Virgo, and the 3rd and 6th houses.

Venus: Affection, relationships, partnerships, alliances, grace, beauty, harmony, luxury, love, art, music, social activity, marriage, decorating, cosmetics, gifts, income, matters related to Taurus, Libra, and the 2nd and 7th houses.

Mars: Strife, aggression, sex, physical energy, muscular activity, guns, tools, metals, cutting, surgery, police, soldiers, combat, confrontation, matters related to Aries, Scorpio, and the 1st and 8th houses.

Jupiter: Publishing, college education, long-distance travel, foreign interests, religion, philosophy, forecasting, broadcasting, publicity, expansion, luck, growth, sports, horses, the law, matters related to Sagittarius, Pisces, and 9th and 12th house issues.

Saturn: Structure, reality, the laws of society, limits, obstacles, tests, hard work, endurance, real estate, dentists, bones, teeth, matters related to Capricorn, Aquarius, and the 10th and 11th houses.

Uranus: Astrology, the New Age, technology, computers, modern gadgets, lecturing, advising, counseling, inventions, reforms, electricity, new methods, originality, sudden events, matters related to Aquarius and the 11th house.

Neptune: Mysticism, music, creative imagination, dance, illusion, sacrifice, service oil, chemicals, paint, drugs, anesthesia, sleep, religious experience, matters related to Pisces and the 12th house.

Pluto: Probing, penetration, goods of the dead, investigation, insurance, taxes, other people's money, loans, the masses, the underworld, transformation, death, matters related to Scorpio and the 8th house.

World Map of Time Zones

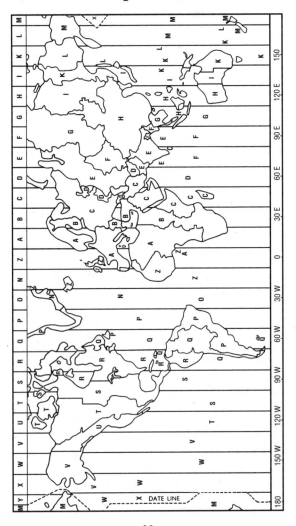

Time Zone Conversions

World Time Zones
Compared to Eastern Standard Time

( ) From Map

(S) Subtract 1 hour

(R) EST—Used in *Planner*

(Q) Add 1 hour

(P) Add 2 hours

(O) Add 3 hours

(N) Add 4 hours

(Z) Add 5 hours

(T) MST—Subtract 2 hours

(U) PST—Used in *Planner* (Subtract 3 hours)

(V) Subtract 4 hours

(W) Subtract 5 hours

(X) Subtract 6 hours

(Y) Subtract 7 hours

(A) Add 6 hours

(B) Add 7 hours

(C) Add 8 hours

(D) Add 9 hours

(E) Add 10 hours

(F) Add 11 hours

(G) Add 12 hours

(H) Add 13 hours

(I) Add 14 hours

(K) Add 15 hours

(L) Add 16 hours

(M) Add 17 hours

Standard Time = Universal Time
+ value from table

	h m			h m			h m			h m
Z	0 00		F* +	6 30		N −	1 00		V −	9 00
A +	1 00		G +	7 00		O −	2 00		V* −	9 30
B +	2 00		H +	8 00		P −	3 00		W −	10 00
C +	3 00		I +	9 00		P* −	3 30		W* −	10 30
C* +	3 30		I* +	9 30		Q −	4 00		X −	11 00
D +	4 00		K +	10 00		R −	5 00		Y −	12 00
D* +	4 30		K* +	10 30		S −	6 00			
E +	5 00		L +	11 00		T −	7 00			
E* +	5 30		M +	12 00		U −	8 00			
F +	6 00		M* +	13 00		U* −	8 30			

29 Monday
4th ♑
New Moon **11:57 am** 8:57 am

30 Tuesday
1st ♑
☽ v/c   9:08 pm
☽ enters ≈   10:59 pm

31 Wednesday
1st ♑
☽ v/c   **12:08 am**
☽ enters ≈   **1:59 am**

January 1, 1998 Thursday
1st ≈
☽ v/c   **4:08 pm** 1:08 pm

New Year's Day • Kwanzaa ends

Eastern Standard Time in bold type
Pacific Standard Time in medium type

2 Friday
1st ≈
☽ enters ♓ **4:56 am** 1:56 am

3 Saturday
1st ♓

4 Sunday
1st ♓
☽ v/c **6:09 am** 3:09 am
☽ enters ♈ **7:44 am** 4:44 am

December 1997						
S	M	T	W	T	F	S
	1	2	3	4	5	6
7	8	9	10	11	12	13
14	15	16	17	18	19	20
21	22	23	24	25	26	27
28	29	30	31			

January 1998						
S	M	T	W	T	F	S
				1	2	3
4	5	6	7	8	9	10
11	12	13	14	15	16	17
18	19	20	21	22	23	24
25	26	27	28	29	30	31

February 1998						
S	M	T	W	T	F	S
1	2	3	4	5	6	7
8	9	10	11	12	13	14
15	16	17	18	19	20	21
22	23	24	25	26	27	28

Eastern Standard Time in bold type
Pacific Standard Time in medium type

5 Monday
1st ♈
2nd Quarter **9:19 am** 6:19 am

6 Tuesday
2nd ♈
☽ v/c **9:25 am** 6:25 am
☽ enters ♉ **10:53 am** 7:53 am

7 Wednesday
2nd ♉

8 Thursday
2nd ♉
☽ v/c **1:22 pm** 10:22 am
☽ enters ♊ **2:42 pm** 11:42 am

Eastern Standard Time in bold type
Pacific Standard Time in medium type

9 Friday
2nd ♊
♀ enters ♑ **4:04 pm** 1:04 pm

10 Saturday
2nd ♊
☽ v/c **3:45 pm** 12:45 pm
☽ enters ♋ **7:43 pm** 4:43 pm

11 Sunday
2nd ♋

December 1997						
S	M	T	W	T	F	S
	1	2	3	4	5	6
7	8	9	10	11	12	13
14	15	16	17	18	19	20
21	22	23	24	25	26	27
28	29	30	31			

January 1998						
S	M	T	W	T	F	S
				1	2	3
4	5	6	7	8	9	10
11	12	13	14	15	16	17
18	19	20	21	22	23	24
25	26	27	28	29	30	31

February 1998						
S	M	T	W	T	F	S
1	2	3	4	5	6	7
8	9	10	11	12	13	14
15	16	17	18	19	20	21
22	23	24	25	26	27	28

Eastern Standard Time in bold type
Pacific Standard Time in medium type

12 Monday

2nd ♋
☿ enters ♑ **11:20 am** 8:20 am
Full Moon **12:24 pm** 9:24 am
☽ v/c 10:37 pm
☽ enters ♌ 11:45 pm

13 Tuesday

3rd ♋
☽ v/c **1:37 am**
☽ enters ♌ **2:45 am**

14 Wednesday

3rd ♌

15 Thursday

3rd ♌
☽ v/c **3:23 am** 12:23 am
☽ enters ♍ **12:31 pm** 9:31 am

Birthday of Martin Luther King, Jr.

Eastern Standard Time in bold type
Pacific Standard Time in medium type

16 Friday
3rd ♍

17 Saturday
3rd ♍
☽ v/c   **11:54 pm**   8:54 pm
☽ enters ♎   9:45 pm

18 Sunday
3rd ♍
☽ enters ♎ **12:45 am**

December 1997						
S	M	T	W	T	F	S
	1	2	3	4	5	6
7	8	9	10	11	12	13
14	15	16	17	18	19	20
21	22	23	24	25	26	27
28	29	30	31			

January 1998						
S	M	T	W	T	F	S
				1	2	3
4	5	6	7	8	9	10
11	12	13	14	15	16	17
18	19	20	21	22	23	24
25	26	27	28	29	30	31

February 1998						
S	M	T	W	T	F	S
1	2	3	4	5	6	7
8	9	10	11	12	13	14
15	16	17	18	19	20	21
22	23	24	25	26	27	28

Eastern Standard Time in bold type
Pacific Standard Time in medium type

19 Monday
3rd ♎
⊙ enters ≈   10:46 pm

Sun enters Aquarius—PST • Birthday of Martin Luther King, Jr. (Observed)

20 Tuesday
3rd ♎
⊙ enters ≈   **1:46 am**
☽ v/c   **12:57 pm** 9:57 am
☽ enters ♏   **1:35 pm** 10:35 am
4th Quarter   **2:41 pm** 11:41 am

Sun enters Aquarius—EST

21 Wednesday
4th ♏

22 Thursday
4th ♏
☽ v/c   9:00 pm
☽ enters ♐   9:26 pm

Eastern Standard Time in bold type
Pacific Standard Time in medium type

23 Friday

4th ♐
☽ v/c   **12:00 am**
☽ enters ♐ **12:26 am**

24 Saturday

4th ♐

25 Sunday

4th ♐
☽ v/c   **3:27 am** 12:27 am
♂ enters ♓ **4:26 am** 1:26 am
☽ enters ♑ **7:40 am** 4:40 am
♀ ℞   **3:25 pm** 12:25 pm

December 1997						
S	M	T	W	T	F	S
	1	2	3	4	5	6
7	8	9	10	11	12	13
14	15	16	17	18	19	20
21	22	23	24	25	26	27
28	29	30	31			

January 1998						
S	M	T	W	T	F	S
				1	2	3
4	5	6	7	8	9	10
11	12	13	14	15	16	17
18	19	20	21	22	23	24
25	26	27	28	29	30	31

February 1998						
S	M	T	W	T	F	S
1	2	3	4	5	6	7
8	9	10	11	12	13	14
15	16	17	18	19	20	21
22	23	24	25	26	27	28

Eastern Standard Time in bold type
Pacific Standard Time in medium type

26 Monday
4th ♑

27 Tuesday
4th ♑
☽ v/c **11:22 am** 8:22 am
☽ enters ♒ **11:27 am** 8:27 am
New Moon 10:01 pm

28 Wednesday
4th ♒
New Moon **1:01 am**
♆ enters ♒ **9:49 pm** 6:49 pm

29 Thursday
1st ♒
☽ v/c **10:54 am** 7:54 am
☽ enters ♓ **1:09 pm** 10:09 am

30 Friday
1st ♓

31 Saturday
1st ♓
☽ v/c **9:06 am** 6:06 am
☽ enters ♈ **2:21 pm** 11:21 am

February 1 Sunday
1st ♈

January 1998						
S	M	T	W	T	F	S
				1	2	3
4	5	6	7	8	9	10
11	12	13	14	15	16	17
18	19	20	21	22	23	24
25	26	27	28	29	30	31

February 1998						
S	M	T	W	T	F	S
1	2	3	4	5	6	7
8	9	10	11	12	13	14
15	16	17	18	19	20	21
22	23	24	25	26	27	28

March 1998						
S	M	T	W	T	F	S
1	2	3	4	5	6	7
8	9	10	11	12	13	14
15	16	17	18	19	20	21
22	23	24	25	26	27	28
29	30	31				

Eastern Standard Time in bold type
Pacific Standard Time in medium type

2 Monday

1st ♈
☿ enters ≈ **10:15 am** 7:15 am
☽ v/c **3:46 pm** 12:46 pm
☽ enters ♉ **4:25 pm** 1:25 pm

Imbolc

3 Tuesday

1st ♉
2nd Quarter **5:53 pm** 2:53 pm
☽ v/c 9:08 pm

4 Wednesday

2nd ♉
☽ v/c **12:08 am**
♃ enters ♓ **5:52 am** 2:52 am
☽ enters ♊ **8:09 pm** 5:09 pm

5 Thursday

2nd ♊
♀ D **4:26 pm** 1:26 pm
☽ v/c 11:58 pm

6 Friday

2nd ♊
☽ v/c   **2:58 am**
☽ enters ♋   10:58 pm

7 Saturday

2nd ♋
☽ enters ♋   **1:58 am**

8 Sunday

2nd ♋
☽ v/c   **12:28 pm** 9:28 am

January 1998						
S	M	T	W	T	F	S
				1	2	3
4	5	6	7	8	9	10
11	12	13	14	15	16	17
18	19	20	21	22	23	24
25	26	27	28	29	30	31

February 1998						
S	M	T	W	T	F	S
1	2	3	4	5	6	7
8	9	10	11	12	13	14
15	16	17	18	19	20	21
22	23	24	25	26	27	28

March 1998						
S	M	T	W	T	F	S
1	2	3	4	5	6	7
8	9	10	11	12	13	14
15	16	17	18	19	20	21
22	23	24	25	26	27	28
29	30	31				

Eastern Standard Time in bold type
Pacific Standard Time in medium type

9 Monday
2nd ♋
☽ enters ♌   **9:57 am**   6:57 am

*chinook breeze in after-
noon & evening.*

*AIDAN JEDREK OLLEY   6 lb. 12 oz.
GRANDE PRAIRIE ALTA
8:57 p.m. MST.
1st child*

10 Tuesday
2nd ♌

11 Wednesday
2nd ♌
Full Moon   **5:23 am**   2:23 am
☽ v/c   **5:23 am**   2:23 am

12 Thursday
3rd ♍

13 Friday
3rd ♍
☽ v/c **11:21 am** 8:21 am

14 Saturday
3rd ♍
☽ enters ♎ **8:18 am** 5:18 am

Valentine's Day

15 Sunday
3rd ♎

January 1998						
S	M	T	W	T	F	S
				1	2	3
4	5	6	7	8	9	10
11	12	13	14	15	16	17
18	19	20	21	22	23	24
25	26	27	28	29	30	31

February 1998						
S	M	T	W	T	F	S
1	2	3	4	5	6	7
8	9	10	11	12	13	14
15	16	17	18	19	20	21
22	23	24	25	26	27	28

March 1998						
S	M	T	W	T	F	S
1	2	3	4	5	6	7
8	9	10	11	12	13	14
15	16	17	18	19	20	21
22	23	24	25	26	27	28
29	30	31				

Eastern Standard Time in bold type
Pacific Standard Time in medium type

16 Monday
3rd ♎︎
☽ v/c   **5:15 pm** 2:15 pm
☽ enters ♏︎ **9:14 pm** 6:14 pm

Washington's Birthday (Observed)

17 Tuesday
3rd ♏︎

18 Wednesday
3rd ♏︎
☉ enters ♓︎ **3:55 pm** 12:55 pm

Sun enters Pisces

19 Thursday
3rd ♏︎
☽ v/c   **5:26 am** 2:26 am
☽ enters ♐︎ **8:56 am** 5:56 am
4th Quarter **10:27 am** 7:27 am
♃ enters ♈︎ **11:50 am** 8:50 am

Eastern Standard Time in bold type
Pacific Standard Time in medium type

20 Friday
4th ♐

☿ enters ♓	**5:22 am**	2:22 am
☽ v/c		10:08 pm

21 Saturday
4th ♐

☽ v/c	**1:08 am**	
☽ enters ♑	**5:30 pm**	2:30 pm

22 Sunday
4th ♑

Washington's Birthday

January 1998						
S	M	T	W	T	F	S
				1	2	3
4	5	6	7	8	9	10
11	12	13	14	15	16	17
18	19	20	21	22	23	24
25	26	27	28	29	30	31

February 1998						
S	M	T	W	T	F	S
1	2	3	4	5	6	7
8	9	10	11	12	13	14
15	16	17	18	19	20	21
22	23	24	25	26	27	28

March 1998						
S	M	T	W	T	F	S
1	2	3	4	5	6	7
8	9	10	11	12	13	14
15	16	17	18	19	20	21
22	23	24	25	26	27	28
29	30	31				

Eastern Standard Time in bold type
Pacific Standard Time in medium type

23 Monday
4th ♑
☽ v/c   **12:01 pm** 9:01 am
☽ enters ♒ **10:10 pm** 7:10 pm

24 Tuesday
4th ♒

25 Wednesday
4th ♒
☽ v/c   **3:41 am** 12:41 am
☽ enters ♓ **11:42 pm** 8:42 pm

Ash Wednesday

26 Thursday
4th ♓
New Moon **12:26 pm** 9:26 am

Solar Eclipse 7° ♓ 55'

Eastern Standard Time in bold type
Pacific Standard Time in medium type

27 Friday
1st ♓
♀ enters ♓ **12:42 pm** 9:42 am
☽ v/c **6:25 pm** 3:25 pm
☽ enters ♈ **11:42 pm** 8:42 pm

28 Saturday
1st ♈

March 1 Sunday
1st ♈
☽ v/c **8:57 pm** 5:57 pm
☽ enters ♉ 9:01 pm
☿ ℞ **11:20 pm** 8:20 pm

February 1998						
S	M	T	W	T	F	S
1	2	3	4	5	6	7
8	9	10	11	12	13	14
15	16	17	18	19	20	21
22	23	24	25	26	27	28

March 1998						
S	M	T	W	T	F	S
1	2	3	4	5	6	7
8	9	10	11	12	13	14
15	16	17	18	19	20	21
22	23	24	25	26	27	28
29	30	31				

April 1998						
S	M	T	W	T	F	S
			1	2	3	4
5	6	7	8	9	10	11
12	13	14	15	16	17	18
19	20	21	22	23	24	25
26	27	28	29	30		

Eastern Standard Time in bold type
Pacific Standard Time in medium type

2 Monday
1st ♉
☽ enters ♉ **12:01 am**

3 Tuesday
1st ♉
☽ v/c   10:45 pm
☽ enters ♊   11:15 pm

4 Wednesday
1st ♊
☽ v/c   **1:45 am**
☽ enters ♊   **2:15 am**
♀ enters ≈ **11:15 am** 8:15 am
♂ enters ♈ **11:18 am** 8:18 am

5 Thursday
1st ♊
2nd Quarter **3:41 am** 12:41 am
☽ v/c   9:09 pm

6 Friday
2nd ♊

☽ v/c **12:09 am**

☽ enters ♋ **7:27 am** 4:27 am

7 Saturday
2nd ♋

☽ v/c **6:33 pm** 3:33 pm

8 Sunday
2nd ♋

☿ enters ♈ **3:28 am** 12:28 am

☽ enters ♌ **3:46 pm** 12:46 pm

February 1998						
S	M	T	W	T	F	S
1	2	3	4	5	6	7
8	9	10	11	12	13	14
15	16	17	18	19	20	21
22	23	24	25	26	27	28

March 1998						
S	M	T	W	T	F	S
1	2	3	4	5	6	7
8	9	10	11	12	13	14
15	16	17	18	19	20	21
22	23	24	25	26	27	28
29	30	31				

April 1998						
S	M	T	W	T	F	S
			1	2	3	4
5	6	7	8	9	10	11
12	13	14	15	16	17	18
19	20	21	22	23	24	25
26	27	28	29	30		

Eastern Standard Time in bold type
Pacific Standard Time in medium type

9 Monday
2nd ♌

10 Tuesday
2nd ♌
☽ v/c   **5:06 am** 2:06 am
♇ R̥   **7:19 pm** 4:19 pm
☽ enters ♍   11:36 pm

11 Wednesday
2nd ♍
☽ enters ♍   **2:36 am**

Purim begins

12 Thursday
2nd ♍
Full Moon   **11:35 pm** 8:35 pm
☽ v/c   **11:35 pm** 8:35 pm

Purim ends • Lunar Eclipse 22° ♍ 24'

Eastern Standard Time in bold type
Pacific Standard Time in medium type

13 Friday
3rd ♍
☿ enters ♍ **5:43 am** 2:43 am
☽ enters ♎ **2:59 pm** 11:59 am

14 Saturday
3rd ♎

15 Sunday
3rd ♎
☽ v/c **7:04 am** 4:04 am

February 1998						
S	M	T	W	T	F	S
1	2	3	4	5	6	7
8	9	10	11	12	13	14
15	16	17	18	19	20	21
22	23	24	25	26	27	28

March 1998						
S	M	T	W	T	F	S
1	2	3	4	5	6	7
8	9	10	11	12	13	14
15	16	17	18	19	20	21
22	23	24	25	26	27	28
29	30	31				

April 1998						
S	M	T	W	T	F	S
			1	2	3	4
5	6	7	8	9	10	11
12	13	14	15	16	17	18
19	20	21	22	23	24	25
26	27	28	29	30		

Eastern Standard Time in bold type
Pacific Standard Time in medium type

16 Monday
3rd ♎
☽ enters ♏ **3:51 am** 12:51 am

17 Tuesday
3rd ♏

St. Patrick's Day

18 Wednesday
3rd ♏
☽ v/c **11:45 am** 8:45 am
☽ enters ♐ **3:56 pm** 12:56 pm

19 Thursday
3rd ♐

20 Friday

3rd ♐

☽ v/c	**7:29 am**	4:29 am
☉ enters ♈	**2:54 pm**	11:54 am
☽ enters ♑		10:43 pm
4th Quarter		11:38 pm

Sun enters Aries • Spring Equinox • Ostara

late 3rd quarter

21 Saturday

3rd ♐

☽ enters ♑	**1:43 am**
4th Quarter	**2:38 am**

22 Sunday

4th ♑

☽ v/c	**3:29 pm**	12:29 pm

February 1998							March 1998							April 1998						
S	M	T	W	T	F	S	S	M	T	W	T	F	S	S	M	T	W	T	F	S
1	2	3	4	5	6	7	1	2	3	4	5	6	7				1	2	3	4
8	9	10	11	12	13	14	8	9	10	11	12	13	14	5	6	7	8	9	10	11
15	16	17	18	19	20	21	15	16	17	18	19	20	21	12	13	14	15	16	17	18
22	23	24	25	26	27	28	22	23	24	25	26	27	28	19	20	21	22	23	24	25
							29	30	31					26	27	28	29	30		

Eastern Standard Time in bold type
Pacific Standard Time in medium type

23 Monday
4th ♑
☽ enters ♒ **8:02 am** 5:02 am

24 Tuesday
4th ♒
☽ v/c **7:51 pm** 4:51 pm

25 Wednesday
4th ♒
☽ enters ♓ **10:43 am** 7:43 am

26 Thursday
4th ♓
☽ v/c **6:03 am** 3:03 am

27 Friday

4th ♓
☽ enters ♈ **10:49 am** 7:49 am
☿ R̥ **2:37 pm** 11:37 pm
New Moon **10:14 pm** 7:14 pm

28 Saturday

1st ♈
☽ v/c **8:59 pm** 5:59 pm

29 Sunday

1st ♈
☽ enters ♉ **10:07 am** 7:07 am

February 1998						
S	M	T	W	T	F	S
1	2	3	4	5	6	7
8	9	10	11	12	13	14
15	16	17	18	19	20	21
22	23	24	25	26	27	28

March 1998						
S	M	T	W	T	F	S
1	2	3	4	5	6	7
8	9	10	11	12	13	14
15	16	17	18	19	20	21
22	23	24	25	26	27	28
29	30	31				

April 1998						
S	M	T	W	T	F	S
			1	2	3	4
5	6	7	8	9	10	11
12	13	14	15	16	17	18
19	20	21	22	23	24	25
26	27	28	29	30		

Eastern Standard Time in bold type
Pacific Standard Time in medium type

30 Monday
1st ♉
☽ v/c   9:30 pm

31 Tuesday
1st ♉
☽ v/c   **12:30 am**
☽ enters ♊   **10:38 am** 7:38 am

April 1 Wednesday
1st ♊

April Fool's Day

2 Thursday
1st ♊
☽ v/c   **7:23 am** 4:23 am
☽ enters ♋   **2:10 pm** 11:10 am

Eastern Standard Time in bold type
Pacific Standard Time in medium type

3 Friday

1st ♋
2nd Quarter **3:19 pm** 12:19 pm

Spring rain
Edmonton.

Ryan Lee Mostowich
9:56 p.m. MST.
Edmonton, Alta.
1st child.

4 Saturday

2nd ♋
☽ v/c   **9:35 am**   6:35 am
☽ enters ♌   **9:36 pm**   6:36 pm

5 Sunday

2nd ♌
♀ enters ♓   9:38 pm

Palm Sunday • Daylight Saving Time begins at 2 AM

March 1998						
S	M	T	W	T	F	S
1	2	3	4	5	6	7
8	9	10	11	12	13	14
15	16	17	18	19	20	21
22	23	24	25	26	27	28
29	30	31				

April 1998						
S	M	T	W	T	F	S
			1	2	3	4
5	6	7	8	9	10	11
12	13	14	15	16	17	18
19	20	21	22	23	24	25
26	27	28	29	30		

May 1998						
S	M	T	W	T	F	S
					1	2
3	4	5	6	7	8	9
10	11	12	13	14	15	16
17	18	19	20	21	22	23
24	25	26	27	28	29	30
31						

Eastern Standard Time in bold type
Pacific Standard Time in medium type

6 Monday
2nd ♌
♀ enters ♓ **12:38 am**
☽ v/c **11:41 pm** 8:41 pm

7 Tuesday
2nd ♌
☽ enters ♍ **8:26 am** 5:26 am

8 Wednesday
2nd ♍
☽ v/c **2:30 pm** 11:30 am

9 Thursday
2nd ♍
☽ enters ♎ **9:05 pm** 6:05 pm

10 Friday
2nd ♎︎

Good Friday • Passover begins

11 Saturday
2nd ♎︎
Full Moon   **5:24 pm** 2:24 pm

12 Sunday
3rd ♎︎
☽ v/c   **9:15 am** 6:15 am
☽ enters ♏︎   **9:55 am** 6:55 am
♂ enters ♉︎   **8:04 pm** 5:04 pm

Easter

March 1998						
S	M	T	W	T	F	S
1	2	3	4	5	6	7
8	9	10	11	12	13	14
15	16	17	18	19	20	21
22	23	24	25	26	27	28
29	30	31				

April 1998						
S	M	T	W	T	F	S
			1	2	3	4
5	6	7	8	9	10	11
12	13	14	15	16	17	18
19	20	21	22	23	24	25
26	27	28	29	30		

May 1998						
S	M	T	W	T	F	S
					1	2
3	4	5	6	7	8	9
10	11	12	13	14	15	16
17	18	19	20	21	22	23
24	25	26	27	28	29	30
31						

Eastern Standard Time in bold type
Pacific Standard Time in medium type

13 Monday

3rd ♏
☽ v/c   **6:10 pm**   3:10 pm

14 Tuesday

3rd ♏
☽ enters ♐   **9:52 pm**   6:52 pm

15 Wednesday

3rd ♐

16 Thursday

3rd ♐
☽ v/c   11:33 pm

Eastern Standard Time in bold type
Pacific Standard Time in medium type

17 Friday

3rd ♐
☽ v/c   **2:33 am**
☽ enters ♑   **8:05 am**   5:05 am

18 Saturday

3rd ♑

Passover ends

19 Sunday

3rd ♑
4th Quarter **2:53 pm** 11:53 am
☽ v/c   **2:53 pm** 11:53 am
☽ enters ♒ **3:42 pm** 12:42 pm
☉ enters ♉   10:56 pm
☿ D   11:28 pm

Sun enters Taurus—PST • Orthodox Easter

March 1998						
S	M	T	W	T	F	S
1	2	3	4	5	6	7
8	9	10	11	12	13	14
15	16	17	18	19	20	21
22	23	24	25	26	27	28
29	30	31				

April 1998						
S	M	T	W	T	F	S
			1	2	3	4
5	6	7	8	9	10	11
12	13	14	15	16	17	18
19	20	21	22	23	24	25
26	27	28	29	30		

May 1998						
S	M	T	W	T	F	S
					1	2
3	4	5	6	7	8	9
10	11	12	13	14	15	16
17	18	19	20	21	22	23
24	25	26	27	28	29	30
31						

Eastern Standard Time in bold type
Pacific Standard Time in medium type

20 Monday

4th ≈
☉ enters ♉ **1:56 am**
☿ D **2:28 am**

Sun enters Taurus—EST

21 Tuesday

4th ≈
☽ v/c **10:32 am** 7:32 am
☽ enters ♓ **8:07 pm** 5:07 pm

22 Wednesday

4th ♓
☽ v/c 11:35 pm

23 Thursday

4th ♓
☽ v/c **2:35 am**
☽ enters ♈ **9:31 pm** 6:31 pm

24 Friday
4th ♈

25 Saturday
4th ♈
| ☽ v/c | **1:06 pm** | 10:06 am |
| ☽ enters ♉ | **9:09 pm** | 6:09 pm |

26 Sunday
4th ♉
| New Moon | **6:42 am** | 3:42 am |
| ⚷ enters ♊ | | 10:53 pm |

March 1998								April 1998								May 1998						
S	M	T	W	T	F	S		S	M	T	W	T	F	S		S	M	T	W	T	F	S
1	2	3	4	5	6	7				1	2	3	4							1	2
8	9	10	11	12	13	14		5	5	7	8	9	10	11		3	4	5	6	7	8	9
15	16	17	18	19	20	21		12	13	14	15	16	17	18		10	11	12	13	14	15	16
22	23	24	25	26	27	28		19	20	21	22	23	24	25		17	18	19	20	21	22	23
29	30	31						26	27	28	29	30				24	25	26	27	28	29	30
																31						

Eastern Standard Time in bold type
Pacific Standard Time in medium type

27 Monday

1st ♉
‑♇ enters ♊ **1:53 am**
☽ v/c **9:47 am** 6:47 am
☽ enters ♊ **8:56 pm** 5:56 pm

28 Tuesday

1st ♊

29 Wednesday

1st ♊
☽ v/c **3:21 pm** 12:21 pm
☽ enters ♋ **10:57 pm** 7:57 pm

30 Thursday

1st ♋

Eastern Standard Time in bold type
Pacific Standard Time in medium type

May 1 Friday
1st ♋
☽ v/c   10:38 pm

Beltane

---

2 Saturday
1st ♋
☽ v/c   **1:38 am**
☽ enters ♌   **4:49 am** 1:49 am

---

3 Sunday
1st ♌
2nd Quarter **5:04 am** 2:04 am
♀ enters ♈   **2:16 pm** 11:16 am
♆ ℞   9:26 pm

April 1998								May 1998								June 1998						
S	M	T	W	T	F	S		S	M	T	W	T	F	S		S	M	T	W	T	F	S
			1	2	3	4							1	2			1	2	3	4	5	6
5	6	7	8	9	10	11		3	4	5	6	7	8	9		7	8	9	10	11	12	13
12	13	14	15	16	17	18		10	11	12	13	14	15	16		14	15	16	17	18	19	20
19	20	21	22	23	24	25		17	18	19	20	21	22	23		21	22	23	24	25	26	27
26	27	28	29	30	31			24	25	26	27	28	29	30		28	29	30				
								31														

Eastern Standard Time in bold type
Pacific Standard Time in medium type

4 Monday
2nd ♌
Ψ ℞   **12:26 am**
☽ v/c   **6:49 am** 3:49 am
☽ enters ♍ **2:47 pm** 11:47 am

5 Tuesday
2nd ♍

6 Wednesday
2nd ♍
☽ v/c   **8:11 am** 5:11 am
♀ enters ♉ **4:16 pm** 1:16 pm

7 Thursday
2nd ♍
☽ enters ♎ **3:19 am** 12:19 am

Eastern Standard Time in bold type
Pacific Standard Time in medium type

8 Friday
2nd ♎

9 Saturday
2nd ♎
☽ v/c   **9:19 am**   6:19 am
☽ enters ♏   **4:10 pm**   1:10 pm

10 Sunday
2nd ♏
☿ D   **5:15 am**   2:15 am

Mother's Day

April 1998						
S	M	T	W	T	F	S
			1	2	3	4
5	6	7	8	9	10	11
12	13	14	15	16	17	18
19	20	21	22	23	24	25
26	27	28	29	30	31	

May 1998						
S	M	T	W	T	F	S
					1	2
3	4	5	6	7	8	9
10	11	12	13	14	15	16
17	18	19	20	21	22	23
24	25	26	27	28	29	30
31						

June 1998						
S	M	T	W	T	F	S
	1	2	3	4	5	6
7	8	9	10	11	12	13
14	15	16	17	18	19	20
21	22	23	24	25	26	27
28	29	30				

Eastern Standard Time in bold type
Pacific Standard Time in medium type

11 Monday

2nd ♏
| Full Moon | **9:30 am** | 6:30 am |
| ☽ v/c | **11:06 am** | 8:06 am |

12 Tuesday

3rd ♏
☽ enters ♐ **3:48 am** 12:48 am

13 Wednesday

3rd ♐

14 Thursday

3rd ♐
☽ v/c	**12:43 pm**	9:43 am
☽ enters ♑	**1:40 pm**	10:40 am
☿ enters ♉	**9:10 pm**	6:10 pm

Eastern Standard Time in bold type
Pacific Standard Time in medium type

15 Friday
3rd ♑

16 Saturday
3rd ♑
☽ v/c   **4:54 pm**   1:54 pm
☽ enters ♒ **9:31 pm**   6:31 pm

17 Sunday
3rd ♒
♅ ℞   **5:54 am**   2:54 am

April 1998						
S	M	T	W	T	F	S
			1	2	3	4
5	6	7	8	9	10	11
12	13	14	15	16	17	18
19	20	21	22	23	24	25
26	27	28	29	30	31	

May 1998						
S	M	T	W	T	F	S
					1	2
3	4	5	6	7	8	9
10	11	12	13	14	15	16
17	18	19	20	21	22	23
24	25	26	27	28	29	30
31						

June 1998						
S	M	T	W	T	F	S
	1	2	3	4	5	6
7	8	9	10	11	12	13
14	15	16	17	18	19	20
21	22	23	24	25	26	27
28	29	30				

Eastern Standard Time in bold type
Pacific Standard Time in medium type

18 Monday

3rd ≈
4th Quarter **11:36 pm** 8:36 pm
☽ v/c **11:36 pm** 8:36 pm

19 Tuesday

4th ≈
☽ enters ⊬ **3:04 am** 12:04 am

20 Wednesday

4th ⊬
☉ enters ♊ 10:05 pm
☽ v/c 11:45 pm

Sun enters Gemini

21 Thursday

4th ⊬
☉ enters ♊ **1:05 am**
☽ v/c **2:45 am**
☽ enters ♈ **6:06 am** 3:06 am

Eastern Standard Time in bold type
Pacific Standard Time in medium type

22 Friday
4th ♈

23 Saturday
4th ♈
☽ v/c   **4:13 am**   1:13 am
☽ enters ♉   **7:06 am**   4:06 am
♂ enters ♊   **10:42 pm**   7:42 pm

24 Sunday
4th ♉
☽ v/c   **9:15 pm**   6:15 pm

April 1998						
S	M	T	W	T	F	S
			1	2	3	4
5	6	7	8	9	10	11
12	13	14	15	16	17	18
19	20	21	22	23	24	25
26	27	28	29	30	31	

May 1998						
S	M	T	W	T	F	S
					1	2
3	4	5	6	7	8	9
10	11	12	13	14	15	16
17	18	19	20	21	22	23
24	25	26	27	28	29	30
31						

June 1998						
S	M	T	W	T	F	S
	1	2	3	4	5	6
7	8	9	10	11	12	13
14	15	16	17	18	19	20
21	22	23	24	25	26	27
28	29	30				

Eastern Standard Time in bold type
Pacific Standard Time in medium type

25 Monday

4th ♉
New Moon **2:32 pm** 11:32 am
☽ enters ♊ **7:25 am** 4:25 am

Memorial Day (Observed)

26 Tuesday

1st ♊

27 Wednesday

1st ♊
☽ v/c **6:43 am** 3:43 am
☽ enters ♋ **8:58 am** 5:58 am

28 Thursday

1st ♋

29 Friday
1st ♋
☽ v/c	**1:09 pm**	10:09 am
☽ enters ♌	**1:38 pm**	10:38 am
♀ enters ♉	**6:32 pm**	3:32 pm

30 Saturday
1st ♌

Memorial Day

31 Sunday
1st ♌
| ☽ v/c | **9:24 pm** | 6:24 pm |
| ☽ enters ♍ | **10:21 pm** | 7:21 pm |

April 1998							May 1998							June 1998					
S	M	T	W	T	F	S
			1	2	3	4
5	6	7	8	9	10	11
12	13	14	15	16	17	18
19	20	21	22	23	24	25
26	27	28	29	30	31	

April 1998	S	M	T	W	T	F	S

May 1998
S M T W T F S
            1 2
3 4 5 6 7 8 9
10 11 12 13 14 15 16
17 18 19 20 21 22 23
24 25 26 27 28 29 30
31

June 1998
S M T W T F S
 1 2 3 4 5 6
7 8 9 10 11 12 13
14 15 16 17 18 19 20
21 22 23 24 25 26 27
28 29 30

June 1 Monday

1st ♍
☿ enters ♊   **3:07 am** 12:07 am
2nd Quarter   **8:45 pm** 5:45 pm

2 Tuesday

2nd ♍
☽ v/c   9:08 pm

3 Wednesday

2nd ♍
☽ v/c   **12:08 am**
☽ enters ♎ **10:17 am** 7:17 am

4 Thursday

2nd ♎

5 Friday
2nd ♎
☽ v/c **10:29 pm** 7:29 pm
☽ enters ♏ **11:06 pm** 8:06 pm

6 Saturday
2nd ♏

7 Sunday
2nd ♏
☽ v/c 11:01 pm

	May 1998					
S	M	T	W	T	F	S
					1	2
3	4	5	6	7	8	9
10	11	12	13	14	15	16
17	18	19	20	21	22	23
24	25	26	27	28	29	30
31						

	June 1998					
S	M	T	W	T	F	S
	1	2	3	4	5	6
7	8	9	10	11	12	13
14	15	16	17	18	19	20
21	22	23	24	25	26	27
28	29	30				

	July 1998					
S	M	T	W	T	F	S
			1	2	3	4
5	6	7	8	9	10	11
12	13	14	15	16	17	18
19	20	21	22	23	24	25
26	27	28	29	30	31	

Eastern Standard Time in bold type
Pacific Standard Time in medium type

8 Monday
2nd ♏
☽ v/c	**2:01 am**	
☽ enters ♐	**10:35 am**	7:35 am
♄ enters ♉		10:08 pm

9 Tuesday
2nd ♐
♄ enters ♉	**1:08 am**	
Full Moon	**11:19 pm**	8:19 pm

10 Wednesday
3rd ♐
☽ v/c	**12:08 pm**	9:08 am
☽ enters ♑	**7:51 pm**	4:51 pm

11 Thursday
3rd ♑

12 Friday

3rd ♑
☽ v/c   **8:04 pm** 5:04 pm

13 Saturday

3rd ♑
☽ enters ♒   **3:03 am** 12:03 am

14 Sunday

3rd ♒
☽ v/c   **9:39 pm** 6:39 pm
☿ enters ♋   9:33 pm

May 1998						
S	M	T	W	T	F	S
					1	2
3	4	5	6	7	8	9
10	11	12	13	14	15	16
17	18	19	20	21	22	23
24	25	26	27	28	29	30
31						

June 1998						
S	M	T	W	T	F	S
	1	2	3	4	5	6
7	8	9	10	11	12	13
14	15	16	17	18	19	20
21	22	23	24	25	26	27
28	29	30				

July 1998						
S	M	T	W	T	F	S
			1	2	3	4
5	6	7	8	9	10	11
12	13	14	15	16	17	18
19	20	21	22	23	24	25
26	27	28	29	30	31	

Eastern Standard Time in bold type
Pacific Standard Time in medium type

15 Monday
3rd ≈
☿ enters ♋ **12:33 am**
☽ enters ♓ **8:32 am** 5:32 am

16 Tuesday
3rd ♓

17 Wednesday
3rd ♓
4th Quarter **5:38 am** 2:38 am
☽ v/c **6:34 am** 3:34 am
☽ enters ♈ **12:23 pm** 9:23 am

18 Thursday
4th ♈

19 Friday

4th ♈
)) v/c   **11:48 am** 8:48 am
)) enters ♉   **2:47 pm** 11:47 am
♀ enters ♈ **10:12 pm** 7:12 pm

20 Saturday

4th ♉

21 Sunday

4th ♉
☉ enters ♋   **9:02 am** 6:02 am
)) v/c   **11:24 am** 8:24 am
)) enters ♊   **4:26 pm** 1:26 pm

Sun enters Cancer • Summer Solstice • Litha • Father's Day

May 1998						
S	M	T	W	T	F	S
					1	2
3	4	5	6	7	8	9
10	11	12	13	14	15	16
17	18	19	20	21	22	23
24	25	26	27	28	29	30
31						

June 1998						
S	M	T	W	T	F	S
	1	2	3	4	5	6
7	8	9	10	11	12	13
14	15	16	17	18	19	20
21	22	23	24	25	26	27
28	29	30				

July 1998						
S	M	T	W	T	F	S
			1	2	3	4
5	6	7	8	9	10	11
12	13	14	15	16	17	18
19	20	21	22	23	24	25
26	27	28	29	30	31	

Eastern Standard Time in bold type
Pacific Standard Time in medium type

22 Monday
4th ♊

23 Tuesday
4th ♊
☽ v/c   **1:46 pm** 10:46 am
☽ enters ♋   **6:39 pm** 3:39 pm
New Moon **10:50 pm** 7:50 pm

24 Wednesday
1st ♋
♀ enters ♊   **7:27 am** 4:27 am

25 Thursday
1st ♋
☽ v/c   **6:11 pm** 3:11 pm
☽ enters ♌ **11:04 pm** 8:04 pm

26 Friday
1st ♌

27 Saturday
1st ♌
☽ v/c   **8:05 pm**   5:05 pm

28 Sunday
1st ♌
☽ enters ♍   **6:55 am**   3:55 am

		May 1998				
S	M	T	W	T	F	S
					1	2
3	4	5	6	7	8	9
10	11	12	13	14	15	16
17	18	19	20	21	22	23
24	25	26	27	28	29	30
31						

		June 1998				
S	M	T	W	T	F	S
	1	2	3	4	5	6
7	8	9	10	11	12	13
14	15	16	17	18	19	20
21	22	23	24	25	26	27
28	29	30				

		July 1998				
S	M	T	W	T	F	S
			1	2	3	4
5	6	7	8	9	10	11
12	13	14	15	16	17	18
19	20	21	22	23	24	25
26	27	28	29	30	31	

Eastern Standard Time in bold type
Pacific Standard Time in medium type

29 Monday
1st ♍

30 Tuesday
1st ♍
☽ v/c   **5:58 pm** 2:58 pm
☽ enters ♎   **6:06 pm** 3:06 pm
☿ enters ♌   **6:51 pm** 3:51 pm

July 1 Wednesday
1st ♎
2nd Quarter **1:44 pm** 10:44 am

2 Thursday
2nd ♎
☽ v/c   11:35 pm

Eastern Standard Time in bold type
Pacific Standard Time in medium type

3 Friday

2nd ♎
☽ v/c   **2:35 am**
☽ enters ♏,   **6:46 am**   3:46 am

4 Saturday

2nd ♏,

Independence Day

5 Sunday

2nd ♏,
☽ v/c   **2:09 pm** 11:09 am
⚷ enters ♋   **3:08 pm** 12:08 pm
☽ enters ♐   **6:24 pm**   3:24 pm

June 1998						
S	M	T	W	T	F	S
	1	2	3	4	5	6
7	8	9	10	11	12	13
14	15	16	17	18	19	20
21	22	23	24	25	26	27
28	29	30				

July 1998						
S	M	T	W	T	F	S
			1	2	3	4
5	6	7	8	9	10	11
12	13	14	15	16	17	18
19	20	21	22	23	24	25
26	27	28	29	30	31	

August 1998						
S	M	T	W	T	F	S
						1
2	3	4	5	6	7	8
9	10	11	12	13	14	15	16
17	18	19	20	21	22	23
24	25	26	27	28	29	30
31						

Eastern Standard Time in bold type
Pacific Standard Time in medium type

6 Monday

2nd ♐
♂ enters ♋ **3:59 am** 12:59 am

7 Tuesday

2nd ♐
☽ v/c **11:34 pm** 8:34 pm

8 Wednesday

2nd ♐
☽ enters ♑ **3:28 am** 12:28 am

9 Thursday

2nd ♑
Full Moon **11:01 am** 8:01 am

10 Friday

3rd ♈
☽ v/c **6:15 am** 3:15 am
☽ enters ≈ **9:52 am** 6:52 am

11 Saturday

3rd ≈
♯ D **7:14 pm** 4:14 pm
✳ enters ♎ **7:20 pm** 4:20 pm
☽ v/c **10:48 pm** 7:48 pm

12 Sunday

3rd ≈
☽ enters ♓ **2:22 pm** 11:22 am

June 1998						
S	M	T	W	T	F	S
	1	2	3	4	5	6
7	8	9	10	11	12	13
14	15	16	17	18	19	20
21	22	23	24	25	26	27
28	29	30				

July 1998						
S	M	T	W	T	F	S
			1	2	3	4
5	6	7	8	9	10	11
12	13	14	15	16	17	18
19	20	21	22	23	24	25
26	27	28	29	30	31	

August 1998						
S	M	T	W	T	F	S
						1
2	3	4	5	6	7	8
9	10	11	12	13	14	15
16	17	18	19	20	21	22
23	24	25	26	27	28	29
30	31					

Eastern Standard Time in bold type
Pacific Standard Time in medium type

13 Monday
3rd ♓

14 Tuesday
3rd ♓
☽ v/c   **2:25 pm** 11:25 am
☽ enters ♈   **5:45 pm** 2:45 pm

15 Wednesday
3rd ♈

16 Thursday
3rd ♈
4th Quarter **10:14 am** 7:14 am
☽ v/c   **2:51 pm** 11:51 am
☽ enters ♉   **8:33 pm** 5:33 pm

17 Friday
4th ♉
♃ ℞   **7:55 pm** 4:55 pm

18 Saturday
4th ♉
☽ v/c   **8:01 pm** 5:01 pm
☽ enters ♊ **11:18 pm** 8:18 pm

19 Sunday
4th ♊
♀ enters ♋ **10:17 am** 7:17 am
☿ ℞   **10:45 pm** 7:45 pm

June 1998						
S	M	T	W	T	F	S
	1	2	3	4	5	6
7	8	9	10	11	12	13
14	15	16	17	18	19	20
21	22	23	24	25	26	27
28	29	30				

July 1998						
S	M	T	W	T	F	S
			1	2	3	4
5	6	7	8	9	10	11
12	13	14	15	16	17	18
19	20	21	22	23	24	25
26	27	28	29	30	31	

August 1998						
S	M	T	W	T	F	S
						1
2	3	4	5	6	7	8
9	10	11	12	13	14	15
16	17	18	19	20	21	22
23	24	25	26	27	28	29
30	31					

Eastern Standard Time in bold type
Pacific Standard Time in medium type

20 Monday
4th ♊
☽ v/c   **11:20 pm** 8:20 pm
☽ enters ♋   11:43 pm

21 Tuesday
4th ♊
☽ enters ♋ **2:43 am**

22 Wednesday
4th ♋
☉ enters ♌ **7:55 pm** 4:55 pm

Sun enters Leo

23 Thursday
4th ♋
☽ v/c   **4:14 am** 1:14 am
☽ enters ♌ **7:49 am** 4:49 am
New Moon **8:44 am** 5:44 am

24 Friday
1st ♌

25 Saturday
1st ♌
☽ v/c   **9:57 am**   6:57 am
☽ enters ♍   **3:34 pm** 12:34 pm

26 Sunday
1st ♍

June 1998						
S	M	T	W	T	F	S
	1	2	3	4	5	6
7	8	9	10	11	12	13
14	15	16	17	18	19	20
21	22	23	24	25	26	27
28	29	30				

July 1998						
S	M	T	W	T	F	S
			1	2	3	4
5	6	7	8	9	10	11
12	13	14	15	16	17	18
19	20	21	22	23	24	25
26	27	28	29	30	31	

August 1998						
S	M	T	W	T	F	S
						1
2	3	4	5	6	7	8
9	10	11	12	13	14	15
16	17	18	19	20	21	22
23	24	25	26	27	28	29	30
31						

Eastern Standard Time in bold type
Pacific Standard Time in medium type

27 Monday
1st ♍
☽ v/c   **10:03 pm**   7:03 pm
☽ enters ♎   11:15 pm

28 Tuesday
1st ♍
☽ enters ♎   **2:15 am**
♀ enters ♊   **12:33 pm**   9:33 am

29 Wednesday
1st ♎

30 Thursday
1st ♎
☽ v/c   **11:13 am**   8:13 am
☽ enters ♏   **2:45 pm** 11:45 am
☿ ℞   **9:23 pm**   6:23 pm

Eastern Standard Time in bold type
Pacific Standard Time in medium type

31 Friday
1st ♏
2nd Quarter **7:05 am** 4:05 am

August 1 Saturday
2nd ♏
☽ v/c   **11:02 pm** 8:02 pm
☽ enters ♐   11:48 pm

Lammas

2 Sunday
2nd ♏
☽ enters ♐ **2:48 am**

July 1998						
S	M	T	W	T	F	S
			1	2	3	4
5	6	7	8	9	10	11
12	13	14	15	16	17	18
19	20	21	22	23	24	25
26	27	28	29	30	31	

August 1998						
S	M	T	W	T	F	S
						1
2	3	4	5	6	7	8
9	10	11	12	13	14	15
16	17	18	19	20	21	22
23	24	25	26	27	28	29
30	31					

September 1998						
S	M	T	W	T	F	S
		1	2	3	4	5
6	7	8	9	10	11	12
13	14	15	16	17	18	19
20	21	22	23	24	25	26
27	28	29	30			

Eastern Standard Time in bold type
Pacific Standard Time in medium type

3 Monday
2nd ♐

4 Tuesday
2nd ♐
☽ v/c   **7:45 am**   4:45 am
☽ enters ♑   **12:18 pm**   9:18 am

5 Wednesday
2nd ♑

6 Thursday
2nd ♑
☽ v/c   **1:59 pm**   10:59 am
☽ enters ≈   **6:31 pm**   3:31 pm

7 Friday
2nd ≈≈
Full Moon   **9:10 pm** 6:10 pm

Lunar Eclipse 15° ≈≈ 21'

8 Saturday
3rd ≈≈
☽ enters ♓ **10:04 pm** 7:04 pm
☽ v/c   **1:47 pm** 10:47 am

9 Sunday
3rd ♓

July 1998						
S	M	T	W	T	F	S
			1	2	3	4
5	6	7	8	9	10	11
12	13	14	15	16	17	18
19	20	21	22	23	24	25
26	27	28	29	30	31	

August 1998						
S	M	T	W	T	F	S
						1
2	3	4	5	6	7	8
9	10	11	12	13	14	15
16	17	18	19	20	21	22
23	24	25	26	27	28	29
30	31					

September 1998						
S	M	T	W	T	F	S
		1	2	3	4	5
6	7	8	9	10	11	12
13	14	15	16	17	18	19
20	21	22	23	24	25	26
27	28	29	30			

Eastern Standard Time in bold type
Pacific Standard Time in medium type

10 Monday
3rd ♓
| ☽ v/c | **7:25 pm** | 4:25 pm |
| ☽ enters ♈ | | 9:11 pm |

11 Tuesday
3rd ♓
☽ enters ♈ **12:11 am**

12 Wednesday
3rd ♈
| ☽ v/c | 10:53 pm |
| ☽ enters ♉ | 11:05 pm |

13 Thursday
3rd ♈
☽ v/c	**1:53 am**	
☽ enters ♉	**2:05 am**	
♀ enters ♌	**4:19 am**	1:19 am

Eastern Standard Time in bold type
Pacific Standard Time in medium type

14 Friday

3rd ♉
4th Quarter **2:49 pm** 11:49 am
☽ v/c **11:18 pm** 8:18 pm

15 Saturday

4th ♉
☽ enters ♊ **4:46 am** 1:46 am
♄ ℞ **12:17 pm** 9:17 am
♇ D **11:14 pm** 8:14pm

16 Sunday

4th ♊
♀ enters ♓ **7:43 pm** 4:43 pm
☽ v/c 11:56 pm

July 1998						
S	M	T	W	T	F	S
			1	2	3	4
5	6	7	8	9	10	11
12	13	14	15	16	17	18
19	20	21	22	23	24	25
26	27	28	29	30	31	

August 1998						
S	M	T	W	T	F	S
						1
2	3	4	5	6	7	8
9	10	11	12	13	14	15
16	17	18	19	20	21	22
23	24	25	26	27	28	29
30	31					

September 1998						
S	M	T	W	T	F	S
		1	2	3	4	5
6	7	8	9	10	11	12
13	14	15	16	17	18	19
20	21	22	23	24	25	26
27	28	29	30			

Eastern Standard Time in bold type
Pacific Standard Time in medium type

17 Monday

4th ♊
☽ v/c   **2:56 am**
☽ enters ♋ **8:56 am** 5:56 am

18 Tuesday

4th ♋

19 Wednesday

4th ♋
☽ v/c   **1:48 pm** 10:48 am
☽ enters ♌ **3:01 pm** 12:01 pm

20 Thursday

4th ♌
♂ enters ♌ **2:16 pm** 11:16 am

21 Friday
4th ♌
New Moon	**9:03 pm**	6:03 pm
☽ v/c	**9:03 pm**	6:03 pm
☽ enters ♍	**11:22 pm**	8:22 pm

Solar Eclipse 28° ♌ 48'

22 Saturday
1st ♍
♆ enters ♑	**7:27 pm**	4:27 pm
☉ enters ♍		11:59 pm

Sun enters Virgo—PST

23 Sunday
1st ♍
☉ enters ♍	**2:59 am** .	
☿ D	**5:30 pm**	2:30 pm

Sun enters Virgo—EST

July 1998							August 1998							September 1998						
S	M	T	W	T	F	S	S	M	T	W	T	F	S	S	M	T	W	T	F	S
			1	2	3	4							1			1	2	3	4	5
5	6	7	8	9	10	11	2	3	4	5	6	7	8	6	7	8	9	10	11	12
12	13	14	15	16	17	18	9	10	11	12	13	14	15	13	14	15	16	17	18	19
19	20	21	22	23	24	25	16	17	18	19	20	21	22	20	21	22	23	24	25	26
26	27	28	29	30	31		23	24	25	26	27	28	29	27	28	29	30			
							30	31												

Eastern Standard Time in bold type
Pacific Standard Time in medium type

24 Monday
1st ℳ
☽ v/c   **9:58 am**   6:58 am
☽ enters ♎ **10:02 am**   7:02 am

25 Tuesday
1st ♎

26 Wednesday
1st ♎
☽ v/c   **10:14 pm**   7:14 pm
☽ enters ♏ **10:25 pm**   7:25 pm

27 Thursday
1st ♏

Eastern Standard Time in bold type
Pacific Standard Time in medium type

28 Friday
1st ♏

29 Saturday
1st ♏

☽ v/c	**10:38 am**	7:38 am
☽ enters ♐	**10:55 am**	7:55 am
2nd Quarter		9:07 pm

30 Sunday
2nd ♐
2nd Quarter **12:07 am**

July 1998							August 1998							September 1998						
S	M	T	W	T	F	S	S	M	T	W	T	F	S	S	M	T	W	T	F	S
			1	2	3	4							1			1	2	3	4	5
5	6	7	8	9	10	11	2	3	4	5	6	7	8	6	7	8	9	10	11	12
12	13	14	15	16	17	18	9	10	11	12	13	14	15	13	14	15	16	17	18	19
19	20	21	22	23	24	25	16	17	18	19	20	21	22	20	21	22	23	24	25	26
26	27	28	29	30	31		23	24	25	26	27	28	29	27	28	29	30			
							30	31												

Eastern Standard Time in bold type
Pacific Standard Time in medium type

31 Monday
2nd ♐
| ☽ v/c | **11:57 am** | 8:57 am |
| ☽ enters ♑ | **9:23 pm** | 6:23 pm |

September 1 Tuesday
2nd ♑

2 Wednesday
2nd ♑

3 Thursday
2nd ♑
| ☽ v/c | **3:56 am** | 12:56 am |
| ☽ enters ♒ | **4:21 am** | 1:21 am |

4 Friday
2nd ≈

5 Saturday
2nd ≈
☽ v/c **4:56 am** 1:56 am
☽ enters ✸ **7:48 am** 4:48 am

6 Sunday
2nd ✸
Full Moon **6:22 am** 3:22 am
♀ enters ♍ **2:24 pm** 11:24 am

TEAYA ALEXIS WONG 7 lb, 10 oz.
EDMONTON, ALTA
7:30 p.m. MDT
2nd child

Lunar Eclipse 13° ✸ 40'

August 1998						
S	M	T	W	T	F	S
						1
2	3	4	5	6	7	8
9	10	11	12	13	14	15
16	17	18	19	20	21	22
23	24	25	26	27	28	29
30	31					

September 1998						
S	M	T	W	T	F	S
		1	2	3	4	5
6	7	8	9	10	11	12
13	14	15	16	17	18	19
20	21	22	23	24	25	26
27	28	29	30			

October 1998						
S	M	T	W	T	F	S
				1	2	3
4	5	6	7	8	9	10
11	12	13	14	15	16	17
18	19	20	21	22	23	24
25	26	27	28	29	30	31

Eastern Standard Time in bold type
Pacific Standard Time in medium type

7 Monday

3rd ♓
☽ v/c	**8:23 am**	5:23 am
☽ enters ♈	**8:53 am**	5:53 am
☿ enters ♍	**8:57 pm**	5:57 pm

Labor Day

8 Tuesday

3rd ♈

9 Wednesday

3rd ♈
| ☽ v/c | **8:43 am** | 5:43 am |
| ☽ enters ♉ | **9:17 am** | 6:17 am |

10 Thursday

3rd ♉

11 Friday
3rd ♉
| ☽ v/c | **10:03 am** | 7:03 am |
| ☽ enters ♊ | **10:41 am** | 7:41 am |

12 Saturday
3rd ♊
| 4th Quarter | **8:58 pm** | 5:58 pm |
| ☽ v/c | **11:47 pm** | |

13 Sunday
4th ♊
| ☽ enters ♋ | **2:20 pm** | 11:20 am |
| ☽ v/c | **2:47 am** | |

August 1998							September 1998							October 1998						
S	M	T	W	T	F	S	S	M	T	W	T	F	S	S	M	T	W	T	F	S
						1			1	2	3	4	5						1	2	3
2	3	4	5	6	7	8	6	7	8	9	10	11	12	4	5	6	7	8	9	10
9	10	11	12	13	14	15	13	14	15	16	17	18	19	11	12	13	14	15	16	17
16	17	18	19	20	21	22	20	21	22	23	24	25	26	18	19	20	21	22	23	24
23	24	25	26	27	28	29	27	28	29	30				25	26	27	28	29	30	31
30	31																			

Eastern Standard Time in bold type
Pacific Standard Time in medium type

14 Monday
4th ⊗

15 Tuesday
4th ⊗
| ☽ v/c | **7:59 pm** | 4:59 pm |
| ☽ enters ♌ | **8:48 pm** | 5:48 pm |

16 Wednesday
4th ♌
| ⚝ enters ♌ | **6:33 pm** | 3:33 pm |

17 Thursday
4th ♌
| ☽ v/c | **5:57 am** | 2:57 am |

18 Friday
4th ♌
☽ enters ♍ **5:51 am** 2:51 am

19 Saturday
4th ♍

20 Sunday
4th ♍
New Moon **12:01 pm** 9:01 am
☽ v/c **3:57 pm** 12:57 pm
☽ enters ♎ **4:57 pm** 1:57 pm

Rosh Hashanah begins

August 1998						
S	M	T	W	T	F	S
						1
2	3	4	5	6	7	8
9	10	11	12	13	14	15
16	17	18	19	20	21	22
23	24	25	26	27	28	29
30	31					

September 1998						
S	M	T	W	T	F	S
		1	2	3	4	5
6	7	8	9	10	11	12
13	14	15	16	17	18	19
20	21	22	23	24	25	26
27	28	29	30			

October 1998						
S	M	T	W	T	F	S
				1	2	3
4	5	6	7	8	9	10
11	12	13	14	15	16	17
18	19	20	21	22	23	24
25	26	27	28	29	30	31

Eastern Standard Time in bold type
Pacific Standard Time in medium type

21 Monday
1st ♎

22 Tuesday
1st ♎
☉ enters ♎   9:37 pm

Rosh Hashanah ends

23 Wednesday
1st ♎
☉ enters ♎ **12:37 am**
☽ v/c   **4:18 am**   1:18 am
☽ enters ♏   **5:22 am**   2:22 am

Sun enters Libra • Fall Equinox • Mabon

24 Thursday
1st ♏
☿ enters ♎   **5:12 am**   2:12 am

25 Friday
1st ♏
☽ v/c   **4:59 pm**   1:59 pm
☽ enters ♐   **6:05 pm**   3:05 pm

26 Saturday
1st ♐

27 Sunday
1st ♐
☽ v/c   **10:42 pm** 7:42 pm

August 1998						
S	M	T	W	T	F	S
						1
2	3	4	5	6	7	8
9	10	11	12	13	14	15
16	17	18	19	20	21	22
23	24	25	26	27	28	29
30	31					

September 1998						
S	M	T	W	T	F	S
		1	2	3	4	5
6	7	8	9	10	11	12
13	14	15	16	17	18	19
20	21	22	23	24	25	26
27	28	29	30			

October 1998						
S	M	T	W	T	F	S
				1	2	3
4	5	6	7	8	9	10
11	12	13	14	15	16	17
18	19	20	21	22	23	24
25	26	27	28	29	30	31

Eastern Standard Time in bold type
Pacific Standard Time in medium type

28 Monday
1st ♐
☽ enters ♑ **5:31 am** 2:31 am
2nd Quarter **4:12 pm** 1:12 pm

29 Tuesday
2nd ♑

Yom Kippur begins

30 Wednesday
2nd ♑
☽ v/c **1:27 pm** 10:27 am
☽ enters ≈ **1:54 pm** 10:54 am
♀ enters ♎ **6:13 pm** 3:13 pm

Yom Kippur ends

October 1 Thursday
2nd ≈

2 Friday
2nd ≈
☽ v/c   **1:28 pm** 10:28 am
☽ enters ♓   **6:24 pm** 3:24 pm

3 Saturday
2nd ♓

4 Sunday
2nd ♓
☽ v/c   **6:35 pm** 3:35 pm
☽ enters ♈   **7:32 pm** 4:32 pm

Sukkot begins

September 1998
S M T W T F S
1 2 3 4 5
6 7 8 9 10 11 12
13 14 15 16 17 18 19
20 21 22 23 24 25 26
27 28 29 30

October 1998
S M T W T F S
1 2 3
4 5 6 7 8 9 10
11 12 13 14 15 16 17
18 19 20 21 22 23 24
25 26 27 28 29 30 31

November 1998
S M T W T F S
1 2 3 4 5 6 7
8 9 10 11 12 13 14
15 16 17 18 19 20 21
22 23 24 25 26 27 28
29 30

Eastern Standard Time in bold type
Pacific Standard Time in medium type

5 Monday
2nd ♈
Full Moon   **3:12 pm** 12:12 pm

6 Tuesday
3rd ♈
☽ v/c   **6:26 pm** 3:26 pm
☽ enters ♉   **6:58 pm** 3:58 pm

Sukkot ends

7 Wednesday
3rd ♉
♂ enters ♍   **7:28 am** 4:28 am

8 Thursday
3rd ♉
☽ v/c   **5:44 pm** 2:44 pm
☽ enters ♊   **6:44 pm** 3:44 pm

9 Friday
3rd ♊

10 Saturday
3rd ♊
☽ v/c   **5:36 pm**   2:36 pm
♀ ℞   **6:49 pm**   3:49 pm
☽ enters ♋   **8:48 pm**   5:48 pm

11 Sunday
3rd ♋
♆ D   **7:10 am**   4:10 am
☿ enters ♏   **9:44 pm**   6:44 pm

September 1998						
S	M	T	W	T	F	S
		1	2	3	4	5
6	7	8	9	10	11	12
13	14	15	16	17	18	19
20	21	22	23	24	25	26
27	28	29	30			

October 1998						
S	M	T	W	T	F	S
				1	2	3
4	5	6	7	8	9	10
11	12	13	14	15	16	17
18	19	20	21	22	23	24
25	26	27	28	29	30	31

November 1998						
S	M	T	W	T	F	S
1	2	3	4	5	6	7
8	9	10	11	12	13	14
15	16	17	18	19	20	21
22	23	24	25	26	27	28
29	30					

Eastern Standard Time in bold type
Pacific Standard Time in medium type

12 Monday

3rd ♋
4th Quarter **6:11 am** 3:11 am
☽ v/c   10:17 pm
☽ enters ♌   11:25 pm

Columbus' Day

13 Tuesday

4th ♋
☽ v/c   **1:17 am**
☽ enters ♌ **2:25 am**

14 Wednesday

4th ♌
☽ v/c   **6:54 pm** 3:54 pm

15 Thursday

4th ♌
⚹ enters ♏ **3:41 am** 12:41 am
☽ enters ♍ **11:32 am** 8:32 am

Eastern Standard Time in bold type
Pacific Standard Time in medium type

16 Friday
4th ♍

17 Saturday
4th ♍
☽ v/c   **9:50 pm** 6:50 pm
☽ enters ♎ **11:02 pm** 8:02 pm

18 Sunday
4th ♎
♅ D   **1:46 pm** 10:46 am

September 1998						
S	M	T	W	T	F	S
		1	2	3	4	5
6	7	8	9	10	11	12
13	14	15	16	17	18	19
20	21	22	23	24	25	26
27	28	29	30			

October 1998						
S	M	T	W	T	F	S
				1	2	3
4	5	6	7	8	9	10
11	12	13	14	15	16	17
18	19	20	21	22	23	24
25	26	27	28	29	30	31

November 1998						
S	M	T	W	T	F	S
1	2	3	4	5	6	7
8	9	10	11	12	13	14
15	16	17	18	19	20	21
22	23	24	25	26	27	28
29	30					

Eastern Standard Time in bold type
Pacific Standard Time in medium type

19 Monday
4th ♎

20 Tuesday
4th ♎
New Moon **5:10 am** 2:10 am
☽ v/c **10:25 am** 7:25 am
☽ enters ♏ **11:37 am** 8:37 am

21 Wednesday
1st ♏

22 Thursday
1st ♏
☽ v/c **11:07 pm** 8:07 pm
☽ enters ♐ 9:17 pm

Eastern Standard Time in bold type
Pacific Standard Time in medium type

23 Friday
1st ♏
☽ enters ♐ **12:17 am**
☉ enters ♏ **9:59 am** 6:59 am

Sun enters Scorpio

24 Saturday
1st ♐
☽ v/c **1:58 pm** 10:58 am
♀ enters ♏ **6:06 pm** 3:06 pm

25 Sunday
1st ♐
☽ enters ♑ **12:05 pm** 9:05 am
♄ enters ♈ **1:42 pm** 10:42 am

Daylight Saving Time ends at 2 AM

September 1998						
S	M	T	W	T	F	S
			1	2	3	4	5
6	7	8	9	10	11	12
13	14	15	16	17	18	19
20	21	22	23	24	25	26
27	28	29	30			

October 1998						
S	M	T	W	T	F	S
				1	2	3
4	5	6	7	8	9	10
11	12	13	14	15	16	17
18	19	20	21	22	23	24
25	26	27	28	29	30	31

November 1998						
S	M	T	W	T	F	S
1	2	3	4	5	6	7
8	9	10	11	12	13	14
15	16	17	18	19	20	21
22	23	24	25	26	27	28
29	30					

Eastern Standard Time in bold type
Pacific Standard Time in medium type

26 Monday
1st ♑

27 Tuesday
1st ♑
☽ v/c **9:24 pm** 6:24 pm
☽ enters ♒ **9:45 pm** 6:45 pm

28 Wednesday
1st ♒
2nd Quarter **6:46 am** 3:46 am

29 Thursday
2nd ♒

30 Friday

2nd ≈
☽ v/c   **3:20 am** 12:20 am
☽ enters ♓ **3:58 am** 12:58 am

31 Saturday

2nd ♓

Halloween • Samhain

November 1 Sunday

2nd ♓
☽ v/c   **5:59 am** 2:59 am
☽ enters ♈ **6:27 am** 3:27 am
☿ enters ♐ **11:03 am** 8:03 am

October 1998						
S	M	T	W	T	F	S
				1	2	3
4	5	6	7	8	9	10
11	12	13	14	15	16	17
18	19	20	21	22	23	24
25	26	27	28	29	30	31

November 1998						
S	M	T	W	T	F	S
1	2	3	4	5	6	7
8	9	10	11	12	13	14
15	16	17	18	19	20	21
22	23	24	25	26	27	28
29	30					

December 1998						
S	M	T	W	T	F	S
		1	2	3	4	5
6	7	8	9	10	11	12
13	14	15	16	17	18	19
20	21	22	23	24	25	26
27	28	29	30	31		

Eastern Standard Time in bold type
Pacific Standard Time in medium type

2 Monday
2nd ♈

3 Tuesday
2nd ♈
☽ v/c	**5:28 am**	2:28 am
☽ enters ♉	**6:12 am**	3:12 am
Full Moon		9:18 pm

4 Wednesday
3rd ♉
Full Moon   **12:18 am**

5 Thursday
3rd ♉
| ☽ v/c | **4:29 am** | 1:29 am |
| ☽ enters ♊ | **5:11 am** | 2:11 am |

Eastern Standard Time in bold type
Pacific Standard Time in medium type

6 Friday
3rd ♊

7 Saturday
3rd ♊
☽ v/c   **4:01 am**   1:01 am
☽ enters ♋ **5:39 am**   2:39 am

8 Sunday
3rd ♋

October 1998						
S	M	T	W	T	F	S
				1	2	3
4	5	6	7	8	9	10
11	12	13	14	15	16	17
18	19	20	21	22	23	24
25	26	27	28	29	30	31

November 1998						
S	M	T	W	T	F	S
1	2	3	4	5	6	7
8	9	10	11	12	13	14
15	16	17	18	19	20	21
22	23	24	25	26	27	28
29	30					

December 1998						
S	M	T	W	T	F	S
		1	2	3	4	5
6	7	8	9	10	11	12
13	14	15	16	17	18	19
20	21	22	23	24	25	26
27	28	29	30	31		

Eastern Standard Time in bold type
Pacific Standard Time in medium type

9 Monday
3rd ⊗
☽ v/c   **8:52 am** 5:52 am
☽ enters ♌   **9:33 am** 6:33 am

10 Tuesday
3rd ♌
4th Quarter   **7:29 pm** 4:29 pm

11 Wednesday
4th ♌
☽ v/c   **3:06 pm** 12:06 pm
☽ enters ♍   **5:38 pm** 2:38 pm

Veterans' Day

12 Thursday
4th ♍
☿ D   **10:58 pm** 7:58 pm

Eastern Standard Time in bold type
Pacific Standard Time in medium type

13 Friday
4th ♍
♃ D   **7:33 am** 4:33 am

14 Saturday
4th ♍
☽ v/c   **4:22 am** 1:22 am
☽ enters ♎ **4:58 am** 1:58 am

15 Sunday
4th ♎

October 1998						
S	M	T	W	T	F	S
				1	2	3
4	5	6	7	8	9	10
11	12	13	14	15	16	17
18	19	20	21	22	23	24
25	26	27	28	29	30	31

November 1998						
S	M	T	W	T	F	S
1	2	3	4	5	6	7
8	9	10	11	12	13	14
15	16	17	18	19	20	21
22	23	24	25	26	27	28
29	30					

December 1998						
S	M	T	W	T	F	S
		1	2	3	4	5
6	7	8	9	10	11	12
13	14	15	16	17	18	19
20	21	22	23	24	25	26
27	28	29	30	31		

Eastern Standard Time in bold type
Pacific Standard Time in medium type

16 Monday
4th ♎
☽ v/c · · · **5:11 pm** · 2:11 pm
☽ enters ♏ · **5:42 pm** · 2:42 pm

17 Tuesday
4th ♏
♀ enters ♐ · **4:06 pm** · 1:06 pm

18 Wednesday
4th ♏
New Moon · **11:27 pm** · 8:27 pm

19 Thursday
1st ♏
☽ v/c · · · **5:49 am** · 2:49 am
☽ enters ♐ · **6:13 am** · 3:13 am

Eastern Standard Time in bold type
Pacific Standard Time in medium type

20 Friday
1st ♐

21 Saturday
1st ♐
☿ R̥   **6:40 am**   3:40 am
☽ v/c   **1:52 pm** 10:52 am
☽ enters ♑ **5:46 pm**   2:46 pm

22 Sunday
1st ♑
☉ enters ♐ **7:34 am**   4:34 am

Sun enters Sagittarius

October 1998						
S	M	T	W	T	F	S
				1	2	3
4	5	6	7	8	9	10
11	12	13	14	15	16	17
18	19	20	21	22	23	24
25	26	27	28	29	30	31

November 1998						
S	M	T	W	T	F	S
1	2	3	4	5	6	7
8	9	10	11	12	13	14
15	16	17	18	19	20	21
22	23	24	25	26	27	28
29	30					

December 1998						
S	M	T	W	T	F	S
		1	2	3	4	5
6	7	8	9	10	11	12
13	14	15	16	17	18	19
20	21	22	23	24	25	26
27	28	29	30	31		

Eastern Standard Time in bold type
Pacific Standard Time in medium type

23 Monday
1st ♑

24 Tuesday
1st ♑
☽ v/c   **3:33 am** 12:33 am
☽ enters ♒   **3:43 am** 12:43 am

25 Wednesday
1st ♒

26 Thursday
1st ♒
☽ v/c   **7:10 am** 4:10 am
☽ enters ♓   **11:14 am** 8:14 am
2nd Quarter **7:22 pm** 4:22 pm

Thanksgiving Day

Eastern Standard Time in bold type
Pacific Standard Time in medium type

27 Friday
2nd ♓
♂ enters ♎ **5:10 am** 2:10 am
☽ v/c **7:56 pm** 4:56 pm
♆ enters ≈ **8:09 pm** 5:09 pm

28 Saturday
2nd ♓
☽ enters ♈ **3:34 pm** 12:34 pm

29 Sunday
2nd ♈

October 1998						
S	M	T	W	T	F	S
				1	2	3
4	5	6	7	8	9	10
11	12	13	14	15	16	17
18	19	20	21	22	23	24
25	26	27	28	29	30	31

November 1998						
S	M	T	W	T	F	S
1	2	3	4	5	6	7
8	9	10	11	12	13	14
15	16	17	18	19	20	21
22	23	24	25	26	27	28
29	30					

December 1998						
S	M	T	W	T	F	S
		1	2	3	4	5
6	7	8	9	10	11	12
13	14	15	16	17	18	19
20	21	22	23	24	25	26
27	28	29	30	31		

Eastern Standard Time in bold type
Pacific Standard Time in medium type

30 Monday
2nd ♈
☽ v/c   **12:53 pm** 9:53 am
☽ enters ♉ **4:52 pm** 1:52 pm

December 1 Tuesday
2nd ♉
☽ v/c   **10:43 pm** 7:43 pm

2 Wednesday
2nd ♉
☽ enters ♊ **4:30 pm** 1:30 pm

3 Thursday
2nd ♊
Full Moon **10:20 am** 7:20 am

Eastern Standard Time in bold type
Pacific Standard Time in medium type

4 Friday

3rd ♊
☽ v/c   **12:08 pm** 9:08 am
☽ enters ♋   **4:28 pm** 1:28 pm

5 Saturday

3rd ♋

6 Sunday

3rd ♋
☽ v/c   **2:09 pm** 11:09 am
☽ enters ♌   **6:56 pm** 3:56 pm

November 1998						
S	M	T	W	T	F	S
1	2	3	4	5	6	7
8	9	10	11	12	13	14
15	16	17	18	19	20	21
22	23	24	25	26	27	28
29	30					

December 1998						
S	M	T	W	T	F	S
		1	2	3	4	5
6	7	8	9	10	11	12
13	14	15	16	17	18	19
20	21	22	23	24	25	26
27	28	29	30	31		

January 1999						
S	M	T	W	T	F	S
					1	2
3	4	5	6	7	8	9
10	11	12	13	14	15	16
17	18	19	20	21	22	23
24	25	26	27	28	29	30
31						

Eastern Standard Time in bold type
Pacific Standard Time in medium type

7 Monday
3rd ♌

---

8 Tuesday
3rd ♌
☽ v/c   **8:02 pm**   5:02 pm
☽ enters ♍   10:22 pm

---

9 Wednesday
3rd ♍
☽ enters ♍   **1:22 am**

---

10 Thursday
3rd ♍
4th Quarter **12:54 pm**   9:54 am
☿ D   10:24 pm

Eastern Standard Time in bold type
Pacific Standard Time in medium type

11 Friday
4th ♍
☿ D	**1:24 am**	
☽ v/c	**11:31 am**	8:31 am
☽ enters ♎	**11:44 am**	8:44 am
♀ enters ♑	**1:33 pm**	10:33 am

12 Saturday
4th ♎

13 Sunday
4th ♎
☽ v/c	**6:11 pm**	3:11 pm
☽ enters ♏		9:17 pm

November 1998							December 1998							January 1999						
S	M	T	W	T	F	S	S	M	T	W	T	F	S	S	M	T	W	T	F	S
1	2	3	4	5	6	7			1	2	3	4	5						1	2
8	9	10	11	12	13	14	6	7	8	9	10	11	12	3	4	5	6	7	8	9
15	16	17	18	19	20	21	13	14	15	16	17	18	19	10	11	12	13	14	15	16
22	23	24	25	26	27	28	20	21	22	23	24	25	26	17	18	19	20	21	22	23
29	30						27	28	29	30	31			24	25	26	27	28	29	30
														31						

Eastern Standard Time in bold type
Pacific Standard Time in medium type

14 Monday
4th ♎
☽ enters ♏ **12:17 am**

Chanukkah begins

15 Tuesday
4th ♏
☽ v/c   **4:33 pm**   1:33 pm

16 Wednesday
4th ♏
☽ enters ♐ **12:47 pm**   9:47 am

17 Thursday
4th ♐

18 Friday

4th ♐

New Moon	**5:42 pm**	2:42 pm
☽ v/c	**5:50 pm**	2:50 pm
☽ enters ♑	**11:55 pm**	8:55 pm

19 Saturday

1st ♑

| ♇ ℞ | **9:31 pm** | 6:31 pm |

20 Sunday

1st ♑

November 1998							December 1998							January 1999						
S	M	T	W	T	F	S	S	M	T	W	T	F	S	S	M	T	W	T	F	S
1	2	3	4	5	6	7			1	2	3	4	5						1	2
8	9	10	11	12	13	14	6	7	8	9	10	11	12	3	4	5	6	7	8	9
15	16	17	18	19	20	21	13	14	15	16	17	18	19	10	11	12	13	14	15	16
22	23	24	25	26	27	28	20	21	22	23	24	25	26	17	18	19	20	21	22	23
29	30						27	28	29	30	31			24	25	26	27	28	29	30
														31						

Eastern Standard Time in bold type
Pacific Standard Time in medium type

21 Monday

1st ♑
☽ v/c   **3:18 am** 12:18 am
☽ enters ♒   **9:17 am** 6:17 am
☉ enters ♑   **8:56 pm** 5:56 pm

Sun enters Capricorn • Winter Solstice • Yule • Chanukkah ends

22 Tuesday

1st ♒

23 Wednesday

1st ♒
☽ v/c   **10:56 am** 7:56 am
☽ enters ♓   **4:45 pm** 1:45 pm

24 Thursday

1st ♓

Christmas Eve

Eastern Standard Time in bold type
Pacific Standard Time in medium type

25 Friday

1st ♓
☽ v/c **6:23 am** 3:23 am
☽ enters ♈ **10:04 pm** 7:04 pm

Christmas Day

26 Saturday

1st ♈
2nd Quarter **5:46 am** 2:46 am

Kwanzaa begins

27 Sunday

2nd ♈
☽ v/c **7:42 pm** 4:42 pm
☽ enters ♉ 10:05 pm

November 1998						
S	M	T	W	T	F	S
1	2	3	4	5	6	7
8	9	10	11	12	13	14
15	16	17	18	19	20	21
22	23	24	25	26	27	28
29	30					

December 1998						
S	M	T	W	T	F	S
		1	2	3	4	5
6	7	8	9	10	11	12
13	14	15	16	17	18	19
20	21	22	23	24	25	26
27	28	29	30	31		

January 1999						
S	M	T	W	T	F	S
					1	2
3	4	5	6	7	8	9
10	11	12	13	14	15	16
17	18	19	20	21	22	23
24	25	26	27	28	29	30
31						

Eastern Standard Time in bold type
Pacific Standard Time in medium type

28 Monday
2nd ♈
☽ enters ♉ **1:05 am**

29 Tuesday
2nd ♉
♄ D **10:14 am** 7:14 am
☽ v/c **2:22 pm** 11:22 am
☽ enters ♊ 11:22 pm

30 Wednesday
2nd ♉
☽ enters ♊ **2:22 am**

31 Thursday
2nd ♊
☽ v/c **9:58 pm** 6:58 pm

New Year's Eve

Eastern Standard Time in bold type
Pacific Standard Time in medium type

1•4 Monday	1•11 Monday	1•18 Monday
1•5 Tuesday	1•12 Tuesday	1•19 Tuesday
1•6 Wednesday	1•13 Wednesday	1•20 Wednesday
1•7 Thursday	1•14 Thursday	1•21 Thursday
1•1 Friday 1•8 Friday	1•15 Friday	1•22 Friday
1•2 Saturday 1•9 Saturday	1•16 Saturday	1•23 Saturday
1•3 Sunday 1•10 Sunday	1•17 Sunday	1•24 Sunday

Llewellyn's 1998 Pocket Planner and Ephemeris

1•25 Monday	2•1 Monday	2•8 Monday
1•26 Tuesday	2•2 Tuesday	2•9 Tuesday
1•27 Wednesday	2•3 Wednesday	2•10 Wednesday
1•28 Thursday	2•4 Thursday	2•11 Thursday
1•29 Friday	2•5 Friday	2•12 Friday
1•30 Saturday	2•6 Saturday	2•13 Saturday
1•31 Sunday	2•7 Sunday	2•14 Sunday

2·15 Monday	2·22 Monday	3·1 Monday
2·16 Tuesday	2·23 Tuesday	3·2 Tuesday
2·17 Wednesday	2·24 Wednesday	3·3 Wednesday
2·18 Thursday	2·25 Thursday	3·4 Thursday
2·19 Friday	2·26 Friday	3·5 Friday
2·20 Saturday	2·27 Saturday	3·6 Saturday
2·21 Sunday	2·28 Sunday	3·7 Sunday

3•8 Monday	3•15 Monday	3•22 Monday
3•9 Tuesday	3•16 Tuesday	3•23 Tuesday
3•10 Wednesday	3•17 Wednesday	3•24 Wednesday
3•11 Thursday	3•18 Thursday	3•25 Thursday
3•12 Friday	3•19 Friday	3•26 Friday
3•13 Saturday	3•20 Saturday	3•27 Saturday
3•14 Sunday	3•21 Sunday	3•28 Sunday

3·29 Monday	4·5 Monday	4·12 Monday
3·30 Tuesday	4·6 Tuesday	4·13 Tuesday
3·31 Wednesday	4·7 Wednesday	4·14 Wednesday
4·1 Thursday	4·8 Thursday	4·15 Thursday
4·2 Friday	4·9 Friday	4·16 Friday
4·3 Saturday	4·10 Saturday	4·17 Saturday
4·4 Sunday	4·11 Sunday	4·18 Sunday

4•19 Monday	4•26 Monday	5•3 Monday
4•20 Tuesday	4•27 Tuesday	5•4 Tuesday
4•21 Wednesday	4•28 Wednesday	5•5 Wednesday
4•22 Thursday	4•29 Thursday	5•6 Thursday
4•23 Friday	4•30 Friday	5•7 Friday
4•24 Saturday	5•1 Saturday	5•8 Saturday
4•25 Sunday	5•2 Sunday	5•9 Sunday

5•10 Monday	5•17 Monday	5•24 Monday
5•11 Tuesday	5•18 Tuesday	5•25 Tuesday
5•12 Wednesday	5•19 Wednesday	5•26 Wednesday
5•13 Thursday	5•20 Thursday	5•27 Thursday
5•14 Friday	5•21 Friday	5•28 Friday
5•15 Saturday	5•22 Saturday	5•29 Saturday
5•16 Sunday	5•23 Sunday	5•30 Sunday

Llewellyn's 1998 Pocket Planner and Ephemeris

5•31 Monday	6•7 Monday	6•14 Monday
6•1 Tuesday	6•8 Tuesday	6•15 Tuesday
6•2 Wednesday	6•9 Wednesday	6•16 Wednesday
6•3 Thursday	6•10 Thursday	6•17 Thursday
6•4 Friday	6•11 Friday	6•18 Friday
6•5 Saturday	6•12 Saturday	6•19 Saturday
6•6 Sunday	6•13 Sunday	6•20 Sunday

6•21 Monday	6•28 Monday	7•5 Monday
6•22 Tuesday	6•29 Tuesday	7•6 Tuesday
6•23 Wednesday	6•30 Wednesday	7•7 Wednesday
6•24 Thursday	7•1 Thursday	7•8 Thursday
6•25 Friday	7•2 Friday	7•9 Friday
6•26 Saturday	7•3 Saturday	7•10 Saturday
6•27 Sunday	7•4 Sunday	7•11 Sunday

7•12 Monday	7•19 Monday	7•26 Monday
7•13 Tuesday	7•20 Tuesday	7•27 Tuesday
7•14 Wednesday	7•21 Wednesday	7•28 Wednesday
7•15 Thursday	7•22 Thursday	7•29 Thursday
7•16 Friday	7•23 Friday	7•30 Friday
7•17 Saturday	7•24 Saturday	7•31 Saturday
7•18 Sunday	7•25 Sunday	8•1 Sunday

8•2 Monday	8•9 Monday	8•16 Monday
8•3 Tuesday	8•10 Tuesday	8•17 Tuesday
8•4 Wednesday	8•11 Wednesday	8•18 Wednesday
8•5 Thursday	8•12 Thursday	8•19 Thursday
8•6 Friday	8•13 Friday	8•20 Friday
8•7 Saturday	8•14 Saturday	8•21 Saturday
8•8 Sunday	8•15 Sunday	8•22 Sunday

Llewellyn's 1998 Pocket Planner and Ephemeris

8•23 Monday	8•30 Monday	9•6 Monday
8•24 Tuesday	8•31 Tuesday	9•7 Tuesday
8•25 Wednesday	9•1 Wednesday	9•8 Wednesday
8•26 Thursday	9•2 Thursday	9•9 Thursday
8•27 Friday	9•3 Friday	9•10 Friday
8•28 Saturday	9•4 Saturday	9•11 Saturday
8•29 Sunday	9•5 Sunday	9•12 Sunday

9•13 Monday	9•20 Monday	9•27 Monday
9•14 Tuesday	9•21 Tuesday	9•28 Tuesday
9•15 Wednesday	9•22 Wednesday	9•29 Wednesday
9•16 Thursday	9•23 Thursday	9•30 Thursday
9•17 Friday	9•24 Friday	10•1 Friday
9•18 Saturday	9•25 Saturday	10•2 Saturday
9•19 Sunday	9•26 Sunday	10•3 Sunday

Llewellyn's 1998 Pocket Planner and Ephemeris

10•4 Monday	10•11 Monday	10•18 Monday
10•5 Tuesday	10•12 Tuesday	10•19 Tuesday
10•6 Wednesday	10•13 Wednesday	10•20 Wednesday
10•7 Thursday	10•14 Thursday	10•21 Thursday
10•8 Friday	10•15 Friday	10•22 Friday
10•9 Saturday	10•16 Saturday	10•23 Saturday
10•10 Sunday	10•17 Sunday	10•24 Sunday

10•25 Monday	11•1 Monday	11•8 Monday
10•26 Tuesday	11•2 Tuesday	11•9 Tuesday
10•27 Wednesday	11•3 Wednesday	11•10 Wednesday
10•28 Thursday	11•4 Thursday	11•11 Thursday
10•29 Friday	11•5 Friday	11•12 Friday
10•30 Saturday	11•6 Saturday	11•13 Saturday
10•31 Sunday	11•7 Sunday	11•14 Sunday

11•15 Monday	11•22 Monday	11•29 Monday
11•16 Tuesday	11•23 Tuesday	11•30 Tuesday
11•17 Wednesday	11•24 Wednesday	12•1 Wednesday
11•18 Thursday	11•25 Thursday	12•2 Thursday
11•19 Friday	11•26 Friday	12•3 Friday
11•20 Saturday	11•27 Saturday	12•4 Saturday
11•21 Sunday	11•28 Sunday	12•5 Sunday

12•6 Monday	12•13 Monday	12•20 Monday 12•27 Monday
12•7 Tuesday	12•14 Tuesday	12•21 Tuesday 12•28 Tuesday
12•8 Wednesday	12•15 Wednesday	12•22 Wednesday 12•29 Wednesday
12•9 Thursday	12•16 Thursday	12•23 Thursday 12•30 Thursday
12•10 Friday	12•17 Friday	12•24 Friday 12•31 Friday
12•11 Saturday	12•18 Saturday	12•25 Saturday
12•12 Sunday	12•19 Sunday	12•26 Sunday

JANUARY 1997

1 WEDNESDAY

☽☍♄	**12:14 am**	
☽△♅	**4:07 am**	1:07 am
☽⚹♇	**6:20 am**	3:20 am
♀⚺⚳	**6:41 am**	3:41 am
☿☌☉	**8:21 pm**	5:21 pm
☽□☿	**8:42 pm**	5:42 pm
☽□☉	**8:46 pm**	5:46 pm

2 THURSDAY

☽☍⚵	**3:32 am**	12:32 am
☽□⚳	**12:03 pm**	9:03 am
☽⚹♀	**2:18 pm**	11:18 am
☽□♃	**11:50 pm**	8:50 pm
☽□♆		11:11 pm

3 FRIDAY

☽□♆	**2:11 am**	
☽□⚶	**5:02 am**	2:02 am
☽⚹⚴	**5:12 am**	2:12 am
☽⚺♂	**8:10 am**	5:10 am
☽☌⚷	**8:50 am**	5:50 am
☽⚻♄	**10:49 am**	7:49 am
☽□♅	**2:29 pm**	11:29 am
☽⚺♇	**4:27 pm**	1:27 pm
☽⚹☿		9:26 pm
⚴⚺⚶		9:25 pm

4 SATURDAY

☽⚹☿	**12:26 am**	
⚴⚺⚶	**12:25 am**	
☽⚹☉	**10:35 am**	7:35 am
☽⚻⚵	**1:41 pm**	10:41 am
♂⚺⚷	**8:01 pm**	5:01 pm
☽⚹⚳	**9:42 pm**	6:42 pm

5 SUNDAY

☽⚺♀	**3:46 am**	12:46 am
☽⚹♃	**7:51 am**	4:51 am
☽⚹♆	**9:13 am**	6:13 am
☽⚺⚴	**1:32 pm**	10:32 am
☽⚹⚶	**1:51 pm**	10:51 am
☽⚺⚷	**3:30 pm**	12:30 pm
☽⚹♂	**3:50 pm**	12:50 pm
☽△♄	**5:15 pm**	2:15 pm
☽⚹♅	**8:37 pm**	5:37 pm
☽☌♇	**10:21 pm**	7:21 pm
☽⚺☿		10:31 pm

Eastern Standard Time in bold type
Pacific Standard Time in medium type

6 MONDAY

☽⚺☿	**1:31 am**	
☽⚺☉	**6:59 pm**	3:59 pm
☽△⚵	**7:16 pm**	4:16 pm
☉□⚵		9:48 pm
☽⚺⚳		11:45 pm

7 TUESDAY

☉□⚵	**12:48 am**	
☽⚺⚳	**2:45 am**	
♀⚺♃	**9:20 am**	6:20 am
☽⚺♃	**11:33 am**	8:33 am
☽☌♀	**11:43 am**	8:43 am
☽⚺♆	**12:08 pm**	9:08 am
⚶□⚷	**4:11 pm**	1:11 pm
♀⚺♆	**4:40 pm**	1:40 pm
☽☌⚴	**5:29 pm**	2:29 pm
☽⚹⚷	**6:08 pm**	3:08 pm
☽⚺⚶	**6:11 pm**	3:11 pm
☽□♂	**7:13 pm**	4:13 pm
☽□♄	**7:43 pm**	4:43 pm
☽⚺♅	**10:53 pm**	7:53 pm
☽⚺♇		9:25 pm
☽☌☿		9:27 pm
☿⚺♇		10:14 pm

8 WEDNESDAY

☽⚺♇	**12:25 am**	
☽☌☿	**12:27 am**	
☿⚺♇	**1:14 am**	
☽□⚵	**9:25 pm**	6:25 pm
⚴⚹⚷	**9:46 pm**	6:46 pm
☽☌☉	**11:26 pm**	8:26 pm

9 THURSDAY

☽☌⚳	**4:37 am**	1:37 am
♂☍♄	**5:53 am**	2:53 am
♃☌♆	**6:40 am**	3:40 am
☿⚺♅	**10:37 am**	7:37 am
☽☌♆	**12:29 pm**	9:29 am
☽☌♃	**12:33 pm**	9:33 am
☽⚺♀	**4:19 pm**	1:19 pm
☽□⚷	**6:24 pm**	3:24 pm
☽⚺⚴	**6:52 pm**	3:52 pm
♄⚹⚶	**7:21 pm**	4:21 pm
☽⚹♄	**7:56 pm**	4:56 pm
☽☌⚶	**7:57 pm**	4:57 pm
☽△♂	**8:08 pm**	5:08 pm
☽⚺☿	**10:35 pm**	7:35 pm
☽☌♅	**11:00 pm**	8:00 pm
☽⚹♇		9:25 pm

10 FRIDAY

☽⚹♇	**12:25 am**	
♂△⚶	**6:26 am**	3:26 am
♀⚹⚷	**6:46 pm**	3:46 pm
☽⚹⚵	**10:24 pm**	7:24 pm
☽⚺☉		11:35 pm

11 SATURDAY

☽⚺☉	**2:35 am**	
☽⚺⚳	**5:38 am**	2:38 am
☽⚺♆	**12:23 pm**	9:23 am
♀☌⚴	**12:43 pm**	9:43 am
☽⚺♃	**1:06 pm**	10:06 am
♀□♄	**2:16 pm**	11:16 am
♄□⚴	**6:14 pm**	3:14 pm
☽△⚷	**6:29 pm**	3:29 pm
☽⚺♄	**8:03 pm**	5:03 pm
☽⚹⚴	**8:06 pm**	5:06 pm
☽⚹♀	**8:33 pm**	5:33 pm
☽⚻♂	**8:54 pm**	5:54 pm
☽⚺⚶	**9:36 pm**	6:36 pm
☽⚹☿	**9:42 pm**	6:42 pm
☽⚺♅	**11:09 pm**	8:09 pm
☿⚺⚶		9:05 pm
☽□♇		9:31 pm
♀□♂		10:36 pm

12 SUNDAY

☿⚺⚶	**12:05 am**	
☽□♇	**12:31 am**	
♀□♂	**1:36 am**	
☿☌♀	**9:30 am**	6:30 am
♀⚺⚶	**5:05 pm**	2:05 pm
☽⚺⚵		9:29 pm

13 MONDAY

☽⚺⚵	**12:29 am**	
♀⚺♅	**4:41 am**	1:41 am
☽⚹☉	**7:11 am**	4:11 am
☽⚹⚳	**8:02 am**	5:02 am
☽⚹♆	**1:48 pm**	10:48 am
☽⚹♃	**3:15 pm**	12:15 pm
☽⚻⚷	**8:18 pm**	5:18 pm
♀⚺♇	**8:24 pm**	5:24 pm
☽☌♄	**9:58 pm**	6:58 pm
♅☌⚶	**10:57 pm**	7:57 pm
☽□⚴	**11:14 pm**	8:14 pm
☽☍♂	**11:30 pm**	8:30 pm
☽□☿	**11:36 pm**	8:36 pm
☽⚹♅		10:12 pm
☽⚹⚶		10:16 pm
☉☌⚳		11:15 pm
☽△♇		11:31 pm

14 TUESDAY

☽⚹♅	**1:12 am**	
☽⚹⚶	**1:16 am**	
☉☌⚳	**2:15 am**	
☽△♇	**2:31 am**	
☽□♀	**3:07 am**	12:07 am
♂□⚴	**9:27 pm**	6:27 pm

15 WEDNESDAY

☽☌⚵	**5:21 am**	2:21 am
♇⚹⚶	**12:52 pm**	9:52 am
☽□⚳	**1:18 pm**	10:18 am
☽□☉	**3:02 pm**	12:02 pm
☽□♆	**5:59 pm**	2:59 pm
☽□♃	**8:19 pm**	5:19 pm
☽☍⚷		9:57 pm
☽⚺♄		11:47 pm

16 THURSDAY

☽☍⚷	**12:57 am**	
☽⚺♄	**2:47 am**	
☽⚻♂	**5:02 am**	2:02 am
☽△⚴	**5:28 am**	2:28 am
☽△☿	**5:31 am**	2:31 am
☽□♅	**6:09 am**	3:09 am
☽⚻♇	**7:26 am**	4:26 am
☽□⚶	**8:09 am**	5:09 am
☽△♀	**1:28 pm**	10:28 am
☿⚺♅		9:59 pm

17 FRIDAY

☿⚺♅	**12:59 am**	
☉☌♆	**7:34 am**	4:34 am
♅⚺⚴	**7:47 am**	4:47 am
☽⚺⚵	**1:30 pm**	10:30 am
☽△⚳	**9:48 pm**	6:48 pm
☽△♆		10:09 pm
☽△☉		11:37 pm

18 SATURDAY

☽△♆	**1:09 am**	
☽△☉	**2:37 am**	
☽△♃	**4:27 am**	1:27 am
☿⚺♇	**6:34 am**	3:34 am
☽⚻⚷	**8:31 am**	5:31 am
☽⚹♄	**10:32 am**	7:32 am
☽△♂	**1:30 pm**	10:30 am
☽△♅	**1:59 pm**	10:59 am
☽⚻⚴	**2:50 pm**	11:50 am
☽☍♇	**3:12 pm**	12:12 pm
☽⚻☿	**3:39 pm**	12:39 pm
☽△⚶	**6:14 pm**	3:14 pm

19 SUNDAY

♇⚺⚴	**3:34 am**	12:34 am
☽⚻♀	**3:36 am**	12:36 am
☉☌♃	**8:07 am**	5:07 am
☽⚹⚵		9:32 pm

20 MONDAY

☽⚹⚵	**12:32 am**	
☽⚻⚳	**8:59 am**	5:59 am
☽⚻♆	**10:45 am**	7:45 am
♂△♅	**1:54 pm**	10:54 am
☽⚻♃	**3:07 pm**	12:07 pm
☽⚻☉	**5:16 pm**	2:16 pm
☽△⚷	**6:27 pm**	3:27 pm
☽□♄	**8:40 pm**	5:40 pm
☽⚻♅		9:09 pm
☽□♂		9:15 pm
☽⚻♇		10:15 pm
☽☍⚴		11:41 pm

21 TUESDAY

☽⚻♅	**12:09 am**	
☽□♂	**12:15 am**	
☽⚻♇	**1:15 am**	
☽☍⚴	**2:41 am**	
☽☍☿	**5:29 am**	2:29 am
☽⚻⚶	**6:50 am**	3:50 am
☉□⚷	**8:03 am**	5:03 am
☽☍♀	**8:38 pm**	5:38 pm

22 WEDNESDAY

☉⚹♄	**1:31 pm**	10:31 am
☽□⚵	**1:44 pm**	10:44 am
♆☌⚳	**8:39 pm**	5:39 pm
☽☍♆	**10:10 pm**	7:10 pm
☽☍⚳	**10:13 pm**	7:13 pm
☿⚺⚶	**10:39 pm**	7:39 pm

23 THURSDAY

☽☍♃	**3:39 am**	12:39 am
☽□⚷	**6:06 am**	3:06 am
☽△♄	**8:34 am**	5:34 am
☽☍☉	**10:12 am**	7:12 am
☽☍♅	**12:01 pm**	9:01 am
☽⚹♂	**12:39 pm**	9:39 am
☽△♇	**12:59 pm**	9:59 am
☽⚻⚴	**4:21 pm**	1:21 pm
☽☍⚶	**9:18 pm**	6:18 pm
☽⚻☿	**10:16 pm**	7:16 pm

24 FRIDAY

☉☌♅	**8:53 am**	5:53 am
☽⚻♀	**3:46 pm**	12:46 pm
☉△♂	**7:25 pm**	4:25 pm
☉⚹♇	**7:38 pm**	4:38 pm
♂⚹♇	**9:19 pm**	6:19 pm

25 SATURDAY

☽△⚵	**4:30 am**	1:30 am
☽⚻♆	**10:53 am**	7:53 am
☽⚻⚳	**12:51 pm**	9:51 am
☽⚻♃	**5:30 pm**	2:30 pm
☽⚹⚷	**6:58 pm**	3:58 pm
☽⚻♄	**9:42 pm**	6:42 pm
☽⚻♅		10:03 pm
☽□♇		10:51 pm
☽⚺♂		11:06 pm

26 SUNDAY

☽⚻♅	**1:03 am**	
☽□♇	**1:51 am**	
☽⚺♂	**2:06 am**	
☽⚻☉	**4:38 am**	1:38 am
☽△⚴	**7:13 am**	4:13 am
☽⚻⚶	**12:57 pm**	9:57 am
☽△☿	**5:10 pm**	2:10 pm

27 MONDAY

☽△♀	**11:57 am**	8:57 am
☽⚻⚵	**7:55 pm**	4:55 pm
☽△♆		9:02 pm

28 TUESDAY

☽△♆	**12:02 am**	
☉⚺⚴	**3:39 am**	12:39 am
☽△⚳	**3:53 am**	12:53 am
☽△♃	**7:38 am**	4:38 am
☽⚺⚷	**8:01 am**	5:01 am
☽☍♄	**11:00 am**	8:00 am
☽△♅	**2:10 pm**	11:10 am
☽⚹♇	**2:46 pm**	11:46 am
☽☌♂	**3:28 pm**	12:28 pm
☽□⚴	**9:58 pm**	6:58 pm
☽△☉	**11:01 pm**	8:01 pm

29 WEDNESDAY

☽△⚶	**4:19 am**	1:19 am
♃□⚷	**6:49 am**	3:49 am
☽□☿	**12:12 pm**	9:12 am

30 THURSDAY

☽□♀	**6:49 am**	3:49 am
☽☍⚵	**10:02 am**	7:02 am
☽□♆	**11:49 am**	8:49 am
☽□⚳	**5:18 pm**	2:18 pm
☽☌⚷	**7:27 pm**	4:27 pm
☽□♃	**8:04 pm**	5:04 pm
☽⚻♄	**10:35 pm**	7:35 pm
☽□♅		10:27 pm
☽⚺♇		10:50 pm
☽⚺♂		11:48 pm

31 FRIDAY

☽□♅	**1:27 am**	
☽⚺♇	**1:50 am**	
☽⚺♂	**2:48 am**	
☽⚹⚴	**10:26 am**	7:26 am
☽□☉	**2:40 pm**	11:40 am
☽□⚶	**5:03 pm**	2:03 pm

JANUARY 1997

☽ Last Aspect day	EST / hr:mn / PST	asp	☽ Ingress sign	day	EST / hr:mn / PST
2	11:11 pm	□ ♆	♏	3	5:02 am
3	**2:11 am**	□ ♆	♏	3	**8:02 am**
5	**9:13 am** 6:13 am	⚹ ♆	♐	5	**2:28 pm** 11:28 am
7	**11:43 am** 8:43 am	☌ ♀	♑	7	**4:55 pm** 1:55 pm
9	**12:33 pm** 9:33 am	☌ ♃	♒	9	**4:59 pm** 1:59 pm
9	9:25 pm	⚹ ♇	♓	11	1:51 pm
10	**12:25 am**	⚹ ♇	♓	11	**4:51 pm**
13	**3:15 pm** 12:15 pm	⚹ ♃	♈	13	**6:21 pm** 3:21 pm
15	**8:19 pm** 5:19 pm	□ ♃	♉	15	**10:40 pm** 7:40 pm
18	**4:27 am** 1:27 am	△ ♃	♊	18	**5:53 am** 2:53 am

☽ Last Aspect day	EST / hr:mn / PST	asp	☽ Ingress sign	day	EST / hr:mn / PST
18	**3:12 pm** 12:12 pm	☍ ♇	♋	20	**3:29 pm** 12:29 pm
22	7:10 pm	☍ ♆	♌	22	11:51 pm
22	**10:10 pm**	☍ ♆	♌	23	**2:51 am**
23	**12:59 pm** 9:59 am	△ ♇	♍	25	**3:27 pm** 12:27 pm
27	9:02 pm	△ ♆	♎	28	1:22 am
28	**12:02 am**	△ ♆	♎	28	**4:22 am**
30	**11:49 am** 8:49 am	□ ♆	♏	30	**3:48 pm** 12:48 pm

☽ Phases & Eclipses phase	day	EST / hr:mn / PST
4th Quarter	1	**8:46 pm** 5:46 pm
New Moon	8	**11:26 pm** 8:26 pm
2nd Quarter	15	**3:02 pm** 12:02 pm
Full Moon	23	**10:12 am** 7:12 am
4th Quarter	31	**2:40 pm** 11:40 am

Planet Ingress		day	EST / hr:mn / PST
♂	♎	3	**3:10 am** 12:10 am
⚵	♒	6	**6:10 am** 3:10 am
⚵	♑	6	**9:04 pm** 6:04 pm
♀	♑	9	9:32 pm
♀	♑	10	**12:32 am**
☉	♒	19	**7:42 pm** 4:42 pm
♃	♒	21	**10:12 am** 7:12 am
⚳	♒	28	**6:14 pm** 3:14 pm

Planetary Motion		day	EST / hr:mn / PST
☿	D	12	**3:36 pm** 12:36 pm

DAY		SID.TIME	SUN	MOON	NODE	MERCURY	VENUS	MARS	JUPITER	SATURN	URANUS	NEPTUNE	PLUTO	CERES	PALLAS	JUNO	VESTA	CHIRON
W	1	6:42:44	10 ♑ 36 27	28 ♍ 44	02 ♎ ℞ 27	13 ♑ ℞ 07	18 ♐ 27	29 ♍ 14	25 ♑ 10	01 ♈ 20	03 ♒ 16	26 ♑ 50	04 ♐ 24	18 ♑ 52	27 ♐ 30	14 ♈ 40	27 ♑ 09	00 ♏ 13
T	2	6:46:41	11 37 37	10 ♎ 48	02 27	11 46	19 42	29 34	25 24	01 23	03 19	26 52	04 26	19 16	27 55	15 02	27 40	00 18
F	3	6:50:37	12 38 46	23 09	02 26	10 24	20 57	29 53	25 38	01 26	03 23	26 54	04 28	19 40	28 20	15 23	28 11	00 22
S	4	6:54:34	13 39 57	05 ♏ 51	02 23	09 05	22 12	00 ♎ 12	25 52	01 30	03 26	26 57	04 30	20 03	28 44	15 45	28 43	00 27
S	5	6:58:31	14 41 07	18 59	02 19	07 50	23 27	00 31	26 06	01 33	03 29	26 59	04 32	20 27	29 09	16 07	29 14	00 32
M	6	7:02:27	15 42 17	02 ♐ 37	02 11	06 41	24 42	00 49	26 20	01 36	03 33	27 01	04 34	20 51	29 33	16 30	29 45	00 36
T	7	7:06:24	16 43 28	16 44	02 02	05 41	25 57	01 07	26 34	01 40	03 36	27 03	04 36	21 15	29 58	16 53	00 ♒ 17	00 41
W	8	7:10:20	17 44 38	01 ♑ 17	01 51	04 49	27 12	01 25	26 48	01 44	03 40	27 06	04 38	21 39	00 ♑ 22	17 16	00 48	00 45
T	9	7:14:17	18 45 49	16 11	01 40	04 07	28 28	01 41	27 02	01 47	03 43	27 08	04 40	22 03	00 47	17 39	01 19	00 49
F	10	7:18:13	19 46 59	01 ♒ 16	01 29	03 35	29 43	01 58	27 16	01 51	03 47	27 10	04 41	22 27	01 11	18 03	01 51	00 53
S	11	7:22:10	20 48 09	16 22	01 21	03 14	00 ♑ 58	02 14	27 30	01 55	03 50	27 12	04 43	22 51	01 35	18 27	02 22	00 57
S	12	7:26:06	21 49 19	01 ♓ 20	01 15	03 01	02 13	02 29	27 44	01 59	03 53	27 15	04 45	23 15	02 00	18 51	02 53	01 01
M	13	7:30:03	22 50 28	16 02	01 11	02 D 58	03 28	02 44	27 58	02 03	03 57	27 17	04 47	23 39	02 24	19 15	03 25	01 05
T	14	7:34:00	23 51 36	00 ♈ 23	01 D 10	03 03	04 43	02 59	28 12	02 07	04 00	27 19	04 49	24 03	02 48	19 40	03 56	01 08
W	15	7:37:56	24 52 44	14 21	01 ℞ 09	03 17	05 58	03 13	28 26	02 11	04 04	27 21	04 50	24 27	03 12	20 05	04 27	01 12
T	16	7:41:53	25 53 51	27 57	01 09	03 37	07 13	03 27	28 40	02 16	04 07	27 24	04 52	24 51	03 36	20 30	04 58	01 15
F	17	7:45:49	26 54 57	11 ♉ 13	01 09	04 04	08 29	03 40	28 55	02 20	04 11	27 26	04 54	25 15	04 00	20 55	05 30	01 19
S	18	7:49:46	27 56 02	24 12	01 06	04 37	09 44	03 52	29 09	02 25	04 14	27 28	04 55	25 39	04 24	21 21	06 01	01 22
S	19	7:53:42	28 57 07	06 ♊ 55	01 01	05 15	10 59	04 04	29 23	02 29	04 18	27 31	04 57	26 02	04 48	21 47	06 32	01 25
M	20	7:57:39	29 58 11	19 27	00 53	05 59	12 14	04 16	29 37	02 34	04 21	27 33	04 58	26 26	05 12	22 13	07 04	01 28
T	21	8:01:35	00 ♒ 59 14	01 ♋ 48	00 43	06 46	13 29	04 27	29 51	02 39	04 25	27 35	05 00	26 50	05 35	22 39	07 35	01 31
W	22	8:05:32	02 00 16	14 00	00 32	07 38	14 44	04 37	00 ♒ 05	02 44	04 28	27 37	05 02	27 14	05 59	23 05	08 06	01 34
T	23	8:09:29	03 01 17	26 05	00 20	08 33	15 59	04 47	00 19	02 48	04 32	27 40	05 03	27 38	06 23	23 32	08 37	01 36
F	24	8:13:25	04 02 18	08 ♌ 03	00 10	09 32	17 15	04 56	00 33	02 53	04 36	27 42	05 05	28 02	06 46	23 59	09 08	01 39
S	25	8:17:22	05 03 18	19 56	00 01	10 33	18 30	05 04	00 48	02 59	04 39	27 44	05 06	28 26	07 10	24 26	09 40	01 41
S	26	8:21:18	06 04 17	01 ♍ 45	29 ♍ 54	11 37	19 45	05 12	01 02	03 04	04 43	27 46	05 07	28 49	07 33	24 53	10 11	01 44
M	27	8:25:15	07 05 15	13 33	29 50	12 44	21 00	05 19	01 16	03 09	04 46	27 49	05 09	29 13	07 57	25 21	10 42	01 46
T	28	8:29:11	08 06 13	25 22	29 49	13 52	22 15	05 26	01 30	03 14	04 50	27 51	05 10	29 37	08 20	25 48	11 13	01 48
W	29	8:33:08	09 07 10	07 ♎ 17	29 49	15 03	23 30	05 32	01 44	03 19	04 53	27 53	05 11	00 ♒ 01	08 43	26 16	11 44	01 50
T	30	8:37:04	10 08 06	19 21	29 50	16 15	24 45	05 37	01 58	03 25	04 57	27 55	05 13	00 24	09 06	26 44	12 15	01 52
F	31	8:41:01	11 09 01	01 ♏ 40	29 51	17 30	26 01	05 42	02 12	03 30	05 00	27 58	05 14	00 48	09 29	27 12	12 47	01 53

EPHEMERIS CALCULATED FOR 12 MIDNIGHT GREENWICH MEAN TIME. ALL OTHER DATA AND FACING ASPECTARIAN PAGE IN **EASTERN STANDARD TIME (BOLD)** AND PACIFIC STANDARD TIME (REGULAR).

FEBRUARY 1997

1 SATURDAY

☽✶☿	**4:14 am**	1:14 am
♀□⚵	**7:38 am**	4:38 am
♀☌♆	**9:27 am**	6:27 am
♆□⚵	**12:42 pm**	9:42 am
☽✶♆	**8:18 pm**	5:18 pm
☽⚻⚵	**8:34 pm**	5:34 pm
☽✶♀	**9:24 pm**	6:24 pm
☽✶⚳		11:56 pm

2 SUNDAY

☽✶⚳	**2:56 am**	
☽⚺⚷	**3:21 am**	12:21 am
☽✶♃	**4:48 am**	1:48 am
☽△♄	**6:32 am**	3:32 am
☽✶♅	**9:03 am**	6:03 am
☽☌♇	**9:15 am**	6:15 am
☽✶♂	**10:17 am**	7:17 am
⚳□⚷	**5:37 pm**	2:37 pm
☽⚺♀	**6:42 pm**	3:42 pm
☽✶☉		10:22 pm
☽✶⚶		10:22 pm
☉☌⚶		10:28 pm

3 MONDAY

☽✶☉	**1:22 am**	
☽✶⚶	**1:22 am**	
☉☌⚶	**1:28 am**	
☽⚺☿	**3:05 pm**	12:05 pm
☽⚺♆		9:35 pm
☽△⚵		11:30 pm

4 TUESDAY

☽⚺♆	**12:35 am**	
☽△⚵	**2:30 am**	
☽⚺♀	**6:26 am**	3:26 am
☽✶⚷	**7:04 am**	4:04 am
☽⚺⚳	**8:03 am**	5:03 am
☽⚺♃	**9:11 am**	6:11 am
☽□♄	**10:17 am**	7:17 am
☽⚺♅	**12:29 pm**	9:29 am
☽⚺♇	**12:32 pm**	9:32 am
☽□♂	**1:32 pm**	10:32 am
♀□⚷	**1:50 pm**	10:50 am
☽☌♀	**10:35 pm**	7:35 pm

5 WEDNESDAY

☽⚺⚶	**5:18 am**	2:18 am
♅✶♇	**5:46 am**	2:46 am
☽⚺☉	**7:10 am**	4:10 am
♀☌⚳	**9:04 am**	6:04 am
♀☌♃	**8:48 pm**	5:48 pm
☽☌☿	**9:17 pm**	6:17 pm
☽☌♆		10:29 pm

6 THURSDAY

☽☌♆	**1:29 am**	
☽□⚵	**4:47 am**	1:47 am
♀✶♄	**6:34 am**	3:34 am
☽□⚷	**7:34 am**	4:34 am
☽☌⚳	**9:45 am**	6:45 am
☽☌♃	**10:17 am**	7:17 am
☽✶♄	**10:55 am**	7:55 am
☽☌♀	**11:16 am**	8:16 am
☽✶♇	**12:48 pm**	9:48 am
☽☌♅	**12:53 pm**	9:53 am
☽△♂	**1:43 pm**	10:43 am
☽⚺♀	**11:37 pm**	8:37 pm

7 FRIDAY

♀✶♇	**6:06 am**	3:06 am
☽☌⚶	**6:35 am**	3:35 am
♀☌♅	**7:44 am**	4:44 am
☽☌☉	**10:06 am**	7:06 am
♀△♂	**4:33 pm**	1:33 pm
☿☌♆	**7:31 pm**	4:31 pm
☽⚺♆		9:49 pm
☽⚺☿		10:21 pm

8 SATURDAY

☽⚺♆	**12:49 am**	
☽⚺☿	**1:21 am**	
☽✶⚵	**5:33 am**	2:33 am
☽△⚷	**6:48 am**	3:48 am
☽⚺⚳	**10:11 am**	7:11 am
☽⚺♃	**10:12 am**	7:12 am
☽⚺♄	**10:25 am**	7:25 am
♃☌⚳	**11:40 am**	8:40 am
☽□♇	**12:02 pm**	9:02 am
☽⚺♅	**12:15 pm**	9:15 am
☽⚻♂	**12:50 pm**	9:50 am
☽⚺♀	**2:42 pm**	11:42 am
♄✶⚳	**9:54 pm**	6:54 pm
☽✶♀		9:04 pm

9 SUNDAY

☽✶♀	**12:04 am**	
☽⚺⚶	**7:38 am**	4:38 am
♃✶♄	**10:36 am**	7:36 am
☽⚺☉	**12:59 pm**	9:59 am
⚵☍⚷	**8:36 pm**	5:36 pm
☽✶♆		9:46 pm

10 MONDAY

☽✶♆	**12:46 am**	
☽✶☿	**6:24 am**	3:24 am
☽⚻⚷	**6:53 am**	3:53 am
☽⚺⚵	**7:14 am**	4:14 am
☽☌♄	**10:57 am**	7:57 am
☽✶♃	**11:10 am**	8:10 am
☿□⚷	**11:16 am**	8:16 am
☽✶⚳	**11:42 am**	8:42 am
☽△♇	**12:21 pm**	9:21 am
☽✶♅	**12:43 pm**	9:43 am
☽☍♂	**12:58 pm**	9:58 am
☿□⚵	**6:39 pm**	3:39 pm
☽✶♀	**7:39 pm**	4:39 pm
☽□♀		11:12 pm

11 TUESDAY

☽□♀	**2:12 am**	
☽✶⚶	**10:43 am**	7:43 am
♇✶⚳	**1:07 pm**	10:07 am
☽✶☉	**6:22 pm**	3:22 pm
♂△♅	**7:08 pm**	4:08 pm

12 WEDNESDAY

☽□♆	**3:11 am**	12:11 am
♂△⚳	**4:08 am**	1:08 am
☿✶♄	**6:33 am**	3:33 am
♅☌⚳	**7:48 am**	4:48 am
☽☍⚷	**9:35 am**	6:35 am
☽☌⚵	**11:51 am**	8:51 am
☿☌♃	**1:22 pm**	10:22 am
☽⚺♄	**2:17 pm**	11:17 am
☽□♃	**2:59 pm**	11:59 am
☽□☿	**3:10 pm**	12:10 pm
☽⚻♇	**3:27 pm**	12:27 pm
☽⚻♂	**3:47 pm**	12:47 pm
☽□♅	**3:59 pm**	12:59 pm
☽□⚳	**4:12 pm**	1:12 pm
☿✶♇	**5:47 pm**	2:47 pm
☿△♂	**8:29 pm**	5:29 pm
☿☌♅	**10:56 pm**	7:56 pm

13 THURSDAY

☿☌⚳	**3:29 am**	12:29 am
☽□♀	**4:29 am**	1:29 am
☽△♀	**7:40 am**	4:40 am
☽□⚶	**5:27 pm**	2:27 pm
♃✶♇	**7:42 pm**	4:42 pm
♂△♃		9:08 pm

14 FRIDAY

♂△♃	**12:08 am**	
☽□☉	**3:58 am**	12:58 am
♂✶♇	**8:06 am**	5:06 am
☽△♆	**9:05 am**	6:05 am
☽⚻⚷	**3:47 pm**	12:47 pm
☽⚺⚵	**8:27 pm**	5:27 pm
☽✶♄	**9:16 pm**	6:16 pm
☽△♂	**9:59 pm**	6:59 pm
☽☍♇	**10:07 pm**	7:07 pm
☽△♃	**10:34 pm**	7:34 pm
☽△♅	**10:53 pm**	7:53 pm
☽△⚳		9:35 pm

15 SATURDAY

☽△⚳	**12:35 am**	
♀⚺♀	**3:08 am**	12:08 am
☽△☿	**5:08 am**	2:08 am
☽⚻♀	**4:59 pm**	1:59 pm
☽△♀	**6:05 pm**	3:05 pm
♃☌♅	**9:23 pm**	6:23 pm
♄⚺⚵	**10:31 pm**	7:31 pm

16 SUNDAY

♂⚻⚵	**3:42 am**	12:42 am
☽△⚶	**4:09 am**	1:09 am
♂☍♄	**12:14 pm**	9:14 am
♇⚻⚵	**3:22 pm**	12:22 pm
☽△☉	**5:56 pm**	2:56 pm
☽⚻♆	**6:25 pm**	3:25 pm
☉⚺♆	**11:54 pm**	8:54 pm
☽△⚷		10:18 pm

17 MONDAY

☽△⚷	**1:18 am**	
☽□♂	**7:11 am**	4:11 am
☽□♄	**7:35 am**	4:35 am
☽⚻♇	**8:01 am**	5:01 am
☽✶⚵	**8:43 am**	5:43 am
☽⚻♅	**9:01 am**	6:01 am
☽⚻♃	**9:32 am**	6:32 am
☽⚻⚳	**12:27 pm**	9:27 am
♅□⚵	**4:34 pm**	1:34 pm
☽⚻☿	**11:53 pm**	8:53 pm

18 TUESDAY

☽☍♀	**5:29 am**	2:29 am
☽⚻♀	**11:38 am**	8:38 am
☽⚻⚶	**5:54 pm**	2:54 pm
♃□⚵	**6:22 pm**	3:22 pm

19 WEDNESDAY

☽☍♆	**6:10 am**	3:10 am
☽⚻☉	**11:01 am**	8:01 am
♄△♇	**11:44 am**	8:44 am
☽□⚷	**1:02 pm**	10:02 am
☽✶♂	**6:19 pm**	3:19 pm
☽△♇	**8:01 pm**	5:01 pm
☽△♄	**8:05 pm**	5:05 pm
☽☍♅	**9:17 pm**	6:17 pm
☽☍♃	**10:41 pm**	7:41 pm
☽□⚵	**11:25 pm**	8:25 pm
☽☍⚳		11:31 pm

20 THURSDAY

☽☍⚳	**2:31 am**	
☿⚺♀	**4:42 am**	1:42 am
☉△⚷	**10:37 am**	7:37 am
☽⚻♀	**7:45 pm**	4:45 pm
☽☍☿	**9:36 pm**	6:36 pm

21 FRIDAY

☽☍♀	**7:17 am**	4:17 am
☽☍⚶	**9:14 am**	6:14 am
☽⚻♆	**7:04 pm**	4:04 pm
☽✶⚷		10:45 pm

22 SATURDAY

☽✶⚷	**1:45 am**	
☽☍☉	**5:27 am**	2:27 am
☽⚺♂	**6:09 am**	3:09 am
☽□♇	**8:54 am**	5:54 am
☽⚻♄	**9:30 am**	6:30 am
☽⚻♅	**10:24 am**	7:24 am
☉⚻♂	**12:21 pm**	9:21 am
☽⚻♃	**12:43 pm**	9:43 am
♀☌⚶	**12:59 pm**	9:59 am
☽△⚵	**3:03 pm**	12:03 pm
☽⚻⚳	**5:25 pm**	2:25 pm

23 SUNDAY

☽△♀	**10:28 am**	7:28 am
☽⚻☿	**8:17 pm**	5:17 pm
☉□♇	**10:17 pm**	7:17 pm
☽⚻⚶		9:47 pm

24 MONDAY

☽⚻⚶	**12:47 am**	
☽⚻♀	**3:17 am**	12:17 am
☽△♆	**7:59 am**	4:59 am
☉⚺♄	**10:41 am**	7:41 am
☽⚺⚷	**2:22 pm**	11:22 am
☽☌♂	**5:40 pm**	2:40 pm
☉⚺♅	**6:35 pm**	3:35 pm
☽✶♇	**9:33 pm**	6:33 pm
☽☍♄	**10:42 pm**	7:42 pm
☽△♅	**11:16 pm**	8:16 pm
☽⚻☉	**11:40 pm**	8:40 pm
☽△♃		11:25 pm

25 TUESDAY

☽△♃	**2:25 am**	
☽⚻⚵	**6:21 am**	3:21 am
☽△⚳	**7:54 am**	4:54 am
☿☌⚶	**3:58 pm**	12:58 pm
☽□♀		9:25 pm
♀⚺♆		10:16 pm

26 WEDNESDAY

☽□♀	**12:25 am**	
♀⚺♆	**1:16 am**	
☽△⚶	**3:13 pm**	12:13 pm
☉⚺♃	**4:53 pm**	1:53 pm
☽△☿	**5:52 pm**	2:52 pm
☽□♆	**7:47 pm**	4:47 pm
☽△♀	**9:49 pm**	6:49 pm
☽☌⚷		10:41 pm

27 THURSDAY

☽☌⚷	**1:41 am**	
☽⚺♂	**3:48 am**	12:48 am
☿⚺♆	**7:46 am**	4:46 am
☽⚺♇	**8:47 am**	5:47 am
☽⚻♄	**10:24 am**	7:24 am
☽□♅	**10:39 am**	7:39 am
☽□♃	**2:30 pm**	11:30 am
☽△☉	**3:59 pm**	12:59 pm
☽☍⚵	**7:49 pm**	4:49 pm
☽□⚳	**8:34 pm**	5:34 pm

28 FRIDAY

♀△⚷	**11:15 am**	8:15 am
☽✶♀	**12:08 pm**	9:08 am
♀⚻♂	**11:06 pm**	8:06 pm
☿△⚷		9:37 pm
☽□⚶		11:59 pm

Eastern Standard Time in bold type
Pacific Standard Time in medium type

FEBRUARY 1997

☽ Last Aspect day	EST / hr:mn / PST		asp	☽ Ingress sign	day	EST / hr:mn / PST	
1	**9:24 pm**	6:24 pm	⚹ ♀	♐	1	**11:51 pm**	8:51 pm
2		10:22 pm	⚹ ☉	♑	4		12:44 am
3	**1:22 am**		⚹ ☉	♑	4	**3:44 am**	
5		10:29 pm	☌ ♆	♒	6		1:21 am
6	**1:29 am**		☌ ♆	♒	6	**4:21 am**	
7	**10:06 am**	7:06 am	☌ ☉	♓	8	**3:34 am**	12:34 am
9		9:46 am	⚹ ♆	♈	10		12:30 am
10	**12:46 am**		⚹ ♆	♈	10	**3:30 am**	
12	**3:11 am**	12:11 am	□ ♆	♉	12	**5:57 am**	2:57 am
14	**9:05 am**	6:05 am	△ ♆	♊	14	**11:54 am**	8:54 am
16	**5:56 pm**	2:56 pm	△ ☉	♋	16	**9:13 pm**	6:13 pm
19	**6:10 am**	3:10 am	☍ ♆	♌	19	**8:53 am**	5:53 am
21	**7:17 am**	4:17 am	☍ ♀	♍	21	**9:38 pm**	6:38 pm
24	**7:59 pm**	4:59 pm	△ ♆	♎	24	**10:23 am**	7:23 am
26	**9:49 pm**	6:49 pm	△ ♀	♏	26	**9:56 pm**	6:56 pm

☽ Phases & Eclipses phase	day	EST / hr:mn / PST	
New Moon	7	**10:06 am**	7:06 am
2nd Quarter	14	**3:58 am**	12:58 am
Full Moon	22	**5:27 am**	2:27 am

Planet Ingress		day	EST / hr:mn / PST	
♀	♒	2	**11:27 pm**	8:27 pm
⚵	♉	5	**3:23 pm**	12:23 pm
☿	♒	8		9:53 pm
☿	♒	9	**12:53 pm**	
☉	♓	18	**9:51am**	6:51 am
♀	♓	26	**11:01 pm**	8:01 pm
☿	♓	27	**10:54 pm**	7:54 pm

Planetary Motion		day	EST / hr:mn / PST	
♂	℞	5	**7:24 pm**	4:24 pm
⚷	℞	13	**9:27 pm**	6:27 pm

DAY		SID.TIME	SUN	MOON	NODE	MERCURY	VENUS	MARS	JUPITER	SATURN	URANUS	NEPTUNE	PLUTO	CERES	PALLAS	JUNO	VESTA	CHIRON
S	1	8:44:58	12 ♒ 09 56	14 ♏ 17	29 ♍℞ 51	18 ♑ 46	27 ♑ 16	05 ♎ 46	02 ♒ 26	03 ♈ 36	05 ♒ 04	28 ♑ 00	05 ♐ 15	01 ♒ 12	09 ♑ 52	27 ♈ 40	13 ♒ 18	01 ♏ 55
S	2	8:48:54	13 10 50	27 19	29 49	20 03	28 31	05 49	02 40	03 42	05 07	28 02	05 16	01 36	10 15	28 09	13 49	01 57
M	3	8:52:51	14 11 43	10 ♐ 48	29 46	21 22	29 46	05 52	02 54	03 47	05 11	28 04	05 18	01 59	10 38	28 37	14 20	01 58
T	4	8:56:47	15 12 36	24 47	29 40	22 42	01 ♒ 01	05 54	03 08	03 53	05 14	28 07	05 19	02 23	11 01	29 06	14 51	01 59
W	5	9:00:44	16 13 27	09 ♑ 15	29 34	24 03	02 16	05 55	03 22	03 59	05 18	28 09	05 20	02 47	11 23	29 35	15 22	02 00
T	6	9:04:40	17 14 18	24 07	29 27	25 25	03 31	05 ℞ 55	03 36	04 05	05 21	28 11	05 21	03 10	11 46	00 ♉ 04	15 53	02 01
F	7	9:08:37	18 15 07	09 ♒ 17	29 21	26 49	04 47	05 55	03 50	04 11	05 25	28 13	05 22	03 34	12 09	00 34	16 24	02 02
S	8	9:12:33	19 15 55	24 33	29 16	28 13	06 02	05 54	04 04	04 17	05 28	28 15	05 23	03 57	12 31	01 03	16 55	02 03
S	9	9:16:30	20 16 42	09 ♓ 46	29 13	29 39	07 17	05 52	04 18	04 23	05 31	28 17	05 24	04 21	12 53	01 33	17 26	02 04
M	10	9:20:27	21 17 27	24 46	29 D 11	01 ♒ 05	08 32	05 49	04 32	04 29	05 35	28 20	05 25	04 44	13 16	02 02	17 57	02 04
T	11	9:24:23	22 18 10	09 ♈ 25	29 11	02 33	09 47	05 46	04 45	04 35	05 38	28 22	05 26	05 08	13 38	02 32	18 28	02 05
W	12	9:28:20	23 18 52	23 39	29 12	04 01	11 02	05 42	04 59	04 41	05 42	28 24	05 27	05 31	14 00	03 02	18 59	02 05
T	13	9:32:16	24 19 33	07 ♉ 27	29 14	05 31	12 17	05 37	05 13	04 48	05 45	28 26	05 27	05 54	14 22	03 32	19 29	02 05
F	14	9:36:13	25 20 12	20 49	29 ℞ 15	07 01	13 32	05 31	05 27	04 54	05 48	28 28	05 28	06 18	14 44	04 02	20 00	02 ℞ 05
S	15	9:40:09	26 20 50	03 ♊ 48	29 15	08 32	14 47	05 25	05 41	05 00	05 52	28 30	05 29	06 41	15 05	04 33	20 31	02 05
S	16	9:44:06	27 21 25	16 28	29 14	10 05	16 02	05 17	05 54	05 07	05 55	28 32	05 30	07 04	15 27	05 03	21 02	02 05
M	17	9:48:02	28 22 00	28 52	29 11	11 38	17 17	05 09	06 08	05 13	05 58	28 34	05 30	07 28	15 49	05 34	21 33	02 05
T	18	9:51:59	29 22 32	11 ♋ 03	29 07	13 12	18 33	05 00	06 21	05 20	06 02	28 36	05 31	07 51	16 10	06 05	22 03	02 04
W	19	9:55:56	00 ♓ 23 02	23 05	29 02	14 47	19 48	04 51	06 35	05 26	06 05	28 38	05 32	08 14	16 32	06 35	22 34	02 04
T	20	9:59:52	01 23 31	05 ♌ 01	28 57	16 22	21 03	04 40	06 49	05 33	06 08	28 40	05 32	08 37	16 53	07 06	23 05	02 03
F	21	10:03:49	02 23 57	16 53	28 52	17 59	22 18	04 29	07 02	05 40	06 12	28 42	05 33	09 00	17 14	07 37	23 35	02 03
S	22	10:07:45	03 24 22	28 42	28 48	19 37	23 33	04 17	07 15	05 47	06 15	28 44	05 33	09 23	17 35	08 09	24 06	02 02
S	23	10:11:42	04 24 46	10 ♍ 31	28 45	21 15	24 48	04 04	07 29	05 53	06 18	28 46	05 34	09 46	17 56	08 40	24 36	02 01
M	24	10:15:38	05 25 08	22 22	28 D 44	22 55	26 03	03 51	07 42	06 00	06 21	28 48	05 34	10 09	18 17	09 11	25 07	02 00
T	25	10:19:35	06 25 28	04 ♎ 17	28 44	24 35	27 18	03 37	07 55	06 07	06 24	28 50	05 35	10 32	18 38	09 43	25 37	01 58
W	26	10:23:31	07 25 47	16 19	28 46	26 17	28 33	03 22	08 09	06 14	06 28	28 52	05 35	10 55	18 58	10 14	26 08	01 57
T	27	10:27:28	08 26 04	28 30	28 47	28 00	29 47	03 06	08 22	06 21	06 31	28 54	05 36	11 18	19 19	10 46	26 38	01 56
F	28	10:31:25	09 26 20	10 ♏ 53	28 49	29 43	01 ♓ 02	02 50	08 35	06 28	06 34	28 56	05 36	11 41	19 39	11 17	27 09	01 54

EPHEMERIS CALCULATED FOR 12 MIDNIGHT GREENWICH MEAN TIME. ALL OTHER DATA AND FACING ASPECTARIAN PAGE IN **EASTERN STANDARD TIME (BOLD)** AND PACIFIC STANDARD TIME (REGULAR).

MARCH 1997

1 SATURDAY

☿ △ ⚷	**12:37 am**	
☽ □ ⚶	**2:59 am**	
☽ ⚹ ♆	**5:06 am**	2:06 am
☿ ⚻ ♂	**7:48 am**	4:48 am
♄ ⚹ ♅	**8:24 am**	5:24 am
☽ ⚺ ⚷	**10:26 am**	7:26 am
☽ ⚹ ♂	**11:21 am**	8:21 am
☽ □ ☿	**11:59 am**	8:59 am
☽ □ ♀	**12:57 pm**	9:57 am
☽ ☌ ♇	**5:17 pm**	2:17 pm
☽ ⚹ ♅	**7:15 pm**	4:15 pm
☽ △ ♄	**7:18 pm**	4:18 pm
☽ ⚹ ♃	**11:36 pm**	8:36 pm

2 SUNDAY

☽ □ ☉	**4:38 am**	1:38 am
☽ ⚻ ⚵	**5:58 am**	2:58 am
☽ ⚹ ⚳	**5:59 am**	2:59 am
⚳ □ ⚵	**7:29 am**	4:29 am
☿ ☌ ♀	**9:32 am**	6:32 am
☽ ⚺ ⚴	**8:22 pm**	5:22 pm
☿ □ ♇		11:59 pm

3 MONDAY

☿ □ ♇	**2:59 am**	
♂ ⚺ ⚷	**6:49 am**	3:49 am
☉ ⚺ ⚳	**8:47 am**	5:47 am
♀ □ ♇	**10:31 am**	7:31 am
☽ ⚹ ⚶	**10:55 am**	7:55 am
☽ ⚺ ♆	**10:59 am**	7:59 am
♆ ⚺ ⚶	**12:33 pm**	9:33 am
☽ □ ♂	**3:34 pm**	12:34 pm
☽ ⚹ ⚷	**3:44 pm**	12:44 pm
☉ ⚹ ⚵	**5:15 pm**	2:15 pm
☿ ⚺ ♅	**6:39 pm**	3:39 pm
☿ ⚺ ♄	**8:59 pm**	5:59 pm
☽ ⚺ ♇	**10:16 pm**	7:16 pm
☽ ⚹ ♀	**11:24 pm**	8:24 pm
☽ ⚺ ♅		9:17 pm
☽ □ ♄		9:35 pm
☽ ⚹ ☿		10:05 pm

4 TUESDAY

☽ ⚺ ♅	**12:17 am**	
☽ □ ♄	**12:35 am**	
☽ ⚹ ☿	**1:05 am**	
☽ ⚺ ♃	**4:58 am**	1:58 am
♀ ⚺ ♅	**9:38 am**	6:38 am
☽ ⚺ ⚳	**11:33 am**	8:33 am
☽ △ ⚵	**12:09 pm**	9:09 am
☽ ⚹ ☉	**12:48 pm**	9:48 am
♀ ⚺ ♄	**2:02 pm**	11:02 am
☽ ☌ ⚴		9:48 pm

5 WEDNESDAY

☽ ☌ ⚴	**12:48 am**	
☿ ⚺ ♃	**10:47 am**	7:47 am
☽ ☌ ♆	**1:26 pm**	10:26 am
☽ ⚺ ⚶	**3:04 pm**	12:04 pm
☽ △ ♂	**4:35 pm**	1:35 pm
☽ □ ⚷	**5:43 pm**	2:43 pm
☽ ⚹ ♇	**9:00 pm**	
☽ ☌ ♅	**11:04 pm**	
☽ ⚹ ♄	**11:36 pm**	

6 THURSDAY

☽ ⚹ ♇	**12:00 am**	
☽ ☌ ♅	**2:04 am**	
☽ ⚹ ♄	**2:36 am**	
☽ ⚺ ♀	**5:38 am**	2:38 am
☽ ☌ ♃	**7:05 am**	4:05 am
☽ ⚺ ☿	**9:36 am**	6:36 am
☽ ☌ ⚳	**1:53 pm**	10:53 am
☽ □ ⚵	**3:01 pm**	12:01 pm
☽ ⚺ ☉	**5:20 pm**	2:20 pm
♂ ⚻ ⚶	**5:56 pm**	2:56 pm
♀ ⚺ ♃		11:15 pm
☽ ⚺ ⚴		11:23 pm

7 FRIDAY

♀ ⚺ ♃	**2:15 am**	
☽ ⚺ ⚴	**2:23 am**	
☽ ⚺ ♆	**1:37 pm**	10:37 am
☽ ⚻ ♂	**3:30 pm**	12:30 pm
☽ ☌ ⚶	**4:45 pm**	1:45 pm
☽ △ ⚷	**5:33 pm**	2:33 pm
☽ □ ♇	**11:49 pm**	8:49 pm
☽ ⚺ ♅		10:59 pm
☽ ⚺ ♄		11:45 pm

8 SATURDAY

☽ ⚺ ♅	**1:59 am**	
☽ ⚺ ♄	**2:45 am**	
☿ ⚺ ⚳	**3:26 am**	12:26 am
☽ ⚺ ♃	**7:26 am**	4:26 am
☽ ☌ ♀	**9:36 am**	6:36 am
☽ ⚺ ⚳	**2:40 pm**	11:40 am
⚶ △ ⚷	**3:04 pm**	12:04 pm
☽ ☌ ☿	**3:57 pm**	12:57 pm
☽ ⚹ ⚵	**4:21 pm**	1:21 pm
☽ ☌ ☉	**8:15 pm**	5:15 pm
☿ ⚹ ⚵	**8:17 pm**	5:17 pm
☽ ⚹ ⚴		11:56 pm

9 SUNDAY

☽ ⚹ ⚴	**2:56 am**	
☽ ⚹ ♆	**1:17 pm**	10:17 am
☽ ☍ ♂	**1:59 pm**	10:59 am
☽ ⚻ ⚷	**5:03 pm**	2:03 pm
☽ ⚺ ⚶	**6:01 pm**	3:01 pm
☽ △ ♇	**11:33 pm**	8:33 pm
☽ ⚹ ♅	**10:55 pm**	
☽ ☌ ♄	**11:55 pm**	

10 MONDAY

☽ ⚹ ♅	**1:55 am**	
☽ ☌ ♄	**2:55 am**	
☽ ⚹ ♃	**8:01 am**	5:01 am
☽ ⚺ ♀	**1:59 pm**	10:59 am
☽ ⚹ ⚳	**4:01 pm**	1:01 pm
♂ △ ♆	**4:59 pm**	1:59 pm
☽ ⚺ ⚵	**6:21 pm**	3:21 pm
☽ ⚺ ☿	**11:20 pm**	8:20 pm
☽ ⚺ ☉		9:06 pm

11 TUESDAY

☽ ⚺ ☉	**12:06 am**	
☽ □ ⚴	**4:34 am**	1:34 am
☿ ☌ ☉	**10:34 am**	7:34 am
☽ ⚻ ♂	**1:48 pm**	10:48 am
☽ □ ♆	**2:23 pm**	11:23 am
☽ ☍ ⚷	**6:06 pm**	3:06 pm
☽ ⚹ ⚶	**9:05 pm**	6:05 pm
♀ ⚺ ⚳	**10:53 pm**	7:53 pm
☽ ⚻ ♇		10:06 pm

12 WEDNESDAY

☽ ⚻ ♇	**1:06 am**	
☽ □ ♅	**3:46 am**	12:46 am
☽ ⚺ ♄	**5:06 am**	2:06 am
☽ □ ♃	**10:49 am**	7:49 am
☽ □ ⚳	**7:57 pm**	4:57 pm
☿ ⚹ ⚴	**8:56 pm**	5:56 pm
☽ ⚹ ♀	**9:26 pm**	6:26 pm
☽ ☌ ⚵	**11:09 pm**	8:09 pm

13 THURSDAY

☽ ⚹ ☉	**7:14 am**	4:14 am
☽ △ ⚴	**9:10 am**	6:10 am
☽ ⚹ ☿	**10:55 am**	7:55 am
☽ △ ♂	**4:24 pm**	1:24 pm
☽ △ ♆	**6:35 pm**	3:35 pm
☽ ⚻ ⚷	**10:16 pm**	7:16 pm

14 FRIDAY

☽ □ ⚶	**3:43 am**	12:43 am
♀ ⚹ ⚵	**5:46 am**	2:46 am
☽ ☍ ♇	**5:58 am**	2:58 am
☽ △ ♅	**9:02 am**	6:02 am
☽ ⚹ ♄	**10:47 am**	7:47 am
☽ △ ♃	**5:17 pm**	2:17 pm
☿ ☍ ♂	**7:06 pm**	4:06 pm
☉ ⚹ ⚴	**8:03 pm**	5:03 pm

15 SATURDAY

☽ △ ⚳	**3:50 am**	12:50 am
☽ ⚺ ⚵	**8:08 am**	5:08 am
☽ □ ♀	**9:44 am**	6:44 am
☿ ⚹ ♆	**3:30 pm**	12:30 pm
☽ ⚻ ⚴	**5:48 pm**	2:48 pm
☽ □ ☉	**7:06 pm**	4:06 pm
☽ □ ♂	**10:31 pm**	7:31 pm
☽ ⚻ ♆		11:38 pm

16 SUNDAY

☽ ⚻ ♆	**2:38 am**	
☽ □ ☿	**4:44 am**	1:44 am
☽ △ ⚷	**6:14 am**	3:14 am
☿ ⚻ ⚷	**1:58 pm**	10:58 am
♇ □ ⚶	**2:35 pm**	11:35 am
☽ △ ⚶	**2:40 pm**	11:40 am
☽ ⚻ ♇	**2:40 pm**	11:40 am
☽ ⚻ ♅	**6:10 pm**	3:10 pm
☽ □ ♄	**8:24 pm**	5:24 pm
☉ ☍ ♂		11:55 pm

17 MONDAY

☉ ☍ ♂	**2:55 am**	
☽ ⚻ ♃	**3:42 am**	12:42 am
☽ ⚻ ⚳	**3:43 pm**	12:43 pm
☽ ⚹ ⚵	**9:14 pm**	6:14 pm
☽ △ ♀		11:54 pm

18 TUESDAY

☽ △ ♀	**2:54 am**	
☽ ☍ ⚴	**6:08 am**	3:08 am
☽ ⚹ ♂	**7:42 am**	4:42 am
☽ △ ☉	**11:20 am**	8:20 am
☽ ☍ ♆	**1:59 pm**	10:59 am
☽ □ ⚷	**5:22 pm**	2:22 pm
☿ △ ♇	**6:17 pm**	3:17 pm
☽ △ ♇		11:22 pm

19 WEDNESDAY

☽ △ ♇	**2:22 am**	
☽ △ ☿	**4:01 am**	1:01 am
☽ ⚻ ⚶	**5:00 am**	2:00 am
☽ ☍ ♅	**6:14 am**	3:14 am
☽ △ ♄	**8:58 am**	5:58 am
♂ △ ⚴	**10:26 am**	7:26 am
☿ ⚺ ⚶	**11:32 am**	8:32 am
♀ ☍ ♂	**3:08 pm**	12:08 pm
☽ ☍ ♃	**4:54 pm**	1:54 pm
☿ ⚹ ♅	**5:30 pm**	2:30 pm
♀ ⚹ ⚴	**6:30 pm**	3:30 pm
☉ ⚹ ♆	**7:51 pm**	4:51 pm

20 THURSDAY

☽ ☍ ⚳	**6:06 am**	3:06 am
☿ ☌ ♄	**11:15 am**	8:15 am
☽ □ ⚵	**12:48 pm**	9:48 am
♅ ⚺ ⚶	**1:14 pm**	10:14 am
☽ ⚺ ♂	**6:31 pm**	3:31 pm
☽ ⚻ ⚴	**8:24 pm**	5:24 pm
☽ ⚻ ♀	**10:45 pm**	7:45 pm
☽ ⚻ ♆		11:57 pm

21 FRIDAY

☽ ⚻ ♆	**2:57 am**	
☽ ⚻ ☉	**5:44 am**	2:44 am
☽ ⚹ ⚷	**5:56 am**	2:56 am
☉ ⚻ ⚷	**7:57 am**	4:57 am
☽ □ ♇	**3:16 pm**	12:16 pm
☽ ⚻ ♅	**7:23 pm**	4:23 pm
☽ ☍ ⚶	**8:35 pm**	5:35 pm
☽ ⚻ ♄	**10:34 pm**	7:34 pm

22 SATURDAY

☽ ⚻ ☿	**5:10 am**	2:10 am
☽ ⚻ ♃	**6:51 am**	3:51 am
♀ ⚹ ♆	**3:12 pm**	12:12 pm
☿ ⚹ ♃	**4:23 pm**	1:23 pm
☽ ⚻ ⚳	**8:50 pm**	5:50 pm

23 SUNDAY

☽ △ ⚵	**4:33 am**	1:33 am
☽ ☌ ♂	**5:21 am**	2:21 am
☽ △ ⚴	**10:36 am**	7:36 am
♂ △ ⚵	**8:59 am**	11:59 am
☽ △ ♆	**3:40 pm**	12:40 pm
♀ ⚻ ⚷	**4:03 pm**	1:03 pm
☽ ⚺ ⚷	**6:12 pm**	3:12 pm
☽ ☍ ♀	**6:27 pm**	3:27 pm
☽ ☍ ☉	**11:45 pm**	8:45 pm

24 MONDAY

☽ ⚹ ♇	**3:37 am**	12:37 am
☽ △ ♅	**7:54 am**	4:54 am
☽ ⚻ ⚶	**11:25 am**	8:25 am
☽ ☍ ♄	**11:26 am**	8:26 am
♄ ⚺ ⚶	**11:58 am**	8:58 am
☽ △ ♃	**7:52 pm**	4:52 pm

25 TUESDAY

♂ △ ⚵	**2:38 am**	
☽ ☍ ☿	**4:28 am**	1:28 am
☽ △ ⚳	**10:19 am**	7:19 am
☽ ⚺ ♂	**3:02 pm**	12:02 pm
☽ ⚻ ⚵	**6:50 pm**	3:50 pm
☉ △ ♇	**10:23 pm**	7:23 pm
☽ □ ⚴	**11:15 pm**	8:15 pm
☽ □ ♆		11:55 pm

26 WEDNESDAY

☽ □ ♆	**2:55 am**	
☽ ☌ ⚷	**4:57 am**	1:57 am
☽ ⚻ ♀	**12:05 am**	9:05 am
☽ ⚺ ♇	**2:20 pm**	11:20 am
☽ ⚻ ☉	**3:43 pm**	12:43 pm
☽ □ ♅	**6:41 pm**	3:41 pm
☽ ⚻ ♄	**10:31 pm**	7:31 pm
☽ △ ⚶		9:17 pm

27 THURSDAY

☽ △ ⚶	**12:17 am**	
☿ ⚹ ⚳	**3:42 am**	12:42 am
☽ □ ♃	**6:57 am**	3:57 am
♀ △ ♇	**10:35 am**	7:35 am
☿ ⚻ ♂	**5:51 pm**	2:51 pm
☽ □ ⚳	**9:35 pm**	6:35 pm
☽ ⚹ ♂	**10:54 pm**	7:54 pm
☽ ⚻ ☿	**11:52 pm**	8:52 pm

28 FRIDAY

☉ ⚹ ♅	**6:30 am**	3:30 am
☽ ☍ ⚵	**6:45 am**	3:45 am
☽ ⚹ ⚴	**9:37 am**	6:37 am
☽ ⚹ ♆	**11:59 am**	8:59 am
☽ ⚺ ⚷	**1:35 pm**	10:35 am
♂ ⚻ ⚳	**10:07 pm**	7:07 pm
☽ ☌ ♇	**10:49 pm**	7:49 pm
☽ △ ♀	**11:40 pm**	

29 SATURDAY

☽ △ ♀	**2:40 am**	
☽ ⚹ ♅	**3:11 am**	12:11 am
☽ △ ☉	**1:49 am**	1:49 am
☽ △ ♄	**7:14 am**	4:14 am
♀ ⚹ ♅	**8:17 am**	5:17 am
☽ □ ⚶	**10:32 am**	7:32 am
☽ ⚹ ♃	**3:33 pm**	12:33 pm

30 SUNDAY

☽ □ ♂	**4:35 am**	1:35 am
☽ ⚹ ⚳	**6:12 am**	3:12 am
☽ △ ☿	**2:32 pm**	11:32 am
☽ ⚻ ⚵	**3:51 pm**	12:51 pm
☽ ⚺ ⚴	**5:17 pm**	2:17 pm
☉ ☌ ♄	**5:19 pm**	2:19 pm
☽ ⚺ ♆	**6:33 pm**	3:33 pm
☽ ⚹ ⚷	**7:43 pm**	4:43 pm

31 MONDAY

☽ ⚺ ♇	**4:45 am**	1:45 am
♀ ☌ ♄	**7:48 am**	4:48 am
☿ ⚺ ⚵	**8:19 am**	5:19 am
☽ ⚺ ♅	**9:05 am**	6:05 am
☽ □ ♄	**1:18 pm**	10:18 am
☽ □ ♀	**1:48 pm**	10:48 am
☽ □ ☉	**2:39 pm**	11:39 am
☽ ⚹ ⚶	**5:54 pm**	2:54 pm
☿ □ ⚴	**8:05 pm**	5:05 pm
☽ ⚺ ♃	**9:25 pm**	6:25 pm

Eastern Standard Time in bold type
Pacific Standard Time in medium type

MARCH 1997

☽ Last Aspect day	EST / hr:mn / PST	asp	☽ Ingress sign	day	EST / hr:mn / PST
1	**5:06 am** 2:06 am	⚹♆	♐	1	**7:01 am** 4:01 am
2	**4:38 am** 1:38 am	□☉	♑	3	**12:39 pm** 9:39 am
5	**1:26 pm** 10:26 am	☌♆	♒	5	**2:55 pm** 11:55 am
6	**7:05 am** 4:05 am	☌♃	♓	7	**2:57 pm** 11:57 am
9	**1:59 pm** 10:59 am	☍♂	♈	9	**2:33 pm** 11:33 am
11	**2:23 pm** 11:23 am	□♆	♉	11	**3:38 pm** 12:38 pm
13	**6:35 pm** 3:35 pm	△♆	♊	13	**7:49 pm** 4:49 pm
15	**10:31 pm** 7:31 pm	□♂	♋	16	**3:51 am** 12:51 am
18	**1:59 pm** 10:59 am	☍♆	♌	18	**3:08 pm** 12:08 pm
19	**4:54 pm** 1:54 pm	☍♃	♍	21	**3:59 am** 12:59 am
23	**3:40 pm** 12:40 pm	△♆	♎	23	**4:35 pm** 1:35 pm
25	11:55 pm	□♆	♏	26	12:43 am
26	**2:55 am**	□♆	♏	26	**3:43 am**
28	**11:59 am** 8:59 am	⚹♆	♐	28	**12:40 pm** 9:40 am
30	**2:32 pm** 11:32 am	△☿	♑	30	**7:07 pm** 4:07 pm

☽ Phases & Eclipses phase	day	EST / hr:mn / PST
4th Quarter	2	**4:38 am** 1:38 am
New Moon	8	**8:15 pm** 5:15 pm
2nd Quarter	15	**7:06 pm** 4:06 pm
●	16	18° ♓ 31'
Full Moon	23	**11:45 pm** 8:45 pm
●	24	03° ♎ 35'
4th Quarter	31	**2:39 pm** 11:39 am

Planet Ingress	day	EST / hr:mn / PST
⚵ ♓	5	**10:32 am** 7:32 am
♂ ♍	8	**2:49 pm** 11:49 am
☿ ♈	15	**11:13 pm** 8:13 pm
☉ ♈	20	**8:55 am** 5:55 am
♀ ♈	22	9:26 pm
♀ ♈	23	**12:26 am**

Planetary Motion	day	EST / hr:mn / PST
♇ ℞	8	**3:36 am** 12:36 am

DAY		SID.TIME	SUN	MOON	NODE	MERCURY	VENUS	MARS	JUPITER	SATURN	URANUS	NEPTUNE	PLUTO	CERES	PALLAS	JUNO	VESTA	CHIRON
S	1	10:35:21	10 ♓ 26 34	23 ♏ 33	28 ♍ ℞ 50	01 ♓ 28	02 ♓ 17	02 ♎ ℞ 33	08 ♒ 48	06 ♈ 35	06 ♒ 37	28 ♑ 57	05 ♐ 36	12 ♒ 03	19 ♑ 59	11 ♉ 49	27 ♒ 39	01 ♏ ℞ 53
S	2	10:39:18	11 26 47	06 ♐ 32	28 51	03 13	03 32	02 16	09 01	06 42	06 40	28 59	05 36	12 26	20 19	12 21	28 10	01 51
M	3	10:43:14	12 26 58	19 54	28 50	05 00	04 47	01 57	09 14	06 49	06 43	29 01	05 37	12 49	20 39	12 53	28 40	01 49
T	4	10:47:11	13 27 07	03 ♑ 41	28 49	06 48	06 02	01 38	09 27	06 56	06 46	29 03	05 37	13 11	20 59	13 25	29 10	01 47
W	5	10:51:07	14 27 15	17 54	28 47	08 36	07 17	01 19	09 40	07 03	06 49	29 04	05 37	13 34	21 19	13 57	29 40	01 45
T	6	10:55:04	15 27 22	02 ♒ 31	28 45	10 26	08 32	00 59	09 53	07 10	06 52	29 06	05 37	13 56	21 39	14 29	00 ♓ 11	01 43
F	7	10:59:00	16 27 27	17 26	28 43	12 17	09 47	00 39	10 06	07 17	06 55	29 08	05 37	14 19	21 58	15 02	00 41	01 41
S	8	11:02:57	17 27 30	02 ♓ 33	28 42	14 09	11 02	00 18	10 18	07 25	06 58	29 10	05 ℞ 37	14 41	22 17	15 34	01 11	01 38
S	9	11:06:54	18 27 31	17 43	28 D 41	16 02	12 17	29 ♍ 56	10 31	07 32	07 01	29 11	05 37	15 03	22 37	16 06	01 41	01 36
M	10	11:10:50	19 27 31	02 ♈ 46	28 41	17 56	13 31	29 34	10 44	07 39	07 03	29 13	05 37	15 25	22 56	16 39	02 11	01 33
T	11	11:14:47	20 27 28	17 34	28 42	19 51	14 46	29 12	10 56	07 46	07 06	29 14	05 37	15 48	23 15	17 12	02 41	01 31
W	12	11:18:43	21 27 23	02 ♉ 00	28 43	21 47	16 01	28 50	11 08	07 54	07 09	29 16	05 37	16 10	23 33	17 44	03 11	01 28
T	13	11:22:40	22 27 17	16 00	28 44	23 44	17 16	28 27	11 21	08 01	07 12	29 18	05 37	16 32	23 52	18 17	03 41	01 25
F	14	11:26:36	23 27 07	29 33	28 45	25 42	18 31	28 04	11 33	08 08	07 14	29 19	05 37	16 54	24 10	18 50	04 11	01 22
S	15	11:30:33	24 26 56	12 ♊ 40	28 45	27 40	19 45	27 41	11 45	08 16	07 17	29 21	05 37	17 16	24 29	19 22	04 41	01 19
S	16	11:34:29	25 26 43	25 24	28 ℞ 46	29 39	21 00	27 17	11 58	08 23	07 20	29 22	05 36	17 37	24 47	19 55	05 11	01 16
M	17	11:38:26	26 26 27	07 ♋ 48	28 46	01 ♈ 38	22 15	26 54	12 10	08 31	07 22	29 24	05 36	17 59	25 05	20 28	05 40	01 13
T	18	11:42:22	27 26 09	19 57	28 46	03 38	23 30	26 30	12 22	08 38	07 25	29 25	05 36	18 21	25 23	21 01	06 10	01 09
W	19	11:46:19	28 25 49	01 ♌ 55	28 45	05 38	24 44	26 07	12 34	08 45	07 27	29 26	05 35	18 43	25 40	21 34	06 40	01 06
T	20	11:50:16	29 25 27	13 46	28 D 45	07 37	25 59	25 43	12 45	08 53	07 30	29 28	05 35	19 04	25 58	22 07	07 09	01 03
F	21	11:54:12	00 ♈ 25 02	25 35	28 46	09 36	27 14	25 20	12 57	09 00	07 32	29 29	05 35	19 26	26 15	22 40	07 39	00 59
S	22	11:58:09	01 24 35	07 ♍ 23	28 46	11 35	28 28	24 57	13 09	09 08	07 35	29 30	05 34	19 47	26 32	23 13	08 08	00 56
S	23	12:02:05	02 24 06	19 15	28 ℞ 46	13 32	29 43	24 33	13 20	09 15	07 37	29 32	05 34	20 08	26 49	23 47	08 38	00 52
M	24	12:06:02	03 23 35	01 ♎ 12	28 46	15 27	00 ♈ 58	24 10	13 32	09 23	07 40	29 33	05 33	20 30	27 06	24 20	09 07	00 48
T	25	12:09:58	04 23 02	13 17	28 46	17 21	02 12	23 48	13 43	09 30	07 42	29 34	05 33	20 51	27 23	24 53	09 37	00 44
W	26	12:13:55	05 22 27	25 31	28 46	19 13	03 27	23 25	13 55	09 38	07 44	29 35	05 32	21 12	27 39	25 26	10 06	00 40
T	27	12:17:51	06 21 50	07 ♏ 56	28 45	21 02	04 42	23 03	14 06	09 45	07 46	29 37	05 31	21 33	27 56	26 00	10 35	00 37
F	28	12:21:48	07 21 11	20 34	28 44	22 47	05 56	22 41	14 17	09 53	07 49	29 38	05 31	21 54	28 12	26 33	11 05	00 33
S	29	12:25:45	08 20 30	03 ♐ 25	28 43	24 30	07 11	22 20	14 28	10 00	07 51	29 39	05 30	22 15	28 28	27 07	11 34	00 28
S	30	12:29:41	09 19 48	16 32	28 41	26 08	08 25	21 59	14 39	10 08	07 53	29 40	05 29	22 35	28 43	27 40	12 03	00 24
M	31	12:33:38	10 19 04	29 56	28 40	27 42	09 40	21 39	14 50	10 15	07 55	29 41	05 29	22 56	28 59	28 13	12 32	00 20

EPHEMERIS CALCULATED FOR 12 MIDNIGHT GREENWICH MEAN TIME. ALL OTHER DATA AND FACING ASPECTARIAN PAGE IN **EASTERN STANDARD TIME (BOLD)** AND PACIFIC STANDARD TIME (REGULAR).

APRIL 1997

1 TUESDAY

2 WEDNESDAY

3 THURSDAY

4 FRIDAY

5 SATURDAY

6 SUNDAY

7 MONDAY

8 TUESDAY

9 WEDNESDAY

10 THURSDAY

11 FRIDAY

12 SATURDAY

13 SUNDAY

14 MONDAY

15 TUESDAY

16 WEDNESDAY

17 THURSDAY

18 FRIDAY

19 SATURDAY

20 SUNDAY

21 MONDAY

22 TUESDAY

23 WEDNESDAY

24 THURSDAY

25 FRIDAY

26 SATURDAY

27 SUNDAY

28 MONDAY

29 TUESDAY

30 WEDNESDAY

APRIL 1997

☽ Last Aspect day	EST / hr:mn / PST	asp	☽ Ingress sign day	EST / hr:mn / PST
1	**10:31 pm** 7:31 pm	☌ ♆	♒ 1	**10:59 pm** 7:59 pm
2	9:45 pm	☌ ♃	♓ 3	9:43 am
3	**12:45 am**	☌ ♃	♓ 4	**12:43 am**
5	9:58 pm	⚹ ♆	♈ 5	10:20 pm
6	**12:58 am**	⚹ ♆	♈ 6	**1:20 am**
7	11:01 pm	□ ♆	♉ 7	11:21 pm
8	**2:01 am**	□ ♆	♉ 8	**2:21 am**
10	**5:10 am** 2:10 am	△ ♆	♊ 10	**5:28 am** 2:28 am
11	11:34 pm	⚹ ♀	♋ 12	9:03 am
12	**2:34 am**	⚹ ♀	♋ 12	**12:03 pm**
14	**10:07 pm** 7:07 pm	☍ ♆	♌ 14	**10:22 pm** 7:22 pm
17	**5:52 am** 2:52 am	△ ☉	♍ 17	**11:00 am** 8:00 am
19	**11:27 pm** 8:27 pm	△ ♆	♎ 19	**11:37 pm** 8:37 pm
22	**10:12 am** 7:12 am	□ ♆	♏ 22	**10:20 am** 7:20 am
24	**6:26 pm** 3:26 pm	⚹ ♆	♐ 24	**6:33 pm** 3:33 pm
26	1:52 am	⚹ ♃	♑ 26	9:33 pm
26	**4:52 am**	⚹ ♃	♑ 27	**12:33 am**
29	**4:46 am** 1:46 am	☌ ♆	♒ 29	**4:51 am** 1:51 am
30	**2:05 pm** 11:05 am	☌ ♃	♓ 5/1	**7:50 am** 4:50 am

☽ Phases & Eclipses phase	day	EST / hr:mn / PST
New Moon	7	**6:02 pm** 3:02 pm
2nd Quarter	14	**11:59 am** 8:59 am
Full Moon	22	**3:34 pm** 12:34 pm
4th Quarter	29	**9:37 pm** 6:37 pm

Planet Ingress	day	EST / hr:mn / PST
☿ ♉	1	**8:44 am** 5:44 am
⚵ ♊	2	**11:15 pm** 8:15 pm
⚴ ♒	3	**8:26 pm** 5:26 pm
⚷ ♎	4	**11:59 am** 8:59 am
♀ ♉	16	**4:42 am** 1:42 am
☉ ♉	19	**8:03 pm** 5:03 pm
⚳ ♓	21	**11:18 am** 8:18 am

Planetary Motion	day	EST / hr:mn / PST
☿ ℞	14	**6:56 pm** 3:56 pm
♂ D	27	**2:10 pm** 11:10 am

DAY		SID.TIME	SUN	MOON	NODE	MERCURY	VENUS	MARS	JUPITER	SATURN	URANUS	NEPTUNE	PLUTO	CERES	PALLAS	JUNO	VESTA	CHIRON
T	1	12:37:34	11 ♈ 18 18	13 ♑ 38	28 ♍ 40	29 ♈ 11	10 ♈ 54	21 ♍ ℞ 19	15 ♒ 01	10 ♈ 23	07 ♒ 57	29 ♑ 42	05 ♐ ℞ 28	23 ♒ 17	29 ♑ 14	28 ♉ 47	13 ♓ 01	00 ♏ ℞ 16
W	2	12:41:31	12 17 31	27 38	28 40	00 ♉ 35	12 09	20 59	15 11	10 30	07 59	29 43	05 27	23 37	29 29	29 20	13 30	00 12
T	3	12:45:27	13 16 41	11 ♒ 57	28 41	01 54	13 23	20 41	15 22	10 38	08 01	29 44	05 26	23 58	29 44	29 54	13 59	00 07
F	4	12:49:24	14 15 49	26 30	28 41	03 08	14 38	20 22	15 32	10 46	08 03	29 45	05 26	24 18	29 59	00 ♊ 28	14 28	00 03
S	5	12:53:20	15 14 56	11 ♓ 15	28 42	04 15	15 52	20 05	15 43	10 53	08 05	29 46	05 25	24 38	00 ♒ 14	01 01	14 56	29 ♎ 59
S	6	12:57:17	16 14 00	26 05	28 ℞ 42	05 16	17 07	19 48	15 53	11 01	08 06	29 47	05 24	24 58	00 28	01 35	15 25	29 54
M	7	13:01:13	17 13 03	10 ♈ 54	28 42	06 12	18 21	19 31	16 03	11 08	08 08	29 47	05 23	25 18	00 42	02 09	15 54	29 50
T	8	13:05:10	18 12 04	25 34	28 41	07 01	19 35	19 16	16 13	11 16	08 10	29 48	05 22	25 38	00 56	02 42	16 23	29 45
W	9	13:09:07	19 11 03	09 ♉ 58	28 39	07 43	20 50	19 01	16 23	11 23	08 12	29 49	05 21	25 58	01 10	03 16	16 51	29 41
T	10	13:13:03	20 10 00	24 00	28 36	08 19	22 04	18 47	16 33	11 31	08 13	29 50	05 20	26 18	01 23	03 50	17 20	29 36
F	11	13:17:00	21 08 54	07 ♊ 38	28 33	08 48	23 18	18 33	16 43	11 38	08 15	29 50	05 19	26 37	01 36	04 23	17 48	29 32
S	12	13:20:56	22 07 47	20 51	28 31	09 11	24 33	18 21	16 52	11 45	08 16	29 51	05 18	26 57	01 49	04 57	18 16	29 27
S	13	13:24:53	23 06 37	03 ♋ 40	28 29	09 27	25 47	18 09	17 02	11 53	08 18	29 52	05 17	27 16	02 02	05 31	18 45	29 22
M	14	13:28:49	24 05 26	16 08	28 D 27	09 36	27 01	17 58	17 11	12 00	08 19	29 52	05 16	27 36	02 14	06 05	19 13	29 18
T	15	13:32:46	25 04 11	28 19	28 27	09 ℞ 39	28 16	17 47	17 20	12 08	08 21	29 53	05 15	27 55	02 26	06 38	19 41	29 13
W	16	13:36:42	26 02 55	10 ♌ 17	28 28	09 36	29 30	17 38	17 29	12 15	08 22	29 53	05 13	28 14	02 38	07 12	20 09	29 08
T	17	13:40:39	27 01 36	22 08	28 30	09 27	00 ♉ 44	17 29	17 38	12 23	08 23	29 54	05 12	28 33	02 50	07 46	20 37	29 04
F	18	13:44:36	28 00 15	03 ♍ 56	28 32	09 13	01 58	17 21	17 47	12 30	08 25	29 54	05 11	28 52	03 02	08 20	21 05	28 59
S	19	13:48:32	28 58 52	15 46	28 34	08 53	03 13	17 14	17 56	12 37	08 26	29 55	05 10	29 10	03 13	08 54	21 33	28 54
S	20	13:52:29	29 57 26	27 41	28 ℞ 34	08 28	04 27	17 07	18 04	12 45	08 27	29 55	05 09	29 29	03 24	09 27	22 01	28 50
M	21	13:56:25	00 ♉ 55 59	09 ♊ 46	28 34	07 59	05 41	17 02	18 13	12 52	08 28	29 56	05 07	29 47	03 34	10 01	22 29	28 45
T	22	14:00:22	01 54 30	22 03	28 31	07 26	06 55	16 57	18 21	12 59	08 29	29 56	05 06	00 ♓ 06	03 45	10 35	22 56	28 40
W	23	14:04:18	02 52 59	04 ♏ 33	28 27	06 51	08 09	16 53	18 29	13 06	08 30	29 56	05 05	00 24	03 55	11 09	23 24	28 36
T	24	14:08:15	03 51 26	17 17	28 21	06 13	09 23	16 50	18 38	13 14	08 31	29 57	05 03	00 42	04 05	11 43	23 51	28 31
F	25	14:12:11	04 49 51	00 ♐ 15	28 15	05 33	10 37	16 47	18 45	13 21	08 32	29 57	05 02	01 00	04 14	12 16	24 19	28 26
S	26	14:16:08	05 48 14	13 27	28 09	04 53	11 51	16 45	18 53	13 28	08 33	29 57	05 01	01 18	04 24	12 50	24 46	28 22
S	27	14:20:05	06 46 36	26 52	28 03	04 12	13 05	16 45	19 01	13 35	08 34	29 57	04 59	01 36	04 33	13 24	25 14	28 17
M	28	14:24:01	07 44 56	10 ♑ 29	27 59	03 32	14 19	16 D 44	19 08	13 42	08 35	29 57	04 58	01 53	04 41	13 58	25 41	28 13
T	29	14:27:58	08 43 14	24 17	27 57	02 54	15 33	16 45	19 16	13 49	08 35	29 58	04 56	02 11	04 50	14 32	26 08	28 08
W	30	14:31:54	09 41 31	08 ♒ 16	27 D 56	02 17	16 47	16 46	19 23	13 56	08 36	29 58	04 55	02 28	04 58	15 05	26 35	28 04

EPHEMERIS CALCULATED FOR 12 MIDNIGHT GREENWICH MEAN TIME. ALL OTHER DATA AND FACING ASPECTARIAN PAGE IN **EASTERN STANDARD TIME (BOLD)** AND PACIFIC STANDARD TIME (REGULAR).

MAY 1997

1 THURSDAY

☽ ⚺ ⚶	**3:06 am**	12:06 am
☽ △ ⚷	**4:24 am**	1:24 am
☽ ⚺ ♆	**7:46 am**	4:46 am
☽ ⚹ ☿	**10:10 am**	7:10 am
☽ ☌ ⚳	**12:49 pm**	9:49 am
☽ □ ♇	**3:59 pm**	12:59 pm
☽ ⚺ ♀	**4:35 pm**	1:35 pm
☽ ⚺ ♅	**10:19 pm**	7:19 pm
♀ □ ♃		11:43 pm

2 FRIDAY

♀ □ ♃	**2:43 am**	
☽ ⚹ ☉	**3:57 am**	12:57 am
☽ ⚺ ♄	**7:42 am**	4:42 am
☽ □ ⚵	**11:40 am**	8:40 am
☽ ☍ ♂	**12:08 pm**	9:08 am
⚶ ⚻ ⚷	**2:48 pm**	11:48 am
☽ ⚺ ♃	**4:52 pm**	1:52 pm
☽ ⚹ ♀	**6:04 pm**	3:04 pm
♂ □ ⚵		9:57 pm

3 SATURDAY

♂ □ ⚵	**12:57 am**	
☽ ⚻ ⚷	**6:20 am**	3:20 am
☽ ☌ ⚶	**6:54 am**	3:54 am
☽ ⚹ ♆	**9:55 am**	6:55 am
☽ ⚺ ☿	**10:46 am**	7:46 am
☽ ⚺ ⚳	**3:54 pm**	12:54 pm
☽ △ ♇	**5:59 pm**	2:59 pm
☽ ⚹ ♀	**7:04 pm**	4:04 pm
☽ ⚹ ♅		9:22 pm

4 SUNDAY

☽ ⚹ ♅	**12:22 am**	
☽ ⚺ ☉	**9:34 am**	6:34 am
☽ ☌ ♄	**10:06 am**	7:06 am
☽ ⚻ ♂	**2:22 pm**	11:22 am
☽ ⚹ ⚵	**3:41 pm**	12:41 pm
☉ ⚺ ♄	**6:20 pm**	3:20 pm
☽ ⚹ ♃	**7:14 pm**	4:14 pm
☿ □ ♆		9:42 pm
☽ ⚺ ♀		9:45 pm

5 MONDAY

☿ □ ♆	**12:42 am**	
☽ ⚺ ♀	**12:45 am**	
☽ ☍ ⚷	**8:08 am**	5:08 am
☽ ⚺ ⚶	**10:34 am**	7:34 am
☽ ☌ ☿	**11:48 am**	8:48 am
☽ □ ♆	**11:59 am**	8:59 am
☽ ⚹ ⚳	**7:03 pm**	4:03 pm
☽ ⚻ ♇	**8:04 pm**	5:04 pm
☽ □ ♀	**9:39 pm**	6:39 pm
☽ □ ♅		11:41 pm

6 TUESDAY

☽ □ ♅	**2:41 am**	
☽ ⚺ ♄	**12:59 pm**	9:59 am
☿ ⚺ ⚶	**2:32 pm**	11:32 am
☽ ☌ ☉	**3:47 pm**	12:47 pm
☽ △ ♂	**5:18 pm**	2:18 pm
☽ ⚺ ⚵	**8:25 pm**	5:25 pm
☽ □ ♃	**10:20 pm**	7:20 pm

7 WEDNESDAY

♆ ⚹ ⚶	**8:26 am**	5:26 am
☽ ☌ ♀	**8:35 am**	5:35 am
☽ ⚻ ⚷	**10:59 am**	7:59 am
☽ ⚺ ☿	**2:29 pm**	11:29 am
☽ △ ♆	**3:15 pm**	12:15 pm
☽ ⚹ ⚶	**3:29 pm**	12:29 pm
☉ △ ♂	**4:30 pm**	1:30 pm
♇ □ ⚳	**8:39 pm**	5:39 pm
☽ ☍ ♇	**11:34 pm**	8:34 pm
☽ □ ⚳	**11:38 pm**	8:38 pm
☽ △ ♀		10:40 pm

8 THURSDAY

☽ △ ♀	**1:40 am**	
☽ △ ♅	**6:35 am**	3:35 am
♀ ⚻ ⚷	**10:20 am**	7:20 am
☽ ⚹ ♄	**5:49 pm**	2:49 pm
☽ □ ♂	**10:22 pm**	7:22 pm
☽ ⚺ ☉		9:25 pm

9 FRIDAY

☽ ⚺ ☉	**12:25 am**	
☽ ☌ ⚵	**3:32 am**	12:32 am
☽ △ ♃	**3:36 am**	12:36 am
♃ △ ⚵	**5:18 am**	2:18am
☽ △ ⚷	**4:19 pm**	1:19 pm
☽ ⚺ ♀	**7:38 pm**	4:38 pm
☽ ⚹ ☿	**8:22 pm**	5:22 pm
☽ ⚻ ♆	**9:06 pm**	6:06 pm
☽ □ ⚶	**11:15 pm**	8:15 pm

10 SATURDAY

☿ ⚺ ♀	**4:06 am**	1:06 am
☽ ⚻ ♇	**5:50 am**	2:50 am
☽ △ ⚳	**7:09 am**	4:09 am
☽ ⚻ ♀	**8:32 am**	5:32 am
♀ △ ♆	**11:07 am**	8:07 am
☽ ⚻ ♅	**1:25 pm**	10:25 am
☉ □ ♃		9:16 pm
☽ □ ♄		10:52 pm

11 SUNDAY

☉ □ ♃	**12:16 am**	
☽ □ ♄	**1:52 am**	
☽ ⚹ ♂	**6:54 am**	3:54 am
☽ ⚻ ♃	**12:13 pm**	9:13 am
☽ ⚹ ☉	**1:08 pm**	10:08 am
☽ ⚺ ⚵	**2:24 pm**	11:24 am
☿ □ ♆	**11:16 pm**	8:16 pm
☽ □ ⚷		10:03 pm

12 MONDAY

☽ □ ⚷	**1:03 am**	
♀ ⚹ ⚶	**4:32 am**	1:32 am
☽ ☍ ♆	**6:25 am**	3:25 am
☽ □ ☿	**6:35 am**	3:35 am
☽ △ ⚶	**10:50 am**	7:50 am
☽ ⚹ ♀	**11:18 am**	8:18 am
☽ △ ♇	**3:35 pm**	12:35 pm
☽ ⚻ ⚳	**6:21 pm**	3:21 pm
☽ ☍ ♀	**6:53 pm**	3:53 pm
☽ ☍ ♅	**11:44 pm**	8:44 pm
☉ ⚺ ⚵		11:02 pm

13 TUESDAY

☉ ⚺ ⚵	**2:02 am**	
☽ △ ♄	**1:24 pm**	10:24 am
☽ ⚺ ♂	**6:59 pm**	3:59 pm
☽ ☍ ♃		9:08 pm

14 WEDNESDAY

☽ ☍ ♃	**12:08 am**	
⚳ ⚺ ♀	**3:22 am**	12:22 am
♀ ☍ ♇	**4:45 am**	1:45 am
☽ ⚹ ⚵	**4:56 am**	1:56 am
☽ □ ☉	**5:56 am**	2:56 am
☽ ⚹ ⚷	**12:43 pm**	9:43 am
☽ ⚻ ♆	**6:34 pm**	3:34 pm
☽ △ ☿	**8:46 pm**	5:46 pm
☽ ⚻ ⚶		10:26 pm

15 THURSDAY

☽ ⚻ ⚶	**1:26 am**	
☽ □ ♇	**3:53 am**	12:53 am
☽ □ ♀	**6:38 am**	3:38 am
☽ ⚻ ♀	**7:41 am**	4:41 am
☽ ☍ ⚳	**8:10 am**	5:10 am
☽ ⚻ ♅	**12:22 pm**	9:22 am
♀ △ ♀	**5:02 pm**	2:02 pm
♀ □ ⚳		9:35 pm
☽ ⚻ ♄		11:46 pm

16 FRIDAY

♀ □ ⚳	**12:35 am**	
☽ ⚻ ♄	**2:46 am**	
☽ ☌ ♂	**8:50 am**	5:50 am
☽ ⚻ ♃	**1:24 pm**	10:24 am
☽ □ ⚵	**8:47 pm**	5:47 pm
☽ △ ☉		9:08 pm
☽ ⚺ ⚷		10:12 pm

17 SATURDAY

☽ △ ☉	**12:08 am**	
☽ ⚺ ⚷	**1:12 am**	
☽ △ ♆	**7:15 am**	4:15 am
☽ ⚻ ☿	**12:27 pm**	9:27 am
☉ ⚻ ⚷	**12:42 pm**	9:42 am
♀ △ ♅	**1:31 pm**	10:31 am
☽ ☍ ⚶	**4:16 pm**	1:16 pm
☽ ⚹ ♇	**4:19 pm**	1:19 pm
♇ △ ⚶	**5:45 pm**	2:45 pm
☽ △ ♀	**8:21 pm**	5:21 pm
☽ ⚻ ⚳	**9:52 pm**	6:52 pm
☽ △ ♅		9:43 pm
☽ △ ♀		10:58 pm

18 SUNDAY

☽ △ ♅	**12:43 am**	
☽ △ ♀	**1:58 am**	
☽ ☍ ♄	**3:13 pm**	12:13 pm
☽ ⚺ ♂	**9:37 pm**	6:37 pm
☽ △ ♃		10:16 pm

19 MONDAY

☽ △ ♃	**1:16 am**	
☽ △ ⚵	**10:47 am**	7:47 am
☽ ☌ ⚷	**11:57 am**	8:57 am
☽ ⚻ ☉	**4:07 pm**	1:07 pm
☽ □ ♆	**5:57 pm**	2:57 pm
☿ ⚻ ♇		10:59 pm
☽ ⚺ ♇		11:30 pm
☽ ☍ ☿		11:32 pm

20 TUESDAY

☿ ⚻ ♇	**1:59 am**	
☽ ⚺ ♇	**2:30 am**	
☽ ☍ ☿	**2:32 am**	
☽ ⚻ ⚶	**4:34 am**	1:34 am
☽ □ ♀	**6:34 am**	3:34 am
☽ △ ⚳	**8:58 am**	5:58 am
☽ □ ♅	**10:34 am**	7:34 am
⚵ △ ⚷	**10:37 am**	7:37 am
☉ △ ♆	**3:52 pm**	12:52 pm
☽ ⚻ ♀	**5:54 pm**	2:54 pm
☽ ⚻ ♄		9:47 pm

21 WEDNESDAY

☽ ⚻ ♄	**12:47 am**	
☽ ⚹ ♂	**7:27 am**	4:27 am
☽ □ ♃	**10:07 am**	7:07 am
☽ ⚺ ⚷	**7:42 pm**	4:42 pm
☽ ⚻ ⚵	**9:18 pm**	6:18 pm
☽ ⚹ ♆		10:35 pm

22 THURSDAY

☽ ⚹ ♆	**1:35 am**	
☽ ☍ ☉	**4:14 am**	1:14 am
☿ ⚺ ⚶	**9:10 am**	6:10 am
☽ ☌ ♇	**9:36 am**	6:36 am
☿ □ ♀	**1:14 pm**	10:14 am
☽ △ ⚶	**1:26 pm**	10:26 am
☽ ⚹ ♀	**1:36 pm**	10:36 am
☽ ⚻ ☿	**1:37 pm**	10:37 am
☽ □ ⚳	**4:46 pm**	1:46 pm
☽ ⚹ ♅	**5:20 pm**	2:20 pm
♀ ⚹ ⚶	**6:24 pm**	3:24 pm

23 FRIDAY

☽ ☍ ♀	**5:44 am**	2:44 am
☽ △ ♄	**7:17 am**	4:17 am
☽ □ ♂	**2:16 pm**	11:16 am
☽ ⚹ ♃	**3:59 pm**	12:59 pm
♀ ⚹ ♄		9:23 pm
☽ ⚹ ⚷		9:45 pm
♅ ⚺ ⚳		10:57 pm

24 SATURDAY

♀ ⚹ ♄	**12:23 am**	
☽ ⚹ ⚷	**12:45 am**	
♅ ⚺ ⚳	**1:57 am**	
☽ ☍ ⚵	**4:43 am**	1:43 am
☽ ⚺ ♆	**6:33 am**	3:33 am
☽ ⚻ ☉	**1:05 pm**	10:05 am
☽ ⚺ ♇	**2:12 pm**	11:12 am
☿ □ ♅	**2:59 pm**	11:59 am
☽ ⚺ ♀	**6:08 pm**	3:08 pm
☿ ⚹ ⚳	**6:25 pm**	3:25 pm
☽ □ ⚶	**7:37 pm**	4:37 pm
☽ ⚺ ♅	**9:44 pm**	6:44 pm
☽ ⚹ ⚳	**10:04 pm**	7:04 pm
☽ △ ☿	**10:18 pm**	7:18 pm

25 SUNDAY

☉ ☍ ♇	**4:57 am**	1:57 am
☽ □ ♄	**11:40 am**	8:40 am
☽ ⚻ ♀	**2:47 pm**	11:47 am
☽ △ ♂	**7:09 pm**	4:09 pm
☽ ⚺ ♃	**7:59 pm**	4:59 pm
♆ ⚻ ⚵		10:07 pm

26 MONDAY

♆ ⚻ ⚵	**1:07 am**	
☽ □ ⚷	**4:10 am**	1:10 am
☽ ☌ ♆	**9:59 am**	6:59 am
☽ ⚻ ⚵	**10:22 am**	7:22 am
☽ ⚹ ♇	**5:28 pm**	2:28 pm
☽ △ ☉	**8:12 pm**	5:12 pm
☽ ☌ ♀	**9:22 pm**	6:22 pm
☽ ⚹ ⚶		9:26 pm
☽ ☌ ♅		9:57 pm
☽ ⚺ ⚳		11:05 pm

27 TUESDAY

☽ ⚹ ⚶	**12:26 am**	
☽ ☌ ♅	**12:57 am**	
☽ ⚺ ⚳	**2:05 am**	
☽ □ ☿	**6:00 am**	3:00 am
☉ △ ♀	**12:45 pm**	9:45 am
☽ ⚹ ♄	**3:07 pm**	12:07 pm
♅ ⚹ ⚶	**6:14 pm**	3:14 pm
♂ ⚻ ♃	**6:17 pm**	3:17 pm
☽ △ ♀	**10:42 pm**	7:42 pm
☽ ☌ ♃	**11:10 pm**	8:10 pm
☽ ⚻ ♂	**11:16 pm**	8:16 pm

28 WEDNESDAY

♀ △ ♃	**4:19 am**	1:19 am
☽ △ ⚷	**6:59 am**	3:59 am
♀ □ ♂	**7:10 am**	4:10 am
☽ ⚺ ♆	**12:54 pm**	9:54 am
☽ △ ⚵	**3:24 pm**	12:24 pm
☽ □ ♇	**8:19 pm**	5:19 pm
☽ ⚺ ♀		9:10 pm
☽ □ ☉		11:51 pm

29 THURSDAY

☽ ⚺ ♀	**12:10 am**	
☽ □ ☉	**2:51 am**	
☽ ⚺ ♅	**3:51 am**	12:51 am
☽ ⚺ ⚶	**4:52 am**	1:52 am
☽ ☌ ⚳	**5:45 am**	2:45 am
☽ ⚹ ☿	**1:51 pm**	10:51 am
☉ △ ♅	**5:16 pm**	2:16 pm
☽ ⚺ ♄	**6:24 pm**	3:24 pm
☽ ⚺ ♃		11:16 pm

30 FRIDAY

☽ ⚺ ♃	**2:16 am**	
☽ ☍ ♂	**3:22 am**	12:22 am
☽ □ ♀	**6:30 am**	3:30 am
☽ ⚻ ⚷	**9:48 am**	6:48 am
☽ ⚹ ♆	**3:51 pm**	12:51 pm
☽ □ ⚵	**8:30 pm**	5:30 pm
☽ △ ♇	**11:14 pm**	8:14 pm

31 SATURDAY

☽ ⚹ ♀	**3:03 am**	12:03 am
☉ ⚹ ⚶	**4:11 am**	1:11 am
☽ ⚹ ♅	**6:51 am**	3:51 am
☉ □ ⚳	**7:34 am**	4:34 am
☽ ☌ ⚶	**9:26 am**	6:26 am
☽ ⚺ ⚳	**9:32 am**	6:32 am
☽ ⚹ ☉	**9:39 am**	6:39 am
⚳ ⚺ ⚶	**4:41 pm**	1:41 pm
☿ ⚺ ♄	**4:47 pm**	1:47 pm
♀ △ ⚷	**7:30 pm**	4:30 pm
☽ ☌ ♄	**9:54 pm**	6:54 pm
☽ ⚺ ☿	**10:26 pm**	7:26 pm

Eastern Standard Time in bold type
Pacific Standard Time in medium type

MAY 1997

☽ Last Aspect day	EST / hr:mn / PST	asp	☽ Ingress sign day	EST / hr:mn / PST
4/30	**2:05 pm** 11:05 am	☌ ♃	♓ 1	**7:50 am** 4:50 am
3	**9:55 am** 6:55 am	⚹ ♆	♈ 3	**9:59 am** 6:59 am
5	**11:59 am** 8:59 am	□ ♆	♉ 5	**12:04 pm** 9:04 am
7	**3:15 pm** 12:15 pm	△ ♆	♊ 7	**3:21 pm** 12:21 pm
9	**8:22 pm** 5:22 pm	⚹ ☿	♋ 9	**9:13 pm** 6:13 pm
12	**6:25 am** 3:25 am	☍ ♆	♌ 12	**6:33 am** 3:33 am
14	**5:56 am** 2:56 am	□ ☉	♍ 14	**6:44 pm** 3:44 pm
17	**7:15 am** 4:15 am	△ ♆	♎ 17	**7:28 am** 4:28 am
19	**5:57 pm** 2:57 pm	□ ♆	♏ 19	**6:12 pm** 3:12 pm
21	10:35 pm	⚹ ♆	♐ 21	10:51 pm
22	**1:35 am**	⚹ ♆	♐ 22	**1:51 am**
23	**3:59 pm** 12:59 pm	⚹ ♃	♑ 24	**6:51 am** 3:51 am
26	**9:59 am** 6:59 am	☌ ♆	♒ 26	**10:20 am** 7:20 am
27	**11:10 pm** 8:10 pm	☌ ♃	♓ 28	**1:18 pm** 10:18 am
30	**3:51 pm** 12:51 pm	⚹ ♆	♈ 30	**4:18 pm** 1:18 pm

☽ Phases & Eclipses phase	day	EST / hr:mn / PST
New Moon	6	**3:47 pm** 12:47 pm
2nd Quarter	14	**5:56 am** 2:56 am
Full Moon	22	**4:14 am** 1:14 am
4th Quarter	28	11:51 pm
4th Quarter	29	**2:51 am**

Planet Ingress	day	EST / hr:mn / PST
☿ ♈	4	**8:48 pm** 5:48 pm
⯓ ♈	7	**11:12 am** 8:12 am
♀ ♊	10	**12:20 pm** 9:20 am
☿ ♉	12	**5:25 am** 2:25 am
☉ ♊	20	**7:18 pm** 4:18 pm
✱ ♋	26	**9:40 am** 6:40 am

Planetary Motion	day	EST / hr:mn / PST
♆ ℞	1	**1:29 pm** 10:29 am
☿ D	8	**1:02 pm** 10:02 am
♅ ℞	12	**7:16 pm** 4:16 pm
⚶ ℞	22	**2:02 pm** 11:02 am

DAY		SID.TIME	SUN	MOON	NODE	MERCURY	VENUS	MARS	JUPITER	SATURN	URANUS	NEPTUNE	PLUTO	CERES	PALLAS	JUNO	VESTA	CHIRON
T	1	14:35:51	10 ♉ 39 47	22 ♒ 23	27 ♍ 56	01 ♉ ℞ 43	18 ♉ 01	16 ♍ 48	19 ♒ 30	14 ♈ 03	08 ♒ 37	29 ♑ ℞ 58	04 ♐ ℞ 54	02 ♓ 45	05 ♈ 06	15 ♊ 39	27 ♓ 02	27 ♎ ℞ 59
F	2	14:39:47	11 38 01	06 ♓ 39	27 57	01 12	19 15	16 51	19 37	14 10	08 37	29 58	04 52	03 02	05 13	16 13	27 29	27 55
S	3	14:43:44	12 36 14	21 00	27 ℞ 58	00 44	20 29	16 54	19 44	14 17	08 38	29 58	04 51	03 19	05 20	16 47	27 56	27 50
S	4	14:47:40	13 34 25	05 ♈ 25	27 57	00 21	21 43	16 58	19 50	14 24	08 38	29 58	04 49	03 36	05 27	17 21	28 22	27 46
M	5	14:51:37	14 32 34	19 49	27 55	00 01	22 57	17 03	19 57	14 31	08 39	29 58	04 48	03 52	05 34	17 54	28 49	27 42
T	6	14:55:34	15 30 42	04 ♉ 07	27 51	29 ♈ 46	24 11	17 09	20 03	14 38	08 39	29 57	04 46	04 08	05 40	18 28	29 16	27 37
W	7	14:59:30	16 28 49	18 14	27 45	29 36	25 25	17 15	20 09	14 45	08 39	29 57	04 45	04 25	05 46	19 02	29 42	27 33
T	8	15:03:27	17 26 53	02 ♊ 06	27 38	29 D 30	26 39	17 22	20 15	14 52	08 40	29 57	04 43	04 41	05 52	19 36	00 ♈ 09	27 29
F	9	15:07:23	18 24 56	15 38	27 29	29 29	27 53	17 29	20 21	14 58	08 40	29 57	04 41	04 57	05 57	20 09	00 35	27 25
S	10	15:11:20	19 22 57	28 48	27 21	29 32	29 07	17 37	20 27	15 05	08 40	29 57	04 40	05 12	06 02	20 43	01 01	27 21
S	11	15:15:16	20 20 57	11 ♋ 37	27 14	29 40	00 ♊ 20	17 46	20 32	15 12	08 40	29 56	04 38	05 28	06 06	21 17	01 27	27 17
M	12	15:19:13	21 18 55	24 06	27 08	29 53	01 34	17 55	20 38	15 18	08 40	29 56	04 37	05 43	06 10	21 50	01 53	27 13
T	13	15:23:09	22 16 51	06 ♌ 18	27 05	00 ♉ 10	02 48	18 05	20 43	15 25	08 ℞ 40	29 56	04 35	05 59	06 14	22 24	02 19	27 09
W	14	15:27:06	23 14 45	18 17	27 D 04	00 32	04 02	18 16	20 48	15 31	08 40	29 55	04 34	06 14	06 18	22 58	02 45	27 05
T	15	15:31:03	24 12 38	00 ♍ 08	27 04	00 58	05 16	18 27	20 53	15 38	08 40	29 55	04 32	06 28	06 21	23 31	03 11	27 01
F	16	15:34:59	25 10 29	11 56	27 06	01 28	06 29	18 39	20 58	15 44	08 40	29 55	04 30	06 43	06	23 24	05 03	36 26
S	17	15:38:56	26 08 17	23 48	27 ℞ 07	02 02	07 43	18 51	21 02	15 51	08 40	29 54	04 29	06 58	06 26	24 38	04 02	26 54
S	18	15:42:52	27 06 04	05 ♎ 47	27 06	02 41	08 57	19 04	21 06	15 57	08 40	29 54	04 27	07 12	06 28	25 12	04 27	26 50
M	19	15:46:49	28 03 50	17 58	27 04	03 23	10 10	19 18	21 11	16 03	08 40	29 53	04 25	07 26	06 30	25 46	04 53	26 46
T	20	15:50:45	29 01 34	00 ♏ 25	26 58	04 08	11 24	19 31	21 15	16 09	08 39	29 52	04 24	07 40	06 31	26 19	05 18	26 43
W	21	15:54:42	29 59 17	13 10	26 51	04 57	12 38	19 46	21 18	16 15	08 39	29 52	04 22	07 54	06 32	26 53	05 43	26 40
T	22	15:58:38	00 ♊ 56 58	26 13	26 41	05 50	13 51	20 01	21 22	16 22	08 38	29 51	04 21	08 07	06 32	27 26	06 08	26 37
F	23	16:02:35	01 54 38	09 ♐ 34	26 30	06 46	15 05	20 16	21 26	16 28	08 38	29 51	04 19	08 20	06 32	27 59	06 33	26 33
S	24	16:06:32	02 52 17	23 12	26 19	07 45	16 18	20 32	21 29	16 34	08 37	29 50	04 17	08 34	06 32	28 33	06 58	26 30
S	25	16:10:28	03 49 55	07 ♑ 02	26 09	08 48	17 32	20 49	21 32	16 40	08 37	29 49	04 16	08 47	06 31	29 06	07 22	26 27
M	26	16:14:25	04 47 32	21 01	26 02	09 53	18 46	21 06	21 35	16 45	08 36	29 49	04 14	08 59	06 30	29 40	07 47	26 24
T	27	16:18:21	05 45 07	05 ♒ 05	25 56	11 02	19 59	21 23	21 38	16 51	08 36	29 48	04 12	09 12	06 29	00 ♋ 13	08 11	26 21
W	28	16:22:18	06 42 42	19 13	25 53	12 13	21 13	21 41	21 40	16 57	08 35	29 47	04 11	09 24	06 27	00 46	08 36	26 18
T	29	16:26:14	07 40 15	03 ♓ 22	25 52	13 27	22 26	21 59	21 43	17 03	08 34	29 46	04 09	09 36	06 25	01 20	09 00	26 16
F	30	16:30:11	08 37 48	17 29	25 D 52	14 44	23 40	22 18	21 45	17 08	08 33	29 45	04 07	09 48	06 22	01 53	09 24	26 13
S	31	16:34:07	09 35 20	01 ♈ 35	25 ℞ 52	16 04	24 53	22 37	21 47	17 14	08 33	29 44	04 06	09 59	06 19	02 26	09 48	26 11

EPHEMERIS CALCULATED FOR 12 MIDNIGHT GREENWICH MEAN TIME. ALL OTHER DATA AND FACING ASPECTARIAN PAGE IN **EASTERN STANDARD TIME (BOLD)** AND PACIFIC STANDARD TIME (REGULAR).

JUNE 1997

1 SUNDAY

	5:36 am	
	7:48 am	
	12:57 pm	
	2:41 pm	
	7:09 pm	
		9:37 pm
		10:49 pm

2 MONDAY

2:02 am · 2:34 am · 6:18 am · 10:21 am · 1:49 pm · 2:31 pm · 2:55 pm · 5:04 pm · 2:36 am · 4:48 am · 9:57 am · 11:41 am · 4:09 pm · 11:31 am · 11:55 am · 2:04 pm · 11:02 pm

3 TUESDAY

2:02 am · 8:23 am · 9:37 am · 1:07 pm · 4:55 pm · 7:19 pm · 8:56 pm · 5:23 am · 6:37 am · 10:07 am · 10:49 am · 1:57 pm · 4:39 pm · 8:20 pm · 8:59 pm · 11:20 pm · 11:59 pm

4 WEDNESDAY

6:55 am · 8:43 am · 10:33 am · 2:57 pm · 7:19 pm · 8:56 pm · 3:55 am · 5:43 am · 7:33 am · 11:57 am · 4:19 pm · 5:56 pm · 11:04 pm

5 THURSDAY

2:04 am · 7:36 am · 12:42 pm · 3:12 pm · 8:16 pm · 9:05 pm · 10:36 pm · 4:36 am · 9:42 am · 12:12 pm · 4:07 pm · 5:16 pm · 6:05 pm · 7:36 pm

6 FRIDAY

	11:46 pm	8:46 pm

5:22 am · 8:57 am · 11:45 am · 4:47 pm · 5:41 pm · 9:43 pm · 2:22 am · 5:57 am · 8:45 am · 1:47 pm · 2:41 pm · 6:43 pm

7 SATURDAY

3:06 am · 3:24 am · 5:48 am · 6:18 am · 3:42 pm · 2:55 pm · 11:20 pm · 11:22 pm · 12:06 am · 12:24 am · 2:48 pm · 11:02 am · 12:42 pm · 8:22 pm

8 SUNDAY

6:23 am · 6:59 am · 12:49 pm · 1:04 pm · 1:51 pm · 2:11 pm · 10:28 pm · 3:23 am · 3:59 am · 9:49 am · 10:04 am · 10:51 am · 11:11 am · 7:28 pm · 9:43 pm · 10:49 pm

9 MONDAY

	12:43 am	

1:49 am · 7:59 am · 3:22 pm · 3:57 pm · 5:54 pm · 10:51 am · 12:22 pm · 12:57 pm · 2:54 pm · 11:49 pm

10 TUESDAY

2:49 am · 10:28 am · 12:39 pm · 6:17 pm · 7:07 pm · 7:46 pm · 9:04 pm · 2:45 am · 7:28 am · 3:17 pm · 4:07 pm · 4:46 pm · 6:04 pm

---

11 WEDNESDAY

	12:37 am	

1:49 am · 10:22 am · 12:52 pm · 3:37 pm · 9:11 pm · 10:30 pm · 7:22 am · 9:52 am · 10:19 am · 12:37 pm · 6:11 pm · 7:30 pm

12 THURSDAY

3:11 am · 8:28 am · 3:50 pm · 4:22 pm · 11:52 pm · 12:11 am · 12:58 pm · 1:22 pm · 8:16 pm · 8:52 pm

13 FRIDAY

6:30 am · 7:03 am · 10:46 am · 2:35 pm · 11:03 pm · 3:30 am · 4:03 am · 7:46 am · 11:35 am · 8:03 pm

14 SATURDAY

	12:50 am	

1:24 am · 9:11 am · 12:44 pm · 1:14 pm · 4:24 pm · 5:58 pm · 10:45 pm · 5:11 am · 6:11 am · 10:14 am · 1:24 pm · 2:58 pm · 7:45 pm

15 SUNDAY

4:32 am · 9:24 am · 11:08 am · 4:49 pm · 6:37 pm · 1:32 am · 6:24 am · 8:08 am · 1:49 pm · 3:37 pm · 9:17 pm · 10:47 pm

---

16 MONDAY

	12:17 am	

9:49 am · 11:27 am · 3:41 pm · 6:29 pm · 6:49 am · 8:27 am · 12:41 pm · 3:29 pm · 10:29 pm · 11:54 pm

17 TUESDAY

1:29 am · 2:54 am · 4:42 am · 8:10 am · 9:51 am · 9:58 am · 10:15 am · 11:36 am · 6:33 pm · 7:50 pm · 1:42 pm · 5:10 pm · 6:51 pm · 6:58 pm · 7:15 pm · 8:36 pm · 3:33 pm · 4:50 pm · 11:53 pm

18 WEDNESDAY

2:53 am · 5:39 am · 9:34 am · 10:05 am · 10:35 am · 5:04 pm · 6:00 pm · 7:17 pm · 2:39 am · 6:34 am · 7:05 am · 7:35 am · 2:04 pm · 3:04 pm · 4:10 pm

19 THURSDAY

1:10 am · 9:12 am · 9:35 am · 10:04 am · 5:12 pm · 7:54 pm · 8:45 pm · 8:53 pm · 6:12 am · 6:35 am · 7:04 am · 2:12 pm · 4:54 pm · 5:45 pm · 10:43 pm

20 FRIDAY

	12:57 am	

1:43 am · 7:40 am · 4:37 pm · 4:40 pm

---

21 SATURDAY

	10:57 am	7:57 am
	1:56 pm	10:56 am
		11:09 am
	4:11 pm	1:11 pm
	9:02 pm	6:02 pm
	9:21 pm	6:21 pm

4:44 am · 1:14 am · 6:11 am · 3:11 am · 11:01 am · 8:01 am · 11:45 am · 8:45 am · 1:44 am · 12:21 am

22 SUNDAY

3:32 am · 12:32 am · 4:26 am · 1:26 am · 10:10 am · 7:10 am · 1:22 pm · 10:22 am · 4:11 pm · 1:11 pm · 8:02 pm · 5:02 pm · 8:49 pm · 5:49 pm · 10:51 pm · 7:51 pm · 11:07 pm · 8:07 pm

23 MONDAY

6:39 am · 3:39 am · 7:49 am · 4:49 am · 2:37 pm · 11:37 am · 3:27 pm · 12:27 pm · 7:10 pm · 4:10 pm · 9:30 pm · 10:04 pm

24 TUESDAY

	12:30 am	

1:04 am · 2:12 am · 5:12 am · 2:12 pm · 7:44 am · 4:44 am · 11:57 am · 8:57 am · 5:54 pm · 2:54 pm · 5:55 pm · 2:55 pm · 11:26 pm · 8:26 pm · 11:59 pm · 8:59 pm

---

25 WEDNESDAY

	12:05 am	
	12:23 am	
	1:23 am	

5:16 am · 2:16 am · 6:21 am · 3:21 am · 9:43 am · 6:43 am · 2:14 pm · 11:14 am · 5:44 pm · 2:44 pm · 11:12 pm · 8:12 pm

26 THURSDAY

3:26 am · 12:26 am · 3:51 am · 12:51 am · 7:15 am · 4:15 am · 2:19 pm · 11:19 am · 4:09 pm · 1:09 pm · 5:53 pm · 2:53 pm · 8:17 pm · 5:17 pm · 10:49 pm

27 FRIDAY

1:49 am · 3:50 am · 12:50 am · 7:43 am · 4:43 am · 11:08 am · 8:08 am · 12:01 pm · 9:01 am · 9:00 pm · 6:00 pm · 9:21 pm · 6:21 pm

28 SATURDAY

	12:25 am	

4:25 am · 1:25 am · 6:55 am · 3:55 am · 8:22 am · 5:22 am · 10:25 am · 7:25 am · 5:54 pm · 2:54 pm · 11:54 pm · 8:54 pm · 11:32 pm

29 SUNDAY

	2:32 am	

4:50 am · 1:50 am · 7:15 am · 4:15 am

---

30 MONDAY

8:25 am	5:25 am
9:37 am	6:37 am
3:07 pm	12:07 pm
3:38 pm	12:38 pm
11:39 pm	8:39 pm
	9:35 pm
	10:36 pm
	10:57 pm

12:35 am · 1:36 am · 1:57 am · 11:11 am · 8:11 am · 11:48 am · 8:48 am · 11:11 am · 2:22 pm · 11:22 am · 2:56 pm · 11:56 am · 10:56 pm · 7:56 pm

JUNE 1997

☽ Last Aspect day	EST / hr:mn	PST	asp	☽ Ingress sign	day	EST / hr:mn	PST
1	**7:09 pm**	4:09 pm	□♆	♉	1	**7:39 pm**	4:39 pm
3	**11:20 pm**	8:20 pm	△♆	♊	3	**11:55 pm**	8:55 pm
5	**8:16 pm**	5:16 pm	□♂	♋	6	**6:03 am**	3:03 am
8	**2:25 pm**	11:25 am	✶☿	♌	8	**2:59 pm**	11:59 am
10		7:28 am	☍♃	♍	10		11:44 pm
10	**10:28 am**		☍♃	♍	11	**2:44 am**	
13	**2:35 pm**	11:35 am	△♆	♎	13	**3:36 pm**	12:36 pm
15		10:47 pm	□♆	♏	15		11:51 pm
16	**1:47 am**		□♆	♏	16	**2:51 am**	
18	**10:05 am**	7:05 am	✶♂	♐	18	**10:39 am**	7:39 am
20	**2:09 pm**	11:09 am	☍☉	♑	20	**3:02 pm**	12:02 pm
22	**4:11 pm**	1:11 pm	☌♆	♒	22	**5:21 pm**	2:21 pm
24	**5:12 am**	2:12 am	☌♃	♓	24	**7:09 pm**	4:09 pm
26	**8:17 pm**	5:17 pm	✶♆	♈	26	**9:39 pm**	6:39 pm
28		8:54 pm	□♆	♉	28		10:24 pm
28	**11:54 pm**		□♆	♉	29	**1:24 am**	

☽ Phases & Eclipses phase	day	EST / hr:mn	PST
New Moon	4		11:04 pm
New Moon	5	**2:04 am**	
2nd Quarter	12	**11:52 pm**	8:52 pm
Full Moon	20	**2:09 pm**	11:09 am
4th Quarter	27	**7:43 am**	4:43 am

Planet Ingress	day	EST / hr:mn	PST
♀ ♋	3	**11:18 pm**	8:18 pm
☿ ♊	8	**6:25 pm**	3:25 pm
♂ ♎	19	**3:30 am**	12:30 am
☉ ♋	21	**3:20 am**	12:20 am
☿ ♋	23	**3:40 pm**	12:40 pm
♀ ♌	28	**1:38 pm**	10:38 am

Planetary Motion	day	EST / hr:mn	PST
♃ ℞	9	**6:28 pm**	3:28 pm
⚷ D	23	**9:26 am**	6:26 am

DAY		SID.TIME	SUN	MOON	NODE	MERCURY	VENUS	MARS	JUPITER	SATURN	URANUS	NEPTUNE	PLUTO	CERES	PALLAS	JUNO	VESTA	CHIRON
S	1	16:38:04	10 ♊ 32 51	15 ♈ 38	25 ♍ ℞ 51	17 ♉ 27	26 ♊ 07	22 ♍ 56	21 ♒ 49	17 ♈ 19	08 ♒ ℞ 32	29 ♑ ℞ 44	04 ♐ ℞ 04	10 ♓ 11	06 ♒ ℞ 16	02 ♋ 59	10 ♈ 12	26 ♎ ℞ 08
M	2	16:42:01	11 30 21	29 37	25 47	18 52	27 20	23 16	21 50	17 25	08 31	29 43	04 02	10 22	06 12	03 32	10 36	26 06
T	3	16:45:57	12 27 51	13 ♉ 30	25 41	20 20	28 33	23 36	21 52	17 30	08 30	29 42	04 01	10 33	06 08	04 06	10 59	26 04
W	4	16:49:54	13 25 20	27 13	25 33	21 50	29 47	23 57	21 53	17 36	08 29	29 41	03 59	10 44	06 03	04 39	11 23	26 01
T	5	16:53:50	14 22 48	10 ♊ 44	25 22	23 24	01 ♋ 00	24 18	21 54	17 41	08 28	29 40	03 58	10 54	05 58	05 12	11 46	25 59
F	6	16:57:47	15 20 15	23 59	25 09	25 00	02 14	24 40	21 55	17 46	08 27	29 39	03 56	11 04	05 53	05 45	12 09	25 58
S	7	17:01:43	16 17 41	06 ♋ 58	24 57	26 38	03 27	25 02	21 56	17 51	08 26	29 38	03 54	11 14	05 47	06 18	12 33	25 56
S	8	17:05:40	17 15 06	19 39	24 46	28 19	04 40	25 24	21 56	17 56	08 24	29 37	03 53	11 24	05 41	06 51	12 56	25 54
M	9	17:09:36	18 12 30	02 ♌ 04	24 36	00 ♊ 03	05 54	25 47	21 ℞ 56	18 01	08 23	29 36	03 51	11 33	05 34	07 24	13 18	25 52
T	10	17:13:33	19 09 53	14 13	24 30	01 49	07 07	26 09	21 56	18 06	08 22	29 34	03 50	11 42	05 27	07 57	13 41	25 51
W	11	17:17:30	20 07 15	26 11	24 26	03 37	08 20	26 33	21 56	18 11	08 21	29 33	03 48	11 51	05 19	08 30	14 04	25 49
T	12	17:21:26	21 04 36	08 ♍ 01	24 25	05 28	09 34	26 56	21 56	18 16	08 19	29 32	03 47	12 00	05 12	09 03	14 26	25 48
F	13	17:25:23	22 01 56	19 50	24 25	07 22	10 47	27 20	21 56	18 20	08 18	29 31	03 45	12 08	05 03	09 36	14 48	25 47
S	14	17:29:19	22 59 16	01 ♎ 41	24 25	09 18	12 00	27 45	21 55	18 25	08 16	29 30	03 43	12 16	04 55	10 08	15 10	25 46
S	15	17:33:16	23 56 34	13 42	24 25	11 16	13 13	28 09	21 54	18 29	08 15	29 28	03 42	12 24	04 46	10 41	15 32	25 45
M	16	17:37:12	24 53 51	25 56	24 22	13 17	14 27	28 34	21 53	18 34	08 14	29 27	03 40	12 31	04 36	11 14	15 54	25 44
T	17	17:41:09	25 51 08	08 ♏ 29	24 17	15 19	15 40	28 59	21 52	18 38	08 12	29 26	03 39	12 38	04 27	11 46	16 15	25 43
W	18	17:45:05	26 48 24	21 23	24 09	17 24	16 53	29 25	21 50	18 43	08 10	29 25	03 37	12 45	04 17	12 19	16 37	25 42
T	19	17:49:02	27 45 39	04 ♐ 40	23 58	19 30	18 06	29 51	21 49	18 47	08 09	29 23	03 36	12 52	04 06	12 52	16 58	25 42
F	20	17:52:59	28 42 54	18 20	23 46	21 37	19 19	00 ♎ 17	21 47	18 51	08 07	29 22	03 34	12 58	03 55	13 24	17 19	25 41
S	21	17:56:55	29 40 08	02 ♑ 20	23 34	23 46	20 32	00 43	21 45	18 55	08 05	29 21	03 33	13 04	03 44	13 57	17 40	25 41
S	22	18:00:52	00 ♋ 37 21	16 35	23 23	25 56	21 45	01 10	21 43	18 59	08 04	29 19	03 32	13 10	03 33	14 29	18 01	25 41
M	23	18:04:48	01 34 35	01 ♒ 00	23 14	28 07	22 58	01 37	21 40	19 03	08 02	29 18	03 30	13 16	03 21	15 02	18 22	25 41
T	24	18:08:45	02 31 48	15 28	23 08	00 ♋ 18	24 11	02 04	21 38	19 07	08 00	29 17	03 29	13 21	03 09	15 34	18 42	25 D 41
W	25	18:12:41	03 29 01	29 55	23 04	02 30	25 24	02 32	21 35	19 10	07 58	29 15	03 27	13 25	02 56	16 07	19 03	25 41
T	26	18:16:38	04 26 14	14 ♓ 15	23 D 03	04 41	26 37	02 59	21 32	19 14	07 57	29 14	03 26	13 30	02 43	16 39	19 23	25 41
F	27	18:20:34	05 23 27	28 27	23 ℞ 02	06 52	27 50	03 27	21 29	19 18	07 55	29 12	03 25	13 34	02 30	17 11	19 43	25 41
S	28	18:24:31	06 20 40	12 ♈ 28	23 02	09 02	29 03	03 55	21 26	19 21	07 53	29 11	03 23	13 38	02 17	17 43	20 02	25 42
S	29	18:28:28	07 17 53	26 20	23 02	11 12	00 ♌ 16	04 24	21 22	19 24	07 51	29 09	03 22	13 41	02 03	18 16	20 22	25 42
M	30	18:32:24	08 15 06	10 ♉ 01	22 59	13 20	01 29	04 53	21 19	19 28	07 49	29 08	03 21	13 45	01 ℞ 50	18 48	20 41	25 43

EPHEMERIS CALCULATED FOR 12 MIDNIGHT GREENWICH MEAN TIME. ALL OTHER DATA AND FACING ASPECTARIAN PAGE IN **EASTERN STANDARD TIME (BOLD)** AND PACIFIC STANDARD TIME (REGULAR).

JULY 1997

10:57 pm

1 TUESDAY

2 WEDNESDAY

3 THURSDAY

4 FRIDAY

5 SATURDAY

6 SUNDAY

7 MONDAY

8 TUESDAY

9 WEDNESDAY

10 THURSDAY

11 FRIDAY

12 SATURDAY

13 SUNDAY

14 MONDAY

15 TUESDAY

16 WEDNESDAY

17 THURSDAY

18 FRIDAY

19 SATURDAY

20 SUNDAY

21 MONDAY

22 TUESDAY

23 WEDNESDAY

24 THURSDAY

25 FRIDAY

26 SATURDAY

27 SUNDAY

28 MONDAY

29 TUESDAY

30 WEDNESDAY

31 THURSDAY

Eastern Standard Time in bold type
Pacific Standard Time in medium type

JULY 1997

D Last Aspect

day	EST / hr:mn / PST	asp
2	4:58 am 1:58 am	△♥
5	9:03 pm 6:03 pm	△♀
8	8:45 am 5:45 am	♂♄
10	3:44 pm 12:44 pm	△♂
12	8:59 pm 5:59 pm	□♀
15	8:57 am 5:57 am	△♂
17	12:46 am	
19	9:12 pm	

D Ingress

sign	day	EST / hr:mn / PST
△	2	6:36 am 3:36 am
♏	3	1:33 pm 10:33 am
✕	5	10:45 pm 7:45 pm
✕	8	10:22 am 7:22 am
♒	10	10:11 pm 7:11 pm
⏀	13	11:20 am 8:20 am
♈	15	11:03 pm 8:03 pm
♉	17	9:46 pm
♊	19	11:29 pm

D Last Aspect

day	EST / hr:mn / PST	asp
20	12:12 am	△♥
22	9:25 pm	♂♀
22	12:25 pm	♂♀
24	1:33 am	△♀
26	5:35 am 2:35 am	△♥
28	9:08 am 6:08 am	△♂
30	11:47 am 8:47 am	△♂

D Ingress

sign	day	EST / hr:mn / PST
⋍	20	4:29 am
✕	22	3:00 am 12:00 am
✕	24	4:04 am 1:04 am
♉	26	6:54 am 3:54 am
♊	28	12:04 pm 9:04 am
⏀	30	7:38 pm 4:38 pm

D Phases & Eclipses

phase	day	EST / hr:mn / PST
New Moon	4	1:40 pm 10:40 am
2nd Quarter	12	4:44 pm 1:44 pm
Full Moon	19	10:21 pm 7:21 pm
4th Quarter	26	1:29 pm 10:29 am

Planet Ingress

	day	EST / hr:mn / PST
♀ ≈	7	3:42 pm 12:42 pm
♂ ♍	7	9:28 pm
♀ ♍	8	12:28 am
⚷ ♍	20	9:19 pm
⊙ ♌	22	11:15 am 1:15 am
⊙ ♌	22	2:15 pm 8:16 am
♀ ♍	23	8:16 am 5:16 am
♂ ♍	26	7:42 pm 4:42 pm

Planetary Motion

	day	EST / hr:mn / PST
♃ R	8	1:56 pm 10:56 am

EPHEMERIS CALCULATED FOR 12 MIDNIGHT GREENWICH MEAN TIME. ALL OTHER DATA AND FACING ASPECTARIAN PAGE IN **EASTERN STANDARD TIME (BOLD)** AND PACIFIC STANDARD TIME (REGULAR).

AUGUST 1997

Eastern Standard Time in bold type
Pacific Standard Time in medium type

---

1 FRIDAY
6:09 am · 3:09 am
10:32 am · 7:32 am
10:38 am · 7:38 am
2:45 pm · 1:49 pm
4:14 pm · 6:18 pm
11:44 pm · 8:44 pm
· 11:00 pm

2 SATURDAY
2:00 am
3:55 am · 12:55 am
10:48 am · 7:48 am
11:04 am · 8:04 am
5:23 pm · 2:23 pm
6:18 pm · 3:18 pm
6:21 pm · 3:21 pm
9:21 pm · 6:21 pm

3 SUNDAY
3:14 am · 12:14 am
5:14 am · 2:14 am
7:30 am · 4:30 am
4:35 pm · 1:35 pm
9:50 pm · 6:50 pm
· 10:16 pm
· 11:28 pm

4 MONDAY
1:58 am
6:22 am · 3:22 am
8:39 am · 5:39 am
10:16 am · 7:16 am
1:58 pm · 10:58 am
2:58 pm · 11:58 am
7:40 pm · 4:40 pm
9:00 pm

5 TUESDAY
12:27 am
3:02 am · 12:02 am
9:55 am · 6:55 am
5:34 am · 2:34 am
4:56 am · 1:56 am
9:50 am · 6:50 am
11:00 pm · 8:00 pm
· 10:23 pm

6 WEDNESDAY
2:50 am

---

7 THURSDAY
4:37 am · 1:37 am
10:35 am · 7:35 am
2:09 pm · 11:09 am
4:49 pm · 1:49 pm
9:18 pm · 6:18 pm
· 11:26 pm

8 FRIDAY
1:03 am
5:26 am · 2:26 am
12:03 pm · 9:03 am
7:10 pm · 4:10 pm
· 10:03 pm

9 SATURDAY
1:58 am
6:24 am · 3:24 am
8:09 am · 5:09 am
4:58 pm · 1:58 pm
7:42 pm · 4:42 pm
11:28 pm · 8:28 pm
· 10:58 pm

10 SUNDAY
1:50 am
6:22 am · 3:22 am
2:10 pm · 11:10 am
7:16 pm · 4:16 pm
· 11:58 am
9:27 pm

11 MONDAY
1:23 am

---

12 TUESDAY
2:44 am · 12:39 am
7:43 am · 4:43 am
10:23 am · 7:23 am
11:53 am · 8:53 am
3:54 pm · 12:54 pm
· 9:59 pm
· 9:44 pm
· 11:25 pm

13 WEDNESDAY
2:24 am
5:49 am · 2:49 am
7:15 am · 4:15 am
9:03 am · 6:03 am
10:53 am · 7:53 am
6:18 pm · 3:18 pm
7:26 pm · 4:26 pm

14 THURSDAY
4:02 am · 1:02 am
7:08 am · 4:08 am
9:02 am · 6:02 am
11:20 am · 8:20 am
2:24 pm · 11:24 am
3:36 pm · 12:36 pm
9:08 pm · 6:08 pm

15 FRIDAY
3:45 am · 12:45 am
8:41 am · 5:41 am
1:50 pm · 10:59 am
2:14 pm · 11:14 am
3:13 pm · 12:13 pm
8:52 pm · 5:52 pm
8:58 pm · 5:58 pm
11:09 pm · 8:09 pm
· 11:11 pm
· 11:17 pm

---

16 SATURDAY
3:39 am · 12:39 am
7:43 am · 4:43 am
10:23 am · 7:23 am
11:53 am · 8:53 am
3:54 pm · 12:54 pm
· 4:46 am
7:46 am
11:06 am · 8:11 am
11:54 am
2:54 pm · 2:35 pm
5:35 pm · 2:35 pm
7:41 pm

17 SUNDAY
4:25 am · 1:25 am
11:27 am · 8:27 am
2:39 pm · 11:39 am
3:08 pm · 12:08 pm
9:00 pm · 6:00 pm
9:21 pm

18 MONDAY
5:56 am · 2:56 am
9:36 am · 6:36 am
10:31 am · 7:31 am
12:27 pm · 9:27 am
3:22 pm · 12:22 pm
5:40 pm · 2:31 pm
· 2:31 pm
10:23 pm · 7:23 pm

19 TUESDAY
3:31 am · 12:31 am
12:43 pm · 9:43 am
1:54 pm · 10:54 am
2:28 pm · 11:28 am
6:54 pm · 3:54 pm
8:06 pm · 5:06 pm
8:53 pm · 5:53 pm

20 WEDNESDAY
8:52 am · 5:52 am
10:13 am · 7:13 am
10:31 am · 7:31 am
2:13 pm · 11:13 am
3:08 pm · 12:08 pm
5:20 pm · 2:20 pm
5:57 pm · 2:57 pm
7:16 pm · 4:16 pm
7:24 pm · 4:24 pm

---

21 THURSDAY
10:09 am · 7:09 am
10:56 am · 7:56 am
· 9:58 pm
· 11:51 pm

22 FRIDAY
2:59 am
4:09 am · 1:09 am
6:07 am · 3:07 am
8:44 am · 5:44 am
11:46 am · 8:46 am
2:51 am
1:16 am
1:47 am · 10:47 am
1:53 pm · 10:53 am
2:39 pm · 11:39 am
4:03 pm · 11:39 pm
8:13 pm · 5:11 pm
9:19 pm · 6:19 pm

23 SATURDAY
6:34 am · 3:34 am
10:11 am · 7:11 am
11:57 am · 8:57 am
1:26 pm · 10:26 am
4:39 pm · 1:39 pm
6:46 pm · 3:46 pm
7:15 pm · 8:15 pm
11:42 pm · 8:42 pm
· 10:19 pm

24 SUNDAY
1:19 am
3:59 am · 12:59 am
8:53 am · 5:53 am
2:44 pm · 11:44 am
3:52 pm · 12:52 pm
7:04 pm · 4:04 pm
10:35 pm · 7:35 pm
· 9:08 pm

25 MONDAY
1:41 am
4:41 am · 1:41 am
1:50 pm · 10:50 am
3:02 pm · 12:02 pm
4:11 pm · 1:11 pm
8:57 pm · 5:57 pm
9:24 pm · 6:24 pm
11:04 pm · 8:04 pm

---

26 TUESDAY
5:43 am · 2:43 am
8:47 am · 5:47 am
8:59 am · 5:59 am
· 11:59 pm

27 WEDNESDAY
2:59 am
4:09 am · 1:09 am
6:07 am · 3:07 am
8:44 am · 5:44 am
11:46 am · 8:46 am
4:28 am · 1:28 am
4:34 am · 1:34 am
6:39 am · 3:39 am
9:08 am · 6:08 am
9:26 am · 6:26 am
3:05 pm · 12:05 pm
5:26 pm · 2:26 pm
10:50 pm · 7:50 pm
· 10:19 pm

28 THURSDAY
1:19 am
5:14 am · 2:14 am
12:49 pm · 9:49 am
2:24 pm · 11:24 am
3:09 pm · 12:09 pm
3:48 pm · 12:48 pm

29 FRIDAY
6:35 am · 3:35 am
8:05 am · 5:05 am
10:21 am · 7:21 am
2:47 pm · 11:47 am
3:16 pm · 12:16 pm
3:58 pm · 12:58 pm
5:03 pm · 2:03 pm
10:12 pm · 7:12 pm
10:16 pm · 7:16 pm
· 9:44 pm
· 10:01 pm

30 SATURDAY
12:34 am
1:01 am
6:27 am · 3:27 am
7:34 am · 4:34 am
3:56 pm · 12:56 pm

---

31 SUNDAY
2:30 am
4:27 am · 1:27 am
8:42 am · 5:42 am
6:30 pm · 3:30 pm
8:01 pm · 5:01 pm
· 11:57 pm
6:53 am · 3:53 am
11:52 am · 8:52 am
· 11:30 pm

AUGUST 1997

☽ Last Aspect day	EST / hr:mn / PST	asp	☽ Ingress sign day	EST / hr:mn / PST
1	11:00 pm	☍ ♆	♌ 2	2:27 am
2	**2:00 am**	☍ ♆	♌ 2	**5:27 am**
4	**5:10 am** 2:10 am	✶ ♂	♍ 4	**5:15 pm** 2:15 pm
6	11:26 pm	△ ♆	♎ 7	3:17 am
7	**2:26 am**	△ ♆	♎ 7	**6:17 am**
9	**2:58 pm** 11:58 am	□ ♆	♏ 9	**6:50 pm** 3:50 pm
11	9:59 pm	✶ ♆	♐ 12	1:46 am
12	**12:59 am**	✶ ♆	♐ 12	**4:46 am**
14	**4:02 am** 1:02 am	□ ♀	♑ 14	**10:43 am** 7:43 am
16	**11:11 am** 8:11 am	△ ♀	♒ 16	**12:59 pm** 9:59 am
18	**5:56 am** 2:56 am	☍ ☉	♓ 18	**1:02 pm** 10:02 am
20	**9:13 am** 6:13 am	✶ ♆	♈ 20	**12:45 pm** 9:45 am
22	**1:26 pm** 10:26 am	△ ☉	♉ 22	**1:57 pm** 10:57 am
24	**1:50 pm** 10:50 am	△ ♆	♊ 24	**5:56 pm** 2:56 pm
26	3:07 am	✶ ♄	♋ 26	10:10 pm
26	**6:07 am**	✶ ♄	♋ 27	**1:10 am**
29	**6:35 am** 3:35 am	☍ ♆	♌ 29	**11:19 am** 8:19 am
30	11:30 pm	△ ♄	♍ 31	8:27 pm
31	**2:30 am**	△ ♄	♍ 31	**11:27 pm**

☽ Phases & Eclipses phase	day	EST / hr:mn / PST
New Moon	3	**3:14 am** 12:14 am
2nd Quarter	11	**7:43 am** 3:43 am
Full Moon	18	**5:56 am** 2:56 am
4th Quarter	24	**9:24 pm** 6:24 pm

Planet Ingress	day	EST / hr:mn / PST
⚶ ♉	6	**9:28 pm** 6:28 pm
♂ ♏	14	**3:42 am** 12:42 am
♀ ♎	17	**9:31 am** 6:31 am
☉ ♍	22	**9:19 pm** 6:19 pm

Planetary Motion	day	EST / hr:mn / PST
♄ ℞	1	**10:01 am** 7:01 am
♇ D	12	10:34 pm
♇ D	13	**1:34 am**
☿ ℞	17	**2:43 pm** 11:43 am
⚶ ℞	29	**5:18 am** 2:18 am

DAY		SID.TIME	SUN	MOON	NODE	MERCURY	VENUS	MARS	JUPITER	SATURN	URANUS	NEPTUNE	PLUTO	CERES	PALLAS	JUNO	VESTA	CHIRON
F	1	20:38:34	08 ♌ 47 24	12 ♋ 16	20 ♍℞ 27	05 ♍ 53	10 ♍ 10	22 ♎ 00	18 ♒℞ 06	20 ♈℞ 22	06 ♒℞ 36	28 ♑℞ 17	02 ♐℞ 53	12 ♓ 23	23 ♑ 27	05 ♌ 33	28 ♈ 58	27 ♎ 00
S	2	20:42:30	09 44 50	24 40	20 19	06 57	11 22	22 35	17 59	20 22	06 34	28 15	02 53	12 ℞ 15	23 ℞ 13	06 03	29 09	27 04
S	3	20:46:27	10 42 16	06 ♌ 53	20 13	07 58	12 34	23 10	17 51	20 22	06 32	28 14	02 52	12 06	22 58	06 34	29 20	27 08
M	4	20:50:24	11 39 44	18 56	20 07	08 57	13 45	23 46	17 43	20 21	06 29	28 12	02 52	11 57	22 44	07 04	29 30	27 13
T	5	20:54:20	12 37 12	00 ♍ 52	20 03	09 52	14 57	24 21	17 36	20 21	06 27	28 11	02 52	11 48	22 30	07 35	29 40	27 17
W	6	20:58:17	13 34 41	12 42	20 D 01	10 45	16 09	24 57	17 28	20 21	06 25	28 09	02 52	11 38	22 16	08 05	29 50	27 21
T	7	21:02:13	14 32 11	24 28	20 01	11 34	17 21	25 32	17 20	20 20	06 22	28 08	02 51	11 29	22 03	08 36	29 59	27 26
F	8	21:06:10	15 29 42	06 ♎ 15	20 03	12 20	18 33	26 08	17 12	20 20	06 20	28 06	02 51	11 19	21 50	09 06	00 ♉ 08	27 31
S	9	21:10:06	16 27 13	18 06	20 05	13 02	19 45	26 44	17 04	20 19	06 17	28 05	02 51	11 08	21 37	09 36	00 17	27 35
S	10	21:14:03	17 24 46	00 ♏ 05	20 07	13 41	20 56	27 21	16 57	20 18	06 15	28 03	02 51	10 58	21 24	10 06	00 25	27 40
M	11	21:17:59	18 22 20	12 18	20 ℞ 08	14 16	22 08	27 57	16 49	20 17	06 13	28 02	02 51	10 47	21 12	10 36	00 33	27 45
T	12	21:21:56	19 19 54	24 48	20 08	14 47	23 20	28 33	16 41	20 16	06 10	28 00	02 51	10 36	21 00	11 06	00 40	27 50
W	13	21:25:53	20 17 29	07 ♐ 42	20 06	15 13	24 31	29 10	16 33	20 15	06 08	27 59	02 51	10 25	20 49	11 36	00 47	27 55
T	14	21:29:49	21 15 05	21 01	20 04	15 35	25 43	29 47	16 25	20 14	06 06	27 57	02 D 51	10 13	20 37	12 06	00 54	28 00
F	15	21:33:46	22 12 42	04 ♑ 49	20 00	15 53	26 54	00 ♏ 23	16 18	20 13	06 04	27 56	02 51	10 02	20 26	12 36	01 00	28 05
S	16	21:37:42	23 10 21	19 04	19 56	16 05	28 06	01 00	16 10	20 11	06 01	27 54	02 51	09 50	20 16	13 06	01 06	28 11
S	17	21:41:39	24 08 00	03 ♒ 42	19 53	16 12	29 17	01 38	16 02	20 10	05 59	27 53	02 51	09 38	20 06	13 35	01 11	28 16
M	18	21:45:35	25 05 41	18 39	19 50	16 ℞ 14	00 ♎ 28	02 15	15 55	20 08	05 57	27 51	02 51	09 25	19 56	14 05	01 17	28 22
T	19	21:49:32	26 03 23	03 ♓ 46	19 48	16 10	01 39	02 52	15 47	20 06	05 55	27 50	02 51	09 13	19 46	14 34	01 21	28 27
W	20	21:53:28	27 01 06	18 54	19 D 47	16 01	02 51	03 30	15 39	20 04	05 52	27 49	02 51	09 00	19 37	15 04	01 26	28 33
T	21	21:57:25	27 58 51	03 ♈ 53	19 48	15 45	04 02	04 07	15 32	20 03	05 50	27 47	02 52	08 48	19 28	15 33	01 29	28 38
F	22	22:01:22	28 56 37	18 36	19 48	15 25	05 13	04 45	15 24	20 01	05 48	27 46	02 52	08 35	19 20	16 03	01 33	28 44
S	23	22:05:18	29 54 25	02 ♉ 59	19 50	14 58	06 24	05 23	15 17	19 59	05 46	27 45	02 52	08 22	19 12	16 32	01 36	28 50
S	24	22:09:15	00 ♍ 52 15	16 59	19 ℞ 51	14 26	07 35	06 01	15 10	19 56	05 44	27 43	02 53	08 09	19 04	17 01	01 39	28 56
M	25	22:13:11	01 50 06	00 ♊ 36	19 51	13 48	08 46	06 39	15 03	19 54	05 42	27 42	02 53	07 56	18 57	17 31	01 41	29 02
T	26	22:17:08	02 47 59	13 50	19 51	13 06	09 57	07 17	14 55	19 52	05 40	27 41	02 53	07 43	18 50	18 00	01 43	29 08
W	27	22:21:04	03 45 54	26 44	19 50	12 19	11 08	07 56	14 48	19 49	05 38	27 40	02 54	07 29	18 43	18 29	01 44	29 14
T	28	22:25:01	04 43 50	09 ♋ 20	19 48	11 28	12 19	08 34	14 42	19 47	05 36	27 38	02 54	07 16	18 37	18 58	01 45	29 20
F	29	22:28:57	05 41 49	21 43	19 47	10 35	13 29	09 13	14 35	19 44	05 34	27 37	02 55	07 03	18 31	19 27	01 45	29 27
S	30	22:32:54	06 39 49	03 ♌ 53	19 45	09 39	14 40	09 51	14 28	19 41	05 32	27 36	02 55	06 49	18 26	19 56	01 ℞ 45	29 33
S	31	22:36:51	07 37 51	15 54	19 43	08 43	15 51	10 30	14 21	19 39	05 30	27 35	02 56	06 36	18 21	20 25	01 45	29 39

EPHEMERIS CALCULATED FOR 12 MIDNIGHT GREENWICH MEAN TIME. ALL OTHER DATA AND FACING ASPECTARIAN PAGE IN **EASTERN STANDARD TIME (BOLD)** AND PACIFIC STANDARD TIME (REGULAR).

SEPTEMBER 1997

Eastern Standard Time in **bold type**
Pacific Standard Time in medium type

1 MONDAY

		am
	2:57	am
	5:23	am 2:23 am
	10:30	am 7:30 am
	12:04	pm 9:04 am
	1:48	pm 10:48 am
	6:52	pm 3:52 pm
	6:57	pm 3:57 pm
	11:41	pm 8:41 pm

2 TUESDAY

	4:06	am 1:06 am
	12:21	pm 9:21 am
	2:23	pm 11:23 am
	3:07	pm 12:07 pm
	7:55	pm 4:55 pm
	10:52	pm 7:52 pm
	11:26	pm 8:26 pm
	10:05	pm 7:05 pm

3 WEDNESDAY

	7:26	am 4:26 am
	1:43	pm 10:43 am
	3:51	pm 12:51 pm
	6:31	pm 3:31 pm
	10:52	pm 7:52 pm
	11:26	pm 8:26 pm

4 THURSDAY

	12:02	pm
	1:24	pm 10:24 am
	4:20	pm 1:20 pm
	4:38	pm 1:38 pm
	9:05	pm 6:05 pm
		10:03 pm

5 FRIDAY

	1:03	am
	3:48	am 12:48 am
	10:01	am 7:01 am
	11:21	am 8:21 am
	1:57	pm 10:57 am
	8:06	pm 5:06 pm
		10:33 pm
		10:53 pm

6 SATURDAY

	1:33	am
	1:53	am
	4:12	am 1:12 am
	7:08	am 4:08 am
	8:01	am 5:01 am
	8:20	am 5:20 am
	11:24	am 8:24 am
	11:44	am 8:44 am

7 SUNDAY

	4:08	am 1:08 am
	6:39	am 3:39 am
	7:44	am 4:44 am
	12:34	pm 9:34 am
	3:09	pm 12:09 pm
	7:37	pm 4:37 pm
		10:02 pm

8 MONDAY

	1:02	am
	3:34	am 12:34 am
	6:59	am 3:59 am
	1:08	pm 10:08 am
	2:29	pm 11:29 am
	5:15	pm 2:15 pm
	5:40	pm 2:40 pm
	8:42	pm 5:42 pm
	9:51	pm 6:51 pm
	11:26	pm 8:26 pm

9 TUESDAY

	1:08	am
	2:39	am
	8:01	am 5:01 am
	8:32	am 5:32 am
	9:22	am 6:22 am
	11:39	am 8:39 am

10 WEDNESDAY

	4:38	am
	11:15	am 8:15 am
	2:44	pm 11:44 am
	4:56	pm 1:56 pm
	9:02	pm 6:02 pm
	9:27	pm 6:27 pm
	10:04	pm 7:04 pm
		9:23 pm
		9:50 pm

11 THURSDAY

	12:23	am
	12:50	am
	2:47	am 1:35 am
	4:35	am 1:35 am
	12:09	pm 9:09 am
	6:37	pm 3:37 pm
	10:54	pm 7:54 pm
		11:00 pm
		11:35 pm

12 FRIDAY

	2:00	am
	2:35	am
	4:02	am 1:02 am
	4:31	am 1:31 am
	5:48	am 2:48 am
	1:22	pm 10:22 am
	5:06	pm 2:06 pm
	5:20	pm 2:20 pm
	6:45	pm 3:45 pm
	9:05	pm 6:05 pm
		9:43 pm
		10:08 pm
		10:27 pm

13 SATURDAY

	12:43	pm
	1:08	pm
	1:27	pm
	4:19	pm 1:19 pm
	5:05	pm 2:05 pm
	5:22	pm 2:22 pm
	7:41	pm 4:41 pm
	10:59	pm 7:59 pm
	8:40	pm 5:40 pm

14 SUNDAY

	4:27	am 1:27 am
	6:03	am 3:03 am
	8:18	am 5:18 am
	10:58	am 7:58 am
	12:25	pm 9:25 am
	1:42	pm 10:42 am
	7:44	pm 4:44 pm
	7:50	pm 4:50 pm
	7:59	pm 4:59 pm
		10:05 pm
		11:15 pm

15 MONDAY

	1:05	am
	2:15	am 1:58 am
	4:58	am 1:58 am
	5:18	am 2:18 am
	6:13	am 3:13 am
	6:51	am 3:51 am
	8:13	am 5:13 am
	11:24	am 8:24 am
	8:26	pm 5:26 pm

16 TUESDAY

	4:16	am 1:16 am
	5:27	am 2:27 am
	5:35	am 2:35 am
	5:50	am 2:50 am
	10:04	am 7:04 am
	1:51	pm 10:51 am
	7:10	pm 4:10 pm
	8:56	pm 5:56 pm
		9:05 pm
		11:03 pm

17 WEDNESDAY

	12:05	pm
	2:03	am
	4:06	am 1:06 am
	4:25	am 1:25 am
	7:22	am 4:22 am
	9:31	am 6:31 am
	10:22	am 7:22 am
	7:37	pm 4:37 pm

18 THURSDAY

	3:50	am 12:50 am
	4:53	am 1:53 am
	11:56	am 8:56 am
	4:52	pm 1:52 pm
	6:57	pm 3:57 pm
	10:19	pm 7:19 pm
	11:34	pm 8:34 pm
		11:29 pm

19 FRIDAY

	2:29	am
	12:37	pm
	1:35	pm
	4:16	pm 1:16 pm
	4:30	pm 1:30 pm
	1:58	pm 10:58 am
	3:01	pm 12:01 pm
	8:09	pm 5:09 pm

20 SATURDAY

	12:06	pm 9:06 pm
	4:37	pm 1:37 pm
	5:06	am 2:06 am
	5:50	am 2:50 am
	4:03	pm 1:03 pm
	8:55	pm 5:55 pm
	10:31	pm 7:31 pm
		10:17 pm
		11:14 pm

21 SUNDAY

	1:17	am
	2:14	am
	5:26	am 2:26 am
	5:34	am 2:34 am
	7:17	am 4:17 am
	10:16	am 7:16 am
	11:28	am 8:28 am
	6:10	pm 3:10 pm
	10:01	pm 7:01 pm
	11:39	pm 8:39 pm
		9:22 pm

22 MONDAY

	12:22	pm
	8:30	am 5:30 am
	9:40	am 6:40 am
	9:59	am 6:59 am
	4:29	pm 1:29 pm
		9:12 pm
		11:27 pm

23 TUESDAY

	12:12	pm
	2:27	am
	8:35	am 5:35 am
	10:09	am 7:09 am
	11:06	am 8:06 am
	12:11	pm 9:11 am
	1:43	pm 10:43 am
	4:45	pm 1:45 pm
	5:14	pm 2:14 pm

24 WEDNESDAY

	6:23	am 3:23 am
	6:59	am 3:59 am
	11:01	pm 8:01 pm
	1:22	pm 10:22 am

25 THURSDAY

	4:02	am 1:02 am
	5:52	am 2:52 am
	5:55	am 2:55 am
	6:11	am 3:11 am
	9:13	am 6:13 am
	5:34	am 2:34 am
	8:43	am 5:43 am
	11:45	am 8:45 am
	12:51	pm 9:51 am
	2:16	pm 11:16 am
	3:10	pm 12:10 pm
	8:16	pm 5:16 pm
	9:12	pm 6:12 pm
	10:45	pm 7:45 pm
	11:23	pm 8:23 pm
	11:51	pm 8:51 pm

26 FRIDAY

	2:52	am
	5:12	am 2:12 am
	5:43	am 2:43 am
	7:05	pm 4:05 pm
	9:01	am 6:01 am

27 SATURDAY

	4:24	am 1:24 am
	4:58	am 1:58 am
	5:59	am 2:59 am
	9:57	am 6:57 am
	1:19	pm 10:19 am
	9:48	pm 2:40 pm
	6:48	pm
	7:10	pm
	10:10	pm 8:49 pm
	11:49	pm
		11:20 pm

28 SUNDAY

	2:20	am
	4:43	am 1:43 am
	7:54	am 4:54 am
	11:50	am 8:50 am
	12:25	pm 9:25 am
	12:57	pm 9:57 am
	3:18	pm 12:18 pm
	5:18	pm 2:18 pm

29 MONDAY

	6:21	am 3:21 am
	5:32	am 2:32 am

30 TUESDAY

	7:25	am 4:25 am
	11:52	am 8:52 am
		11:49 pm
	2:49	am
	11:13	am 8:13 am
	12:52	pm 9:52 am
	1:09	pm 10:09 am
	2:19	pm 11:19 am
	8:06	pm 5:06 pm
	8:21	pm 5:21 pm
	9:39	pm 6:39 pm
		10:36 pm
		10:37 pm
		11:37 pm

SEPTEMBER 1997

☽ Last Aspect / ☽ Ingress

☽ Last Aspect			☽ Ingress		
day	EST / hr:mn / PST	asp	sign day	EST / hr:mn / PST	
3	4:26 am	1:26 am	△♥	≏ 3	12:30 pm	9:30 am
5		5:06 pm	□♥	m, 5		10:10 pm
8	8:06 pm		□♀	✗ 8	1:10 am	
6	6:59 am	3:59 am	✶♥	✗ 8	11:55 am	6:55 am
10	4:56 pm	1:56 pm	♂♄	≈ 10	7:24 am	4:24 am
12	6:45 pm	3:45 pm	♂♀	⋇ 12	12:11:10 pm	8:10 pm
16	8:10 am	5:10 am	⋇♀	♈ 14	11:59 pm	8:59 pm
16	7:10 pm	4:10 pm	□♀	♉ 16	11:25 pm	8:25 pm
18	6:57 pm	3:57 pm	⋇♀	♊ 18	11:21 pm	8:21 pm
20		7:31 pm	△☉	♊ 20	11:38 pm	10:38 pm

☽ Last Aspect			☽ Ingress		
day	EST / hr:mn / PST	asp	sign day	EST / hr:mn / PST	
20	10:31 pm			♊ 21	1:38 am	
22	9:59 am	6:59 am	⋇♄	♋ 23	7:33 am	4:33 am
25	12:51 am		□♀	♌ 25	5:32 pm	2:13 pm
28	4:43 am	1:43 am	♂♀	♍ 28	5:28 am	2:28 am
30	1:09 pm	10:09 am	♂♀	≏ 30	6:33 pm	3:33 pm

☽ Phases & Eclipses

phase	day	EST / hr:mn / PST	
New Moon	1	6:52 pm	3:52 pm
	1	9° ♍ 34′	
2nd Quarter	9	8:32 pm	5:32 pm
Full Moon	16	1:51 pm	10:51 am
	16	23° ⋇ 56′	
4th Quarter	23	8:35 am	5:35 am

Planet Ingress

		EST / hr:mn / PST	
♀ m,	2	10:11 pm	7:11 pm
♀ m,	11	9:17 pm	6:17 pm
♀ ♍	12	7:28 pm	4:28 pm
☉ ≏	22	7:53 am	4:53 am
♀ ≏	26	1:56 pm	3:56 pm
♂ ✗	28	5:22 pm	2:22 pm

Planetary Motion

		EST / hr:mn / PST	
♀ D	9	8:38 pm	5:38 pm
♀ D	12	7:40 pm	4:40 pm

EPHEMERIS CALCULATED FOR 12 MIDNIGHT GREENWICH MEAN TIME. ALL OTHER DATA AND FACING ASPECTARIAN PAGE IN **EASTERN STANDARD TIME (BOLD)** AND PACIFIC STANDARD TIME (REGULAR).

OCTOBER 1997

1 WEDNESDAY
1:36 am
1:37 am
2:38 am
3:34 am 12:34
4:19 am 1:19 pm
4:22 am 1:22 pm
8:53 am
11:53 am
7:11 pm 4:11 pm

2 THURSDAY
2:59 am 5:59 am
5:44 am 8:44 am
7:07 am 10:07 am
3:58 pm 6:58 pm
10:22 pm
10:41 pm

3 FRIDAY
1:22 am
1:41 am
8:11 am 5:11 am
12:17 pm 9:17 am
1:44 pm 10:44 am
2:01 pm 11:01 am
4:28 pm 1:28 pm
6:27 pm 3:27 pm
6:44 pm 3:44 pm
6:50 pm 3:50 pm
9:03 pm

4 SATURDAY
12:03 am
3:22 am 12:22 am
4:29 am 1:29 am
5:11 am 2:11 am
6:38 am 3:38 am
6:56 am 3:56 am
4:21 pm 1:21 pm
5:09 pm 2:09 pm
8:44 pm 5:44 pm
11:41 pm

5 SUNDAY
2:41 am
11:31 am 8:31 am
4:20 am
8:31 am

6 MONDAY
12:01 am
12:08 am
12:18 am
3:05 am
5:27 am
8:22 am

7 TUESDAY
12:38 am
1:39 am
2:51 am
7:13 am
4:46 pm
7:59 pm

8 WEDNESDAY
2:14 am
6:34 am 3:34 am
7:06 am 4:06 am
8:53 am 5:53 am
10:56 pm
11:25 pm

9 THURSDAY
12:43 am
1:56 am
2:25 am
8:46 am
10:43 am
12:17 pm
1:58 pm 11:58 am

10 FRIDAY
2:35 am
7:34 am 4:34 am
11:09 am 8:09 am
12:01 pm 9:01 am
1:56 pm 10:56 am
3:39 pm 12:39 pm
10:17 pm 7:17 pm
10:59 pm 7:59 pm
11:35 pm

11 SATURDAY
4:11 am 1:11 am
11:28 am 8:28 am
12:04 pm 9:04 am
12:09 pm 9:09 am
12:41 pm 9:41 am
2:59 pm 11:59 am
5:33 pm 2:33 pm
10:57 pm

12 SUNDAY
1:57 am
5:21 am 2:21 am
6:41 am 3:38 am
9:53 am 6:53 am
4:13 pm 1:13 pm
4:25 pm 1:25 pm
5:45 pm 2:45 pm
6:16 pm 3:16 pm
6:24 pm 3:24 pm
11:12 pm
11:37 pm

13 MONDAY
2:12 am
2:37 am
5:46 am 2:46 am
10:09 am
12:52 pm 9:52 am
1:00 pm 10:00 am
4:02 pm 1:02 pm
7:01 pm 4:01 pm
7:33 pm 4:33 pm
7:45 pm 4:45 pm
10:48 pm

14 TUESDAY
1:48 am

15 WEDNESDAY
3:36 am 12:36 am
5:03 am 2:03 am
5:48 am 2:48 am
12:38 pm 9:38 am
6:56 pm 3:56 pm
7:22 pm 4:22 pm
9:16 pm 6:16 pm
10:46 pm 7:46 pm
10:40 pm

16 THURSDAY
12:48 am
1:40 am
5:46 am 2:46 am
9:56 am 6:56 am
4:35 pm 1:35 pm
5:54 pm 2:54 pm
7:19 pm 4:19 pm
11:39 pm 8:39 pm
11:14 pm

17 FRIDAY
2:14 am
5:05 am 2:05 am
6:03 am 3:03 am
12:43 pm 9:43 am
2:34 pm 11:34 am
8:29 pm 5:29 pm
9:42 pm

18 SATURDAY
3:02 am 12:02 am
6:45 am 3:45 am
8:52 am 5:52 am
11:03 am 8:03 am
6:12 pm 3:12 pm
6:46 pm 3:46 pm
7:28 pm 4:28 pm
9:27 pm 6:27 pm

19 SUNDAY
3:36 am 12:36 am
7:24 am 4:24 am
8:32 am 5:32 am
8:49 am 5:49 am
12:50 pm 9:50 am
2:18 pm 11:18 am
3:08 pm 12:08 pm
9:23 pm

20 MONDAY
12:23 am
3:15 am 12:15 am
9:07 am 6:07 am
10:44 am 7:44 am
10:52 am 7:52 am
3:19 pm 12:19 pm
8:23 pm 5:23 pm
11:10 pm 8:10 pm
9:26 pm

21 TUESDAY
12:26 am
3:08 am 12:08 am
4:08 am 1:08 am
2:35 pm 11:35 am
4:34 pm 1:34 pm
7:21 pm 4:21 pm
9:18 pm 6:18 pm
10:27 pm 7:27 pm

22 WEDNESDAY
5:14 am 2:14 am
8:25 am 5:25 am
9:37 am 6:37 am
3:51 pm 12:51 pm
10:56 pm 7:56 pm
11:49 pm 8:49 pm

23 THURSDAY
7:36 am 4:36 am
8:17 am 5:17 am
9:31 am 6:31 am
10:02 am
11:47 am 10:47 am
6:57 pm 3:57 pm
9:49 pm

24 FRIDAY
12:49 am
4:42 am 1:42 am
7:22 am 4:22 am
11:31 am 8:31 am
12:46 pm 9:46 am
7:31 pm 4:31 pm
8:27 pm 5:27 pm

25 SATURDAY
2:41 am
5:08 am 3:26 am
8:36 am 5:36 am
9:45 am 6:45 am
11:05 pm

26 SUNDAY
2:05 am
6:34 am 3:34 am
11:33 am 8:33 am
1:46 pm 10:46 am
7:33 pm 4:33 pm
7:47 pm 4:47 pm
10:41 pm

27 MONDAY
1:41 am
4:46 am 1:46 am
5:43 am 2:43 am
6:25 am 3:25 am
7:17 am 4:17 am
10:30 am 7:30 am
11:33 am 8:33 am
2:29 pm 11:29 am
7:34 pm 4:34 pm
9:11 pm
9:56 pm
9:59 pm

28 TUESDAY
12:11 am
12:56 am
12:59 am
9:52 am 6:52 am
10:52 am 7:52 am
11:50 am 8:50 am
11:06 pm 12:51 pm
8:06 pm

29 WEDNESDAY
12:01 am
3:01 am 5:15 am
8:15 am 6:41 am
9:41 am 7:25 am
10:25 am 11:33 am
2:33 pm 2:01 pm
5:01 pm 3:44 pm
6:44 pm 7:19 pm
10:19 pm 9:05 pm
9:49 pm

30 THURSDAY
12:45 am
7:56 am 4:56 am
12:58 pm 10:26 am
6:40 pm 3:40 pm
9:57 pm 6:57 pm
10:48 pm 7:49 pm

31 FRIDAY
4:17 am 1:17 am
5:01 am 2:01 am
1:58 pm 10:58 am
2:45 pm 11:45 am
7:07 pm 4:07 pm
11:26 pm 8:26 pm
9:17 pm

OCTOBER 1997

☽ Last Aspect day	EST / hr:mn / PST	asp	☽ Ingress sign day	EST / hr:mn / PST
2	10:22 pm	□♆	♏ 3	3:58 am
3	**1:22 am**	□♆	♏ 3	**6:58 am**
5	**12:18 pm** 9:18 am	⚹♆	♐ 5	**5:43 pm** 2:43 pm
6	11:14 pm	△♄	♑ 7	11:04 pm
7	**2:14 am**	△♄	♑ 8	**2:04 am**
9	11:35 pm	☌♆	♒ 10	4:29 am
10	**2:35 am**	☌♆	♒ 10	**7:29 am**
11	**2:59 pm** 11:59 am	△☉	♓ 12	**9:59 am** 6:59 am
14	**5:56 am** 2:56 am	⚹♆	♈ 14	**10:25 am** 7:25 am
16	**5:46 am** 2:46 am	□♆	♉ 16	**10:16 am** 7:16 am
18	**6:45 am** 3:45 am	△♆	♊ 18	**11:27 am** 8:27 am
20	**10:52 am** 7:52 am	△☉	♋ 20	**3:46 pm** 12:46 pm
22	8:49 pm	□☉	♌ 22	9:11 pm
22	**11:49 pm**	□☉	♌ 23	**12:11 am**
24	**12:46 pm** 9:46 am	△♂	♍ 25	**12:00 pm** 9:00 am
27	4:34 pm	△♆	♎ 27	10:05 pm
27	**7:34 pm**	△♆	♎ 28	**1:05 am**
30	**7:56 am** 4:56 am	□♆	♏ 30	**1:16 pm** 10:16 am

☽ Phases & Eclipses phase	day	EST / hr:mn / PST
New Moon	1	**11:53 am** 8:53 am
2nd Quarter	9	**7:22 am** 4:22 am
Full Moon	15	**10:46 pm** 7:46 pm
4th Quarter	22	**11:49 pm** 8:49 pm
New Moon	31	**5:01 am** 2:01 am

Planet Ingress	day	EST / hr:mn / PST
☿ ♎	1	9:38 pm
☿ ♎	2	**12:38 am**
♀ ♐	8	**3:25 am** 12:25 am
⚳ ♓	11	**3:51 am** 12:51 am
☿ ♏	19	**7:08 am** 4:08 am
☉ ♏	23	**4:15 am** 1:15 am
⚳ ♓	29	**3:15 am** 12:15 am

Planetary Motion	day	EST / hr:mn / PST
♃ D	7	**11:21 pm** 8:21 pm
♆ D	8	**6:22 pm** 3:22 pm
♅ D	14	**3:06 am** 12:06 am
⚳ D	19	10:29 pm
⚳ D	20	**1:29 am**

DAY		SID.TIME	SUN	MOON	NODE	MERCURY	VENUS	MARS	JUPITER	SATURN	URANUS	NEPTUNE	PLUTO	CERES	PALLAS	JUNO	VESTA	CHIRON
W	1	0:39:04	07 ♎ 51 06	00 ♎ 13	19 ♍℞ 48	27 ♍ 47	21 ♏ 43	01 ♐ 27	12 ♒℞ 11	17 ♈℞ 38	04 ♒℞ 49	27 ♑℞ 12	03 ♐ 29	00 ♓℞ 54	18 ♑ 43	04 ♍ 40	27 ♈℞ 52	03 ♏ 26
T	2	0:43:00	08 50 07	12 04	19 47	29 35	22 51	02 09	12 09	17 33	04 48	27 12	03 31	00 47	18 49	05 06	27 39	03 34
F	3	0:46:57	09 49 11	24 00	19 44	01 ♎ 23	23 59	02 51	12 08	17 28	04 47	27 12	03 32	00 40	18 56	05 33	27 25	03 42
S	4	0:50:53	10 48 17	06 ♏ 04	19 41	03 11	25 07	03 33	12 07	17 24	04 47	27 11	03 34	00 34	19 02	05 59	27 11	03 50
S	5	0:54:50	11 47 24	18 16	19 37	04 58	26 14	04 16	12 07	17 19	04 46	27 11	03 36	00 28	19 09	06 25	26 57	03 58
M	6	0:58:46	12 46 34	00 ♐ 40	19 33	06 46	27 22	04 58	12 06	17 14	04 46	27 11	03 37	00 23	19 16	06 50	26 42	04 06
T	7	1:02:43	13 45 45	13 17	19 29	08 33	28 29	05 41	12 06	17 10	04 46	27 11	03 39	00 18	19 24	07 16	26 27	04 14
W	8	1:06:39	14 44 58	26 09	19 27	10 19	29 36	06 23	12 D 06	17 05	04 45	27 D 11	03 41	00 13	19 31	07 42	26 13	04 23
T	9	1:10:36	15 44 12	09 ♑ 20	19 26	12 06	00 ♐ 43	07 06	12 06	17 00	04 45	27 11	03 42	00 09	19 39	08 07	25 57	04 31
F	10	1:14:33	16 43 29	22 50	19 D 26	13 51	01 50	07 49	12 06	16 55	04 45	27 11	03 44	00 05	19 47	08 33	25 42	04 39
S	11	1:18:29	17 42 47	06 ♒ 42	19 27	15 36	02 57	08 32	12 06	16 51	04 44	27 11	03 46	00 01	19 56	08 58	25 27	04 47
S	12	1:22:26	18 42 07	20 56	19 28	17 20	04 04	09 15	12 07	16 46	04 44	27 11	03 48	29 ♒ 58	20 04	09 24	25 12	04 56
M	13	1:26:22	19 41 29	05 ♓ 30	19 30	19 03	05 10	09 58	12 08	16 41	04 44	27 11	03 50	29 55	20 13	09 49	24 56	05 04
T	14	1:30:19	20 40 53	20 22	19 ℞ 30	20 46	06 16	10 41	12 09	16 36	04 D 44	27 11	03 51	29 53	20 22	10 14	24 41	05 12
W	15	1:34:15	21 40 19	05 ♈ 23	19 29	22 28	07 22	11 24	12 10	16 32	04 44	27 12	03 53	29 50	20 32	10 39	24 25	05 20
T	16	1:38:12	22 39 47	20 28	19 27	24 10	08 28	12 08	12 12	16 27	04 44	27 12	03 55	29 49	20 41	11 04	24 09	05 29
F	17	1:42:08	23 39 16	05 ♉ 25	19 23	25 50	09 34	12 51	12 13	16 22	04 44	27 12	03 57	29 47	20 51	11 28	23 54	05 37
S	18	1:46:05	24 38 48	20 08	19 18	27 31	10 39	13 34	12 15	16 18	04 44	27 12	03 59	29 46	21 01	11 53	23 38	05 46
S	19	1:50:02	25 38 22	04 ♊ 28	19 13	29 10	11 45	14 18	12 17	16 13	04 45	27 13	04 01	29 46	21 12	12 17	23 23	05 54
M	20	1:53:58	26 37 58	18 22	19 07	00 ♏ 49	12 50	15 02	12 19	16 08	04 45	27 13	04 03	29 45	21 22	12 42	23 07	06 02
T	21	1:57:55	27 37 36	01 ♋ 47	19 03	02 27	13 54	15 45	12 22	16 04	04 45	27 13	04 05	29 D 45	21 33	13 06	22 52	06 11
W	22	2:01:51	28 37 16	14 45	19 00	04 04	14 59	16 29	12 24	15 59	04 46	27 14	04 07	29 46	21 44	13 30	22 37	06 19
T	23	2:05:48	29 36 58	27 20	18 D 58	05 41	16 04	17 13	12 27	15 55	04 46	27 14	04 09	29 47	21 55	13 54	22 21	06 28
F	24	2:09:44	00 ♏ 36 43	09 ♌ 35	18 59	07 18	17 08	17 57	12 30	15 50	04 46	27 15	04 11	29 48	22 06	14 18	22 06	06 36
S	25	2:13:41	01 36 31	21 36	19 00	08 53	18 12	18 41	12 33	15 46	04 47	27 15	04 13	29 49	22 18	14 42	21 51	06 44
S	26	2:17:37	02 36 20	03 ♍ 27	19 02	10 29	19 16	19 25	12 37	15 41	04 48	27 16	04 15	29 51	22 30	15 06	21 37	06 53
M	27	2:21:34	03 36 12	15 13	19 03	12 03	20 19	20 09	12 40	15 37	04 48	27 16	04 17	29 53	22 42	15 29	21 22	07 01
T	28	2:25:31	04 36 05	27 00	19 ℞ 04	13 38	21 22	20 53	12 44	15 32	04 49	27 17	04 19	29 56	22 54	15 52	21 08	07 10
W	29	2:29:27	05 36 01	08 ♎ 51	19 01	15 11	22 25	21 38	12 48	15 28	04 50	27 18	04 21	29 59	23 06	16 16	20 54	07 18
T	30	2:33:24	06 35 59	20 48	18 57	16 45	23 28	22 22	12 52	15 24	04 50	27 18	04 24	00 ♓ 02	23 19	16 39	20 40	07 27
F	31	2:37:20	07 35 58	02 ♏ 55	18 50	18 17	24 30	23 06	12 57	15 20	04 51	27 19	04 26	00 06	23 31	17 02	20 26	07 35

EPHEMERIS CALCULATED FOR 12 MIDNIGHT GREENWICH MEAN TIME. ALL OTHER DATA AND FACING ASPECTARIAN PAGE IN **EASTERN STANDARD TIME (BOLD)** AND PACIFIC STANDARD TIME (REGULAR).

NOVEMBER 1997

1 SATURDAY
12:17 am
1:32 am
2:13 am
5:13 am
11:46 am
12:45 pm
3:52 pm
11:55 pm

2 SUNDAY
7:59 am
8:44 am
1:13 pm
2:34 pm
7:32 pm

3 MONDAY
12:21 am
3:55 am
10:05 am
7:04 pm
9:15 pm
9:29 pm

4 TUESDAY
12:38 am
2:41 am
5:48 am
8:20 am
3:54 am
4:32 am
10:41 am

5 WEDNESDAY
7:24 am
7:53 am
10:42 am
1:07 pm
2:27 pm
5:30 pm
6:19 pm
6:28 pm

6 THURSDAY
6:49 pm 3:49 pm
9:23 pm

12:23 am
4:36 am
8:58 am
10:06 am
10:42 am
2:43 pm
4:15 pm
9:48 pm
10:19 pm

7 FRIDAY
12:37 am
4:44 am
1:24 pm
4:44 pm
10:22 pm

1:44 am
10:24 am
12:29 am
1:44 pm
9:04 pm
9:21 pm

8 SATURDAY
12:38 am
1:53 am
9:51 am
1:13 pm
10:22 pm

6:51 am
10:13 am
2:11 pm
9:38 am
11:41 pm

9 SUNDAY
12:04 am
1:32 pm
2:05 am
7:06 pm
6:57 am

1:46 am
2:06 am
6:57 am
7:53 am
12:17 am
5:04 pm
5:23 pm
10:53 pm
11:47 pm

10 MONDAY
12:34 am

1:53 am
2:47 am
9:13 pm
1:04 am
1:32 pm

11 TUESDAY
1:39 pm
2:59 am
8:21 am
9:09 am
10:07 am
12:35 pm
4:17 pm
6:37 pm
7:05 pm
8:17 pm

12:41 am
1:04 am
1:35 pm
2:36 am
3:44 pm
7:53 pm
4:36 pm
10:22 pm

12 WEDNESDAY
6:13 am
6:23 am
10:04 am
2:07 pm
3:01 pm

1:53 am
2:47 pm
9:13 pm
9:23 pm

13 THURSDAY
12:10 am
4:11 am
2:12 am
5:47 am
8:47 am
9:04 pm
11:59 pm

14 FRIDAY
2:59 am
4:10 am
5:11 am
5:11 am
1:13 pm
1:22 pm
6:14 pm
6:32 pm

15 SATURDAY
10:56 pm 7:56 pm
9:56 pm

12:56 am
1:15 am
2:58 am
3:45 am
3:12 pm
3:11 pm
6:27 pm
7:19 pm
7:36 pm

16 SUNDAY
3:48 am
12:48 pm
10:25 am
12:57 pm
3:57 pm
9:16 am
9:19 am
9:06 pm

17 MONDAY
12:36 am
5:08 am
10:29 am
10:35 am
10:52 am

2:08 am
7:29 am
7:35 am
7:52 pm
9:02 pm

18 TUESDAY
12:10 am
1:11 am
2:12 am
5:47 am

3:35 pm
4:39 pm
8:42 pm

19 WEDNESDAY
2:59 am
4:10 am
5:11 am
5:11 am
1:13 pm
1:22 pm
10:22 am
6:14 pm
6:32 pm

20 THURSDAY
6:47 pm 3:47 pm
9:22 pm
9:39 pm

12:22 am
12:39 pm
4:45 am
11:58 am
12:55 pm
1:51 pm
5:43 pm
9:28 pm

1:45 pm
8:58 am
9:55 am
11:35 am
12:12 pm
12:27 pm
2:43 pm
6:28 pm

21 FRIDAY
4:19 am
8:55 am
5:13 pm
6:58 pm

1:19 pm
5:55 pm
11:56 pm
2:13 pm
3:58 pm
10:14 pm

22 SATURDAY
1:14 am
6:10 am
4:30 pm
11:56 pm

3:10 pm
3:24 pm
1:30 pm
2:42 pm
8:56 pm
11:49 pm

23 SUNDAY
2:49 am
3:26 am
5:42 am
5:54 am
8:22 am
5:21 pm
11:24 am

2:49 pm
4:39 pm
12:26 pm
2:42 pm
2:54 pm
5:22 pm
2:21 pm
8:24 pm

24 MONDAY
3:56 am
1:37 pm
7:23 am
7:34 am

12:56 pm
4:34 am
2:10 pm
10:37 am
4:23 pm
4:34 pm

25 TUESDAY
7:02 am
9:41 pm

7:02 am
4:02 pm
3:14 pm
3:32 pm

26 WEDNESDAY
11:42 am
12:40 pm
6:15 pm
11:17 pm

8:42 am
9:40 am
1:26 pm
3:15 pm
8:17 pm

9:36 am
12:36 pm
1:29 pm
4:26 pm
9:13 pm

10:29 am
1:26 pm
6:13 pm
10:38 pm

27 THURSDAY
1:38 am
4:09 am
6:05 am
7:05 am
7:36 am
11:34 am
1:34 pm
7:07 pm
11:42 pm

1:09 am
3:05 am
4:05 am
4:36 am
8:34 am
10:34 am
4:07 pm
8:42 pm
9:54 pm

28 FRIDAY
12:54 am
4:10 am
5:01 am
8:34 am
1:58 am

1:10 am
2:01 am
5:34 am
10:58 am
10:00 am
11:30 am

29 SATURDAY
1:00 am
2:30 am
3:59 am
8:14 am
2:28 am
4:52 pm
5:01 am
9:14 pm

1:10 am
4:10 am
5:14 am
11:28 am
7:52 pm
7:01 pm
8:04 pm
6:14 pm

30 SUNDAY
3:56 am
8:04 am
12:53 pm
1:07 pm
1:10 pm
4:51 pm

1:24 am
5:04 am
9:53 am
12:59 am
10:07 am
10:10 am
1:51 pm

2:35 pm
2:47 pm
10:14 pm

5:35 pm
5:47 pm

Eastern Standard Time in bold type
Pacific Standard Time in medium type

NOVEMBER 1997

☽ Last Aspect day	EST / hr:mn / PST	asp	☽ Ingress sign	day	EST / hr:mn / PST
1	**6:22 pm** 3:22 pm	✶♆	♐	1	**11:27 pm** 8:27 pm
4	**5:48 am** 2:48 am	☌♀	♑	4	**7:31 am** 4:31 am
6	**10:42 am** 7:42 am	✶☿	♒	6	**1:33 pm** 10:33 am
8	**5:11 pm** 2:11 pm	✶♂	♓	8	**5:35 pm** 2:35 pm
10	**3:35 pm** 12:35 pm	✶♆	♈	10	**7:44 pm** 4:44 pm
12	**4:43 pm** 1:43 pm	□♆	♉	12	**8:46 pm** 5:46 pm
14	**6:01 pm** 3:01 pm	△♆	♊	14	**10:05 pm** 7:05 pm
15	7:36 pm	△♃	♋	16	10:33 pm
15	**10:36 pm**	△♃	♋	17	**1:33 am**
19	**4:10 am** 1:10 am	☍♆	♌	19	**8:38 am** 5:38 am
21	**6:58 pm** 3:58 pm	□☉	♍	21	**7:33 pm** 4:33 pm
24	**3:56 am** 12:56 am	△♆	♎	24	**8:29 am** 5:29 am
26	**4:26 pm** 1:26 pm	□♆	♏	26	**8:43 pm** 5:43 pm
28	11:30 pm	✶♆	♐	29	3:29 am
29	**2:30 am**	✶♆	♐	29	**6:28 am**
30	**1:07 pm** 10:07 am	✶♃	♑	12/1	**1:38 pm** 10:38 am

☽ Phases & Eclipses phase	day	EST / hr:mn / PST
2nd Quarter	7	**4:44 pm** 1:44 pm
Full Moon	14	**9:13 am** 6:13 am
4th Quarter	21	**6:58 pm** 3:58 pm
New Moon	29	**9:14 pm** 6:14 pm

Planet Ingress	day	EST / hr:mn / PST
♀ ♑	5	**3:50 am** 12:50 am
☿ ♐	7	**12:42 pm** 9:42 am
♂ ♑	8	9:33 pm
♂ ♑	9	**12:33 am**
☉ ♐	21	10:47 pm
☉ ♐	22	**1:47 am**
♀ ♒	25	**11:26 pm** 8:26 pm
☿ ♑	30	**2:11 pm** 11:11 am

Planetary Motion	day	EST / hr:mn / PST

DAY		SID.TIME	SUN	MOON	NODE	MERCURY	VENUS	MARS	JUPITER	SATURN	URANUS	NEPTUNE	PLUTO	CERES	PALLAS	JUNO	VESTA	CHIRON
S	1	2:41:17	08 ♏ 36 00	15 ♏ 12	18 ♍℞ 41	19 ♏ 50	25 ♐ 32	23 ♐ 51	13 ♒ 01	15 ♈℞ 15	04 ♒ 52	27 ♑ 20	04 ♐ 28	00 ♓ 10	23 ♑ 44	17 ♍ 25	20 ♈℞ 13	07 ♏ 44
S	2	2:45:13	09 36 04	27 40	18 31	21 22	26 34	24 36	13 06	15 11	04 53	27 21	04 30	00 14	23 57	17 47	20 00	07 52
M	3	2:49:10	10 36 09	10 ♐ 20	18 22	22 53	27 36	25 20	13 11	15 07	04 54	27 21	04 32	00 19	24 11	18 10	19 47	08 01
T	4	2:53:06	11 36 16	23 13	18 13	24 24	28 37	26 05	13 16	15 03	04 55	27 22	04 34	00 24	24 24	18 33	19 35	08 09
W	5	2:57:03	12 36 25	06 ♑ 17	18 06	25 54	29 38	26 50	13 21	14 59	04 56	27 23	04 37	00 29	24 38	18 55	19 23	08 18
T	6	3:01:00	13 36 35	19 34	18 01	27 25	00 ♑ 38	27 35	13 26	14 56	04 57	27 24	04 39	00 35	24 51	19 17	19 11	08 26
F	7	3:04:56	14 36 47	03 ♒ 05	17 D 58	28 54	01 38	28 20	13 32	14 52	04 58	27 25	04 41	00 41	25 05	19 39	19 00	08 34
S	8	3:08:53	15 37 01	16 50	17 58	00 ♐ 23	02 38	29 05	13 38	14 48	04 59	27 26	04 43	00 47	25 19	20 01	18 49	08 43
S	9	3:12:49	16 37 15	00 ♓ 50	17 58	01 52	03 37	29 50	13 43	14 44	05 01	27 27	04 46	00 54	25 34	20 23	18 38	08 51
M	10	3:16:46	17 37 31	15 05	17 ℞ 58	03 20	04 36	00 ♑ 35	13 50	14 41	05 02	27 28	04 48	01 01	25 48	20 44	18 28	09 00
T	11	3:20:42	18 37 49	29 33	17 57	04 48	05 34	01 20	13 56	14 37	05 03	27 29	04 50	01 08	26 03	21 05	18 18	09 08
W	12	3:24:39	19 38 08	14 ♈ 12	17 55	06 15	06 32	02 05	14 02	14 34	05 05	27 30	04 52	01 15	26 17	21 27	18 08	09 16
T	13	3:28:35	20 38 29	28 55	17 49	07 42	07 30	02 50	14 09	14 30	05 06	27 31	04 55	01 23	26 32	21 48	17 59	09 25
F	14	3:32:32	21 38 51	13 ♉ 37	17 42	09 08	08 26	03 36	14 15	14 27	05 08	27 32	04 57	01 31	26 47	22 09	17 51	09 33
S	15	3:36:29	22 39 15	28 09	17 32	10 34	09 23	04 21	14 22	14 24	05 09	27 34	04 59	01 40	27 02	22 29	17 43	09 41
S	16	3:40:25	23 39 40	12 ♊ 24	17 21	11 58	10 19	05 07	14 29	14 21	05 11	27 35	05 02	01 48	27 17	22 50	17 35	09 50
M	17	3:44:22	24 40 08	26 17	17 11	13 22	11 14	05 52	14 37	14 18	05 13	27 36	05 04	01 57	27 33	23 10	17 28	09 58
T	18	3:48:18	25 40 37	09 ♋ 45	17 01	14 45	12 09	06 38	14 44	14 15	05 14	27 37	05 06	02 07	27 48	23 31	17 21	10 06
W	19	3:52:15	26 41 08	22 47	16 54	16 07	13 03	07 23	14 52	14 12	05 16	27 39	05 09	02 16	28 04	23 51	17 14	10 15
T	20	3:56:11	27 41 40	05 ♌ 24	16 48	17 29	13 57	08 09	14 59	14 09	05 18	27 40	05 11	02 26	28 20	24 11	17 08	10 23
F	21	4:00:08	28 42 14	17 42	16 46	18 48	14 50	08 55	15 07	14 07	05 20	27 41	05 13	02 36	28 36	24 30	17 03	10 31
S	22	4:04:04	29 42 50	29 44	16 D 45	20 07	15 42	09 40	15 15	14 04	05 22	27 43	05 16	02 46	28 52	24 50	16 58	10 3
S	23	4:08:01	00 ♐ 43 28	11 ♍ 35	16 ℞ 45	21 24	16 33	10 26	15 23	14 01	05 23	27 44	05 18	02 57	29 08	25 09	16 53	10 47
M	24	4:11:58	01 44 07	23 23	16 45	22 39	17 24	11 12	15 31	13 59	05 25	27 46	05 21	03 08	29 24	25 28	16 49	10 55
T	25	4:15:54	02 44 48	05 ♎ 11	16 43	23 52	18 14	11 58	15 40	13 57	05 27	27 47	05 23	03 19	29 40	25 47	16 45	11 04
W	26	4:19:51	03 45 30	17 04	16 40	25 03	19 04	12 44	15 48	13 55	05 29	27 49	05 25	03 31	29 57	26 06	16 42	11 12
T	27	4:23:47	04 46 14	29 08	16 33	26 12	19 52	13 30	15 57	13 52	05 32	27 50	05 28	03 42	00 ♒ 13	26 25	16 39	11 20
F	28	4:27:44	05 47 00	11 ♏ 24	16 23	27 17	20 40	14 16	16 06	13 50	05 34	27 52	05 30	03 54	00 30	26 43	16 37	11 28
S	29	4:31:40	06 47 47	23 55	16 11	28 19	21 26	15 02	16 15	13 48	05 36	27 53	05 32	04 06	00 47	27 01	16 35	11 36
S	30	4:35:37	07 48 35	06 ♐ 42	15 58	29 17	22 12	15 49	16 24	13 47	05 38	27 55	05 35	04 19	01 04	27 19	16 33	11 44

EPHEMERIS CALCULATED FOR 12 MIDNIGHT GREENWICH MEAN TIME. ALL OTHER DATA AND FACING ASPECTARIAN PAGE IN **EASTERN STANDARD TIME (BOLD)** AND PACIFIC STANDARD TIME (REGULAR).

DECEMBER 1997

1 MONDAY

☽⚺♀	**1:14 am**	
☽□⚵	**9:40 am**	6:40 am
☽⚺♆	**9:57 am**	6:57 am
☽☌☿	**3:11 pm**	12:11 pm
☽⚺♀	**4:32 pm**	1:32 pm
☽⚹⚳	**10:13 pm**	7:13 pm
☽⚺♇	**11:48 pm**	8:48 pm
♆△⚵	**11:55 pm**	8:55 pm
☽⚺♅	**11:55 pm**	8:55 pm

2 TUESDAY

☽⚺☉	**8:18 am**	5:18 am
☽⚹⚷	**11:17 am**	8:17 am
☽□♄	**2:11 pm**	11:11 am
☽□⚴	**7:11 pm**	4:11 pm
☽⚺♃	**7:48 pm**	4:48 pm
☽☌♂	**10:13 pm**	7:13 pm

3 WEDNESDAY

☽☌♀	**9:53 am**	6:53 am
☿⚺♀	**11:19 am**	8:19 am
☽☌♆	**3:29 pm**	12:29 pm
☽△⚵	**4:15 pm**	1:15 pm
☽☌♀	**10:56 pm**	7:56 pm
☽⚺☿	**11:10 pm**	8:10 pm

4 THURSDAY

☽⚺⚳	**4:11 am**	1:11 am
☽⚹♇	**5:01 am**	2:01 am
☽☌♅	**5:09 am**	2:09 am
☉⚺⚷	**5:18 am**	2:18 am
☽□⚷	**4:35 pm**	1:35 pm
☽⚹☉	**5:22 pm**	2:22 pm
☽⚹♄	**6:50 pm**	3:50 pm
☽⚹⚴	**11:52 pm**	8:52 pm
☽☌♃		10:03 pm

5 FRIDAY

☽☌♃	**1:03 am**	
☽⚺♂	**5:54 am**	2:54 am
☉△♄	**12:53 pm**	9:53 am
☽⚺♀	**4:52 pm**	1:52 pm
☽⚺♆	**7:49 pm**	4:49 pm
☽⚻⚵	**9:32 pm**	6:32 pm

6 SATURDAY

☽⚺♀	**4:08 am**	1:08 am
☽⚹☿	**4:41 am**	1:41 am
☽☌⚳	**9:03 am**	6:03 am
☽□♇	**9:09 am**	6:09 am
☽⚺♅	**9:16 am**	6:16 am
♇□⚳	**4:04 pm**	1:04 pm
☽△⚷	**8:50 pm**	5:50 pm
☽⚺♄	**10:30 pm**	7:30 pm
☽□☉		10:10 pm
♅⚺⚳		10:31 pm

7 SUNDAY

☽□☉	**1:10 am**	
♅⚺⚳	**1:31 am**	
☽⚺⚴	**3:37 am**	12:37 am
☽⚺♃	**5:18 am**	2:18 am
☽⚹♂	**12:27 pm**	9:27 am
☿⚺♀	**5:45 pm**	2:45 pm
☽⚹♀	**10:38 pm**	7:38 pm
☽⚹♆	**11:16 pm**	8:16 pm
☽☍⚵		10:50 pm

8 MONDAY

☽☍⚵	**1:50 am**	
☽□☿	**8:01 am**	5:01 am
☽⚹♀	**8:25 am**	5:25 am
☉△⚴	**12:12 pm**	9:12 am
☽△♇	**12:24 pm**	9:24 am
☽⚹♅	**12:33 pm**	9:33 am
☽⚺⚳	**1:02 pm**	10:02 am
♀☌♆	**2:31 pm**	11:31 am
☽⚻⚷		9:15 pm
☽☌♄		10:23 pm

9 TUESDAY

☽⚻⚷	**12:15 am**	
☽☌♄	**1:23 am**	
☽☌⚴	**6:37 am**	3:37 am
☽△☉	**7:58 am**	4:58 am
☽⚹♃	**8:45 am**	5:45 am
☽□♂	**6:07 pm**	3:07 pm
☉⚹♃	**8:59 pm**	5:59 pm
☽□♆		10:59 pm

10 WEDNESDAY

☽□♆	**1:59 am**	
☽□♀	**3:23 am**	12:23 am
☽⚻⚵	**5:24 am**	2:24 am
☽△☿	**9:24 am**	6:24 am
☽□♀	**12:03 pm**	9:03 am
☽⚻♇	**3:04 pm**	12:04 pm
☽□♅	**3:14 pm**	12:14 pm
☽⚹⚳	**4:26 pm**	1:26 pm

11 THURSDAY

☽☍⚷	**3:10 am**	12:10 am
☽⚺♄	**3:49 am**	12:49 am
☽⚺⚴	**9:17 am**	6:17 am
☽□♃	**11:51 am**	8:51 am
☽⚻☉	**2:19 pm**	11:19 am
☽△♂	**11:33 pm**	8:33 pm

12 FRIDAY

☽△♆	**4:40 am**	1:40 am
☽△♀	**7:53 am**	4:53 am
☽△⚵	**8:54 am**	5:54 am
☽⚻☿	**9:33 am**	6:33 am
☽△♀	**3:49 pm**	12:49 pm
☿□⚵	**5:06 pm**	2:06 pm
☽☍♇	**5:56 pm**	2:56 pm
☽△♅	**6:06 pm**	3:06 pm
☽□⚳	**8:06 pm**	5:06 pm
☿⚺♀		10:18 pm

13 SATURDAY

☿⚺♀	**1:18 am**	
☽⚻⚷	**6:34 am**	3:34 am
☽⚹♄	**6:45 am**	3:45 am
☽⚹⚴	**12:39 pm**	9:39 am
☽△♃	**3:41 pm**	12:41 pm
☽☍☉	**9:38 pm**	6:38 pm
♄⚻⚷		11:38 pm

14 SUNDAY

♄⚻⚷	**2:38 am**	
☽⚻♂	**6:11 am**	3:11 am
☽⚻♆	**8:30 am**	5:30 am
☽☍☿	**9:40 am**	6:40 am
☽⚻♀	**1:32 pm**	10:32 am
☽□⚵	**1:44 pm**	10:44 am
☽⚻♀	**9:11 pm**	6:11 pm
☿⚺♆	**10:14 pm**	7:14 pm
☽⚻♇	**10:20 pm**	7:20 pm
☽⚻♅	**10:33 pm**	7:33 pm
☽△⚳		10:29 pm

15 MONDAY

☽△⚳	**1:29 am**	
♀△⚵	**4:20 am**	1:20 am
☿⚺♂	**7:40 am**	4:40 am
☽□♄	**11:37 am**	8:37 am
☽△⚷	**11:55 am**	8:55 am
☽□⚴	**6:11 pm**	3:11 pm
☽⚻♃	**9:48 pm**	6:48 pm
♂☌♆		9:19 pm

16 TUESDAY

♂☌♆	**12:19 am**	
☽⚻☉	**7:54 am**	4:54 am
☽⚻☿	**11:05 am**	8:05 am
☽☍♆	**2:59 pm**	11:59 am
☽☍♂	**3:54 pm**	12:54 pm
☽⚹⚵	**9:27 pm**	6:27 pm
☽☍♀	**9:57 pm**	6:57 pm
☿☌☉		11:53 pm

17 WEDNESDAY

☿☌☉	**2:53 am**	
☽☍♀	**5:43 am**	2:43 am
☽△♇	**5:44 am**	2:44 am
☽☍♅	**6:01 am**	3:01 am
♇⚹♀	**6:28 am**	3:28 am
☽⚻⚳	**10:07 am**	7:07 am
♅☌♀	**7:33 pm**	4:33 pm
☽△♄	**7:43 pm**	4:43 pm
☽□⚷	**8:35 pm**	5:35 pm

18 THURSDAY

☽△⚴	**3:11 am**	12:11 am
☽☍♃	**7:26 am**	4:26 am
☽△☿	**2:51 pm**	11:51 am
☽△☉	**10:34 pm**	7:34 pm
☽⚻♆		10:00 pm

19 FRIDAY

☽⚻♆	**1:00 am**	
☽⚻♂	**5:49 am**	2:49 am
☽⚺⚵	**8:48 am**	5:48 am
☽⚻♀	**9:48 am**	6:48 am
☽□♇	**4:38 pm**	1:38 pm
☽⚻♅	**4:58 pm**	1:58 pm
☽⚻♀	**5:59 pm**	2:59 pm
☽☍⚳	**10:26 pm**	7:26 pm

20 SATURDAY

☉⚺♆	**4:35 am**	1:35 am
☽⚻♄	**7:10 am**	4:10 am
☽⚹⚷	**8:38 am**	5:38 am
☽⚻⚴	**3:32 pm**	12:32 pm
☽⚻♃	**8:21 pm**	5:21 pm
☽□☿	**9:23 pm**	6:23 pm

21 SUNDAY

☿⚹♃	**7:01 am**	4:01 am
☽△♆	**1:42 pm**	10:42 am
☽□☉	**4:43 pm**	1:43 pm
♂△⚵	**7:42 am**	4:42 am
☽☌⚵	**10:36 pm**	7:36 pm
☽△♂	**10:46 pm**	7:46 pm
☽△♀	**11:42 pm**	8:42 pm

22 MONDAY

☽⚹♇	**5:39 am**	2:39 am
☽△♅	**6:03 am**	3:03 am
☽△♀	**8:29 am**	5:29 am
☽⚻⚳	**12:48 pm**	9:48 am
♀☌♂	**4:43 pm**	1:43 pm
☽☍♄	**8:09 pm**	5:09 pm
☽⚺⚷	**10:10 pm**	7:10 pm

23 TUESDAY

☽☍⚴	**5:08 am**	2:08 am
☽⚹☿	**5:59 am**	2:59 am
☽△♃	**10:15 am**	7:15 am
☿△⚴	**6:37 pm**	3:37 pm
☽□♆		11:29 pm

24 WEDNESDAY

☽□♆	**2:29 am**	
☽⚹☉	**10:49 am**	7:49 am
☽⚺⚵	**12:00 pm**	9:00 am
☽□♀	**12:44 pm**	9:44 am
☽□♂	**3:18 pm**	12:18 pm
☽⚺♇	**5:59 pm**	2:59 pm
☽□♅	**6:27 pm**	3:27 pm
☽□♀	**10:08 pm**	7:08 pm
☽△⚳		11:08 pm

25 THURSDAY

☽△⚳	**2:08 am**	
☉□⚵	**3:59 am**	12:59 am
☽⚻♄	**7:51 am**	4:51 am
☽☌⚷	**10:14 am**	7:14 am
♀⚺☉	**11:11 am**	8:11 am
☽⚺☿	**2:57 pm**	11:57 am
☽⚻⚴	**5:03 pm**	2:03 pm
☽□♃	**10:10 pm**	7:10 pm

26 FRIDAY

♂⚹♇	**11:05 pm**	8:05 pm
☽⚹♆	**12:47 pm**	9:47 am
♂☌♅	**7:39 am**	4:39 am
☽⚹⚵	**10:29 pm**	7:29 pm
☽⚹♀	**10:29 pm**	7:29 pm
♀△⚵	**10:59 pm**	7:59 pm
☽⚺☉		10:28 pm

27 SATURDAY

☽⚺☉	**1:28 am**	
☽☌♇	**3:26 am**	12:26 am
☽⚹♅	**3:57 am**	12:57 am
☽⚹♂	**4:27 am**	1:27 am
☽⚹♀	**8:36 am**	5:36 am
☽□⚳	**12:15 pm**	9:15 am
☽△♄	**4:25 pm**	1:25 pm
☽⚺⚷	**7:03 pm**	4:03 pm
☽☌☿	**10:40 pm**	7:40 pm
☽△⚴		10:41 pm

28 SUNDAY

☽△⚴	**1:41 am**	
☉⚺♇	**3:25 am**	12:25 am
☽⚹♃	**6:41 am**	3:41 am
☉⚺♅	**10:36 am**	7:36 am
☽⚺♆	**7:45 pm**	4:45 pm

29 MONDAY

☽⚺♀	**4:33 am**	1:33 am
☽□⚵	**5:29 am**	2:29 am
☽⚺♇	**9:36 am**	6:36 am
☽⚺♅	**10:09 am**	7:09 am
☽☌☉	**11:57 am**	8:57 am
☽⚺♂	**1:43 pm**	10:43 am
☽⚺♀	**3:39 pm**	12:39 pm
☽⚹⚳	**7:02 pm**	4:02 pm
☽□♄	**9:53 pm**	6:53 pm
☽⚹⚷		9:43 pm

30 TUESDAY

☽⚹⚷	**12:43 am**	
☽⚺☿	**4:47 am**	1:47 am
☽□⚴	**7:19 am**	4:19 am
☽⚺♃	**12:13 pm**	9:13 am
☽☌♆		9:08 pm

31 WEDNESDAY

☽☌♆	**12:08 am**	
☽☌♀	**7:57 am**	4:57 am
☽△⚵	**10:00 am**	7:00 am
☽⚹♇	**1:31 pm**	10:31 am
☽☌♅	**2:07 pm**	11:07 am
☽⚺☉	**7:42 pm**	4:42 pm
☽☌♂	**8:25 pm**	5:25 pm
☽☌♀	**8:28 pm**	5:28 pm
☽⚺⚳	**11:41 pm**	8:41 pm
☽⚹♄		10:26 pm

Eastern Standard Time in bold type
Pacific Standard Time in medium type

DECEMBER 1997

☽ Last Aspect day	EST / hr:mn / PST	asp	☽ Ingress sign day	EST / hr:mn / PST
11/30	**1:07 pm** 10:07 am	⚹ ♃	♑ 1	**1:38 pm** 10:38 am
3	**3:29 pm** 12:29 pm	☌ ♆	♒ 3	**6:58 pm** 3:58 pm
4	10:03 pm	☌ ♃	♓ 5	8:08 pm
5	**1:03 am**	☌ ♃	♓ 5	**11:08 pm**
7	8:16 pm	⚹ ♆	♈ 7	11:25 pm
7	**11:16 pm**	⚹ ♆	♈ 8	**2:25 am**
10	**3:23 am** 12:23 am	□ ♀	♉ 10	**5:01 am** 2:01 am
12	**4:40 am** 1:40 am	△ ♆	♊ 12	**7:36 am** 4:36 am
14	**9:40 am** 6:40 am	☍ ☿	♋ 14	**11:25 am** 8:25 am
16	**3:54 pm** 12:54 pm	☍ ♂	♌ 16	**5:58 pm** 2:58 pm
18	**10:34 pm** 7:34 pm	△ ☉	♍ 19	**3:59 am** 12:59 am
21	**1:42 pm** 10:42 am	△ ♆	♎ 21	**4:35 pm** 1:35 pm
23	11:29 pm	□ ♆	♏ 24	2:07 am
23	**2:29 am**	□ ♆	♏ 24	**5:07 am**
26	**12:47 pm** 9:47 am	⚹ ♆	♐ 26	**3:08 pm** 12:08 pm
28	**6:41 am** 3:41 am	⚹ ♃	♑ 28	**9:49 pm** 6:49 pm
30	9:08 pm	☌ ♆	♒ 30	10:59 pm
31	**12:08 am**	☌ ♆	♒ 31	**1:59 am**

☽ Phases & Eclipses phase	day	EST / hr:mn / PST
2nd Quarter	6	10:10 pm
2nd Quarter	7	**1:10 am**
Full Moon	13	**9:38 pm** 6:38 pm
4th Quarter	21	**4:43 pm** 1:43 pm
New Moon	29	**11:57 am** 8:57 am

Planet Ingress	day	EST / hr:mn / PST
⚵ ♎	9	**8:18 am** 5:18 am
♀ ♒	11	**11:39 pm** 8:39 pm
☿ ♐	13	**1:06 pm** 10:06 am
♂ ♒	17	10:37 pm
♂ ♒	18	**1:37 am**
☉ ♑	21	**3:07 pm** 12:07 pm

Planetary Motion	day	EST / hr:mn / PST
⚶ D	2	**1:03 pm** 10:03 am
☿ ℞	7	**11:50 am** 8:50 am
♄ D	16	**5:06 am** 2:06 am
♀ ℞	26	**4:17 pm** 1:17 pm
☿ D	27	**6:36 am** 3:36 am

DAY		SID.TIME	SUN	MOON	NODE	MERCURY	VENUS	MARS	JUPITER	SATURN	URANUS	NEPTUNE	PLUTO	CERES	PALLAS	JUNO	VESTA	CHIRON
M	1	4:39:33	08 ♐ 4924	19 ♐ 44	15 ♍℞ 45	00 ♑ 10	22 ♑ 57	16 ♑ 35	16 ♒ 33	13 ♈℞ 45	05 ♒ 40	27 ♑ 56	05 ♐ 37	04 ♓ 31	01 ♒ 21	27 ♍ 37	16 ♈℞ 32	11 ♏ 51
T	2	4:43:30	09 50 15	02 ♑ 59	15 32	00 59	23 41	17 21	16 42	13 43	05 43	27 58	05 39	04 44	01 38	27 55	16 32	11 59
W	3	4:47:27	10 51 06	16 25	15 22	01 42	24 24	18 08	16 52	13 42	05 45	28 00	05 42	04 57	01 55	28 12	16 D 31	12 07
T	4	4:51:23	11 51 59	00 ♒ 01	15 14	02 18	25 06	18 54	17 02	13 40	05 47	28 01	05 44	05 10	02 13	28 29	16 32	12 15
F	5	4:55:20	12 52 52	13 45	15 10	02 47	25 46	19 40	17 11	13 39	05 50	28 03	05 47	05 24	02 30	28 46	16 33	12 23
S	6	4:59:16	13 53 46	27 36	15 07	03 08	26 26	20 27	17 21	13 38	05 52	28 05	05 49	05 38	02 48	29 03	16 34	12 30
S	7	5:03:13	14 54 41	11 ♓ 34	15 06	03 20	27 04	21 13	17 31	13 37	05 55	28 07	05 51	05 52	03 05	29 19	16 35	12 38
M	8	5:07:09	15 55 37	25 38	15 06	03 ℞ 22	27 41	22 00	17 41	13 36	05 57	28 08	05 54	06 06	03 23	29 35	16 38	12 45
T	9	5:11:06	16 56 34	09 ♈ 48	15 04	03 13	28 16	22 46	17 51	13 35	06 00	28 10	05 56	06 20	03 41	29 51	16 40	12 53
W	10	5:15:02	17 57 31	24 03	15 01	02 54	28 50	23 33	18 02	13 34	06 02	28 12	05 58	06 35	03 58	00 ♎ 07	16 43	13 01
T	11	5:18:59	18 58 29	08 ♉ 19	14 54	02 23	29 23	24 20	18 12	13 34	06 05	28 14	06 01	06 49	04 16	00 22	16 46	13 08
F	12	5:22:56	19 59 27	22 34	14 46	01 40	29 54	25 06	18 23	13 33	06 08	28 16	06 03	07 04	04 34	00 38	16 50	13 15
S	13	5:26:52	21 00 26	06 ♊ 42	14 35	00 47	00 ♒ 24	25 53	18 33	13 33	06 10	28 18	06 05	07 20	04 52	00 53	16 54	13 23
S	14	5:30:49	22 01 26	20 38	14 22	29 ♐ 44	00 51	26 40	18 44	13 32	06 13	28 20	06 07	07 35	05 11	01 07	16 59	13 30
M	15	5:34:45	23 02 26	04 ♋ 17	14 10	28 32	01 18	27 27	18 55	13 32	06 16	28 22	06 10	07 50	05 29	01 22	17 04	13 37
T	16	5:38:42	24 03 28	17 36	13 58	27 14	01 42	28 13	19 06	13 D 32	06 19	28 24	06 12	08 06	05 47	01 36	17 09	13 44
W	17	5:42:38	25 04 30	00 ♌ 33	13 49	25 52	02 05	29 00	19 17	13 32	06 21	28 25	06 14	08 22	06 06	01 50	17 15	13 52
T	18	5:46:35	26 05 33	13 10	13 42	24 29	02 25	29 47	19 28	13 32	06 24	28 27	06 17	08 38	06 24	02 04	17 21	13 59
F	19	5:50:31	27 06 37	25 28	13 38	23 08	02 44	00 ♒ 34	19 40	13 32	06 27	28 29	06 19	08 54	06 42	02 17	17 28	14 06
S	20	5:54:28	28 07 41	07 ♍ 31	13 D 36	21 51	03 01	01 21	19 51	13 33	06 30	28 31	06 21	09 11	07 01	02 30	17 35	14 13
S	21	5:58:25	29 08 47	19 23	13 ℞ 36	20 41	03 15	02 08	20 03	13 33	06 33	28 34	06 23	09 27	07 20	02 43	17 42	14 19
M	22	6:02:21	00 ♑ 0953	01 ♎ 11	13 36	19 39	03 28	02 55	20 14	13 34	06 36	28 36	06 26	09 44	07 38	02 56	17 49	14 26
T	23	6:06:18	01 11 00	13 00	13 35	18 47	03 38	03 42	20 26	13 34	06 39	28 38	06 28	10 01	07 57	03 08	17 57	14 33
W	24	6:10:14	02 12 07	24 55	13 32	18 05	03 46	04 29	20 38	13 35	06 42	28 40	06 30	10 18	08 16	03 20	18 06	14 40
T	25	6:14:11	03 13 15	07 ♏ 02	13 27	17 34	03 52	05 16	20 49	13 36	06 45	28 42	06 32	10 35	08 35	03 32	18 15	14 46
F	26	6:18:07	04 14 23	19 24	13 20	17 14	03 ℞ 55	06 03	21 01	13 37	06 48	28 44	06 34	10 53	08 54	03 43	18 24	14 53
S	27	6:22:04	05 15 33	02 ♐ 04	13 10	17 D 05	03 56	06 50	21 13	13 38	06 51	28 46	06 36	11 10	09 13	03 54	18 33	15 00
S	28	6:26:00	06 16 43	15 04	12 58	17 05	03 55	07 37	21 26	13 39	06 54	28 48	06 39	11 28	09 32	04 05	18 43	15 06
M	29	6:29:57	07 17 53	28 25	12 47	17 14	03 51	08 24	21 38	13 41	06 58	28 50	06 41	11 46	09 51	04 16	18 53	15 12
T	30	6:33:54	08 19 03	12 ♑ 03	12 36	17 31	03 44	09 12	21 50	13 42	07 01	28 52	06 43	12 04	10 10	04 26	19 03	15 19
W	31	6:37:50	09 20 14	25 56	12 27	17 57	03 35	09 59	22 02	13 44	07 04	28 55	06 45	12 22	10 30	04 36	19 14	15 25

EPHEMERIS CALCULATED FOR 12 MIDNIGHT GREENWICH MEAN TIME. ALL OTHER DATA AND FACING ASPECTARIAN PAGE IN **EASTERN STANDARD TIME (BOLD)** AND PACIFIC STANDARD TIME (REGULAR).

JANUARY 1998

1 THURSDAY

☽⚹♄	**1:26 am**	
☽□⚷	**4:29 am**	1:29 am
☽⚹☿	**10:05 am**	7:05 am
☉⊻♀	**10:44 am**	7:44 am
☽⚹⚶	**11:14 am**	8:14 am
☽☌♃	**4:08 pm**	1:08 pm

2 FRIDAY

☽⊻♆	**3:14 am**	12:14 am
☽⊻♀	**10:01 am**	7:01 am
☉⊻♂	**1:16 pm**	10:16 am
☽⊼⚵	**1:26 pm**	10:26 am
☽□♇	**4:29 pm**	1:29 pm
☽⊻♅	**5:09 pm**	2:09 pm
☿△⚶	**5:19 pm**	2:19 pm
☽⊻♀		9:27 pm
☽⊻♂		11:13 pm
☽⚹☉		11:26 pm

3 SATURDAY

☽⊻♀	**12:27 am**	
☽⊻♂	**2:13 am**	
☽⚹☉	**2:26 am**	
☽☌⚳	**3:36 am**	12:36 am
☽⊻♄	**4:20 am**	1:20 am
☽△⚷	**7:37 am**	4:37 am
☽⊻⚶	**2:42 pm**	11:42 am
☽□☿	**3:40 pm**	12:40 pm
☽⊻♃	**7:40 pm**	4:40 pm
☉⚹⚳		10:17 pm

4 SUNDAY

☉⚹⚳	**1:17 am**	
☉□♄	**5:34 am**	2:34 am
☽⚹♆	**6:09 am**	3:09 am
☽⚹♀	**11:42 am**	8:42 am
♄⊻⚳	**4:21 pm**	1:21 pm
☽☍⚵	**4:46 pm**	1:46 pm
♂⚹♄	**5:58 pm**	2:58 pm
♂⊻⚳	**6:56 pm**	3:56 pm
☽△♇	**7:27 pm**	4:27 pm
☽⚹♅	**8:12 pm**	5:12 pm

5 MONDAY

☽⚹♀	**4:32 am**	1:32 am
☽☌♄	**7:22 am**	4:22 am
☽⊻⚳	**7:40 am**	4:40 am
☽⚹♂	**8:07 am**	5:07 am
☽□☉	**9:19 am**	6:19 am
☽⊼⚷	**10:54 am**	7:54 am
☽☌⚶	**6:27 pm**	3:27 pm
☽△☿	**10:13 pm**	7:13 pm
☽⚹♃	**11:29 pm**	8:29 pm

Eastern Standard Time in bold type
Pacific Standard Time in medium type

6 TUESDAY

☉⚹⚷	**9:24 am**	6:24 am
☽□♆	**9:25 am**	6:25 am
☽□♀	**1:28 pm**	10:28 am
☿⚹♃	**8:20 pm**	5:20 pm
☽⊼⚵	**8:29 pm**	5:29 pm
☽⊼♇	**10:50 pm**	7:50 pm
☽□♅	**11:41 pm**	8:41 pm

7 WEDNESDAY

☽□♀	**9:08 am**	6:08 am
☽⊻♄	**10:56 am**	7:56 am
☽⚹⚳	**12:18 pm**	9:18 am
☽□♂	**2:39 pm**	11:39 am
☽☍⚷	**2:43 pm**	11:43 am
♂□⚷	**4:07 pm**	1:07 pm
☽△☉	**4:50 pm**	1:50 pm
☽⊻⚶	**10:50 pm**	7:50 pm

8 THURSDAY

☽□♃	**3:56 am**	12:56 am
☽⊼☿	**6:03 am**	3:03 am
☽△♆	**1:22 pm**	10:22 am
☽△♀	**3:37 pm**	12:37 pm
☽△⚵		9:55 pm

9 FRIDAY

☽△⚵	**12:55 am**	
☽☍♇	**3:00 am**	12:00 am
☽△♅	**3:57 am**	12:57 am
☽△♀	**2:41 pm**	11:41 am
☽⚹♄	**3:23 pm**	12:23 pm
☽□⚳	**5:54 pm**	2:54 pm
☽⊼⚷	**7:27 pm**	4:27 pm
☽△♂	**10:15 pm**	7:15 pm
☽⊼☉		10:31 pm

10 SATURDAY

☽⊼☉	**1:31 am**	
☽⚹⚶	**4:19 am**	1:19 am
☽△♃	**9:31 am**	6:31 am
☽☍☿	**3:45 pm**	12:45 pm
☽⊼♆	**6:29 pm**	3:29 pm
☽⊼♀	**6:38 pm**	3:38 pm
♀☌♆	**10:02 pm**	7:02 pm
♄⚹♀		9:16 pm

11 SUNDAY

♄⚹♀	**12:16 am**	
☽□⚵	**6:40 am**	3:40 am
☽⊼♇	**8:32 am**	5:32 am
☽⊼♅	**9:37 am**	6:37 am
☿⊻♀	**2:30 pm**	11:30 am
☽□♄	**9:25 pm**	6:25 pm
☽⊼♀	**9:53 pm**	6:53 pm
☿⊻♆	**10:54 pm**	7:54 pm
☉□⚶		9:43 pm
☽△⚳		10:13 pm
☽△⚷		10:49 pm

12 MONDAY

☉□⚶	**12:43 am**	
☽△⚳	**1:13 am**	
☽△⚷	**1:49 am**	
☽⊼♂	**7:52 am**	4:52 am
☽□⚶	**11:41 am**	8:41 am
☽☍☉	**12:24 pm**	9:24 am
☽⊼♃	**5:03 pm**	2:03 pm
☽☍♀	**11:15 pm**	8:15 pm
☽☍♆		10:37 pm

13 TUESDAY

☽☍♆	**1:37 am**	
☽⊼☿	**4:26 am**	1:26 am
⚳△⚷	**9:01 am**	6:01 am
☽⚹⚵	**2:36 pm**	11:36 am
☽△♇	**4:18 pm**	1:18 pm
☽☍♅	**5:34 pm**	2:34 pm

14 WEDNESDAY

☽△♄	**5:55 am**	2:55 am
☽☍♀	**7:43 am**	4:43 am
☽□⚷	**10:43 am**	7:43 am
☽⊼⚳	**11:14 am**	8:14 am
☽☍♂	**8:33 pm**	5:33 pm
☽△⚶	**9:50 pm**	6:50 pm
☽⊼☉		11:35 pm

15 THURSDAY

☽⊼☉	**2:35 am**	
☽☍♃	**3:23 am**	12:23 am
☽⊼♀	**6:07 am**	3:07 am
☽⊼♆	**11:31 am**	8:31 am
☉⊻♃	**2:41 pm**	11:41 am
☽△☿	**9:13 pm**	6:13 pm
☽⊻⚵		10:18 pm
♂⚹⚶		10:39 pm
☽□♇		11:53 pm

16 FRIDAY

☽⊻⚵	**1:18 am**	
♂⚹⚶	**1:39 am**	
☽□♇	**2:53 am**	
☽⊼♅	**4:21 am**	1:21 am
♀☌☉	**6:20 am**	3:20 am
☽⊼♄	**5:15 pm**	2:15 pm
☽⊼♀	**8:33 pm**	5:33 pm
♀⊻♃	**9:03 pm**	6:03 pm
☽⚹⚷	**10:24 pm**	7:24 pm
☽☍⚳		9:16 pm

17 SATURDAY

☽☍⚳	**12:16 am**	
☽⊼⚶	**10:53 am**	7:53 am
☿□⚵	**11:27 am**	8:27 am
☽⊼♂	**12:28 pm**	9:28 am
☽△♀	**3:10 pm**	12:10 pm
☽⊼♃	**4:28 pm**	1:28 pm
☽△☉	**8:07 pm**	5:07 pm
☽△♆	**11:54 pm**	8:54 pm
☿⊻♇		9:55 pm

18 SUNDAY

☿⊻♇	**12:55 am**	
♀⊻♂	**12:27 pm**	9:27 am
☽☌⚵	**2:09 pm**	11:09 am
☿⊻♅	**3:14 pm**	12:14 pm
☽⚹♇	**3:38 pm**	12:38 pm
☽△♅	**5:16 pm**	2:16 pm
☽□☿	**5:32 pm**	2:32 pm

19 MONDAY

☽☍♄	**6:23 am**	3:23 am
☽△♀	**11:11 am**	8:11 am
☽⊻⚷	**11:41 am**	8:41 am
☽⊼⚳	**2:58 pm**	11:58 am
☉☌♆	**5:34 pm**	2:34 pm
♀□⚶		9:43 pm
☽□♀		10:09 pm
☽☍⚶		10:12 pm

20 TUESDAY

♀□⚶	**12:43 am**	
☽□♀	**1:09 am**	
☽☍⚶	**1:12 am**	
☽△♂	**5:44 am**	2:44 am
☽△♃	**6:34 am**	3:34 am
♀□⚷	**10:03 am**	7:03 am
☽□♆	**12:57 pm**	9:57 am
☽□☉	**2:41 pm**	11:41 am
♂☌♃	**11:07 pm**	8:07 pm
☽⊻⚵		11:58 pm

21 WEDNESDAY

☽⊻⚵	**2:58 am**	
☽⊻♇	**4:21 am**	1:21 am
☽□♅	**6:07 am**	3:07 am
☽⚹☿	**1:59 pm**	10:59 am
☽⊼♄	**6:52 pm**	3:52 pm
☽☌⚷		9:02 pm
☽□♀		9:52 pm

22 THURSDAY

☽☌⚷	**12:02 am**	
☽□♀	**12:52 am**	
☽△⚳	**4:33 am**	1:33 am
☽⚹♀	**10:02 am**	7:02 am
☽⊼⚶	**1:59 pm**	10:59 am
☽□♃	**6:52 pm**	3:52 pm
☽□♂	**8:57 pm**	5:57 pm
☽⚹♆		9:00 pm

23 FRIDAY

☽⚹♆	**12:00 am**	
☽⚹☉	**6:37 am**	3:37 am
☿□♄	**9:08 am**	6:08 am
☽⚹⚵	**1:12 pm**	10:12 am
☽☌♇	**2:31 pm**	11:31 am
☽⚹♅	**4:19 pm**	1:19 pm

24 SATURDAY

☽△♄	**4:19 am**	1:19 am
☽⊻☿	**6:37 am**	3:37 am
☽⊻⚷	**9:10 am**	6:10 am
☽⚹♀	**11:07 am**	8:07 am
☽□⚳	**2:38 pm**	11:38 am
☽⊻♀	**4:11 pm**	1:11 pm
☽△⚶	**11:08 pm**	8:08 pm
♂⊻♆	**11:57 pm**	8:57 pm

25 SUNDAY

☽⚹♃	**3:27 am**	12:27 am
☿⚹⚷	**6:21 am**	3:21 am
☽⊻♆	**7:26 am**	4:26 am
☽⚹♂	**7:52 am**	4:52 am
♀⚹⚳	**5:07 pm**	2:07 pm
☽⊻☉	**5:52 pm**	2:52 pm
☽□⚵	**7:37 pm**	4:37 pm
☽⊻♇	**8:55 pm**	5:55 pm
☽⊻♅	**10:44 pm**	7:44 pm

26 MONDAY

☿⊻♀	**9:09 am**	6:09 am
☽□♄	**9:59 am**	6:59 am
☽⚹⚷	**2:31 pm**	11:31 am
☉△⚵	**5:15 pm**	2:15 pm
☽⊻♀	**5:24 pm**	2:24 pm
☽☌☿	**6:09 pm**	3:09 pm
☽☌♀	**7:17 pm**	4:17 pm
☽⚹⚳	**8:45 pm**	5:45 pm
☿☌♀		11:47 pm

27 TUESDAY

☿☌♀	**2:47 am**	
☽□⚶	**4:29 am**	1:29 am
☽⊻♃	**8:20 am**	5:20 am
☽☌♆	**11:22 am**	8:22 am
☉⚹♇	**11:47 am**	8:47 am
☽⊻♂	**2:40 pm**	11:40 am
☽△⚵	**10:45 pm**	7:45 pm
☽⚹♇		9:06 pm
☽☌☉		10:01 pm
☿⚹⚳		10:17 pm
☽☌♅		10:58 pm

28 WEDNESDAY

☽⚹♇	**12:06 am**	
☽☌☉	**1:01 am**	
☿⚹⚳	**1:17 am**	
☽☌♅	**1:58 am**	
♀⊻♀	**8:14 am**	5:14 am
☽⚹♄	**12:47 pm**	9:47 am
☉☌♅	**3:08 pm**	12:08 pm
☽□⚷	**5:05 pm**	2:05 pm
☽⊻♀	**8:15 pm**	5:15 pm
☽☌♀	**8:50 pm**	5:50 pm
☽⊻⚳		9:08 pm
☽⊻☿		11:09 pm

29 THURSDAY

☽⊻⚳	**12:08 am**	
☽⊻☿	**2:09 am**	
☽⚹⚶	**7:24 am**	4:24 am
☽☌♃	**10:54 am**	7:54 am
☽⊻♆	**1:11 pm**	10:11 am
☽☌♂	**7:06 pm**	4:06 pm
☽⊼⚵		9:07 pm
☽□♇		10:36 pm

30 FRIDAY

☽⊼⚵	**12:07 am**	
☽□♇	**1:36 am**	
☽⊻♅	**3:33 am**	12:33 am
☽⊻☉	**6:06 am**	3:06 am
☽⊻♄	**2:17 pm**	11:17 am
☽△⚷	**6:30 pm**	3:30 pm
☽⚹♀	**8:32 pm**	5:32 pm
☽⊻♀	**11:10 pm**	8:10 pm
☽☌⚳		11:33 pm

31 SATURDAY

☽☌⚳	**2:33 am**	
☽⚹☿	**9:06 am**	6:06 am
☽⊻⚶	**9:38 am**	6:38 am
☽⊻♃	**12:54 pm**	9:54 am
☽⚹♆	**2:31 pm**	11:31 am
☿□⚶	**3:17 pm**	12:17 pm
☽⊻♂	**11:11 pm**	8:11 pm
☽☍⚵		10:17 pm
☽△♇		11:59 pm

JANUARY 1998

☽ Last Aspect day	EST / hr:mn / PST		asp	☽ Ingress sign day	EST / hr:mn / PST	
1	**4:08 pm**	1:08 pm	☌ ♃	♓ 2	**4:56 am**	1:56 am
4	**6:09 am**	3:09 am	✶ ♆	♈ 4	**7:44 am**	4:44 am
6	**9:25 am**	6:25 am	□ ♆	♉ 6	**10:53 am**	7:53 am
8	**1:22 pm**	10:22 am	△ ♆	♊ 8	**2:42 pm**	11:42 am
10	**3:45 pm**	12:45 pm	☍ ☿	♋ 10	**7:43 pm**	4:43 pm
12		10:37 pm	☍ ♆	♌ 12		11:45 pm
13	**1:37 am**		☍ ♆	♌ 13	**2:45 am**	
15	**3:23 am**	12:23 am	☍ ♃	♍ 15	**12:31 pm**	9:31 am
17		8:54 pm	△ ♆	♎ 17		9:45 pm
17	**11:54 pm**		△ ♆	♎ 18	**12:45 am**	
20	**12:57 pm**	9:57 am	□ ♆	♏ 20	**1:35 pm**	10:35 am
22		9:00 pm	✶ ♆	♐ 22		9:26 pm
23	**12:00 am**		✶ ♆	♐ 23	**12:26 am**	
25	**3:27 am**	12:27 am	✶ ♃	♑ 25	**7:40 am**	4:40 am
27	**11:22 am**	8:22 am	☌ ♆	♒ 27	**11:27 am**	8:27 am
29	**10:54 am**	7:54 am	☌ ♃	♓ 29	**1:09 pm**	10:09 am
31	**9:06 am**	6:06 am	✶ ☿	♈ 31	**2:21 pm**	11:21 am

☽ Phases & Eclipses

phase	day	EST / hr:mn / PST	
2nd Quarter	5	**9:19 am**	6:19 am
Full Moon	12	**12:24 pm**	9:24 am
4th Quarter	20	**2:41 pm**	11:41 am
New Moon	27		10:01 pm
New Moon	28	**1:01 am**	

Planet Ingress

	day	EST / hr:mn / PST	
♀ ♑	9	**4:04 pm**	1:04 pm
☿ ♑	12	**11:20 am**	8:20 am
☉ ♒	19		10:46 pm
☉ ♒	20	**1:46 am**	
♂ ♓	25	**4:26 am**	1:26 am
♆ ♒	28	**9:49 pm**	6:49 pm

Planetary Motion

	day	EST / hr:mn / PST	
⚵ ℞	25	**4:25 pm**	12:25 pm

DATE		SID.TIME	SUN	MOON	NODE	MERCURY	VENUS	MARS	JUPITER	SATURN	URANUS	NEPTUNE	PLUTO	CERES	PALLAS	JUNO	VESTA	CHIRON
T	1	6:41:47	10 ♑ 21	09 ♒ 59	12 ♍ ℞ 20	18 ♐ 29	03 ♒ ℞ 24	10 ♒ 46	22 ♒ 15	13 ♈ 45	07 ♒ 07	28 ♑ 57	06 ♐ 46	12 ♓ 40	10 ♒ 49	04 ♎ 45	19 ♈ 25	15 ♏ 31
F	2	6:45:43	11 22	24 07	12 16	19 07	03 10	11 33	22 27	13 47	07 10	28 59	06 48	12 59	11 08	04 54	19 36	15 37
S	3	6:49:40	12 23	08 ♓ 19	12 D 14	19 50	02 54	12 20	22 40	13 49	07 14	29 01	06 50	13 17	11 28	05 03	19 48	15 43
S	4	6:53:36	13 24	22 30	12 14	20 39	02 35	13 08	22 53	13 51	07 17	29 03	06 52	13 36	11 47	05 12	20 00	15 49
M	5	6:57:33	14 26	06 ♈ 38	12 ℞ 14	21 31	02 13	13 55	23 05	13 53	07 20	29 05	06 54	13 55	12 06	05 20	20 12	15 55
T	6	7:01:29	15 27	20 43	12 14	22 28	01 50	14 42	23 18	13 55	07 24	29 08	06 56	14 14	12 26	05 28	20 24	16 01
W	7	7:05:26	16 28	04 ♉ 44	12 12	23 28	01 24	15 30	23 31	13 57	07 27	29 10	06 58	14 33	12 45	05 35	20 37	16 06
T	8	7:09:23	17 29	18 39	12 09	24 32	00 57	16 17	23 44	14 00	07 30	29 12	07 00	14 52	13 05	05 42	20 50	16 12
F	9	7:13:19	18 30	02 ♊ 28	12 03	25 38	00 27	17 04	23 57	14 02	07 34	29 14	07 02	15 11	13 25	05 49	21 04	16 17
S	10	7:17:16	19 31	16 07	11 55	26 46	29 ♑ 56	17 51	24 10	14 05	07 37	29 17	07 03	15 31	13 44	05 55	21 17	16 23
S	11	7:21:12	20 32	29 36	11 46	27 57	29 23	18 39	24 23	14 08	07 40	29 19	07 05	15 50	14 04	06 01	21 31	16 28
M	12	7:25:09	21 34	12 ♋ 51	11 37	29 10	28 49	19 26	24 37	14 10	07 44	29 21	07 07	16 10	14 24	06 07	21 45	16 33
T	13	7:29:05	22 35	25 52	11 28	00 ♑ 24	28 14	20 13	24 50	14 13	07 47	29 23	07 09	16 30	14 43	06 12	22 00	16 38
W	14	7:33:02	23 36	08 ♌ 35	11 21	01 40	27 38	21 01	25 03	14 16	07 51	29 26	07 11	16 50	15 03	06 17	22 14	16 44
T	15	7:36:59	24 37	21 03	11 17	02 58	27 02	21 48	25 16	14 19	07 54	29 28	07 13	17 10	15 23	06 22	22 29	16 49
F	16	7:40:55	25 38	03 ♍ 17	11 14	04 16	26 25	22 35	25 30	14 23	07 57	29 30	07 14	17 30	15 43	06 26	22 44	16 53
S	17	7:44:52	26 39	15 18	11 D 14	05 37	25 48	23 23	25 43	14 26	08 01	29 32	07 16	17 50	16 03	06 30	23 00	16 58
S	18	7:48:48	27 40	27 10	11 15	06 58	25 11	24 10	25 57	14 29	08 04	29 35	07 18	18 10	16 23	06 33	23 15	17 03
M	19	7:52:45	28 41	08 ♎ 58	11 17	08 20	24 35	24 57	26 11	14 33	08 08	29 37	07 19	18 31	16 42	06 36	23 31	17 08
T	20	7:56:41	29 42	20 47	11 ℞ 18	09 44	23 59	25 45	26 24	14 36	08 11	29 39	07 21	18 51	17 02	06 39	23 47	17 12
W	21	8:00:38	00 ♒ 43	02 ♏ 42	11 18	11 08	23 24	26 32	26 38	14 40	08 15	29 42	07 23	19 12	17 22	06 41	24 03	17 17
T	22	8:04:34	01 44	14 48	11 17	12 33	22 51	27 19	26 52	14 44	08 18	29 44	07 24	19 33	17 42	06 43	24 20	17 21
F	23	8:08:31	02 45	27 09	11 14	13 59	22 19	28 07	27 05	14 48	08 22	29 46	07 26	19 53	18 02	06 44	24 36	17 25
S	24	8:12:27	03 47	09 ♐ 51	11 10	15 26	21 48	28 54	27 19	14 52	08 25	29 48	07 27	20 14	18 22	06 45	24 53	17 29
S	25	8:16:24	04 48	22 56	11 04	16 53	21 19	29 41	27 33	14 56	08 29	29 51	07 29	20 35	18 42	06 ℞ 46	25 10	17 33
M	26	8:20:21	05 49	06 ♑ 25	10 58	18 22	20 52	00 ♓ 29	27 47	15 00	08 32	29 53	07 30	20 56	19 02	06 46	25 28	17 37
T	27	8:24:17	06 50	20 17	10 53	19 51	20 28	01 16	28 01	15 04	08 36	29 55	07 32	21 17	19 22	06 46	25 45	17 41
W	28	8:28:14	07 51	04 ♒ 30	10 48	21 21	20 05	02 03	28 15	15 08	08 39	29 57	07 33	21 39	19 43	06 45	26 03	17 45
T	29	8:32:10	08 52	18 58	10 45	22 51	19 44	02 51	28 29	15 13	08 43	30 00	07 35	22 00	20 03	06 44	26 21	17 48
F	30	8:36:07	09 53	03 ♓ 34	10 D 43	24 22	19 26	03 38	28 43	15 17	08 46	00 ♒ 02	07 36	22 21	20 23	06 42	26 39	17 52
S	31	8:40:03	10 54	18 14	10 43	25 54	19 11	04 25	28 57	15 22	08 50	00 04	07 37	22 43	20 43	06 40	26 57	17 55

EPHEMERIS CALCULATED FOR 12 MIDNIGHT GREENWICH MEAN TIME. ALL OTHER DATA AND FACING ASPECTARIAN PAGE IN **EASTERN STANDARD TIME (BOLD)** AND PACIFIC STANDARD TIME (REGULAR).

FEBRUARY 1998

1 SUNDAY
☽☍⚵	**1:17 am**	
☽△♇	**2:59 am**	
☽⚹♅	**5:05 am**	2:05 am
☽⚹☉	**11:13 am**	8:13 am
☽☌♄	**4:03 pm**	1:03 pm
☽⚻⚷	**8:16 pm**	5:16 pm
☽□♀	**9:29 pm**	6:29 pm
☽⚹♀		11:03 pm
☿⚺♃		11:29 pm

2 MONDAY
☽⚹♀	**2:03 am**	
☿⚺♃	**2:29 am**	
☽⚺⚳	**5:36 am**	2:36 am
♂⚻⚵	**11:51 am**	8:51 am
☽☌⚶	**12:41 pm**	9:41 am
☿☌♆	**12:53 pm**	9:53 am
☽⚹♃	**3:46 pm**	12:46 pm
☽□♆	**4:43 pm**	1:43 pm
☽□☿	**5:11 pm**	2:11 pm

3 TUESDAY
☽⚻⚵	**3:29 am**	12:29 am
☽⚹♂	**4:28 am**	1:28 am
☽⚻♇	**5:30 am**	2:30 am
☽□♅	**7:48 am**	4:48 am
☽□☉	**5:53 pm**	2:53 pm
☽⚺♄	**7:13 pm**	4:13 pm
♂□♇	**11:10 pm**	8:10 pm
☽☍⚷	**11:28 pm**	8:28 pm
☽△♀		9:08 pm

4 WEDNESDAY
☽△♀	**12:08 am**	
☽□♀	**6:32 am**	3:32 am
☽⚹⚳	**10:20 am**	7:20 am
☉⚹♄	**1:34 pm**	10:34 am
☽⚺⚶	**5:31 pm**	2:31 pm
☽□♃	**8:24 pm**	5:24 pm
☽△♆	**8:37 pm**	5:37 pm

5 THURSDAY
☽△☿	**3:47 am**	12:47 am
☽△⚵	**7:24 am**	4:24 am
☽☍♇	**9:50 am**	6:50 am
♃⚺♆	**10:12 am**	7:12 am
☽□♂	**11:55 am**	8:55 am
☽△♅	**12:22 pm**	9:22 am
♂⚺♅	**8:09 pm**	5:09 pm
☽⚹♄		9:21 pm
☽△☉		11:58 pm

6 FRIDAY
☽⚹♄	**12:21 am**	
☽△☉	**2:58 am**	
☽⚻⚷	**4:37 am**	1:37 am
☽⚻♀	**5:02 am**	2:02 am
☿△⚵	**8:57 am**	5:57 am
☽△♀	**1:11 pm**	10:11 am
☽□⚳	**5:16 pm**	2:16 pm
☽⚹⚶		9:34 pm
☉□⚷		10:43 pm
☽⚻♆		11:35 pm

7 SATURDAY
☽⚹⚶	**12:34 am**	
☉□⚷	**1:43 am**	
☽⚻♆	**2:35 am**	
☽△♃	**3:13 am**	12:13 am
☿⚹♇	**6:55 am**	3:55 am
♀⚺☉	**7:18 am**	4:18 am
☽□⚵	**1:19 pm**	10:19 am
☽⚻♇	**4:16 pm**	1:16 pm
☽⚻☿	**5:36 pm**	2:36 pm
☽⚻♅	**7:04 pm**	4:04 pm
☽△♂	**9:53 pm**	6:53 pm

8 SUNDAY
☿☌♅	**5:40 am**	2:40 am
☽□♄	**7:40 am**	4:40 am
☽△⚷	**11:56 am**	8:56 am
☽☍♀	**12:28 pm**	9:28 am
☽⚻☉	**2:45 pm**	11:45 am
☽⚻♀	**10:09 pm**	7:09 pm
☽△⚳		11:34 pm

9 MONDAY
☽△⚳	**2:34 am**	
☽□⚶	**9:59 am**	6:59 am
☽☍♆	**10:46 am**	7:46 am
☽⚻♃	**12:21 pm**	9:21 am
☽⚹⚵	**9:20 pm**	6:20 pm
☽△♇		9:55 pm

10 TUESDAY
☽△♇	**12:55 am**	
☽☍♅	**4:01 am**	1:01 am
☿⚺♂	**5:53 am**	2:53 am
☽⚻♂	**10:31 am**	7:31 am
☽☍☿	**10:54 am**	7:54 am
☽△♄	**5:16 pm**	2:16 pm
♆□⚶	**6:32 pm**	3:32 pm
☽□⚷	**9:28 pm**	6:28 pm
☽⚻♀	**10:35 pm**	7:35 pm

11 WEDNESDAY
☽☍☉	**5:23 am**	2:23 am
☽☍♀	**9:33 am**	6:33 am
☽⚻⚳	**2:19 pm**	11:19 am
☽⚻♆	**9:11 pm**	6:11 pm
☽△⚶	**9:52 pm**	6:52 pm
☽☍♃	**11:49 pm**	8:49 pm

12 THURSDAY
☽⚺⚵	**7:26 am**	4:26 am
☽□♇	**11:46 am**	8:46 am
☿⚹♄	**12:01 pm**	9:01 am
☽⚻♅	**3:11 pm**	12:11 pm
☽☍♂		10:46 pm

13 FRIDAY
☽☍♂	**1:46 am**	
☽⚻♄	**5:04 am**	2:04 am
☽⚻☿	**7:45 am**	4:45 am
☽⚹⚷	**9:07 am**	6:07 am
☽△♀	**11:21 am**	8:21 am
☿□⚷	**5:21 pm**	2:21 pm
☽⚻☉	**10:40 pm**	7:40 pm
☽⚻♀	**11:08 pm**	8:08 pm

14 SATURDAY
☽☍⚳	**4:15 am**	1:15 am
☉☌♀	**6:41 am**	3:41 am
☽△♆	**9:31 am**	6:31 am
☽⚻⚶	**11:49 am**	8:49 am
☽⚻♃	**1:18 pm**	10:18 am
☿⚺♀	**1:22 pm**	10:22 am
☽☌⚵	**7:11 pm**	4:11 pm
☽⚹♇		9:20 pm

15 SUNDAY
☽⚹♇	**12:20 am**	
☽△♅	**4:02 am**	1:02 am
♂⚺♄	**10:34 am**	7:34 am
☽☍♄	**6:20 pm**	3:20 pm
☽⚻♂	**6:49 pm**	3:49 pm
☽⚺⚷	**10:05 pm**	7:05 pm
☽□♀		10:58 pm

16 MONDAY
☽□♀	**1:58 am**	
☽△☿	**7:01 am**	4:01 am
☽△♀	**1:49 pm**	10:49 am
☽△☉	**5:15 pm**	2:15 pm
☽⚻⚳	**7:10 pm**	4:10 pm
☽□♆	**10:38 pm**	7:38 pm
☽☍⚶		11:34 pm

17 TUESDAY
☽☍⚶	**2:34 am**	
☽△♃	**3:28 am**	12:28 am
☽⚺⚵	**7:19 am**	4:19 am
☽⚺♇	**1:13 pm**	10:13 am
☽□♅	**5:06 pm**	2:06 pm
♂△⚷	**9:29 pm**	6:29 pm

18 WEDNESDAY
☉⚺⚳	**3:55 am**	12:55 am
☽⚻♄	**7:21 am**	4:21 am
☽☌⚷	**10:39 am**	7:39 am
☽△♂	**11:32 am**	8:32 am
☿☌♀	**1:30 pm**	10:30 am
☽⚹♀	**4:25 pm**	1:25 pm

19 THURSDAY
☽□♀	**3:29 am**	12:29 am
☽□☿	**5:26 am**	2:26 am
☽△⚳	**8:51 am**	5:51 am
☉⚺♆	**10:24 am**	7:24 am
☽□☉	**10:27 am**	7:27 am
☽⚹♆	**10:27 am**	7:27 am
☽⚻⚶	**3:48 pm**	12:48 pm
☽□♃	**4:06 pm**	1:06 pm
☽⚹⚵	**5:52 pm**	2:52 pm
☽☌♇		9:18 pm

20 FRIDAY
☽☌♇	**12:18 am**	
☽⚹♅	**4:13 am**	1:13 am
☿⚺⚳	**9:59 am**	6:59 am
☿⚺♆	**4:11 pm**	1:11 pm
☽△♄	**5:55 pm**	2:55 pm
☽⚺⚷	**8:39 pm**	5:39 pm
♃⚹⚶	**11:06 pm**	8:06 pm
☽□♂		10:08 pm

21 SATURDAY
☽□♂	**1:08 am**	
☽⚺♀	**4:15 am**	1:15 am
☽⚹♀	**1:53 pm**	10:53 am
⚵⚻⚶	**4:59 pm**	1:59 pm
♆⚹⚳	**5:48 pm**	2:48 pm
☽⚺♆	**7:03 pm**	4:03 pm
♃⚻⚵	**9:59 pm**	6:59 pm
☽⚹☿	**11:17 pm**	8:17 pm
☽⚹☉	**11:34 pm**	8:34 pm
☽⚹♃		10:13 pm
☽△⚶		10:27 pm

22 SUNDAY
☽□⚵	**1:07 am**	
☽⚹♃	**1:13 am**	
☽△⚶	**1:27 am**	
☿☌☉	**3:29 am**	12:29 am
☽⚺♇	**7:53 am**	4:53 am
☿⚻⚵	**11:34 am**	8:34 am
☽⚺♅	**11:42 am**	8:42 am
☿☌♃	**3:07 pm**	12:07 pm
☉⚻⚵	**5:15 pm**	2:15 pm
☿⚹⚶	**6:17 pm**	3:17 pm
☽□♄		9:38 pm
☽⚹⚷		11:50 pm

23 MONDAY
☽□♄	**12:38 am**	
☽⚹⚷	**2:50 am**	
☉☌♃	**3:50 am**	12:50 am
☽⚹♂	**10:08 am**	7:08 am
☽☌♀	**12:01 pm**	9:01 am
☉⚹⚶	**1:30 pm**	10:30 am
☽⚺♀	**8:05 pm**	5:05 pm
☽☌♆	**11:45 pm**	8:45 pm
☽⚹⚳		10:06 pm

24 TUESDAY
☽⚹⚳	**1:06 am**	
☽△⚵	**4:37 am**	1:37 am
☽⚺♃	**6:16 am**	3:16 am
☽□⚶	**6:57 am**	3:57 am
☽⚺☉	**7:47 am**	4:47 am
☽⚺☿	**11:21 am**	8:21 am
☽⚹♇	**11:38 am**	8:38 am
☿□♇	**1:32 pm**	10:32 am
☽☌♅	**3:22 pm**	12:22 pm

25 WEDNESDAY
☽⚹♄	**3:41 am**	12:41 am
☽□⚷	**5:25 am**	2:25 am
☽⚺♂	**3:05 pm**	12:05 pm
☽⚺♀	**4:10 pm**	1:10 pm
☿⚺♅	**6:57 pm**	3:57 pm
☽☌♀	**10:51 pm**	7:51 pm
☽⚺♆		10:19 pm

26 THURSDAY
☽⚺♆	**1:19 am**	
☽⚺⚳	**3:48 am**	12:48 am
☽⚻⚵	**5:13 am**	2:13 am
☽☌♃	**8:14 am**	5:14 am
☽⚹⚶	**9:19 am**	6:19 am
☽☌☉	**12:26 pm**	9:26 am
☽□♇	**12:36 pm**	9:36 am
☉□♇	**2:59 pm**	11:59 am
☽⚺♅	**4:21 pm**	1:21 pm
☽☌☿	**7:21 pm**	4:21 pm

27 FRIDAY
☽⚺♄	**4:26 am**	1:26 am
☽△⚷	**5:48 am**	2:48 am
⚳☍⚵	**3:44 pm**	12:44 pm
☽☌♂	**5:51 pm**	2:51 pm
☽⚹♀	**6:25 pm**	3:25 pm
☽⚺♀	**11:57 pm**	8:57 pm
☽⚹♆		10:23 pm

28 SATURDAY
☽⚹♆	**1:23 am**	
☽☍⚵	**4:30 am**	1:30 am
☽☌⚳	**5:01 am**	2:01 am
☽⚺♃	**8:56 am**	5:56 am
☽⚺⚶	**10:26 am**	7:26 am
☽△♇	**12:32 pm**	9:32 am
☽⚺☉	**3:47 pm**	12:47 pm
☽⚹♅	**4:25 pm**	1:25 pm
☉⚺♅		10:49 pm
☽⚺☿		11:16 pm

Eastern Standard Time in bold type
Pacific Standard Time in medium type

FEBRUARY 1998

☽ Last Aspect

day	EST / hr:mn / PST	asp
1	**3:46 pm** 12:46 pm	✱ ♂
3	**9:08 pm**	△ ♀
4	**12:00 am**	△ ♂
5	11:58 am	
7	**2:58 am**	
8	**12:28 pm** 9:28 am	
11	**5:23 am** 2:23 am	
13	**11:21 am** 8:21 am	
16	**5:15 pm** 2:15 pm	
19	**5:26 am** 2:26 am	

☽ Ingress

sign	day	EST / hr:mn / PST
♉	2	**4:25 pm** 1:25 pm
♊	4	12:08 pm
♋	6	**8:09 pm**
♌	9	**1:58 am** 10:58 pm
♍	11	**8:10 pm** 5:10 pm
♎	14	**8:18 am** 5:18 am
♏	16	**9:14 pm** 6:14 pm
♐	19	**8:56 am** 3:56 am

☽ Last Aspect

day	EST / hr:mn / PST	asp	sign	day	EST / hr:mn / PST
21	**1:08 am** 10:08 pm	□ ♂	♑ 21		
23	**12:01 am** 9:01 am	□ ♂	≈ 23	**1:30 pm**	
25	**3:41 am** 12:41 am	♂ ♀	♓ 25	**11:42 am**	7:10 pm
27	**6:25 pm** 3:25 pm	✱ ♀	♈ 27	**11:42 am**	8:42 pm

☽ Phases & Eclipses

phase	day	EST / hr:mn / PST
2nd Quarter	3	**5:53 pm** 2:53 pm
Full Moon	11	**5:23 am** 2:23 am
4th Quarter	19	**10:27 am** 7:27 am
New Moon	26	**12:26 pm** 9:26 am
	26	♓ 7°55′

Planet Ingress

	day	EST / hr:mn / PST
☿ ≈	2	**10:15 am** 7:15 am
♃ ♓	4	**5:52 am** 2:52 am
⊙ ♓	18	**3:55 pm** 12:55 pm
☿ ♓	20	**5:22 am** 2:22 am
♀ ♓	27	**12:42 pm** 9:42 am

Planetary Motion

	day	EST / hr:mn / PST
♀ R	5	**4:26 pm** 1:26 pm

Main Ephemeris

DATE	SID.TIME	SUN	MOON	NODE	MERCURY	VENUS	MARS	JUPITER	SATURN	URANUS	NEPTUNE	PLUTO	CERES	PALLAS	JUNO	VESTA	CHIRON
1 S	8:44:00	11 ≈ 54	02 ♈ 49	10 ♍ 44	27 ♑	18 ♑ R 57	05 ♓ 13	29 ♒ 11	15 ♈ 26	08 ≈ 53	00 ≈ 06	07 ✗ 39	23 ♓ 05	21 ≈ 03	05 ♈ 38	27 ♏ 15	17 ♏ 59
2 M	8:47:56	12 55	16 16	10 R	29	47	06	29	15	55	07	40	23	21	06	34	02
3 T	8:51:53	13 56	01 ♉ 15	10	00 ≈	38	07	29	15	57	09	41	23	22	06	53	05
4 W	8:55:50	14 57	16 33	10 R	03	28	08	00 ♓	15	59	11	42	24	22	06	12	08
5 T	8:59:46	15 58	01 ♊ 53	10	05	21	09	00	15	01	13	43	24	23	06	31	11
6 F	9:03:43	16 59	17 02	10	06	15	10	00	15	03	16	44	24	23	06	10	14
7 S	9:07:39	17 00	01 ♋ 58	10	06	12	11	00	16	05	18	45	25	23	06	29	16
8 S	9:11:36	19 00	16 30	10	06 D	10	12	00	16	07	22	47	25	23	06	19	19
9 M	9:15:32	20 01	00 ♌ 41	10	05	10	13	51	16	09	24	48	26	24	06	49	21
10 T	9:19:29	21 02	14 24	10 R	04	11	14	01	16	12	26	49	26	24	06	08	24
11 W	9:23:25	22 02	27 42	10	02	12	15	01	16	15	28	50	26	24	06	28	26
12 T	9:27:22	23 03	10 ♍ 39	10 D	29 ♑	14	16	02	16	17	31	52	27	25	06	47	28
13 F	9:31:19	24 04	23 19	10	27	17	17	02	16	19	33	52	27	25	06	06	30
14 S	9:35:15	25 04	05 ♎ 46	10	26	19	18	02	16	21	35	53	27	25	06	25	32
15 S	9:39:12	26 05	18 03	10	25	22	19	03	16	40	37	54	28	25	05	50	34
16 M	9:43:08	27 06	00 ♏ 12	10 R	24	25	20	03	16	42	39	55	28	26	05	11	35
17 T	9:47:05	28 06	12 14	10	23	28	21	03	16	46	41	55	29	26	05	33	37
18 W	9:51:01	00 ♓	24 11	10	23	31	22	04	17	49	43	56	29	27	05	14	38
19 T	9:54:58	01 07	06 ♐ 05	10	24	34	23	04	17	52	45	57	52	27	05	35	40
20 F	9:58:54	02 08	17 58	10	25	37	24	04	17	55	47	57	00 ♈	27	05	57	41
21 S	10:02:51	03 08	29 49	10	26	40	25	04	17	59	49	58	01	27	04	18	42
22 S	10:06:48	04 09	11 ♑ 42	10	29 ♑	44	26	05	17	21	51	59	01	28	04	40	43
23 M	10:10:44	05 09	23 38	10 R	01 ≈	48	27	05	17	27	53	59	02	28	04	02	44
24 T	10:14:41	06 10	05 ≈ 41	10	02	52	28	05	17	40	55	00 ♈	03	28	04	23	45
25 W	10:18:37	07 10	17 52	10	04	57	29	05	17	46	57	01	03	28	04	45	46
26 T	10:22:34	08 11	00 ♓ 16	10	06	02	00 ♈	05	17	53	59	02	03	29	03	06	46
27 F	10:26:30	09 11	12 ♓ 56	10 D	08	06	01	05	17	57	01 ♈	03	03	29	03	28	47
28 S	10:30:27	09 11	27	10	09	14	02	05	17	59	01	03	00 ♓	00 ♓	03	29	47

EPHEMERIS CALCULATED FOR 12 MIDNIGHT GREENWICH MEAN TIME. ALL OTHER DATA AND FACING ASPECTARIAN PAGE IN **EASTERN STANDARD TIME (BOLD)** AND PACIFIC STANDARD TIME (REGULAR).

MARCH 1998

1 SUNDAY

☉ ∨ ⚷   1:49 am
☐ ∨ ♀   2:16 am
☐ ∆ ♀   4:45 am
☐ ∨ ⚷   5:48 am
☐ ⚹ ♀   8:42 am
☐ ⚹ ♃   8:57 am
☐ □ ♄   10:35 am
     1:45 pm
     2:48 pm
     5:42 pm
     7:57 pm
    10:23 pm
    10:51 pm

2 MONDAY

  ☐   1:23 am
     1:51 am
     4:15 am
     5:38 am
     6:47 am
     8:20 am
    12:20 pm
     1:14 pm
     5:25 pm
    11:58 pm

3 TUESDAY

     6:27 am
     7:09 am
    11:08 am
    11:34 am

4 WEDNESDAY

     1:43 am
     1:45 am
     4:17 am
     4:55 am
     5:55 am
     7:51 am
    10:51 am
    12:56 pm
     2:02 pm
     4:13 pm
     4:41 pm
     8:49 pm

5 THURSDAY

     3:41 am
     6:13 am

6 FRIDAY

☐ ∨ ♄   10:52 am
    11:10 am
     6:44 pm
     7:10 pm
     7:13 pm
     7:26 pm
     8:40 pm
     9:57 pm
    10:38 pm
     3:15 pm
     3:51 pm
     5:58 pm
     7:17 pm
     9:24 pm

7 SATURDAY

    12:24 am
     3:22 am
     3:06 am
     6:19 am
     6:33 am
     8:40 am
    12:22 pm
    12:06 pm
     3:19 pm
     3:33 pm
     5:40 pm

8 SUNDAY

     3:34 am
     5:25 am
     5:52 am
     5:54 am
     6:19 am
     8:43 am
     9:45 am
    10:28 am
    12:34 pm
    12:54 pm
     2:52 pm
     2:52 pm
     3:19 pm
     6:45 pm
     7:26 pm
     7:28 pm

9 MONDAY

     2:58 am
     7:07 am
     7:22 am
     7:28 am
    11:25 am
     1:58 pm
     4:07 pm
     4:22 pm
     4:28 pm
     8:25 pm

10 TUESDAY

    12:55 am
     4:05 am
     8:30 am
     1:18 pm
     5:06 pm
     6:08 pm
     9:48 pm
     9:55 pm
     1:05 pm
     5:30 pm
    10:18 pm

11 WEDNESDAY

    12:54 am
     3:37 am
     5:22 am
     6:15 am
     6:51 am
     8:58 am
    10:17 am
    12:37 pm
     7:22 pm
    10:26 pm
    10:54 pm
     1:54 pm
     3:01 pm
     6:11 pm
     6:15 pm
     6:43 pm
     7:39 pm

12 THURSDAY

    12:40 am
    12:52 am
     4:04 am
     5:28 am
     5:37 am
     8:16 am
    11:35 am
     5:33 pm
     1:04 pm
     2:28 pm
     2:37 pm
     5:16 pm
     8:35 pm

13 FRIDAY

     5:19 am
     2:47 pm
     5:56 pm
     2:19 am
    11:47 am
     2:56 pm
     9:39 pm

14 SATURDAY

    12:39 am
     6:19 am
     7:12 am
     7:20 am
     8:56 am
     8:58 am
     9:32 am
     3:19 am
     4:12 am
     4:20 am
     5:56 am
     5:58 am
     6:32 am

15 SUNDAY

     1:10 am
     1:36 am
     3:37 am
     4:44 am
     9:46 am
     4:46 am
     7:04 am
     3:21 pm
     6:02 pm
    11:50 pm
    10:10 am
    10:36 am
    12:21 pm
     1:44 pm
     6:46 pm

16 MONDAY

    12:56 am
     3:37 am
     4:25 am
     6:55 am
     3:12 pm
     8:07 pm
    11:19 pm
    11:32 pm
    11:48 pm
     1:22 pm
     3:55 pm
    12:12 pm
     5:07 pm
     8:19 pm
     8:32 pm
     8:48 pm

17 TUESDAY

    12:54 am
     2:47 am
     3:09 am
     6:25 am
     9:55 am
     2:13 pm
     5:12 pm
     8:12 pm
     1:09 pm
     3:25 pm
     6:53 pm
    11:13 pm
     2:12 pm
     5:12 pm
     9:13 pm

18 WEDNESDAY

    12:13 am
     4:35 am
     5:05 am
     7:43 am
    12:12 pm
     1:16 pm
    11:45 am
     1:21 pm
     7:03 pm
     8:45 pm
    10:21 pm
     4:03 pm

19 THURSDAY

     3:44 am
     3:59 am
     5:59 am
    10:23 am
    11:33 am
    12:44 am
     1:35 am
     2:05 am
     4:43 am
     7:23 am
     8:11 am
     8:33 am

20 FRIDAY

♀ ∆ ♄   2:12 am
     2:46 am
     7:38 am
     2:46 am
     3:54 am
     7:29 am
     5:45 pm
    10:10 pm
    10:13 pm
    12:54 pm
     2:45 pm
     7:10 pm
     7:13 pm
    11:38 pm

21 SATURDAY

    12:56 am
     4:25 am
     4:47 am
     6:25 am
     8:07 am
    10:57 am
    11:32 am
    11:48 am
     1:47 pm
    12:08 pm
     1:38 pm
     5:07 pm
     6:54 pm
     7:57 pm
     8:38 pm
    10:24 pm
    11:47 pm

22 SUNDAY

     1:24 am
     5:36 am
     5:48 am
    11:28 am
     2:07 pm
     3:29 pm
     2:36 pm
     2:48 pm
     4:08 pm
     8:28 pm
    11:07 pm
    12:29 pm
    11:35 pm

23 MONDAY

     3:46 am
    10:59 am
     1:05 pm
     9:47 pm
     9:54 pm
    12:46 am
     7:59 am
    10:05 am
     6:47 pm
    11:51 pm

24 TUESDAY

     2:51 am
     3:44 am
     3:59 am
     5:59 am
    10:23 am
    11:11 am
    11:33 am
    12:44 am
    12:59 am
     2:05 am
     4:43 am
     7:23 am
     8:11 am
     8:33 am

25 WEDNESDAY

♀ ∆ ♀   1:59 am
     3:22 am
     7:41 am
     7:51 am
     9:16 am
     5:54 am
     9:40 am
     1:34 pm
     7:06 pm
    11:44 pm
    10:59 pm
    12:22 pm
     4:41 pm
     4:51 pm
     6:16 pm

26 THURSDAY

    12:44 am
     5:38 am
     5:03 am
     7:33 am
     8:44 am
     9:54 am
     2:01 pm
     2:11 pm
     4:09 pm
     6:22 pm
     8:49 pm
     9:18 pm
     2:54 am
     6:40 am
    10:34 am
     4:06 pm
     8:44 pm
     9:44 pm

27 FRIDAY

     5:26 am
     1:37 pm
    10:14 pm
    11:24 pm
     2:26 am
    10:37 am
     7:14 pm
     8:24 pm
    10:25 pm

28 SATURDAY

     1:25 am
     3:11 am
     5:18 am
     6:19 am
     9:29 am
    12:49 pm
     2:43 pm
     3:23 pm
     3:57 pm
    12:11 am
     2:18 am
     3:19 am
     6:29 am
     9:49 am
    11:43 am
    12:23 pm
    12:57 pm

29 SUNDAY

☐ ∆ ⚹   4:01 am
    12:59 pm
     1:27 pm
    10:47 pm
     1:01 am
     9:59 am
    10:27 am
     7:47 pm
     9:59 pm
    10:53 pm

30 MONDAY

    12:59 am
     1:53 am
     4:58 am
     6:37 am
    10:26 am
     3:02 pm
     3:51 pm
     6:29 pm
     7:38 pm
     8:21 pm
     8:54 pm
     1:58 am
     3:37 am
     7:26 am
    12:02 pm
    12:51 pm
     3:29 pm
     4:38 pm
     5:21 pm
     5:54 pm
     9:30 pm

31 TUESDAY

    12:30 am
     3:32 am
     9:36 am
     1:43 pm
    11:55 pm
    12:32 pm
     6:36 pm
     8:55 pm

Eastern Standard Time in bold type
Pacific Standard Time in medium type

MARCH 1998

☽ Last Aspect day	EST / hr:mn / PST	asp	☽ Ingress sign day	EST / hr:mn / PST
1	**8:57 pm** 5:57 pm	□ ♀	♉ 1	**9:01 pm** 6:01 pm
3	10:45 pm	△ ♀	♊ 3	11:15 pm
4	**1:45 am**	△ ♀	♊ 4	**2:15 am**
5	9:09 pm	□ ☿	♋ 6	4:27 am
6	**12:09 am**	□ ☿	♋ 6	**7:27 am**
7	**6:33 pm** 3:33 pm	□ ♄	♌ 8	**3:46 pm** 12:46 pm
10	2:06 am	△ ♄	♍ 10	11:36 pm
10	**5:06 am**	△ ♄	♍ 11	**2:36 am**
12	**11:35 pm** 8:35 pm	☍ ☉	♎ 13	**2:59 pm** 11:59 am
15	**7:04 am** 4:04 am	☍ ♄	♏ 16	**3:51 am** 12:51 am
18	**11:45 am** 8:45 am	△ ☉	♐ 18	**3:56 pm** 12:56 pm
20	4:29 am	△ ♄	♑ 20	10:43 pm
20	**7:29 am**	△ ♄	♑ 21	**1:43 am**
22	**3:29 pm** 12:29 pm	□ ♄	♒ 23	**8:02 am** 5:02 am
24	**7:51 pm** 4:51 pm	✶ ☿	♓ 25	**10:43 am** 7:43 am
26	**6:03 am** 3:03 am	☌ ♃	♈ 27	**10:49 am** 7:49 am
28	**8:59 pm** 5:59 pm	✶ ♀	♉ 29	**10:07 am** 7:07 am
30	9:30 pm	□ ♀	♊ 31	7:38 am
30	**12:30 am**	□ ♀	♊ 31	**10:38 am**

☽ Phases & Eclipses phase	day	EST / hr:mn / PST
2nd Quarter	5	**3:41 am** 12:41 am
Full Moon	12	**11:35 pm** 8:35 pm
●	12	22° ♍ 24'
4th Quarter	20	11:38 pm
4th Quarter	21	**2:38 am**
New Moon	27	**10:14 pm** 7:14 pm

Planet Ingress	day	EST / hr:mn / PST
♀ ♒	4	**11:15 am** 8:15 am
♂ ♈	4	**11:18 am** 8:18 am
☿ ♈	8	**3:28 am** 2:28 am
✱ ♍	13	**5:43 am** 2:43 am
☉ ♈	20	**2:54 pm** 11:54 am

Planetary Motion	day	EST / hr:mn / PST
⚷ ℞	1	**11:20 pm** 8:20 pm
♇ ℞	10	**7:19 pm** 4:19 pm
☿ ℞	27	**2:37 pm** 11:37 am

DATE		SID.TIME	SUN	MOON	NODE	MERCURY	VENUS	MARS	JUPITER	SATURN	URANUS	NEPTUNE	PLUTO	CERES	PALLAS	JUNO	VESTA	CHIRON
S	1	10:34:23	10 ♓ 11	12 ♈ 04	10 ♍ ℞ 31	16 ♓ 01	27 ♑ 23	27 ♓ 09	05 ♓ 53	18 ♈ 06	10 ♒ 28	01 ♒ 05	08 ♐ 02	03 ♈ 34	00 ♓ 25	02 ♎ ℞ 53	06 ♉ 51	18 ♏ ℞ 47
M	2	10:38:20	11 12	26 56	10 31	17 56	28 04	27 55	06 08	18 12	10 31	01 07	08 02	03 57	00 45	02 40	07 14	18 47
T	3	10:42:17	12 12	11 ♉ 31	10 31	19 51	28 47	28 42	06 22	18 19	10 34	01 09	08 03	04 20	01 05	02 27	07 36	18 47
W	4	10:46:13	13 12	25 46	10 D 31	21 46	29 30	29 28	06 37	18 25	10 37	01 10	08 03	04 43	01 25	02 14	07 59	18 47
T	5	10:50:10	14 12	09 ♊ 39	10 31	23 41	00 ♒ 14	00 ♈ 15	06 51	18 32	10 40	01 12	08 03	05 07	01 45	02 00	08 21	18 46
F	6	10:54:06	15 12	23 08	10 31	25 35	01 00	01 01	07 05	18 39	10 43	01 14	08 03	05 30	02 04	01 47	08 44	18 46
S	7	10:58:03	16 12	06 ♋ 17	10 31	27 28	01 46	01 48	07 20	18 46	10 47	01 16	08 03	05 53	02 24	01 33	09 07	18 46
S	8	11:01:59	17 12	19 07	10 31	29 21	02 33	02 34	07 34	18 52	10 50	01 18	08 04	06 17	02 44	01 19	09 30	18 45
M	9	11:05:56	18 12	01 ♌ 41	10 31	01 ♈ 11	03 21	03 21	07 48	18 59	10 52	01 19	08 04	06 40	03 04	01 04	09 53	18 44
T	10	11:09:52	19 12	14 01	10 32	03 00	04 10	04 07	08 03	19 06	10 55	01 21	08 04	07 03	03 23	00 50	10 16	18 43
W	11	11:13:49	20 12	26 11	10 33	04 47	05 00	04 53	08 17	19 13	10 58	01 23	08 04	07 27	03 43	00 36	10 39	18 43
T	12	11:17:46	21 12	08 ♍ 12	10 ℞ 33	06 30	05 50	05 40	08 31	19 20	11 01	01 24	08 ℞ 04	07 50	04 02	00 21	11 02	18 42
F	13	11:21:42	22 12	20 08	10 33	08 10	06 41	06 26	08 46	19 27	11 04	01 26	08 04	08 14	04 22	00 07	11 25	18 40
S	14	11:25:39	23 12	01 ♎ 59	10 32	09 46	07 33	07 12	09 00	19 34	11 07	01 27	08 04	08 37	04 41	29 ♍ 52	11 49	18 39
S	15	11:29:35	24 12	13 48	10 31	11 18	08 26	07 58	09 14	19 41	11 10	01 29	08 03	09 01	05 01	29 37	12 12	18 38
M	16	11:33:32	25 11	25 38	10 29	12 45	09 19	08 44	09 28	19 48	11 12	01 31	08 03	09 25	05 20	29 22	12 36	18 36
T	17	11:37:28	26 11	07 ♏ 30	10 27	14 06	10 12	09 30	09 43	19 56	11 15	01 32	08 03	09 48	05 40	29 08	12 59	18 35
W	18	11:41:25	27 11	19 27	10 25	15 22	11 07	10 16	09 57	20 03	11 18	01 34	08 03	10 12	05 59	28 53	13 23	18 33
T	19	11:45:21	28 10	01 ♐ 33	10 23	16 32	12 01	11 02	10 11	20 10	11 21	01 35	08 03	10 36	06 19	28 38	13 46	18 31
F	20	11:49:18	29 10	13 51	10 22	17 34	12 57	11 48	10 25	20 17	11 23	01 36	08 02	10 59	06 38	28 23	14 10	18 29
S	21	11:53:14	00 ♈ 10	26 25	10 D 21	18 30	13 53	12 34	10 39	20 25	11 26	01 38	08 02	11 23	06 57	28 08	14 34	18 27
S	22	11:57:11	01 09	09 ♑ 19	10 21	19 19	14 49	13 20	10 53	20 32	11 28	01 39	08 02	11 47	07 16	27 54	14 58	18 25
M	23	12:01:08	02 09	22 37	10 22	20 00	15 46	14 06	11 07	20 39	11 31	01 41	08 01	12 10	07 35	27 39	15 22	18 23
T	24	12:05:04	03 08	06 ♒ 20	10 23	20 34	16 44	14 52	11 21	20 47	11 33	01 42	08 01	12 34	07 55	27 25	15 46	18 21
W	25	12:09:01	04 08	20 29	10 24	20 59	17 42	15 38	11 35	20 54	11 36	01 43	08 01	12 58	08 14	27 10	16 10	18 19
T	26	12:12:57	05 07	05 ♓ 05	10 ℞ 25	21 17	18 40	16 23	11 49	21 01	11 38	01 44	08 00	13 22	08 33	26 56	16 34	18 16
F	27	12:16:54	06 07	20 01	10 25	21 ℞ 27	19 39	17 09	12 03	21 09	11 41	01 46	08 00	13 46	08 52	26 42	16 59	18 14
S	28	12:20:50	07 06	05 ♈ 11	10 23	21 30	20 38	17 54	12 16	21 16	11 43	01 47	07 59	14 09	09 11	26 28	17 23	18 11
S	29	12:24:47	08 06	20 26	10 20	21 25	21 37	18 40	12 30	21 24	11 45	01 48	07 58	14 33	09 29	26 14	17 47	18 08
M	30	12:28:43	09 05	05 ♉ 35	10 17	21 12	22 37	19 26	12 44	21 31	11 48	01 49	07 58	14 57	09 48	26 00	18 12	18 05
T	31	12:32:40	10 04	20 29	10 13	20 53	23 37	20 11	12 58	21 39	11 50	01 50	07 57	15 21	10 07	25 47	18 36	18 03

EPHEMERIS CALCULATED FOR 12 MIDNIGHT GREENWICH MEAN TIME. ALL OTHER DATA AND FACING ASPECTARIAN PAGE IN **EASTERN STANDARD TIME (BOLD)** AND PACIFIC STANDARD TIME (REGULAR).

APRIL 1998

1 WEDNESDAY
- 4:21 am
- 5:59 am
- 6:37 am
- 9:04 am
- 1:05 pm
- 1:46 pm
- 2:01 pm
- 3:16 pm
- 4:35 pm
- 7:35 pm
- 8:27 pm
- 11:48 pm
- 11:55 pm
- 3:22 pm
- 5:47 pm
- 8:53 pm
- 10:20 pm
- 10:26 pm
- 11:30 pm

2 THURSDAY
- 2:30 am
- 5:45 am
- 7:23 am
- 7:59 am
- 5:33 pm
- 2:45 am
- 4:23 am
- 4:59 am
- 2:33 pm

3 FRIDAY
- 1:25 am
- 10:29 am
- 11:48 am
- 1:52 pm
- 3:14 pm
- 3:19 pm
- 9:03 pm
- 11:59 pm
- 7:29 am
- 8:48 am
- 10:52 am
- 12:14 pm
- 12:19 pm
- 6:03 pm
- 8:59 pm

4 SATURDAY
- 3:25 am
- 6:50 am
- 9:35 am
- 9:40 am
- 7:11 pm
- 12:25 am
- 3:50 am
- 6:35 am
- 4:11 pm
- 10:18 pm
- 10:45 pm

5 SUNDAY
- 1:18 am
- 1:45 am
- 4:16 pm
- 1:48 pm
- 1:39 am
- 5:16 am
- 9:47 am
- 10:18 am
- 10:48 am

6 MONDAY
- 6:22 am
- 8:47 am
- 8:53 am
- 3:22 pm
- 5:47 pm
- 5:53 pm
- 10:20 pm
- 10:26 pm

7 TUESDAY
- 10:50 am
- 11:27 am
- 12:22 pm
- 10:32 pm
- 7:50 am
- 8:27 am
- 9:22 am
- 7:02 pm
- 9:11 pm

8 WEDNESDAY
- 12:11 pm
- 10:08 pm
- 2:37 pm
- 4:06 pm
- 6:25 pm
- 7:47 pm
- 10:43 pm
- 11:57 pm
- 5:49 am
- 7:08 am
- 11:30 am
- 11:37 am
- 1:06 pm
- 3:25 pm
- 4:47 pm
- 7:43 pm
- 7:57 pm

9 THURSDAY
- 5:50 am
- 6:32 am
- 8:33 am
- 4:16 pm
- 2:50 am
- 3:32 am
- 5:33 am
- 1:16 pm
- 10:09 pm

10 FRIDAY
- 1:09 am
- 6:05 am
- 12:57 pm
- 10:05 am
- 3:57 am
- 3:05 am
- 6:56 am
- 9:57 am

11 SATURDAY
- 3:56 am
- 9:52 am
- 11:55 am
- 12:37 am
- 8:24 am
- 12:41 pm
- 1:47 pm
- 8:06 am
- 8:34 am
- 8:58 am
- 12:56 pm
- 6:52 pm
- 9:37 pm
- 1:34 am
- 5:24 am
- 9:41 am
- 1:56 pm
- 2:24 pm
- 5:06 pm
- 5:34 pm
- 5:58 pm

12 SUNDAY
- 12:48 am
- 1:34 am
- 2:42 am
- 6:41 am
- 9:13 am
- 9:27 am
- 2:43 pm
- 6:10 pm
- 8:31 pm
- 6:15 pm
- 8:09 pm
- 11:02 pm
- 11:42 pm
- 12:00 am
- 9:48 am
- 10:34 am
- 3:41 am
- 6:13 am
- 6:27 am
- 7:36 am
- 11:43 am
- 3:10 pm
- 5:31 pm

13 MONDAY
- 4:11 am
- 7:59 am
- 8:58 am
- 10:59 am
- 11:20 am
- 6:16 pm
- 1:11 am
- 4:59 am
- 5:58 am
- 7:59 am
- 8:20 am
- 3:16 pm
- 10:07 pm
- 10:56 pm

14 TUESDAY
- 1:07 am
- 1:56 am
- 2:36 pm
- 2:21 am
- 6:10 am
- 10:51 am
- 1:51 am
- 4:44 am
- 5:50 am
- 7:47 pm

15 WEDNESDAY
- 1:03 pm
- 11:36 am
- 1:19 am
- 5:21 am
- 9:10 am
- 8:50 am
- 9:22 am
- 10:47 pm
- 6:10 am
- 10:51 am
- 5:50 am
- 6:22 am
- 7:47 pm

16 THURSDAY
- 6:07 pm
- 6:40 pm
- 10:04 pm
- 11:03 pm
- 3:24 am
- 7:15 am
- 5:59 am
- 8:14 am
- 11:57 pm
- 3:07 pm
- 3:40 pm
- 8:03 pm
- 12:24 am
- 4:15 pm
- 2:59 pm
- 5:14 pm
- 8:57 pm
- 11:33 pm

17 FRIDAY
- 2:33 am
- 2:50 am
- 4:08 pm
- 10:36 pm
- 11:36 pm
- 9:03 am
- 11:50 am
- 2:41 pm
- 7:36 pm
- 8:36 pm
- 11:53 pm

18 SATURDAY
- 1:45 am
- 7:25 am
- 8:48 am
- 1:43 pm
- 4:08 pm
- 4:25 am
- 5:48 am
- 10:43 am
- 12:47 pm
- 1:08 pm
- 10:45 pm

19 SUNDAY
- 3:05 am
- 4:59 am
- 9:49 am
- 7:29 pm
- 12:05 am
- 1:59 am
- 6:49 am
- 11:53 am
- 4:29 pm
- 10:19 pm

20 MONDAY
- 1:19 am
- 5:21 am
- 9:10 am
- 1:51 am
- 8:50 am
- 9:22 am
- 10:47 pm
- 2:21 am
- 6:10 am
- 10:51 am
- 4:44 am
- 5:50 am
- 6:22 am
- 7:47 pm

21 TUESDAY
- 6:32 am
- 9:48 am
- 10:32 pm
- 3:01 pm
- 4:13 pm
- 11:13 pm
- 11:42 pm
- 3:32 am
- 6:48 am
- 7:32 am
- 12:01 pm
- 1:53 pm
- 8:13 pm
- 8:42 pm

22 WEDNESDAY
- 6:09 am
- 7:58 am
- 8:52 am
- 12:56 pm
- 5:00 pm
- 6:13 pm
- 11:04 pm
- 11:45 pm
- 3:09 am
- 4:58 am
- 5:52 am
- 9:56 pm
- 2:00 pm
- 3:13 pm
- 8:04 pm
- 8:45 pm
- 9:32 pm
- 9:47 pm
- 11:04 pm
- 11:35 pm

23 THURSDAY
- 12:32 am
- 12:47 pm
- 2:04 am
- 2:35 am
- 8:18 am
- 12:53 pm
- 1:08 pm
- 7:17 pm
- 5:18 pm
- 9:53 pm
- 10:08 pm
- 4:17 pm
- 9:57 pm

24 FRIDAY
- 12:57 pm
- 3:55 am
- 9:35 am
- 12:31 pm
- 5:32 pm
- 11:45 pm
- 12:55 pm
- 6:36 am
- 8:21 am
- 11:31 pm
- 2:32 pm
- 10:38 pm
- 11:52 pm

25 SATURDAY
- 1:38 am
- 6:29 pm
- 3:51 pm
- 4:36 pm
- 8:08 am
- 11:28 pm
- 3:21 pm
- 6:15 pm
- 9:13 pm
- 2:51 pm
- 1:36 pm
- 9:28 am
- 12:21 pm
- 3:15 pm
- 10:08 pm
- 11:41 pm
- 3:29 am

26 SUNDAY
- 12:33 pm
- 1:04 am
- 6:42 am
- 9:01 am
- 1:14 pm
- 5:02 pm
- 10:58 pm
- 3:42 am
- 6:01 am
- 10:14 am
- 12:22 pm
- 2:02 pm
- 7:58 pm
- 10:59 pm
- 11:58 pm

27 MONDAY
- 1:59 am
- 2:58 am
- 9:47 am
- 3:10 pm
- 5:56 pm
- 9:30 pm
- 4:12 am
- 6:47 am
- 1:06 pm
- 2:56 pm
- 6:30 pm
- 9:25 pm

28 TUESDAY
- 12:25 am
- 9:05 am
- 10:11 am
- 12:28 pm
- 4:07 pm
- 5:33 pm
- 5:47 pm
- 11:28 pm
- 6:05 pm
- 7:11 pm
- 9:28 pm
- 1:07 pm
- 2:33 pm
- 2:47 pm
- 8:28 pm

29 WEDNESDAY
- 3:51 pm
- 4:36 pm
- 8:08 am
- 11:28 pm
- 3:21 pm
- 6:15 pm
- 9:13 pm
- 12:51 pm
- 1:36 pm
- 9:28 am
- 12:21 pm
- 3:15 pm
- 6:13 pm
- 10:08 pm
- 11:41 pm

30 THURSDAY
- 1:08 am
- 2:41 am
- 11:52 am
- 9:07 pm
- 10:28 pm
- 8:52 am
- 2:03 pm
- 6:07 pm
- 7:28 pm
- 9:13 pm

Eastern Standard Time in bold type
Pacific Standard Time in medium type

APRIL 1998

☽ Last Aspect day	EST / hr:mn / PST	asp	☽ Ingress sign	day	EST / hr:mn / PST
2	**7:23 am** 4:23 am	△♀	♋	2	**2:10 pm** 11:10 am
4	**9:35 am** 6:35 am	□♂	♌	4	**9:36 pm** 6:36 pm
6	**11:41 pm** 8:41 pm	△♂	♍	7	**8:26 am** 5:26 am
8	**2:30 pm** 11:30 am	☍♃	♎	9	**9:05 pm** 6:05 pm
12	**9:15 am** 6:15 am	☍♂	♏	12	**9:55 am** 6:55 am
13	**6:10 pm** 3:10 pm	△♃	♐	14	**9:52 pm** 6:52 pm
16	11:33 pm	△☉	♑	17	5:05 am
17	**2:33 am**	△☉	♑	17	**8:05 am**
19	**2:53 pm** 11:53 am	□☉	♒	19	**3:42 pm** 12:42 pm
21	**10:32 am** 7:32 am	✶♄	♓	21	**8:07 pm** 5:07 pm
22	11:35 pm	☌♀	♈	23	6:31 pm
23	**2:35 am**	☌♀	♈	23	**9:31 pm**
25	**1:06 pm** 10:06 am	☌♄	♉	25	**9:09 pm** 6:09 pm
27	**9:47 am** 6:47 am	✶♀	♊	27	**8:56 pm** 5:56 pm
29	**3:21 pm** 12:21 pm	□♀	♋	29	**10:57 pm** 7:57 pm

☽ Phases & Eclipses

phase	day	EST / hr:mn / PST
2nd Quarter	3	**3:19 pm** 12:19 pm
Full Moon	11	**5:24 pm** 2:24 pm
4th Quarter	19	**2:53 pm** 11:53 am
New Moon	26	**6:42 am** 3:42 am

Planet Ingress

	day	EST / hr:mn / PST
♀ ♓	5	9:38 pm
♀ ♓	6	**12:38 am**
♂ ♉	12	**8:04 pm** 5:04 pm
☉ ♉	19	10:56 pm
☉ ♉	20	**1:56 am**

Planetary Motion

	day	EST / hr:mn / PST
☿ D	19	11:28 pm
☿ D	20	**2:28 am**

DATE		SID.TIME	SUN	MOON	NODE	MERCURY	VENUS	MARS	JUPITER	SATURN	URANUS	NEPTUNE	PLUTO	CERES	PALLAS	JUNO	VESTA	CHIRON
W	1	12:36:37	11 ♈ 03	05 ♊ 01	10 ♍ ℞ 09	20 ♈ ℞ 28	24 ♒ 38	20 ♈ 57	13 ♓ 11	21 ♈ 46	11 ♒ 52	01 ♒ 51	07 ♐ ℞ 57	15 ♈ 45	10 ♓ 26	25 ♍ ℞ 34	19 ♉ 01	18 ♏ ℞ 00
T	2	12:40:33	12 03	19 05	10 06	19 57	25 39	21 42	13 25	21 54	11 54	01 53	07 56	16 09	10 44	25 20	19 25	17 56
F	3	12:44:30	13 02	02 ♋ 42	10 D 04	19 22	26 40	22 27	13 38	22 01	11 56	01 54	07 55	16 33	11 03	25 08	19 50	17 53
S	4	12:48:26	14 01	15 52	10 03	18 42	27 41	23 13	13 52	22 09	11 58	01 55	07 54	16 56	11 21	24 55	20 15	17 50
S	5	12:52:23	15 00	28 38	10 04	17 58	28 43	23 58	14 05	22 16	12 01	01 56	07 54	17 20	11 40	24 43	20 39	17 47
M	6	12:56:19	15 59	11 ♌ 05	10 05	17 13	29 45	24 43	14 19	22 24	12 02	01 56	07 53	17 44	11 58	24 31	21 04	17 43
T	7	13:00:16	16 58	23 16	10 07	16 26	00 ♓ 48	25 28	14 32	22 32	12 04	01 57	07 52	18 08	12 17	24 19	21 29	17 40
W	8	13:04:12	17 57	05 ♍ 16	10 08	15 38	01 50	26 13	14 45	22 39	12 06	01 58	07 51	18 32	12 35	24 07	21 54	17 36
T	9	13:08:09	18 56	17 09	10 ℞ 08	14 51	02 53	26 58	14 58	22 47	12 08	01 59	07 50	18 56	12 53	23 56	22 19	17 33
F	10	13:12:06	19 55	28 59	10 06	14 05	03 57	27 43	15 12	22 54	12 10	02 00	07 49	19 20	13 11	23 45	22 43	17 29
S	11	13:16:02	20 54	10 ♎ 47	10 02	13 21	05 00	28 28	15 25	23 02	12 12	02 01	07 48	19 44	13 29	23 34	23 08	17 25
S	12	13:19:59	21 53	22 37	09 56	12 40	06 04	29 13	15 38	23 09	12 14	02 01	07 47	20 08	13 47	23 24	23 33	17 22
M	13	13:23:55	22 52	04 ♏ 30	09 48	12 03	07 08	29 58	15 51	23 17	12 15	02 02	07 46	20 31	14 05	23 14	23 58	17 18
T	14	13:27:52	23 50	16 28	09 40	11 29	08 12	00 ♉ 43	16 04	23 25	12 17	02 03	07 45	20 55	14 23	23 04	24 24	17 14
W	15	13:31:48	24 49	28 33	09 31	11 00	09 16	01 28	16 16	23 32	12 18	02 04	07 44	21 19	14 41	22 55	24 49	17 10
T	16	13:35:45	25 48	10 ♐ 46	09 24	10 35	10 21	02 12	16 29	23 40	12 20	02 04	07 43	21 43	14 58	22 46	25 14	17 06
F	17	13:39:41	26 47	23 09	09 18	10 16	11 26	02 57	16 42	23 47	12 22	02 05	07 42	22 07	15 16	22 37	25 39	17 02
S	18	13:43:38	27 45	05 ♑ 46	09 14	10 01	12 31	03 42	16 55	23 55	12 23	02 05	07 41	22 31	15 33	22 29	26 04	16 58
S	19	13:47:34	28 44	18 39	09 D 13	09 52	13 36	04 26	17 07	24 03	12 24	02 06	07 40	22 55	15 51	22 21	26 29	16 54
M	20	13:51:31	29 43	01 ♒ 50	09 13	09 D 48	14 41	05 11	17 20	24 10	12 26	02 06	07 38	23 19	16 08	22 14	26 55	16 49
T	21	13:55:28	00 ♉ 41	15 24	09 13	09 49	15 47	05 55	17 32	24 18	12 27	02 07	07 37	23 42	16 26	22 06	27 20	16 45
W	22	13:59:24	01 40	29 21	09 ℞ 14	09 55	16 53	06 39	17 44	24 25	12 28	02 07	07 36	24 06	16 43	21 59	27 45	16 41
T	23	14:03:21	02 38	13 ♓ 42	09 14	10 06	17 58	07 24	17 57	24 33	12 30	02 08	07 35	24 30	17 00	21 53	28 11	16 37
F	24	14:07:17	03 37	28 26	09 12	10 21	19 05	08 08	18 09	24 40	12 31	02 08	07 34	24 54	17 17	21 47	28 36	16 32
S	25	14:11:14	04 35	13 ♈ 27	09 08	10 42	20 11	08 52	18 21	24 48	12 32	02 08	07 32	25 18	17 34	21 41	29 02	16 28
S	26	14:15:10	05 34	28 38	09 01	11 07	21 17	09 37	18 33	24 56	12 33	02 09	07 31	25 42	17 51	21 35	29 27	16 23
M	27	14:19:07	06 32	13 ♉ 48	08 54	11 36	22 24	10 21	18 45	25 03	12 34	02 09	07 30	26 05	18 07	21 30	29 53	16 19
T	28	14:23:03	07 30	28 48	08 45	12 09	23 30	11 05	18 57	25 11	12 35	02 09	07 28	26 29	18 24	21 26	00 ♊ 18	16 14
W	29	14:27:00	08 29	13 ♊ 28	08 36	12 46	24 37	11 49	19 09	25 18	12 36	02 09	07 27	26 53	18 41	21 21	00 44	16 10
T	30	14:30:57	09 27	27 42	08 29	13 27	25 44	12 33	19 21	25 26	12 37	02 09	07 26	27 17	18 57	21 17	01 09	16 05

EPHEMERIS CALCULATED FOR 12 MIDNIGHT GREENWICH MEAN TIME. ALL OTHER DATA AND FACING ASPECTARIAN PAGE IN **EASTERN STANDARD TIME (BOLD)** AND PACIFIC STANDARD TIME (REGULAR).

MAY 1998

1 FRIDAY

☽ □ ☿	**12:13 am**	
☽ △ ⚷	**3:08 am**	12:08 am
☽ △ ♀	**9:16 am**	6:16 am
☽ △ ♃	**9:45 am**	6:45 am
☽ ⚹ ⚵	**12:33 pm**	9:33 am
☽ □ ♄	**8:48 pm**	5:48 pm
♀ ⚺ ⚳	**10:12 pm**	7:12 pm
☽ □ ⚳		10:26 pm
☽ △ ♀		10:38 pm

2 SATURDAY

☽ □ ⚳	**1:26 am**	
☽ △ ♀	**1:38 am**	
♆ △ ⚶	**3:37 am**	12:37 am
☽ ☍ ♆	**8:52 am**	5:52 am
☽ ⚹ ⚶	**9:03 am**	6:03 am
☽ △ ♇	**6:41 pm**	3:41 pm
☿ ⚻ ⚷	**6:59 pm**	3:59 pm
☉ □ ♅		11:05 pm

3 SUNDAY

☉ □ ♅	**2:05 am**	
☽ ☍ ♅	**4:50 am**	1:50 am
☽ □ ☉	**5:04 am**	2:04 am
☽ □ ♂	**9:43 am**	6:43 am
☽ □ ⚷	**10:56 am**	7:56 am
☽ △ ☿	**12:17 pm**	9:17 am
☽ ⚻ ♀	**7:08 pm**	4:08 pm
☽ ⚻ ♃	**7:17 pm**	4:17 pm
☽ ⚺ ⚵	**9:11 pm**	6:11 pm

4 MONDAY

♂ ☍ ⚷	**4:22 am**	1:22 am
☽ △ ♄	**6:49 am**	3:49 am
☽ △ ⚳	**1:07 pm**	10:07 am
☽ ⚻ ♀	**5:18 pm**	2:18 pm
♃ ☌ ♀	**6:43 pm**	3:43 pm
☽ ⚻ ♆	**7:05 pm**	4:05 pm
☽ □ ⚶	**9:25 pm**	6:25 pm

5 TUESDAY

☽ □ ♇	**5:21 am**	2:21 am
♀ ⚹ ♆	**12:20 pm**	9:20 am
☽ ⚻ ♅	**4:12 pm**	1:12 pm
☽ △ ☉	**9:39 pm**	6:39 pm
☽ ⚹ ⚷	**10:08 pm**	7:08 pm
☽ △ ♂		10:09 pm

6 WEDNESDAY

☽ △ ♂	**1:09 am**	
☉ ☍ ⚷	**3:12 am**	12:12 am
☽ ⚻ ☿	**5:23 am**	2:23 am
☽ ☍ ♃	**8:11 am**	5:11 am
☽ ☍ ♀	**8:26 am**	5:26 am
☽ ☌ ⚵	**9:02 am**	6:02 am
☽ ⚻ ♄	**7:46 pm**	4:46 pm

7 THURSDAY

☽ ⚻ ⚳	**3:42 am**	12:42 am
☽ △ ♆	**7:43 am**	4:43 am
♀ ☍ ⚵	**10:03 am**	7:03 am
☽ ☍ ♀	**12:19 pm**	9:19 am
☽ △ ⚶	**12:23 pm**	9:23 am
♀ ⚹ ⚶	**1:34 pm**	10:34 am
☿ ⚺ ♃	**5:05 pm**	2:05 pm
☽ ⚹ ♇	**6:02 pm**	3:02 pm
☿ ⚻ ⚵	**8:09 pm**	5:09 pm
☿ ⚺ ♀	**11:19 pm**	8:19 pm

8 FRIDAY

☽ △ ♅	**5:10 am**	2:10 am
☽ ⚺ ⚷	**10:43 am**	7:43 am
♃ ☍ ⚵	**11:11 am**	8:11 am
☽ ⚻ ☉	**4:03 pm**	1:03 pm
☽ ⚻ ♂	**6:07 pm**	3:07 pm
☽ ⚺ ⚵	**9:56 pm**	6:56 pm
☽ ⚻ ♃	**10:06 pm**	7:06 pm
☽ ⚻ ♀	**10:46 pm**	7:46 pm
☽ ☍ ☿		9:45 pm

9 SATURDAY

☽ ☍ ☿	**12:45 am**	
☽ ☍ ♄	**9:19 am**	6:19 am
☽ ☍ ⚳	**6:38 pm**	3:38 pm
☽ □ ♆	**8:30 pm**	5:30 pm
♀ △ ♇	**10:37 pm**	7:37 pm

10 SUNDAY

☽ ⚻ ⚶	**3:24 am**	12:24 am
☽ ⚺ ♇	**6:34 am**	3:34 am
☽ ⚻ ♀	**7:25 am**	4:25 am
☽ □ ♅	**5:40 pm**	2:40 pm
☽ ☌ ⚷	**10:41 pm**	7:41 pm

11 MONDAY

♂ △ ⚵	**8:36 am**	5:36 am
☽ ☍ ☉	**9:30 am**	6:30 am
☽ ⚹ ⚵	**10:02 am**	7:02 am
☽ ☍ ♂	**10:07 am**	7:07 am
☽ △ ♃	**11:06 am**	8:06 am
☽ △ ♀	**12:08 pm**	9:08 am
☉ △ ⚵	**4:16 pm**	1:16 pm
☽ ⚻ ☿	**7:37 pm**	4:37 pm
☽ ⚻ ♄	**9:44 pm**	6:44 pm

12 TUESDAY

♆ □ ⚳	**3:21 am**	12:21 am
♂ ⚹ ♃	**7:28 am**	4:28 am
☽ ⚹ ♆	**8:00 am**	5:00 am
☽ ⚻ ⚳	**8:10 am**	5:10 am
☉ ⚹ ♃	**9:43 am**	6:43 am
☉ ☌ ♂	**2:46 pm**	11:46 am
☽ ☍ ⚶	**4:52 pm**	1:52 pm
☿ ☌ ♄	**4:57 pm**	1:57 pm
☽ ☌ ♇	**5:41 pm**	2:41 pm
☽ △ ♀		9:38 pm

13 WEDNESDAY

☽ △ ♀	**12:38 am**	
☽ ⚹ ♅	**4:36 am**	1:36 am
☉ ⚹ ♀	**5:21 am**	2:21 am
☽ ⚺ ⚷	**9:05 am**	6:05 am
♂ ⚹ ♀	**12:52 pm**	9:52 am
♇ ☍ ⚶	**2:49 pm**	11:49 am
☽ □ ⚵	**8:31 pm**	5:31 pm
☽ □ ♃	**10:18 pm**	7:18 pm
☽ □ ♀	**11:40 pm**	8:40 pm
☽ ⚻ ♂		9:06 pm
☽ ⚻ ☉		9:48 pm

14 THURSDAY

☽ ⚻ ♂	**12:06 am**	
☽ ⚻ ☉	**12:48 am**	
☽ △ ♄	**8:20 am**	5:20 am
☽ △ ☿	**12:43 pm**	9:43 am
☽ ⚺ ♆	**5:42 pm**	2:42 pm
♀ ⚹ ♅	**7:42 pm**	4:42 pm
☽ △ ⚳	**7:43 pm**	4:43 pm
☽ ⚺ ♇		11:58 pm

15 FRIDAY

☽ ⚺ ♇	**2:58 am**	
☽ ⚻ ⚶	**4:18 am**	1:18 am
☽ ⚺ ♅	**1:39 pm**	10:39 am
☽ □ ♀	**3:24 pm**	12:24 pm
☽ ⚹ ⚷	**5:39 pm**	2:39 pm

16 SATURDAY

☽ △ ⚵	**5:07 am**	2:07 am
☽ ⚹ ♃	**7:28 am**	4:28 am
☿ □ ♆	**8:21 am**	5:21 am
☽ ⚹ ♀	**9:07 am**	6:07 am
☽ △ ♂	**11:45 am**	8:45 am
☽ △ ☉	**1:37 pm**	10:37 am
♀ ⚻ ⚷	**3:18 pm**	12:18 pm
☽ □ ♄	**4:54 pm**	1:54 pm
☽ ☌ ♆		10:23 pm

17 SUNDAY

☽ ☌ ♆	**1:23 am**	
☽ □ ☿	**3:34 am**	12:34 am
☽ □ ⚳	**5:02 am**	2:02 am
☽ ⚹ ♇	**10:12 am**	7:12 am
☽ △ ⚶	**1:27 pm**	10:27 am
☿ ☌ ⚳	**8:15 pm**	5:15 pm
☽ ☌ ♅	**8:34 pm**	5:34 pm
☽ □ ⚷		9:06 pm

18 MONDAY

☽ □ ⚷	**12:06 am**	
☽ ⚹ ♀	**3:22 am**	12:22 am
☽ ⚻ ⚵	**11:33 am**	8:33 am
☽ ⚺ ♃	**2:18 pm**	11:18 am
☉ ⚺ ♄	**3:40 pm**	12:40 pm
☽ ⚺ ♀	**4:11 pm**	1:11 pm
☽ □ ♂	**8:43 pm**	5:43 pm
☽ ⚹ ♄	**11:07 pm**	8:07 pm
☽ □ ☉	**11:36 pm**	8:36 pm

19 TUESDAY

☽ ⚺ ♆	**6:44 am**	3:44 am
☿ ⚻ ♇	**11:25 am**	8:25 am
☽ ⚹ ⚳	**11:46 am**	8:46 am
☽ □ ♇	**3:04 pm**	12:04 pm
☽ ⚹ ☿	**3:33 pm**	12:33 pm
☽ □ ⚶	**7:57 pm**	4:57 pm
☽ ⚺ ♅		10:03 pm

20 WEDNESDAY

☽ ⚺ ♅	**1:03 am**	
☽ △ ⚷	**4:09 am**	1:09 am
☽ ⚺ ♀	**12:08 pm**	9:08 am
☽ ☍ ⚵	**3:31 pm**	12:31 pm
☽ ☌ ♃	**6:32 pm**	3:32 pm
☽ ☌ ♀	**8:35 pm**	5:35 pm
♂ ⚺ ♄		11:44 pm
☽ ⚺ ♄		11:45 pm
☽ ⚹ ♂		11:45 pm

21 THURSDAY

♂ ⚺ ♄	**2:44 am**	
☽ ⚺ ♄	**2:45 am**	
☽ ⚹ ♂	**2:45 am**	
☽ ⚹ ☉	**6:28 am**	3:28 am
☽ ⚹ ♆	**9:34 am**	6:34 am
☽ ⚺ ⚳	**3:48 pm**	12:48 pm
☿ ⚺ ⚶	**4:57 pm**	1:57 pm
☽ △ ♇	**5:28 pm**	2:28 pm
☽ ⚹ ⚶	**11:45 pm**	8:45 pm
☽ ⚺ ☿		9:25 pm

22 FRIDAY

☽ ⚺ ☿	**12:25 am**	
☽ ⚹ ♅	**3:06 am**	12:06 am
☽ ⚻ ⚷	**5:51 am**	2:51 am
♀ ⚻ ⚵	**8:04 am**	5:04 am
☽ ⚻ ⚵	**5:13 pm**	2:13 pm
☽ ☌ ♀	**5:57 pm**	2:57 pm
☽ ⚺ ♃	**8:26 pm**	5:26 pm
☽ ⚺ ♀	**10:40 pm**	7:40 pm
☿ □ ♅	**11:27 pm**	8:27 pm

23 SATURDAY

☽ ☌ ♄	**4:13 am**	1:13 am
☉ △ ♆	**4:40 am**	1:40 am
☽ ⚺ ♂	**6:19 am**	3:19 am
☽ □ ♆	**10:26 am**	7:26 am
☽ ⚺ ☉	**10:50 am**	7:50 am
☽ ☌ ⚳	**5:50 pm**	2:50 pm
☽ ⚻ ♇	**6:04 pm**	3:04 pm
☿ ☍ ⚷	**9:11 pm**	6:11 pm
☽ ⚺ ⚶		10:46 pm
♇ ⚻ ⚳		11:20 pm

24 SUNDAY

☽ ⚺ ⚶	**1:46 am**	
♇ ⚻ ⚳	**2:20 am**	
☽ □ ♅	**3:35 am**	12:35 am
☽ ☍ ⚷	**6:05 am**	3:05 am
♀ ⚺ ♃	**6:22 am**	3:22 am
☽ ☌ ☿	**7:19 am**	4:19 am
☽ △ ⚵	**5:47 pm**	2:47 pm
☽ ⚹ ♃	**9:15 pm**	6:15 pm
☽ ⚺ ♀	**10:20 pm**	7:20 pm
☽ ⚹ ♀	**11:43 pm**	8:43 pm

25 MONDAY

☽ ⚺ ♄	**4:54 am**	1:54 am
☽ ☌ ♂	**9:04 am**	6:04 am
☽ △ ♆	**10:44 am**	7:44 am
☽ ☌ ☉	**2:32 pm**	11:32 am
☽ ☍ ♇	**6:24 pm**	3:24 pm
☽ ⚺ ⚳	**7:33 pm**	4:33 pm
♀ ⚺ ♀	**7:49 pm**	4:49 pm

26 TUESDAY

☽ ☌ ⚶	**3:48 am**	12:48 am
☽ △ ♅	**4:09 am**	1:09 am
☽ ⚻ ⚷	**6:30 am**	3:30 am
☽ ⚺ ☿	**2:57 pm**	11:57 am
♅ △ ⚶	**3:29 pm**	12:29 pm
☽ □ ⚵	**7:04 pm**	4:04 pm
♂ △ ♆	**7:11 pm**	4:11 pm
☽ □ ♃	**10:53 pm**	7:53 pm
☽ □ ♀		10:42 pm

27 WEDNESDAY

☽ □ ♀	**1:42 am**	
☽ ⚹ ♀	**3:51 am**	12:51 am
☽ ⚹ ♄	**6:43 am**	3:43 am
☽ ⚻ ♆	**12:24 pm**	9:24 am
☽ ⚺ ♂	**1:20 pm**	10:20 am
☽ ⚺ ☉	**8:07 pm**	5:07 pm
☽ ⚻ ♇	**8:24 pm**	5:24 pm
☽ ⚹ ⚳	**11:09 pm**	8:09 pm
☿ △ ⚵		9:02 pm
☉ ☍ ♇		9:14 pm

28 THURSDAY

☿ △ ⚵	**12:02 am**	
☉ ☍ ♇	**12:14 am**	
☽ ⚻ ♅	**6:47 am**	3:47 am
☽ ⚺ ⚶	**8:05 am**	5:05 am
☽ △ ⚷	**9:04 am**	6:04 am
♀ ☌ ♄	**6:25 pm**	3:25 pm
☽ ⚹ ⚵	**11:05 pm**	8:05 pm
☽ ⚹ ☿		11:45 pm

29 FRIDAY

☽ ⚹ ☿	**2:45 am**	
☽ △ ♃	**3:22 am**	12:22 am
☽ △ ♀	**6:40 am**	3:40 am
☿ ⚹ ♃	**7:13 am**	4:13 am
⚶ ⚻ ⚷	**11:20 am**	8:20 am
☽ □ ♄	**11:39 am**	8:39 am
☽ □ ♀	**1:09 pm**	10:09 am
☽ ☍ ♆	**5:16 pm**	2:16 pm
☽ ⚹ ♂	**9:21 pm**	6:21 pm
☽ △ ♇		10:50 pm

30 SATURDAY

☽ △ ♇	**1:50 am**	
☽ ⚹ ☉	**5:55 am**	2:55 am
☽ □ ⚳	**6:32 am**	3:32 am
☿ ⚹ ♀	**8:00 am**	5:00 am
☽ ☍ ♅	**1:06 pm**	10:06 am
☽ □ ⚷	**3:20 pm**	12:20 pm
☽ ⚹ ⚶	**4:28 pm**	1:28 pm
☉ ⚺ ⚳	**7:22 pm**	4:22 pm

31 SUNDAY

☽ ⚺ ⚵	**7:11 am**	4:11 am
♀ □ ♆	**11:09 am**	8:09 am
☽ ⚻ ♃	**11:57 am**	8:57 am
☽ ⚻ ♀	**3:50 pm**	12:50 pm
☿ ⚺ ♄	**5:04 pm**	2:04 pm
☽ △ ♄	**8:43 pm**	5:43 pm
☽ □ ☿	**9:24 pm**	6:24 pm
☽ ⚻ ♆		11:11 pm

Eastern Standard Time in bold type
Pacific Standard Time in medium type

MAY 1998

☽ Last Aspect day	EST / hr:mn	PST	asp	☽ Ingress sign day	EST / hr:mn	PST
1		10:38 pm	△♀	♌ 2		1:49 am
2	**1:38 am**		△♀	♌ 2	**4:49 am**	
4	**6:49 am**	3:49 am	△♄	♍ 4	**2:47 pm**	11:47 am
6	**8:11 am**	5:11 am	☍♃	♎ 7	**3:19 am**	12:19 am
9	**9:19 am**	6:19 am	☍♄	♏ 9	**4:10 pm**	1:10 pm
11	**11:06 am**	8:06 am	△♃	♐ 12	**3:48 am**	12:48 am
14	**12:43 pm**	9:43 am	△☿	♑ 14	**1:40 pm**	10:40 am
16	**4:54 pm**	1:54 pm	□♄	♒ 16	**9:31 pm**	6:31 pm
18	**11:36 pm**	8:36 pm	□☉	♓ 19	**3:04 am**	12:04 am
20		11:45 pm	✶♂	♈ 21		3:06 am
21	**2:45 am**		✶♂	♈ 21	**6:06 am**	
23	**4:13 am**	1:13 am	☌♄	♉ 23	**7:06 am**	4:06 am
24	**9:15 pm**	6:15 pm	✶♃	♊ 25	**7:25 am**	4:25 am
27	**6:43 am**	3:43 am	✶♄	♋ 27	**8:58 am**	5:58 am
29	**1:09 pm**	10:09 am	□♀	♌ 29	**1:38 pm**	10:38 am
31	**9:24 pm**	6:24 pm	□☿	♍ 31	**10:21 pm**	7:21 pm

☽ Phases & Eclipses phase	day	EST / hr:mn	PST
2nd Quarter	3	**5:04 am**	2:04 am
Full Moon	11	**9:30 am**	6:30 am
4th Quarter	18	**11:36 pm**	8:36 pm
New Moon	25	**2:32 pm**	11:32 am

Planet Ingress	day	EST / hr:mn	PST
♀ ♈	3	**2:16 pm**	11:16 am
⚳ ♉	6	**4:16 pm**	1:16 pm
☿ ♉	14	**9:10 pm**	6:10 pm
☉ ♊	20		10:05 pm
☉ ♊	21	**1:05 am**	
♂ ♊	23	**10:43 pm**	7:43 pm
♀ ♉	29	**6:32 pm**	3:32 pm

Planetary Motion	day	EST / hr:mn	PST
♆ ℞	3		9:26 pm
♆ ℞	4	**12:26 am**	
⚵ D	10	**5:15 am**	2:15 am
♅ ℞	17	**5:54 am**	2:54 am

DATE		SID.TIME	SUN	MOON	NODE	MERCURY	VENUS	MARS	JUPITER	SATURN	URANUS	NEPTUNE	PLUTO	CERES	PALLAS	JUNO	VESTA	CHIRON
F	1	14:34:53	10 ♉ 25	11 ♋ 27	08 ♍ ℞ 23	14 ♈ 12	26 ♓ 51	13 ♉ 17	19 ♓ 32	25 ♈ 33	12 ♒ 38	02 ♒ 10	07 ♐ ℞ 24	27 ♈ 41	19 ♓ 13	21 ♍ ℞ 14	01 ♊ 35	16 ♏ ℞ 01
S	2	14:38:50	11 24	24 42	08 19	15 00	27 59	14 01	19 44	25 40	12 39	02 10	07 23	28 04	19 30	21 10	02 01	15 56
S	3	14:42:46	12 22	07 ♌ 31	08 D 18	15 52	29 06	14 45	19 55	25 48	12 39	02 10	07 21	28 28	19 46	21 08	02 26	15 52
M	4	14:46:43	13 20	19 58	08 18	16 47	00 ♈ 13	15 28	20 07	25 55	12 40	02 ℞ 10	07 20	28 52	20 02	21 05	02 52	15 47
T	5	14:50:39	14 18	02 ♍ 07	08 ℞ 19	17 45	01 21	16 12	20 18	26 03	12 41	02 10	07 18	29 15	20 18	21 03	03 18	15 43
W	6	14:54:36	15 16	14 05	08 19	18 45	02 29	16 56	20 29	26 10	12 41	02 10	07 17	29 39	20 34	21 01	03 43	15 38
T	7	14:58:32	16 14	25 55	08 17	19 49	03 36	17 40	20 40	26 17	12 42	02 10	07 15	00 ♉ 03	20 49	21 00	04 09	15 34
F	8	15:02:29	17 12	07 ♎ 42	08 14	20 56	04 44	18 23	20 51	26 25	12 42	02 10	07 14	00 26	21 05	20 59	04 35	15 29
S	9	15:06:26	18 10	19 31	08 07	22 05	05 52	19 07	21 02	26 32	12 43	02 09	07 12	00 50	21 21	20 58	05 00	15 25
S	10	15:10:22	19 08	01 ♏ 24	07 57	23 17	07 00	19 50	21 13	26 39	12 43	02 09	07 11	01 14	21 36	20 D 58	05 26	15 20
M	11	15:14:19	20 06	13 24	07 45	24 31	08 09	20 34	21 23	26 46	12 44	02 09	07 09	01 37	21 51	20 58	05 52	15 15
T	12	15:18:15	21 04	25 31	07 32	25 48	09 17	21 17	21 34	26 53	12 44	02 09	07 08	02 01	22 06	20 58	06 18	15 11
W	13	15:22:12	22 02	07 ♐ 47	07 19	27 07	10 25	22 00	21 44	27 01	12 44	02 09	07 06	02 24	22 21	20 59	06 44	15 06
T	14	15:26:08	23 00	20 13	07 07	28 28	11 34	22 43	21 55	27 08	12 44	02 08	07 05	02 48	22 36	21 00	07 09	15 02
F	15	15:30:05	23 58	02 ♑ 49	06 58	29 52	12 42	23 27	22 05	27 15	12 44	02 08	07 03	03 11	22 51	21 02	07 35	14 58
S	16	15:34:01	24 56	15 37	06 50	01 ♉ 19	13 51	24 10	22 15	27 22	12 45	02 08	07 01	03 34	23 06	21 03	08 01	14 53
S	17	15:37:58	25 54	28 37	06 46	02 47	15 00	24 53	22 25	27 29	12 45	02 07	07 00	03 58	23 20	21 05	08 27	14 49
M	18	15:41:55	26 52	11 ♒ 52	06 D 44	04 18	16 09	25 36	22 35	27 36	12 ℞ 45	02 07	06 58	04 21	23 35	21 08	08 53	14 44
T	19	15:45:51	27 49	25 23	06 44	05 51	17 18	26 19	22 45	27 43	12 45	02 06	06 57	04 45	23 49	21 11	09 19	14 40
W	20	15:49:48	28 47	09 ♓ 13	06 ℞ 44	07 26	18 27	27 02	22 55	27 50	12 44	02 06	06 55	05 08	24 03	21 14	09 45	14 36
T	21	15:53:44	29 45	23 21	06 43	09 03	19 36	27 45	23 04	27 57	12 44	02 05	06 53	05 31	24 17	21 17	10 11	14 31
F	22	15:57:41	00 ♊ 43	07 ♈ 48	06 41	10 43	20 45	28 28	23 14	28 03	12 44	02 05	06 52	05 55	24 31	21 21	10 37	14 27
S	23	16:01:37	01 40	22 31	06 35	12 25	21 54	29 11	23 23	28 10	12 44	02 04	06 50	06 18	24 44	21 25	11 02	14 23
S	24	16:05:34	02 38	07 ♉ 23	06 28	14 09	23 04	29 53	23 32	28 17	12 44	02 04	06 49	06 41	24 58	21 29	11 28	14 19
M	25	16:09:30	03 36	22 19	06 18	15 55	24 13	00 ♊ 36	23 41	28 24	12 43	02 03	06 47	07 04	25 11	21 34	11 54	14 15
T	26	16:13:27	04 33	07 ♊ 07	06 07	17 43	25 23	01 19	23 50	28 30	12 43	02 02	06 45	07 27	25 25	21 39	12 20	14 10
W	27	16:17:24	05 31	21 41	05 56	19 34	26 32	02 01	23 59	28 37	12 42	02 02	06 44	07 50	25 38	21 44	12 46	14 06
T	28	16:21:20	06 29	05 ♋ 53	05 45	21 27	27 42	02 44	24 08	28 44	12 42	02 01	06 42	08 13	25 51	21 49	13 12	14 02
F	29	16:25:17	07 26	19 38	05 37	23 22	28 52	03 26	24 17	28 50	12 41	02 00	06 40	08 36	26 03	21 55	13 38	13 59
S	30	16:29:13	08 24	02 ♌ 56	05 31	25 19	00 ♉ 01	04 09	24 25	28 57	12 41	02 00	06 39	08 59	26 16	22 01	14 04	13 55
S	31	16:33:10	09 21	15 48	05 28	27 18	01 11	04 51	24 33	29 03	12 40	01 59	06 37	09 22	26 29	22 08	14 30	13 51

EPHEMERIS CALCULATED FOR 12 MIDNIGHT GREENWICH MEAN TIME. ALL OTHER DATA AND FACING ASPECTARIAN PAGE IN **EASTERN STANDARD TIME (BOLD)** AND PACIFIC STANDARD TIME (REGULAR).

JUNE 1998

1 MONDAY

☽⚻♆	**2:11 am**	
☽△♀	**3:47 am**	12:47 am
☽□♂	**10:09 am**	7:09 am
☽□♇	**11:16 am**	8:16 am
☽△⚳	**6:19 pm**	3:19 pm
☽□☉	**8:45 pm**	5:45 pm
☽⚻♅	**11:20 pm**	8:20 pm
☽⚹⚷		10:28 pm
☿△♆		10:49 pm

2 TUESDAY

☽⚹⚷	**1:28 am**	
☿△♆	**1:49 am**	
♂☍♇	**4:44 am**	1:44 am
☽□⚶	**5:09 am**	2:09 am
☽☌⚵	**7:04 pm**	4:04 pm
☽☍♃		9:08 pm

3 WEDNESDAY

☽☍♃	**12:08 am**	
☽☍♀	**4:32 am**	1:32 am
☉△♅	**4:47 am**	1:47 am
☽⚻♄	**9:08 am**	6:08 am
☽△♆	**2:11 pm**	11:11 am
☽△☿	**10:06 pm**	7:06 pm
☽⚻♀	**10:30 pm**	7:30 pm
☽⚹♇	**11:29 pm**	8:29 pm
☽△♂		11:18 pm
☿⚺♀		11:41 pm

4 THURSDAY

☽△♂	**2:18 am**	
☿⚺♀	**2:41 am**	
☉⚻⚷	**4:40 am**	1:40 am
☿☍♇	**5:46 am**	2:46 am
♀⚻♇	**8:14 am**	5:14 am
☽⚻⚳	**8:51 am**	5:51 am
☽△♅	**11:54 am**	8:54 am
☽⚺⚷	**1:50 pm**	10:50 am
☽△☉	**2:41 pm**	11:41 am
☽△⚶	**8:11 pm**	5:11 pm

5 FRIDAY

☿☌♂	**6:39 am**	3:39 am
☽⚺⚵	**8:34 am**	5:34 am
☽⚻♃	**1:38 pm**	10:38 am
☽⚻♀	**6:23 pm**	3:23 pm
☽☍♄	**10:29 pm**	7:29 pm
☽□♆		11:54 pm

6 SATURDAY

☽□♆	**2:54 am**	
☽⚺♇	**12:02 pm**	9:02 am
☽☍♀	**5:45 pm**	2:45 pm
☽⚻♂	**6:42 pm**	3:42 pm
☿⚺⚳	**7:25 pm**	4:25 pm
☽☍⚳	**11:20 pm**	8:20 pm
☽⚻☿		9:03 pm
☽□♅		9:17 pm
☿△♅		10:20 pm
☽☌⚷		10:58 pm

7 SUNDAY

☽⚻☿	**12:03 am**	
☽□♅	**12:17 am**	
☿△♅	**1:20 am**	
☽☌⚷	**1:58 am**	
☽⚻☉	**8:16 am**	5:16 am
☿⚻⚷	**10:26 am**	7:26 am
☽⚻⚶	**10:41 am**	7:41 am
♀⚺♂	**4:28 pm**	1:28 pm
☽⚹⚵	**9:12 pm**	6:12 pm
☽△♃		11:01 pm

8 MONDAY

☽△♃	**2:01 am**	
♅□⚳	**4:31 am**	1:31 am
☽△♀	**6:55 am**	3:55 am
☽⚻♄	**10:28 am**	7:28 am
☽⚹♆	**2:10 pm**	11:10 am
☽☌♇	**10:56 pm**	7:56 pm

9 TUESDAY

☽☍♂	**8:58 am**	5:58 am
☽⚻♀	**10:39 am**	7:39 am
☽⚹♅	**10:47 am**	7:47 am
☽⚻⚳	**11:45 am**	8:45 am
♀□♅	**11:59 am**	8:59 am
☽⚺⚷	**12:14 pm**	9:14 am
☉☌⚶	**2:25 pm**	11:25 am
☿☌⚶	**10:32 pm**	7:32 pm
☽☍⚶	**10:56 pm**	7:56 pm
☽☍☿	**11:00 pm**	8:00 pm
☽☍☉	**11:19 pm**	8:19 pm
⚳☍⚷		10:50 pm
☿☌☉		10:56 pm
♀☍⚷		11:54 pm

10 WEDNESDAY

⚳☍⚷	**1:50 am**	
☿☌☉	**1:56 am**	
♀☍⚷	**2:54 am**	
♀☌⚳	**3:27 am**	12:27 am
☽□⚵	**7:40 am**	4:40 am
☽□♃	**12:08 pm**	9:08 am
♂△♅	**4:46 pm**	1:46 pm
☽□♀	**5:08 pm**	2:08 pm
☽△♄	**8:11 pm**	5:11 pm
☽⚺♆	**11:13 pm**	8:13 pm

11 THURSDAY

☽⚺♇	**7:37 am**	4:37 am
♂⚻⚷	**4:00 pm**	1:00 pm
☽⚺♅	**7:04 pm**	4:04 pm
☽⚹⚷	**8:19 pm**	5:19 pm
☽⚻♂	**8:35 pm**	5:35 pm
☽△⚳	**9:45 pm**	6:45 pm
☽△♀		9:36 pm

12 FRIDAY

☽△♀	**12:36 am**	
☿□⚵	**4:06 am**	1:06 am
☽⚻⚶	**8:46 am**	5:46 am
☽⚻☉	**11:37 am**	8:37 am
☽△⚵	**3:57 pm**	12:57 pm
☽⚻☿	**6:08 pm**	3:08 pm
☽⚹♃	**8:04 pm**	5:04 pm
☽⚹♀		10:09 pm

13 SATURDAY

☽⚹♀	**1:09 am**	
☽□♄	**3:46 am**	12:46 am
☽☌♆	**6:14 am**	3:14 am
☿□♃	**6:16 am**	3:16 am
☽⚹♇	**2:20 pm**	11:20 am
♂⚺⚳	**5:53 pm**	2:53 pm
☽☌♅		10:26 pm
☽□⚷		11:33 pm

14 SUNDAY

☽☌♅	**1:26 am**	
☽□⚷	**2:33 am**	
☽□⚳	**5:39 am**	2:39 am
☽△♂	**5:57 am**	2:57 am
☽□♀	**12:04 pm**	9:04 am
☿□♀	**3:42 pm**	12:42 pm
☽△⚶	**4:35 pm**	1:35 pm
☽△☉	**9:39 pm**	6:39 pm
☽⚻⚵	**10:26 pm**	7:26 pm
☽⚺♃		11:09 pm

15 MONDAY

☽⚺♃	**2:09 am**	
☿⚹♄	**7:13 am**	4:13 am
☽⚺♀	**7:19 am**	4:19 am
☽⚹♄	**9:35 am**	6:35 am
☽△☿	**10:01 am**	7:01 am
☉□⚵	**11:09 am**	8:09 am
☽⚺♆	**11:32 am**	8:32 am
☽□♇	**7:22 pm**	4:22 pm
☿⚻♆	**7:43 pm**	4:43 pm

16 TUESDAY

☽⚺♅	**6:08 am**	3:08 am
☽△⚷	**7:09 am**	4:09 am
☽⚹⚳	**11:46 am**	8:46 am
☽□♂	**1:23 pm**	10:23 am
☽⚹♀	**9:23 pm**	6:23 pm
☽□⚶	**10:36 pm**	7:36 pm

17 WEDNESDAY

☽☍⚵	**3:15 am**	12:15 am
☽□☉	**5:38 am**	2:38 am
☽☌♃	**6:34 am**	3:34 am
☽☌♀	**11:47 am**	8:47 am
☽⚺♄	**1:45 pm**	10:45 am
☽⚹♆	**3:13 pm**	12:13 pm
♀⚺⚶	**7:25 pm**	4:25 pm
☉□♃	**8:34 pm**	5:34 pm
☿⚻♇	**10:17 pm**	7:17 pm
☽△♇	**10:48 pm**	7:48 pm
☽□☿	**10:53 pm**	7:53 pm

18 THURSDAY

☽⚹♅	**9:16 am**	6:16 am
☽⚻⚷	**10:11 am**	7:11 am
☽⚺⚳	**4:10 pm**	1:10 pm
☽⚹♂	**6:58 pm**	3:58 pm
☽⚹⚶		11:56 pm

19 FRIDAY

☽⚹⚶	**2:56 am**	
☽⚺♀	**4:43 am**	1:43 am
☽⚻⚵	**6:32 am**	3:32 am
☽⚺♃	**9:26 am**	6:26 am
☽⚹☉	**11:48 am**	8:48 am
☽⚺♀	**2:43 pm**	11:43 am
☽☌♄	**4:26 pm**	1:26 pm
☽□♆	**5:29 pm**	2:29 pm
☽⚻♇		9:53 pm

20 SATURDAY

☽⚻♇	**12:53 am**	
♀△⚵	**6:45 am**	3:45 am
☽⚹☿	**9:16 am**	6:16 am
☽☍⚷	**12:01 pm**	9:01 am
☽☌⚳	**7:19 pm**	4:19 pm
☿⚻♅	**10:58 pm**	7:58 pm
☽⚺♂	**11:17 pm**	8:17 pm

21 SUNDAY

☿△⚷	**5:05 am**	2:05 am
☽⚺⚶	**6:11 am**	3:11 am
☽△⚵	**8:53 am**	5:53 am
☽☌♀	**10:50 am**	7:50 am
☽⚹♃	**11:24 am**	8:24 am
☉□♀	**2:53 pm**	11:53 am
☽⚹♀	**4:50 pm**	1:50 pm
☽⚺☉	**4:57 pm**	1:57 pm
♀⚹♃	**6:14 pm**	3:14 pm
☽⚺♄	**6:22 pm**	3:22 pm
☽△♆	**7:03 pm**	4:03 pm
☽☍♇		11:26 pm

22 MONDAY

☽☍♇	**2:26 am**	
☽△♅	**12:45 pm**	9:45 am
☽⚻⚷	**1:35 pm**	10:35 am
☉⚹♄	**4:18 pm**	1:18 pm
☽⚺☿	**6:46 pm**	3:46 pm
☽⚺⚳	**10:23 pm**	7:23 pm
☉⚻♆		9:06 pm

23 TUESDAY

☉⚻♆	**12:06 am**	
☽☌♂	**3:38 am**	12:38 am
☽☌⚶	**9:43 am**	6:43 am
☽□⚵	**11:37 am**	8:37 am
☽□♃	**1:46 pm**	10:46 am
☽⚺♀	**5:29 pm**	2:29 pm
☽□♀	**7:32 pm**	4:32 pm
☽⚹♄	**8:56 pm**	5:56 pm
☽⚻♆	**9:16 pm**	6:16 pm
☽☌☉	**10:50 pm**	7:50 pm

24 WEDNESDAY

☿⚹⚳	**3:51 am**	12:51 am
☽⚻♇	**4:53 am**	1:53 am
☽⚻♅	**3:35 pm**	12:35 pm
☽△⚷	**4:26 pm**	1:26 pm
♀⚹♀	**8:32 pm**	5:32 pm

25 THURSDAY

☽⚹⚳	**3:07 am**	12:07 am
☽☌☿	**6:03 am**	3:03 am
☽⚺♂	**9:59 am**	6:59 am
♀⚺♄	**1:22 pm**	10:22 am
♀△♆	**1:43 pm**	10:43 am
☽⚺⚶	**3:21 pm**	12:21 pm
☽⚹⚵	**4:26 pm**	1:26 pm
♄□♆	**5:28 pm**	2:28 pm
☽△♃	**6:11 pm**	3:11 pm
☽△♀		9:29 pm
☽☍♆		10:45 pm
☽□♄		10:48 pm
☽⚹♀		11:57 pm

26 FRIDAY

☽△♀	**12:29 am**	
☽☍♆	**1:45 am**	
☽□♄	**1:48 am**	
☽⚹♀	**2:57 am**	
☽⚺☉	**7:36 am**	4:36 am
☽△♇	**9:49 am**	6:49 am
☽☍♅	**9:10 pm**	6:10 pm
☽□⚷	**10:05 pm**	7:05 pm

27 SATURDAY

☿⚺♂	**3:51 am**	12:51 am
☽□⚳	**11:11 am**	8:11 am
☉⚻♇	**1:36 pm**	10:36 am
☽⚹♂	**8:05 pm**	5:05 pm
☽⚺☿	**9:40 pm**	6:40 pm
☽⚹⚶		9:38 pm
☽⚺⚵		9:47 pm
☽⚻♃		10:59 pm

28 SUNDAY

☽⚹⚶	**12:38 am**	
☽⚺⚵	**12:47 am**	
☽⚻♃	**1:59 am**	
⚵□⚶	**8:19 am**	5:19 am
☽⚻♀	**8:56 am**	5:56 am
☽⚻♆	**9:40 am**	6:40 am
☽△♄	**10:12 am**	7:12 am
☽□♀	**5:00 pm**	2:00 pm
☽□♇	**6:17 pm**	3:17 pm
☽⚹☉	**8:45 pm**	5:45 pm
☿⚹⚵	**11:22 pm**	8:22 pm
☿⚺⚶		10:57 pm

29 MONDAY

☿⚺⚶	**1:57 am**	
♀☍♇	**6:06 am**	3:06 am
☽⚻♅	**6:20 am**	3:20 am
☿△♃	**6:35 am**	3:35 am
☽⚹⚷	**7:20 am**	4:20 am
♃□⚶	**10:07 pm**	7:07 pm
☽△⚳	**11:06 pm**	8:06 pm

30 TUESDAY

☽□♂	**10:16 am**	7:16 am
☽☌⚵	**12:45 pm**	9:45 am
☽☍♃	**1:13 pm**	10:13 am
☽□⚶	**1:43 pm**	10:43 am
☽⚹☿	**5:58 pm**	2:58 pm
☽☍♀	**8:42 pm**	5:42 pm
☽△♆	**8:51 pm**	5:51 pm
☽⚻♄	**9:54 pm**	6:54 pm

Eastern Standard Time in bold type
Pacific Standard Time in medium type

JUNE 1998

D Last Aspect / D Ingress

D Last Aspect day EST / hr:mn / PST	asp	D Ingress sign day EST / hr:mn / PST
2 9:06 am 7:17 am	☌ ♀	≏ 3
3 12:08 am	□ ♄	♏ 5 10:17 am 7:17 am
5 10:29 pm 7:29 pm	△ ♄	♐ 8 11:06 pm 8:06 pm
7 11:01 pm	□ ♂	♑ 10 10:35 am 7:35 am
2 2:01 am	✶ ♀	♒ 13 7:51 pm 4:51 pm
10 12:08 pm 9:06 am		♓ 15 3:03 am 12:03 am
12 8:04 pm 5:04 pm		♈ 17 8:32 am 5:32 am
14 9:39 pm 6:39 pm		♉ 19 12:... 9:23 am
17 6:34 am 3:34 am		19 2:47 pm 11:47 am
19 11:48 am 8:48 am		

D Last Aspect / D Ingress

D Last Aspect day EST / hr:mn / PST	asp	D Ingress sign day EST / hr:mn / PST
21 11:24 am 8:24 am	✶ ♀	Ⅱ 21 4:26 pm 1:26 pm
23 1:46 pm 10:46 am	△ ♃	⊙ 23 6:39 pm 3:39 pm
25 6:11 am 3:11 am	△ ♂	♌ 25 11:04 pm 8:04 pm
27 8:05 pm 5:05 pm	□ ♀	♍ 28 6:55 am 3:55 am
30 5:58 pm 2:58 pm	✶ ♀	≏ 30 6:06 pm 3:06 pm

D Phases & Eclipses

phase	day	EST / hr:mn / PST
2nd Quarter	1	8:45 pm 5:45 pm
Full Moon	9	11:19 am 8:19 am
4th Quarter	17	5:38 am 2:38 am
New Moon	23	10:50 pm 7:50 pm

Planet Ingress

	day	EST / hr:mn / PST
♄ →	1	3:47 am 12:07 am
♀ →	8	1:05 am 10:05 pm
♂ →	14	1:05 am
☿ →	15	12:33 am 9:33 pm
⊙ →	21	10:12 pm 7:12 pm
♀ →	24	9:02 am 6:02 am
☿ →	30	6:51 am 3:51 am

Planetary Motion

	day	EST / hr:mn / PST

Ephemeris

DATE	SID.TIME	SUN	MOON	NODE	MERCURY	VENUS	MARS	JUPITER	SATURN	URANUS	NEPTUNE	PLUTO	CERES	PALLAS	JUNO	VESTA	CHIRON
1 M	16:37:06	10 Ⅱ 19	28 Ω 17	05 ♏ R 27	19	21	05 Ⅱ 34	24 ♓ 41	29 ♈	10 ♒ 40	01 ♒ R 58	06 ♐ R 35	09 ♉ 45	26 ♓ 41	22 ♍ 14	14 Ⅱ 56	13 ♏ 47
2 T	16:41:03	11 16	12 ♍ 03	01	22	31	06	24	29	12	57	35	34	53	22	15	43
3 W	16:44:59	12 14	25	28	25	41	06 58	24	29	12	56	32	31	26	22	15	40
4 T	16:48:56	13 11	07 ♏ 55	26	40	04	07	25	29	28	55	31	30	27	22	16	36
5 F	16:52:53	14 08	20	24	50	04	08	25 13	29	34	54	06	54	27	22	16	33
6 S	16:56:49	15 06	04 ♐ 58	22	50	08	09	25	29	40	53	27	11	27	22	16	29
7 S	17:00:46	16 04	09 ♐	17	00	09	09	25	29	47	52	07	02	28	23	17	26
8 M	17:04:42	17 01	18	55	12	11	10	25	29	53	51	58	26	28	23	17	23
9 T	17:08:39	17 58	04 ♑ 11	58	18	23	11	25	29	58	50	44	22	28	23	18	20
10 W	17:12:35	18 56	18	56	29	36	12	25	00 ♉	58	49	20	47	29	23	18	17
11 T	17:20:28	19 53	02 ♒ 50	52	40	48	13	25	00	10	48	19	32	29	24	19	14
12 F	17:24:25	20 50	17	52	45	01	14	25	00	16	47	10	27	29	24	19	11
13 S	17:24:25	21 48	01 ♓ 34	34	57	16	15	25	00	22	46	05	51	14	29	24	08
14 S	17:28:22	22 45	08 ♓	51	20	34	14	26	00	27	45	06	39	04	24	20	05
15 M	17:32:18	23 42	29	49	30	45	15	26	00	33	44	15	23	04	24	21	02
16 T	17:36:15	24 40	12 ♈ 56	56	40	56	16	26	00	38	43	12	12	45	04	24	00
17 W	17:40:11	25 37	03 ♈	54	52	08	17	26	00	44	42	08	10	45	04	25	57
18 T	17:44:08	26 34	18	52	07	22	18	26	00	49	41	05	05	45	04	25	54
19 F	17:48:04	27 32	02 ♉ 08	08	19	35	18	26	00	55	40	01	58	46	24	26	52
20 S	17:52:01	28 29	15 32	29	30	48	18	26	00	00	39	01	57	46	24	26	50
21 S	17:55:57	29 26	26	45	44	11	19	30	26	01	17	36	01	54	13	20	48
22 M	17:59:54	00 ⊙ 00	17	42	57	17	21	26	01	10	35	01	54	13	20	46	46
23 T	18:03:51	01 21	29	35	57	16	22	26	01	15	34	01	53	15	20	44	44
24 W	18:07:47	02 18	11 ♊ 18	18	51	16	23	26	01	21	32	01	58	57	20	43	42
25 T	18:11:44	03 15	00 ⊙ 08	08	44	09	26	27	27	01	26	30	01	58	18	21	40
26 F	18:15:40	04 12	12	44	21	07	27	27	01	31	28	01	06	18	21	46	38
27 S	18:19:37	05 09	24	09	55	21	56	27	01	32	26	01	03	19	21	52	36
29 M	18:23:33	06 06	07 ♌	23	46	52	24	18	27	01	39	12	01	44	00	23	37
30 T	18:27:30	07 03	07 04	18	27	04	22	27	01	43	09	01	40	00	23	03	34
	18:31:26	08 00	18	02 D	53	05	40	25	27	48	07	24	27	01	12	27	33

EPHEMERIS CALCULATED FOR 12 MIDNIGHT GREENWICH MEAN TIME. ALL OTHER DATA AND FACING ASPECTARIAN PAGE IN **EASTERN STANDARD TIME (BOLD)** AND PACIFIC STANDARD TIME (REGULAR).

JULY 1998

(Astrological aspectarian — daily planetary aspects with times. Eastern Standard Time in bold type; Pacific Standard Time in medium type.)

1 WEDNESDAY
5:50 am · 11:07 am · 8:15 am · 11:15 am · 1:44 pm · 3:02 pm · 3:20 pm · 7:16 pm · 7:21 pm · 10:10 pm
2:50 am · 8:07 am · 8:15 am · 10:44 am · 12:02 pm · 3:16 pm · 6:20 pm · 7:11 pm · 9:22 pm

2 THURSDAY
1:26 am · 6:18 am
10:26 am · 3:18 pm · 11:08 pm · 11:11 pm · 11:34 pm · 11:35 pm

3 FRIDAY
2:26 am · 2:44 am · 11:34 am
1:39 am · 6:24 am · 6:51 am · 7:57 am · 10:57 am · 6:24 pm · 8:26 pm

4 SATURDAY
3:34 am · 3:39 am · 4:21 am · 4:33 am · 4:48 am · 7:39 am · 10:39 am · 11:50 am · 6:55 pm
3:22 am · 2:09 pm · 3:30 pm

5 SUNDAY
3:22 am · 2:09 pm · 3:30 pm

6 MONDAY
4:13 am · 5:31 am · 11:03 am · 5:12 pm · 6:24 pm · 11:02 pm · 11:25 pm
1:13 am · 2:31 am · 8:03 am · 2:12 pm · 3:24 pm · 8:02 pm · 8:25 pm · 11:26 pm

7 TUESDAY
12:21 am · 1:00 am · 2:17 am
1:46 am · 5:32 am · 5:39 am · 6:04 am · 6:57 am · 7:53 am · 9:03 am · 1:57 pm · 6:14 pm

8 WEDNESDAY
2:32 am · 2:39 am · 3:04 am · 3:57 am · 4:53 am · 6:03 am · 10:57 am · 3:14 pm · 6:03 pm · 9:21 pm · 10:46 pm · 11:17 pm

9 THURSDAY
3:53 am · 8:01 am · 8:50 am · 3:55 pm
6:34 am · 6:39 am · 7:21 am · 7:33 am · 7:48 am · 10:39 am · 11:50 am · 6:55 pm
10:01 am · 12:36 pm · 6:01 pm · 8:17 pm · 11:08 pm

10 FRIDAY
6:15 am · 6:33 am · 9:15 am · 11:52 am · 1:26 pm · 2:21 pm · 3:13 pm · 7:51 pm
3:15 pm · 3:33 pm · 6:15 pm · 8:52 pm · 10:26 pm · 10:38 pm · 11:21 pm · 12:13 am · 4:51 am

11 SATURDAY
6:26 am · 7:47 am · 12:41 pm · 4:09 pm · 8:11 pm · 10:48 pm
3:26 am · 4:47 am · 9:41 am · 1:09 pm · 5:11 pm · 7:48 pm

12 SUNDAY
5:16 am · 10:56 am · 2:43 pm · 6:00 pm · 6:57 pm · 7:41 pm · 10:14 pm
2:16 am · 7:56 am · 11:43 am · 3:00 pm · 3:57 pm · 4:41 pm · 7:14 pm · 9:01 pm

13 MONDAY
12:01 pm · 10:17 pm · 11:44 pm · 9:10 pm
12:38 pm · 4:15 pm · 7:03 pm · 7:37 pm · 11:25 pm · 4:02 pm · 4:28 pm · 6:27 pm · 7:28 pm

14 TUESDAY
3:38 am · 7:15 am · 10:03 am · 10:37 am · 2:25 pm · 7:02 pm · 7:28 pm · 9:27 pm · 10:28 pm
7:17 pm · 8:44 pm · 6:10 pm

15 WEDNESDAY
12:35 am · 3:12 am · 4:03 am
12:12 am · 1:03 am

16 THURSDAY
1:15 pm · 2:50 pm · 4:33 pm
3:27 am · 4:11 am · 2:08 pm · 5:16 pm · 9:19 pm · 10:46 pm
10:15 am · 11:50 am · 1:33 pm

17 FRIDAY
12:19 am · 1:25 am · 4:56 am · 5:54 am · 9:18 am · 5:35 pm · 7:34 pm
12:27 pm · 1:11 pm · 11:08 am · 2:16 pm · 7:10 pm · 7:46 pm · 10:25 pm
1:56 am · 2:54 am · 6:18 am · 2:35 pm · 4:34 pm

18 SATURDAY
10:27 am · 4:36 pm · 6:03 pm · 8:03 pm · 10:17 pm
7:27 am · 1:11 pm · 1:36 pm · 3:03 pm · 7:01 pm · 9:50 pm · 11:30 pm
9:11 am · 1:49 am · 5:44 am · 6:14 am · 8:50 am · 10:25 am · 10:34 am

19 SUNDAY
12:50 pm · 2:30 pm · 3:07 pm · 4:22 am · 8:39 am · 9:19 am · 2:40 pm · 5:36 pm · 6:33 pm
12:07 am · 1:22 am · 5:39 am · 6:19 am · 11:40 am · 3:36 pm · 9:32 pm

20 MONDAY
12:32 am · 11:24 am
12:34 am · 8:24 am

21 TUESDAY
4:11 am · 6:35 am · 6:37 am · 6:59 am · 7:00 am · 12:15 pm · 12:42 pm · 2:37 pm · 9:08 pm · 10:22 pm
4:46 am · 6:48 am · 10:35 am · 11:20 am · 11:40 pm
1:11 am · 3:35 am · 3:37 am · 3:59 am · 4:00 am · 5:05 am · 9:15 am · 9:42 am · 11:37 am · 6:08 pm · 9:13 pm · 9:35 pm
1:46 pm · 3:48 pm · 7:35 pm · 8:20 pm · 8:40 pm

22 WEDNESDAY
2:13 pm · 2:35 pm · 9:13 pm
12:13 pm · 2:30 am · 5:30 am · 6:13 pm · 9:14 pm

23 THURSDAY
12:14 am · 4:14 am · 8:44 am · 9:14 am · 11:50 am · 1:25 pm · 1:34 am · 3:20 pm · 5:13 pm · 5:43 pm · 10:03 pm · 10:25 pm · 10:35 pm
1:14 am · 1:49 am · 5:44 am · 6:14 am · 8:50 am · 10:25 am · 10:34 am · 12:20 pm · 2:13 pm · 2:43 pm · 7:03 pm · 7:25 pm · 7:35 pm

24 FRIDAY
4:13 am · 5:59 am · 6:47 am · 10:14 am
1:13 am · 2:59 am · 3:47 am · 7:14 pm · 11:33 pm

25 SATURDAY
2:33 am · 9:57 am · 11:42 am · 1:50 pm · 4:56 pm · 9:09 pm · 9:49 pm · 10:45 pm
6:57 am · 8:42 am · 10:50 am · 1:56 pm · 4:41 pm · 6:09 pm · 7:45 pm · 10:57 pm

26 SUNDAY
1:57 pm · 6:05 pm · 7:33 am · 8:35 am · 12:54 pm · 3:54 pm · 6:11 pm · 11:22 pm
3:05 pm · 4:33 pm · 5:35 am · 9:54 am · 12:54 pm · 3:11 pm · 8:22 pm · 10:52 pm

27 MONDAY
1:52 pm · 9:39 pm · 10:03 pm
6:39 pm · 7:03 pm · 10:59 pm

28 TUESDAY
1:59 pm · 3:33 pm · 5:21 pm · 8:56 pm · 11:09 pm · 11:16 pm · 12:48 pm · 1:02 pm · 1:11 pm · 10:09 pm
12:33 am · 3:21 pm · 5:56 pm · 8:09 pm · 8:16 pm · 9:48 pm · 10:11 pm · 10:11 pm · 7:09 pm

29 WEDNESDAY
12:16 pm · 1:36 pm · 3:42 pm · 9:27 pm · 10:50 pm
12:42 am · 6:27 am · 7:50 pm

30 THURSDAY
10:18 am · 10:52 am · 11:13 am · 3:55 pm · 4:04 pm · 6:37 pm · 9:39 pm
7:18 am · 7:52 am · 8:13 am · 12:55 pm · 1:04 pm · 3:37 pm · 9:09 pm · 10:14 pm · 10:35 pm

31 FRIDAY
1:14 am · 1:35 am · 4:51 am · 7:05 am · 12:41 pm · 3:41 pm · 4:29 pm · 9:04 pm
1:51 am · 4:05 am · 9:41 am · 10:00 am · 12:41 pm · 1:00 pm · 12:41 am · 1:29 am · 6:04 pm · 10:33 pm

Eastern Standard Time in bold type
Pacific Standard Time in medium type

JULY 1998

D Last Aspect

day	EST / hr:mm / PST	asp
2	**11:35 pm**	
5	**2:09 pm** 11:09 am	♂♂
7	**11:34 am** 8:34 am	□♀
10	**6:15 am** 3:15 am	△♀
11	**10:48 pm** 7:48 pm	□♂
14	**2:25 pm** 11:25 am	⚹♀
16	**2:51 pm** 11:51 am	△♂
18	**8:01 pm** 5:01 pm	⚹♀
20	8:20 pm	□♀

D Ingress

sign	day	EST / hr:mm / PST
♏	3	**6:46 am** 3:46 am
♐	5	**6:24 am** 3:24 am
♑	8	**3:28 am** 12:28 am
♒	10	**9:52 am** 6:52 am
♓	12	**2:22 pm** 11:22 am
♈	14	**5:45 pm** 2:45 pm
♉	16	**8:34 pm** 5:34 pm
♊	18	**11:18 pm** 8:18 pm
♋	20	11:43 pm

D Last Aspect

day	EST / hr:mm / PST	asp
20	**11:20 pm**	
23	**4:14 am** 1:14 am	□♀
25	**9:57 am** 6:57 am	♂♀
27	7:03 pm	
27	**10:03 pm**	
30	**1:13 am** 8:13 am	□♀

D Ingress

sign	day	EST / hr:mm / PST
♌	21	**2:43 am**
♍	23	**7:49 am** 4:49 am
♎	25	**3:34 pm** 12:34 pm
♏	27	11:15 pm
♏	28	**2:15 am**
♐	30	**2:45 pm** 11:45 am

Planetary Motion

	day	EST / hr:mm / PST
♂ D	11	**7:14 pm** 4:14 pm
♃ R	17	**7:55 pm** 4:55 pm
♀ R	19	**10:45 pm** 7:45 pm
♀ R	30	**9:23 pm** 6:23 pm

Phases & Eclipses

phase	day	EST / hr:mm / PST
2nd Quarter	1	**1:44 pm** 10:44 am
Full Moon	9	**11:01 am** 8:01 am
4th Quarter	16	**10:14 am** 7:14 am
New Moon	23	**8:44 am** 5:44 am
2nd Quarter	31	**7:05 am** 4:05 am

Planet Ingress

		day	EST / hr:mm / PST
♀	♋	5	**3:08 pm** 12:08 pm
♂	♋	6	**3:59 pm** 12:59 pm
♀	♋	11	**7:20 pm** 4:20 pm
♀	♌	19	**10:17 am** 7:17 am
♀	♌	22	**7:55 pm** 4:55 pm
♀	♊	28	**12:33 pm** 9:33 pm

EPHEMERIS CALCULATED FOR 12 MIDNIGHT GREENWICH MEAN TIME. ALL OTHER DATA AND FACING ASPECTARIAN PAGE IN **EASTERN STANDARD TIME (BOLD)** AND PACIFIC STANDARD TIME (REGULAR).

AUGUST 1998

Eastern Standard Time in bold type
Pacific Standard Time in medium type

The following is an aspectarian (daily planetary-aspect listing). Times in bold are Eastern Standard Time; times in medium type are Pacific Standard Time. Exact planetary glyphs are reproduced by time values below.

Top-of-page aspects

Aspect	EST	PST
△□ ☿	3:45 pm	12:45 pm
△⚷ ♇	9:01 pm	6:01 pm

1 SATURDAY
1:33 am · 10:15 am · 11:02 am · 7:15 pm · 8:02 pm

2 SUNDAY
3:49 am · 5:36 am · 6:14 am · 1:16 pm · 11:36 pm · 11:49 pm
12:49 am · 2:36 am · 3:14 am · 10:16 am · 8:36 pm · 8:49 pm · 11:12 pm · 11:22 pm · 11:32 pm

3 MONDAY
2:12 am · 2:22 am · 2:32 am · 3:50 am · 2:20 pm · 2:33 pm · 8:38 pm
12:50 am · 11:20 am · 12:33 pm · 5:38 pm

4 TUESDAY
7:30 am · 7:45 am · 1:08 am · 3:10 am · 4:16 pm · 4:30 pm · 6:50 pm · 6:10 pm
4:30 am · 4:45 am · 10:08 am · 1:16 pm · 1:30 pm · 3:50 pm · 7:10 pm · 9:34 pm · 11:17 pm

5 WEDNESDAY
12:34 am · 1:17 am · 12:05 pm · 12:23 pm · 1:16 pm
4:58 am · 9:05 am · 9:20 am · 9:23 am · 10:48 pm

6 THURSDAY
1:48 am · 3:20 am · 12:10 pm · 1:59 pm · 7:12 pm · 8:51 pm · 11:26 pm
12:20 am · 9:10 am · 10:59 am · 4:12 pm · 5:51 pm · 8:26 pm · 9:46 pm

7 FRIDAY
12:46 pm · 3:49 pm · 7:17 pm · 12:58 pm · 5:12 pm · 6:56 pm · 9:10 pm
12:49 am · 4:17 am · 9:58 am · 2:12 pm · 3:56 pm · 6:10 pm

8 SATURDAY
8:37 am · 1:47 am · 10:38 am · 11:27 am · 3:43 pm · 7:24 pm · 8:08 pm · 11:09 pm
5:37 am · 9:27 am · 10:47 am · 2:29 pm · 7:38 pm · 7:46 pm · 8:55 pm

9 SUNDAY
3:50 am · 7:45 am · 1:08 am · 4:16 pm · 4:30 pm · 6:50 pm · 6:10 pm
12:50 am · 1:07 am · 4:00 am · 4:24 pm · 5:08 pm · 8:09 pm

10 MONDAY
3:25 am · 1:22 am · 3:44 pm · 7:22 pm · 7:25 pm · 7:56 pm
12:25 am · 10:22 am · 1:36 pm · 12:44 pm · 4:22 pm · 4:25 pm

11 TUESDAY
12:39 am · 6:10 am · 8:59 am · 2:28 pm · 5:29 pm · 10:11 pm
3:10 am · 3:50 am · 5:59 am · 11:28 am · 2:29 pm · 7:11 pm · 11:29 pm

12 WEDNESDAY
2:29 am · 12:48 pm · 12:50 pm · 5:35 pm · 9:02 pm
8:50 am · 9:48 am · 2:35 pm · 6:02 pm · 10:53 pm · 11:28 pm

13 THURSDAY
1:53 am · 2:28 am · 3:51 am · 8:09 am · 8:45 am · 9:45 am · 10:57 pm
12:01 am · 5:09 am · 5:45 am · 6:45 am · 7:57 am

14 FRIDAY
12:32 am · 6:12 am · 12:27 pm · 2:49 pm · 10:32 pm
3:12 am · 9:27 am · 11:49 am · 7:32 pm · 8:18 pm

15 SATURDAY
5:05 am · 5:13 am · 9:24 am · 10:59 am · 1:30 pm · 1:37 pm · 1:52 pm · 6:47 pm
2:05 am · 2:13 am · 6:24 am · 7:59 am · 10:30 pm · 10:37 pm · 10:52 pm

16 SUNDAY
9:50 am · 10:25 am
12:36 pm · 3:36 pm · 11:14 am · 1:21 pm · 8:54 pm · 10:26 pm
6:50 pm · 7:25 pm · 11:21 pm
12:36 am · 8:14 am · 5:54 pm · 7:26 pm · 11:56 pm

17 MONDAY
2:56 am · 5:04 am · 8:47 am · 9:09 am · 12:19 pm · 3:11 pm · 3:21 pm
2:04 am · 5:47 am · 6:09 am · 9:19 am · 12:21 pm · 12:21 pm

18 TUESDAY
3:32 am · 9:15 am · 4:11 pm · 6:10 pm
6:20 pm · 6:56 pm · 7:06 pm · 9:24 pm
12:02 am · 6:15 am · 1:11 pm · 3:10 pm
3:20 pm · 3:56 pm · 4:06 pm · 6:24 pm

19 WEDNESDAY
8:20 am · 8:24 am · 9:04 am · 1:48 pm · 3:09 pm · 9:40 pm
5:20 am · 5:24 am · 6:04 am · 10:48 am · 12:09 pm · 4:25 pm

20 THURSDAY
12:48 am · 7:07 am · 7:25 pm · 12:04 pm
2:05 am · 2:13 am · 6:24 am · 7:59 am · 10:30 pm · 10:37 pm · 10:52 pm

21 FRIDAY
3:27 am · 9:30 am · 9:03 am · 9:39 am · 11:24 pm
12:27 pm · 6:30 pm · 1:01 pm · 6:03 pm · 6:39 pm · 8:24 pm · 10:09 pm

22 SATURDAY
1:09 am · 3:36 am · 6:16 am · 9:34 am · 12:41 pm · 6:40 pm · 10:27 pm · 10:49 pm
12:36 pm · 3:16 pm · 6:34 pm · 9:41 pm · 3:40 pm · 7:27 pm · 7:49 pm · 11:22 pm · 11:48 pm

23 SUNDAY
2:22 am · 2:48 am · 3:21 am · 5:20 am · 3:20 am
4:19 pm · 6:58 pm · 9:44 am · 12:13 pm · 10:54 am

24 MONDAY
1:54 am · 7:19 am · 9:58 am · 3:13 pm · 3:53 pm · 5:07 pm · 8:39 pm
12:53 pm · 5:07 pm · 5:39 pm · 10:02 pm

25 TUESDAY
1:02 am · 11:57 am · 2:20 pm · 4:46 pm · 6:35 pm
2:51 am · 8:57 am · 11:20 am · 1:46 pm · 3:35 pm · 11:05 pm

26 WEDNESDAY
2:05 am · 4:04 am · 6:31 am · 6:37 am · 10:14 pm
1:34 am · 4:31 am · 3:31 am · 3:37 am · 7:14 pm · 2:24 am · 10:34 am · 1:04 pm · 3:31 pm · 3:37 pm · 7:14 pm

27 THURSDAY
5:32 am · 6:32 am · 7:09 am · 9:13 am · 6:19 pm
2:32 am · 3:32 am · 4:09 am · 6:13 am · 11:49 pm · 3:19 pm · 11:19 pm

28 FRIDAY
2:19 am · 3:25 am · 3:50 am · 9:38 am · 12:28 pm · 8:12 pm · 9:57 pm
12:25 pm · 12:50 pm · 6:38 pm · 9:28 pm · 12:46 pm · 5:12 pm · 6:57 pm · 10:36 pm

29 SATURDAY
1:36 am · 6:06 am · 10:38 am · 5:47 pm · 9:33 pm · 10:51 pm
3:06 am · 7:38 am · 2:47 pm · 6:33 pm · 7:51 pm · 9:07 pm

30 SUNDAY
12:07 am · 4:04 am · 6:13 am · 7:28 am · 3:46 pm
1:04 am · 3:13 am · 4:13 am · 12:28 pm · 12:36 pm · 12:46 pm · 10:14 pm

31 MONDAY
1:14 am · 6:28 am · 9:17 am · 11:57 pm
3:28 am · 6:17 am · 8:57 am

AUGUST 1998

☽ Last Aspect day	EST / hr:mn	PST	asp	☽ Ingress sign	day	EST / hr:mn	PST
1		8:02 pm	□ ☿	♐	1		11:48 pm
1	**11:02 pm**		□ ☿	♐	2	**2:48 am**	
4	**7:45 am**	4:45 am	□ ♃	♑	4	**12:18 pm**	9:18 am
6	**1:59 pm**	10:59 am	✶ ♃	♒	6	**6:31 pm**	3:31 pm
8	**1:47 pm**	10:47 am	☍ ☿	♓	8	**10:04 pm**	7:04 pm
10		4:25 pm	☌ ♃	♈	10		9:11 pm
10	**7:25 pm**		☌ ♃	♈	11	**12:11 am**	
12		10:53 pm	□ ♀	♉	12		11:05 pm
13	**1:53 am**		□ ♀	♉	13	**2:05 am**	
14	**11:18 pm**	8:18 pm	✶ ♃	♊	15	**4:46 am**	1:46 am

☽ Last Aspect day	EST / hr:mn	PST	asp	☽ Ingress sign	day	EST / hr:mn	PST
16		11:56 pm	□ ♃	♋	17		5:56 am
17	**2:56 am**		□ ♃	♋	17	**8:56 am**	
19	**1:48 pm**	10:48 am	☌ ♂	♌	19	**3:01 pm**	12:01 pm
21	**9:04 pm**	6:04 pm	☌ ☉	♍	21	**11:22 pm**	8:22 pm
24	**9:58 am**	6:58 am	△ ♆	♎	24	**10:02 am**	7:02 am
26	**10:14 pm**	7:14 pm	□ ♆	♏	26	**10:25 pm**	7:25 pm
29	**10:38 am**	7:38 am	✶ ♆	♐	29	**10:55 am**	7:55 am
31	**11:57 am**	8:57 am	□ ♃	♑	31	**9:23 pm**	6:23 pm

☽ Phases & Eclipses phase	day	EST / hr:mn	PST
Full Moon	7	**9:10 pm**	6:10 pm
●	8	15° ♒ 21'	
4th Quarter	14	**2:49 pm**	11:49 am
New Moon	21	**9:03 pm**	6:03 pm
●	22	28° ♌ 48'	
2nd Quarter	29		9:07 pm
2nd Quarter	30	**12:07 pm**	

Planet Ingress	day	EST / hr:mn	PST
♀ ♌	13	**4:19 am**	1:19 am
⚴ ♈	16	**7:43 pm**	4:43 pm
♂ ♌	20	**2:16 pm**	11:16 am
♆ ♑	22	**7:27 pm**	4:27 pm
☉ ♍	22		11:59 pm
☉ ♍	23	**2:59 am**	

Planetary Motion	day	EST / hr:mn	PST
♄ ℞	15	**12:17 pm**	9:17 am
♇ D	15	**11:14 pm**	8:14 pm
☿ D	23	**5:13 pm**	2:13 pm

DATE	SID.TIME	SUN	MOON	NODE	MERCURY	VENUS	MARS	JUPITER	SATURN	URANUS	NEPTUNE	PLUTO	CERES	PALLAS	JUNO	VESTA	CHIRON
S 1	20:37:36	08 ♌ 33	14 ♏ 01	01 ♍ ℞ 41	28 ♌ ℞ 14	14 ♋ 56	17 ♋ 06	27 ♓ ℞ 45	03 ♉ 26	10 ♒ ℞ 51	00 ♒ ℞ 33	05 ♐ ℞ 22	00 ♊ 59	01 ♈ ℞ 51	05 ♎ 24	11 ♋ 08	12 ♏ 46
S 2	20:41:33	09 31	26 03	01 40	28 07	16 09	17 46	27 42	03 28	10 49	00 32	05 21	01 17	01 47	05 41	11 33	12 48
M 3	20:45:29	10 28	08 ♐ 17	01 38	27 54	17 22	18 25	27 39	03 29	10 47	00 30	05 21	01 35	01 42	05 59	11 58	12 50
T 4	20:49:26	11 26	20 48	01 36	27 37	18 34	19 04	27 36	03 30	10 44	00 28	05 20	01 53	01 37	06 16	12 23	12 53
W 5	20:53:22	12 23	03 ♑ 37	01 33	27 14	19 47	19 44	27 32	03 32	10 42	00 27	05 20	02 10	01 32	06 34	12 48	12 55
T 6	20:57:19	13 21	16 46	01 30	26 46	21 00	20 23	27 29	03 33	10 40	00 25	05 19	02 28	01 26	06 52	13 13	12 58
F 7	21:01:16	14 18	00 ♒ 16	01 28	26 14	22 13	21 02	27 25	03 34	10 37	00 24	05 19	02 45	01 20	07 09	13 38	13 00
S 8	21:05:12	15 15	14 06	01 27	25 38	23 26	21 41	27 21	03 35	10 35	00 22	05 19	03 02	01 14	07 27	14 03	13 03
S 9	21:09:09	16 13	28 11	01 D 27	24 57	24 39	22 21	27 17	03 35	10 32	00 20	05 19	03 19	01 07	07 45	14 28	13 06
M 10	21:13:05	17 10	12 ♓ 28	01 27	24 13	25 52	23 00	27 13	03 36	10 30	00 19	05 18	03 36	01 00	08 03	14 53	13 09
T 11	21:17:02	18 08	26 53	01 28	23 27	27 05	23 39	27 08	03 36	10 28	00 17	05 18	03 52	00 53	08 21	15 18	13 12
W 12	21:20:58	19 06	11 ♈ 20	01 28	22 39	28 18	24 18	27 04	03 37	10 25	00 16	05 18	04 09	00 45	08 40	15 43	13 15
T 13	21:24:55	20 03	25 46	01 29	21 50	29 32	24 57	26 59	03 37	10 23	00 14	05 18	04 25	00 37	08 58	16 07	13 18
F 14	21:28:51	21 01	10 ♉ 05	01 ℞ 29	21 00	00 ♌ 45	25 36	26 54	03 38	10 21	00 13	05 18	04 41	00 28	09 16	16 32	13 22
S 15	21:32:48	21 58	24 16	01 29	20 12	01 58	26 15	26 49	03 38	10 18	00 11	05 18	04 57	00 19	09 35	16 57	13 25
S 16	21:36:45	22 56	08 ♊ 17	01 29	19 25	03 11	26 54	26 44	03 ℞ 38	10 16	00 10	05 D 18	05 13	00 10	09 53	17 22	13 28
M 17	21:40:41	23 54	22 05	01 28	18 41	04 25	27 33	26 38	03 38	10 14	00 08	05 18	05 29	00 00	10 12	17 46	13 32
T 18	21:44:38	24 51	05 ♋ 40	01 27	18 01	05 38	28 11	26 33	03 37	10 11	00 07	05 18	05 44	29 ♓ 51	10 31	18 11	13 36
W 19	21:48:34	25 49	19 02	01 26	17 25	06 52	28 50	26 27	03 37	10 09	00 06	05 18	05 59	29 40	10 49	18 35	13 40
T 20	21:52:31	26 47	02 ♌ 10	01 25	16 54	08 05	29 29	26 21	03 37	10 07	00 04	05 18	06 14	29 30	11 08	19 00	13 43
F 21	21:56:27	27 45	15 04	01 D 25	16 30	09 19	00 ♌ 08	26 15	03 36	10 04	00 03	05 18	06 29	29 19	11 27	19 24	13 47
S 22	22:00:24	28 42	27 43	01 25	16 12	10 32	00 46	26 09	03 36	10 02	00 01	05 18	06 44	29 08	11 46	19 48	13 51
S 23	22:04:20	29 40	10 ♍ 10	01 25	16 D 01	11 46	01 25	26 03	03 35	10 00	00 00	05 18	06 58	28 56	12 05	20 13	13 56
M 24	22:08:17	00 ♍ 38	22 25	01 ℞ 25	15 58	13 00	02 04	25 56	03 34	09 58	29 ♑ 59	05 19	07 13	28 44	12 24	20 37	14 00
T 25	22:12:14	01 36	04 ♎ 30	01 25	16 02	14 13	02 42	25 50	03 33	09 56	29 57	05 19	07 27	28 32	12 43	21 01	14 04
W 26	22:16:10	02 34	16 27	01 24	16 14	15 27	03 21	25 43	03 32	09 53	29 56	05 19	07 41	28 20	13 02	21 25	14 09
T 27	22:20:07	03 32	28 19	01 24	16 35	16 41	03 59	25 36	03 31	09 51	29 55	05 20	07 54	28 07	13 21	21 49	14 13
F 28	22:24:03	04 30	10 ♏ 10	01 24	17 03	17 54	04 37	25 29	03 30	09 49	29 53	05 20	08 08	27 54	13 41	22 14	14 18
S 29	22:28:00	05 28	22 03	01 23	17 39	19 08	05 16	25 22	03 29	09 47	29 52	05 20	08 21	27 41	14 00	22 37	14 22
S 30	22:31:56	06 26	04 ♐ 04	01 D 23	18 23	20 22	05 54	25 15	03 27	09 45	29 51	05 21	08 34	27 28	14 20	23 01	14 27
M 31	22:35:53	07 24	16 16	01 24	19 14	21 36	06 32	25 08	03 26	09 43	29 50	05 21	08 47	27 14	14 39	23 25	14 32

EPHEMERIS CALCULATED FOR 12 MIDNIGHT GREENWICH MEAN TIME. ALL OTHER DATA AND FACING ASPECTARIAN PAGE IN **EASTERN STANDARD TIME (BOLD)** AND PACIFIC STANDARD TIME (REGULAR).

SEPTEMBER 1998

1 TUESDAY
12:47 am, 3:47 am, 7:30 am, 8:42 am, 11:42 am, 11:34 am, 2:34 pm, 2:38 pm, 3:29 pm, 8:14 pm, 9:49 pm, 11:04 pm, 11:31 pm, 11:14 pm

2 WEDNESDAY
12:49 am, 2:04 am, 2:31 am, 9:36 am, 2:34 pm, 6:45 pm, 7:02 pm, 8:05 pm, 10:08 pm, 6:36 pm, 11:34 pm, 3:45 pm, 4:02 pm, 5:05 pm, 7:08 pm, 11:22 pm

3 THURSDAY
2:22 am, 3:56 am, 2:55 am, 1:50 am, 2:59 am, 5:40 am, 8:08 am, 8:11 am, 12:56 am, 10:50 am, 11:59 am, 2:40 pm, 5:20 pm, 6:11 pm, 9:26 pm

4 FRIDAY
2:26 am, 6:19 am, 8:25 am, 2:59 am, 10:35 am, 10:53 am, 11:15 am, 3:19 am, 5:16 am, 5:25 am, 9:59 am, 7:35 pm, 7:53 pm, 8:15 pm, 9:14 pm

5 SATURDAY
9:19 am, 10:04 pm
12:14 am, 12:19 am, 1:04 am, 4:56 am, 6:42 am, 7:21 am, 8:14 am, 7:47 am, 11:33 pm, 1:56 am, 3:42 am, 4:21 am, 10:12 am, 1:47 pm, 8:33 pm, 9:23 pm, 10:12 pm

6 SUNDAY
12:23 am, 2:48 am, 6:22 am, 8:42 am, 8:42 am, 11:34 am, 12:29 pm, 3:22 am, 5:42 am, 5:42 am, 8:34 pm, 10:34 pm, 11:55 pm

7 MONDAY
1:34 am, 2:55 am, 7:23 am, 8:23 am, 10:34 am, 4:21 pm, 5:39 pm, 8:57 pm, 4:23 am, 5:23 am, 7:34 am, 11:00 am, 1:21 pm, 2:39 pm, 5:57 pm, 9:08 pm, 10:39 pm

8 TUESDAY
12:08 am, 1:39 am, 4:00 am, 9:30 am, 10:18 am, 1:07 pm, 11:32 pm, 1:00 am, 6:30 am, 7:18 am, 10:07 am, 8:32 pm

9 WEDNESDAY
1:08 am, 2:48 am, 8:43 am, 2:01 pm, 2:18 pm, 3:23 pm, 6:10 pm, 1:36 am, 5:43 am, 11:01 am, 11:18 am, 11:23 am, 3:10 pm, 11:48 pm

10 THURSDAY
12:35 am, 2:48 am, 6:48 am, 10:32 am, 2:31 pm, 3:04 pm, 3:48 am, 7:32 am, 11:31 am, 12:04 pm, 9:40 pm, 9:47 pm, 10:34 pm, 11:55 pm

11 FRIDAY
2:10 am, 12:40 am, 12:45 am, 12:47 am, 1:23 am, 2:41 am, 10:03 am, 3:44 pm, 7:57 pm, 9:45 pm, 10:44 pm, 4:11 pm, 4:57 pm, 6:45 pm, 7:44 pm, 11:29 pm

12 SATURDAY
2:29 am, 2:29 am, 5:29 am, 11:27 am, 6:58 pm, 2:29 pm, 2:51 pm, 3:56 pm, 8:41 pm, 2:29 am, 5:29 am, 1:20 pm, 8:27 pm, 10:20 pm, 3:58 pm

13 SUNDAY
8:58 am, 5:58 pm, 11:47 pm
2:47 am, 3:01 am, 3:36 am, 12:09 pm, 1:37 pm, 7:29 pm, 12:01 am, 12:36 am, 9:09 am, 10:37 am, 11:18 pm, 9:10 pm, 11:27 pm

14 MONDAY
12:10 am, 2:27 am, 6:12 am, 6:53 am, 7:21 am, 10:47 am, 11:29 am, 12:32 pm, 6:50 pm, 7:06 pm, 3:12 am, 3:53 am, 4:21 am, 7:47 am, 8:29 am, 9:32 am, 3:50 pm, 4:06 pm, 10:47 pm

15 TUESDAY
1:47 pm, 3:48 pm, 5:05 pm, 5:24 pm, 11:44 pm, 6:48 am, 8:05 am, 8:24 am, 2:44 pm, 7:59 pm, 10:02 pm, 11:55 pm, 4:59 pm, 7:02 pm, 8:55 pm, 9:45 pm, 10:59 pm

16 WEDNESDAY
12:45 pm, 1:59 am, 7:12 am, 3:24 am, 5:51 am, 6:56 am, 8:41 am, 4:12 pm, 4:57 pm, 6:45 pm, 7:44 pm, 11:05 am, 12:24 pm, 2:51 pm, 5:51 pm, 11:29 pm

17 THURSDAY
3:11 am, 4:44 am, 12:11 am, 1:44 pm

18 FRIDAY
5:57 am, 11:34 am, 3:44 pm, 3:59 pm, 8:03 pm, 2:57 pm, 8:34 pm, 12:44 pm, 12:59 pm, 1:13 pm, 5:03 pm
4:57 am, 6:58 am, 11:02 am, 11:43 am, 1:57 pm, 3:58 pm, 8:02 pm, 8:43 pm

19 SATURDAY
5:30 am, 1:16 am, 10:48 am, 1:55 pm, 7:26 pm, 8:10 pm, 11:46 pm, 2:30 am, 7:48 am, 10:16 am, 10:55 am, 4:26 pm, 7:22 pm, 8:46 pm, 10:08 pm, 11:01 pm

20 SUNDAY
1:08 am, 1:42 am, 2:44 am, 3:39 am, 3:57 pm, 9:59 pm, 3:48 am, 5:05 am, 5:24 am, 11:44 am, 4:59 pm, 7:02 pm, 8:55 pm, 10:59 pm

21 MONDAY
3:41 am, 4:16 am, 11:12 am, 5:49 pm, 12:41 am, 1:16 am, 8:12 am, 2:49 pm, 11:22 pm

22 TUESDAY
6:22 am, 8:09 am, 10:30 am, 10:48 am, 11:54 am, 1:31 pm, 12:40 am, 12:58 am, 5:09 am, 5:39 am, 12:09 pm, 7:11 pm, 7:55 pm, 12:03 am, 2:39 am, 9:09 am, 4:11 pm, 4:55 pm

23 WEDNESDAY
1:39 pm, 1:00 am, 2:41 am, 4:13 am, 4:18 am, 5:47 am, 10:10 am, 10:23 am, 2:48 pm, 4:56 pm, 10:12 pm, 11:43 pm, 1:18 am, 1:43 am, 2:47 am, 7:10 am, 11:48 pm, 1:56 pm, 7:12 pm, 8:43 pm

24 THURSDAY
6:19 am, 7:03 am, 7:05 am, 8:01 am, 3:40 pm, 11:24 pm, 3:19 am, 4:03 am, 5:01 am, 5:40 am, 12:40 pm, 8:24 pm, 10:38 pm, 11:55 pm

25 FRIDAY
1:38 am, 2:55 am, 4:02 am, 4:13 am, 6:19 am, 10:57 am, 2:50 pm, 4:59 pm, 10:32 pm, 11:56 pm, 1:02 am, 1:13 am, 3:19 am, 4:53 am, 7:57 am, 11:50 am, 1:59 pm, 7:32 pm, 8:56 pm, 9:40 pm, 9:58 pm

26 SATURDAY
12:40 am, 12:58 am, 3:03 am, 5:39 am, 12:09 pm, 7:11 pm, 7:55 pm, 5:09 am, 7:30 am, 7:48 am, 8:54 am, 10:31 pm

27 SUNDAY
4:27 am, 8:14 am, 10:11 am, 12:59 pm, 5:49 pm, 6:03 pm, 10:42 pm, 1:27 am, 5:14 am, 7:11 am, 9:59 am, 2:49 pm, 3:03 pm, 7:42 pm

28 MONDAY
4:25 am, 9:29 am, 1:53 pm, 4:12 pm, 4:44 pm, 10:45 pm, 11:08 pm, 1:25 am, 6:29 am, 10:53 am, 1:12 pm, 1:44 pm, 6:38 pm, 7:45 pm, 8:08 pm

29 TUESDAY
5:39 am, 6:35 am, 6:35 am, 2:49 pm, 6:33 pm, 9:49 pm, 2:39 am, 3:35 am, 3:35 am, 11:49 am, 3:33 pm, 6:49 pm

30 WEDNESDAY
4:28 am, 5:59 am, 7:01 am, 12:50 pm, 1:27 pm, 5:20 pm, 11:15 pm, 1:28 am, 2:59 am, 4:01 am, 9:50 am, 10:27 am, 2:20 pm, 8:15 pm, 8:15 pm, 9:29 pm

Eastern Standard Time in **bold type**
Pacific Standard Time in medium type

SEPTEMBER 1998

EPHEMERIS CALCULATED FOR 12 MIDNIGHT GREENWICH MEAN TIME. ALL OTHER DATA AND FACING ASPECTARIAN PAGE IN **EASTERN STANDARD TIME (BOLD)** AND PACIFIC STANDARD TIME (REGULAR).

☽ Last Aspect

day	EST / hr:mn / PST	asp
3	**3:56 am** 12:56 am	□ ♀
5	**4:56 am** 1:56 am	✶ ♂
7	**8:23 am** 5:23 am	□ ♇
8	**8:43 am** 5:43 am	△ ♆
11	**10:03 am** 7:03 am	□ ♀
12	11:47 am	□ ♆
13	**2:47 am**	△ ♂
15	**7:59 pm** 4:59 pm	✶ ♃
20	**3:57 pm** 12:57 pm	✶ ♄

☽ Ingress

sign	day EST / hr:mn / PST
♊ ♉	3 **4:21 am** 1:21 am
♈ ♋	5 **7:48 am** 4:48 am
♌ ♆	7 **8:53 am** 5:53 am
♍ ♉	9 **9:17 am** 6:17 am
♏	11 **10:41 am** 7:41 am
♐	13 **2:20 pm** 11:20 am
♑	15 **8:48 pm** 5:48 pm
♒	18 **5:51 am** 2:51 am
♓	20 **4:57 pm** 1:57 pm

☽ Last Aspect

day	EST / hr:mn / PST	asp
23	**4:18 am** 1:18 am	□ ♀
25	**4:59 pm** 1:59 pm	✶ ♀
27	**10:42 pm** 7:42 pm	□ ♇
30	**1:27 pm** 10:27 am	△ ♄

☽ Ingress

sign	day EST / hr:mn / PST
♈	23 **5:22 am** 2:22 am
♉	25 **6:05 pm** 3:05 pm
♊	28 **5:31 am** 2:31 am
♋	30 **1:54 pm** 10:54 am

☽ Phases & Eclipses

phase	day EST / hr:mn / PST
Full Moon	6 **6:22 am** 3:22 am
4th Quarter	12 **8:58 pm** 5:58 pm
New Moon	20 **12:01 pm** 9:01 am
2nd Quarter	28 **4:12 pm** 1:12 pm

Planet Ingress

	day EST / hr:mn / PST
♀ ♏	6 **2:24 pm** 11:24 am
♀ ♍	7 **8:57 pm** 5:57 pm
♃ ♌	12 **8:58 pm** 5:58 pm
☉ ♎	22 **6:45 pm** 3:45 pm
☿ ♎	23 **12:37 am** 9:37 pm
♀ ♎	24 **5:12 am** 2:12 am
♀ ♎	30 **6:13 pm** 3:13 pm

Planetary Motion

	day EST / hr:mn / PST
♇	6 **13 ♓ 40'**

Ephemeris data table for September 1998 (DATE, SID. TIME, SUN, MOON, NODE, MERCURY, VENUS, MARS, JUPITER, SATURN, URANUS, NEPTUNE, PLUTO, CERES, PALLAS, JUNO, VESTA, CHIRON)

OCTOBER 1998

1 THURSDAY

2 FRIDAY

3 SATURDAY

4 SUNDAY

5 MONDAY

6 TUESDAY

7 WEDNESDAY

8 THURSDAY

9 FRIDAY

10 SATURDAY

11 SUNDAY

12 MONDAY

13 TUESDAY

14 WEDNESDAY

15 THURSDAY

16 FRIDAY

17 SATURDAY

18 SUNDAY

19 MONDAY

20 TUESDAY

21 WEDNESDAY

22 THURSDAY

23 FRIDAY

24 SATURDAY

25 SUNDAY

26 MONDAY

27 TUESDAY

28 WEDNESDAY

29 THURSDAY

30 FRIDAY

31 SATURDAY

Eastern Standard Time in bold type
Pacific Standard Time in medium type

☽ Last Aspect day	EST / hr:mn / PST	asp	☽ Ingress sign day	EST / hr:mn / PST
2	**1:28 pm** 10:28 am	☍ ♂	♓ 2	**6:24 pm** 3:24 pm
4	**6:35 pm** 3:35 pm	⚹ ♆	♈ 4	**7:32 pm** 4:32 pm
6	**6:26 pm** 3:26 pm	△ ♂	♉ 6	**6:58 pm** 3:58 pm
8	**5:44 pm** 2:44 pm	△ ♆	♊ 8	**6:44 pm** 3:44 pm
10	**5:36 pm** 2:36 pm	△ ☿	♋ 10	**8:48 pm** 5:48 pm
12	10:17 pm	☍ ♆	♌ 12	11:25 pm
13	**1:17 am**	☍ ♆	♌ 13	**2:25 am**
14	**6:54 pm** 3:54 pm	⚹ ☉	♍ 15	**11:32 am** 8:32 am
17	**9:50 pm** 6:50 pm	△ ♆	♎ 17	**11:02 pm** 8:02 pm
20	**10:25 am** 7:25 am	□ ♆	♏ 20	**11:37 am** 8:37 am
22	8:07 pm	⚹ ♆	♐ 22	9:17 pm
22	**11:07 pm**	⚹ ♆	♐ 23	**12:17 am**
24	**1:58 pm** 10:58 am	□ ♃	♑ 25	**12:05 pm** 9:05 am
27	**9:24 pm** 6:24 pm	□ ♄	♒ 27	**9:45 pm** 6:45 pm
30	**3:20 am** 12:20 am	⚹ ♄	♓ 30	**3:58 am** 12:58 am

☽ Phases & Eclipses phase	day	EST / hr:mn / PST
Full Moon	5	**3:12 pm** 12:12 pm
4th Quarter	12	**6:11 am** 3:11 am
New Moon	20	**5:10 am** 2:10 am
2nd Quarter	28	**6:46 am** 3:46 am

Planet Ingress	day	EST / hr:mn / PST
♂ ♍	7	**7:28 am** 4:28 am
☿ ♏	11	**9:44 pm** 6:44 pm
⚹ ♏	15	**3:41 am** 12:41 am
☉ ♏	23	**9:59 am** 6:59 am
♀ ♏	24	**6:06 pm** 3:06 pm
♄ ♈	25	**1:42 pm** 10:42 am

Planetary Motion	day	EST / hr:mn / PST
⚳ R	10	**6:49 pm** 3:49 pm
♆ D	11	**7:10 am** 4:10 am
♅ D	18	**1:46 pm** 10:46 am

DATE		SID.TIME	SUN	MOON	NODE	MERCURY	VENUS	MARS	JUPITER	SATURN	URANUS	NEPTUNE	PLUTO	CERES	PALLAS	JUNO	VESTA	CHIRON
T	1	0:38:06	07 ♎ 37	02 ♒ 49	00 ♍ 54	11 ♎ 40	00 ♎ 02	26 ♌ 00	21 ♓ R 08	01 ♉ R 54	08 ♒ R 57	29 ♑ R 25	05 ♐ 52	13 ♊ 12	19 ♓ R 16	25 ♎ 03	05 ♌ 07	17 ♏ 37
F	2	0:42:03	08 36	16 21	00 56	13 23	01 17	26 37	21 00	01 50	08 56	29 25	05 53	13 15	19 02	25 23	05 28	17 44
S	3	0:45:59	09 35	00 ♓ 22	00 R 56	15 06	02 32	27 14	20 53	01 45	08 55	29 24	05 55	13 19	18 47	25 44	05 49	17 51
S	4	0:49:56	10 34	14 49	00 56	16 47	03 47	27 50	20 46	01 41	08 54	29 24	05 56	13 21	18 33	26 05	06 10	17 58
M	5	0:53:52	11 33	29 40	00 53	18 28	05 02	28 27	20 39	01 37	08 53	29 24	05 58	13 24	18 19	26 25	06 31	18 05
T	6	0:57:49	12 32	14 ♈ 47	00 49	20 07	06 17	29 04	20 32	01 32	08 53	29 24	06 00	13 26	18 05	26 46	06 52	18 12
W	7	1:01:45	13 31	00 ♉ 02	00 43	21 46	07 32	29 41	20 26	01 28	08 52	29 23	06 01	13 28	17 52	27 07	07 12	18 19
T	8	1:05:42	14 30	15 13	00 36	23 24	08 47	00 ♍ 18	20 19	01 24	08 52	29 23	06 03	13 29	17 38	27 27	07 33	18 26
F	9	1:09:38	15 29	00 ♊ 10	00 30	25 02	10 01	00 54	20 12	01 19	08 51	29 23	06 04	13 30	17 25	27 48	07 53	18 34
S	10	1:13:35	16 29	14 47	00 24	26 38	11 16	01 31	20 06	01 15	08 51	29 23	06 06	13 R 30	17 12	28 09	08 13	18 41
S	11	1:17:32	17 28	28 57	00 20	28 14	12 31	02 08	20 00	01 10	08 50	29 23	06 08	13 31	17 00	28 29	08 33	18 48
M	12	1:21:28	18 27	12 ♋ 41	00 18	29 49	13 46	02 44	19 54	01 05	08 50	29 D 23	06 09	13 30	16 48	28 50	08 53	18 56
T	13	1:25:25	19 27	25 58	00 D 18	01 ♏ 24	15 01	03 21	19 48	01 01	08 49	29 23	06 11	13 30	16 36	29 11	09 13	19 03
W	14	1:29:21	20 26	08 ♌ 53	00 19	02 57	16 16	03 57	19 42	00 56	08 49	29 23	06 13	13 29	16 24	29 32	09 32	19 10
T	15	1:33:18	21 25	21 29	00 R 20	04 30	17 32	04 33	19 36	00 51	08 49	29 23	06 15	13 27	16 13	29 52	09 52	19 18
F	16	1:37:14	22 25	03 ♍ 49	00 20	06 03	18 47	05 10	19 31	00 47	08 49	29 23	06 17	13 26	16 02	00 ♏ 13	10 11	19 25
S	17	1:41:11	23 24	15 58	00 19	07 34	20 02	05 46	19 25	00 42	08 49	29 24	06 18	13 23	15 52	00 34	10 30	19 33
S	18	1:45:07	24 24	27 59	00 16	09 05	21 17	06 22	19 20	00 37	08 49	29 24	06 20	13 21	15 42	00 55	10 49	19 41
M	19	1:49:04	25 24	09 ♎ 55	00 09	10 36	22 32	06 59	19 15	00 32	08 D 49	29 24	06 22	13 18	15 32	01 16	11 08	19 48
T	20	1:53:00	26 23	21 48	00 01	12 06	23 47	07 35	19 10	00 28	08 49	29 24	06 24	13 15	15 22	01 36	11 26	19 56
W	21	1:56:57	27 23	03 ♏ 39	29 ♌ 50	13 35	25 02	08 11	19 05	00 23	08 49	29 25	06 26	13 11	15 13	01 57	11 45	20 03
T	22	2:00:54	28 23	15 30	29 38	15 03	26 17	08 47	19 01	00 18	08 49	29 25	06 28	13 07	15 04	02 18	12 03	20 11
F	23	2:04:50	29 22	27 23	29 26	16 31	27 32	09 23	18 57	00 13	08 49	29 25	06 30	13 02	14 56	02 39	12 21	20 19
S	24	2:08:47	00 ♏ 22	09 ♐ 19	29 15	17 58	28 48	09 59	18 52	00 09	08 49	29 26	06 32	12 57	14 48	03 00	12 39	20 27
S	25	2:12:43	01 22	21 21	29 07	19 24	00 ♏ 03	10 35	18 48	00 04	08 50	29 26	06 34	12 52	14 40	03 20	12 57	20 34
M	26	2:16:40	02 22	03 ♑ 31	29 01	20 50	01 18	11 11	18 45	29 ♈ 59	08 50	29 27	06 36	12 46	14 33	03 41	13 15	20 42
T	27	2:20:36	03 21	15 54	28 58	22 15	02 33	11 47	18 41	29 54	08 50	29 27	06 38	12 40	14 26	04 02	13 32	20 50
W	28	2:24:33	04 21	28 32	28 D 56	23 39	03 48	12 22	18 38	29 49	08 51	29 28	06 40	12 33	14 20	04 23	13 49	20 58
T	29	2:28:29	05 21	11 ♒ 31	28 57	25 02	05 04	12 58	18 34	29 45	08 51	29 28	06 42	12 27	14 14	04 44	14 06	21 06
F	30	2:32:26	06 21	24 53	28 R 57	26 25	06 19	13 34	18 31	29 40	08 52	29 29	06 44	12 19	14 08	05 04	14 23	21 14
S	31	2:36:23	07 21	08 ♓ 43	28 56	27 46	07 34	14 09	18 28	29 35	08 52	29 29	06 46	12 12	14 03	05 25	14 40	21 22

EPHEMERIS CALCULATED FOR 12 MIDNIGHT GREENWICH MEAN TIME. ALL OTHER DATA AND FACING ASPECTARIAN PAGE IN **EASTERN STANDARD TIME (BOLD)** AND PACIFIC STANDARD TIME (REGULAR).

NOVEMBER 1998

1 SUNDAY
1:42 am
5:35 am
5:35 am
5:39 am
5:59 am
7:44 am
9:04 am
4:17 pm
5:31 pm
8:49 pm
9:45 pm
11:03 pm
10:36 pm

2 MONDAY
1:36 am
1:44 am
4:05 am
7:05 am
7:35 am
8:53 am
11:53 am
5:14 pm
11:40 pm

3 TUESDAY
2:40 am
5:08 am
5:28 am
10:12 am
4:47 pm
5:00 pm
8:09 pm
9:19 pm
9:31 pm
11:29 pm

4 WEDNESDAY
12:18 am
12:19 am
12:31 am
2:29 am
3:39 am
3:40 am
4:22 am
8:32 am
8:52 am
10:48 am
12:39 pm
12:49 pm
1:47 pm
3:26 pm
5:17 pm
7:48 pm

5 THURSDAY
4:25 am
4:37 am
3:52 am
4:29 am
4:15 am
5:01 am
7:23 am
11:07 am
1:25 pm
1:37 pm
12:52 pm
1:29 pm
10:28 am
2:01 pm
4:23 pm
8:07 pm
10:28 pm
11:53 pm
11:59 pm

6 FRIDAY
1:28 am
2:53 am
2:59 am
6:11 am
7:19 am
10:20 am
4:55 pm
5:25 pm
10:32 pm
3:11 pm
4:19 pm
7:02 am
7:20 pm
1:55 pm
2:25 pm
7:32 pm
10:22 pm

7 SATURDAY
1:22 am
4:01 am
4:58 am
5:30 am
6:54 am
7:25 am
8:46 am
1:01 am
1:58 am
2:30 am
3:54 am
4:25 pm
5:46 pm
9:05 pm

8 SUNDAY
12:05 am
2:42 am
6:34 am
8:43 am
10:23 am
12:39 am
1:16 am
2:38 am
6:25 pm
8:17 pm
12:42 pm
1:36 pm
3:34 pm
5:43 pm
7:23 pm
9:39 pm
10:16 pm
11:38 pm

9 MONDAY
7:30 am
8:52 am
2:09 pm
9:03 pm
10:31
4:30 am
5:52 am
1:08 pm
7:31 pm
10:01 pm
10:59 pm

10 TUESDAY
1:53 am
1:59 am
4:20 am
4:46 am
4:49 am
6:00 am
10:17 am
1:20 pm
1:46 pm
1:49 pm
3:00 pm
7:17 pm
10:59

11 WEDNESDAY
1:45 am
3:57 am
3:06 pm
4:58 pm
10:17 am
4:17 pm
4:59 pm
9:43 pm
12:57 am
1:58 pm
1:10 pm

12 THURSDAY
2:10 am
7:42 am
11:18 am
12:45 pm
1:17 pm
7:17 pm
7:59 pm
4:42 am
8:18 am
9:45 am
10:17 am
4:17 pm

13 FRIDAY
12:43 am
4:49 am
5:17 am
5:57 am
11:04 am
3:20 pm
7:13 pm
9:45 pm
1:49 am
1:58 am
2:17 am
8:04 am
10:21 am
12:20 pm
6:45 pm
10:59 pm

14 SATURDAY
1:59 am
4:22 am
7:45 am
11:23 am
1:22 am
4:45 am
8:23 am
9:18 am
11:33

15 SUNDAY
2:34 am
4:14 am
5:43 am
6:19 am
6:30 pm
9:03 pm
11:50 pm
5:14 am
8:55 am
2:43 pm
3:19 pm
3:30 pm
6:03 pm
8:50 pm

16 MONDAY
4:36 am
5:00 am
5:13 am
8:42 am
2:20 pm
3:02 pm
5:11 pm
10:13 pm
1:36 am
2:00 am
2:13 pm
5:42 pm
12:02 pm
2:11 pm
7:13 pm

17 TUESDAY
8:44 am
11:37 am
12:02 pm
12:18 pm
4:07 pm
5:21 pm
6:14 pm
6:42 pm
5:44 am
8:37 am
9:02 am
9:18 am
1:07 pm
2:21 pm
3:14 pm
3:42 pm

18 WEDNESDAY
3:47 am
6:30 am
8:17 am
5:57 am
8:43 am
11:27 pm
12:47 pm
3:30 pm
5:17 pm
2:57 pm
5:43 pm
11:34

19 THURSDAY
2:34 am
5:49 am
9:15 am
10:41 am
11:14 am
2:49 pm
6:15 pm
8:14 pm
9:43 pm

20 FRIDAY
12:43 am
7:06 am
9:28 am
10:13 am
5:10 pm
6:36 pm
9:13 pm
4:06 pm
6:28 pm
7:13 pm
2:10 pm
3:36 pm
6:13 pm

21 SATURDAY
6:24 am
11:23 am
1:52 pm
4:31 pm
5:29 pm
8:55 pm
6:19 pm
9:03 pm
11:50 pm
3:24 pm
8:23 pm
10:52 pm
1:31 am
2:29 pm
3:19 am
3:30 am
6:03 pm
8:50 pm

22 SUNDAY
4:23 am
4:54 am
8:39 am
10:19 am
11:58 am
7:43 pm
8:38 pm
1:36 am
2:00 am
5:42 am
8:42 am
12:02 pm
2:11 pm
7:13 pm
1:23 am
1:54 am
5:39 am
6:19 am
9:17 am
9:26 am
10:40 am
11:06 am
4:56 pm
8:48 pm

23 MONDAY
3:22 am
5:25 am
8:40 am
11:51 am
12:18 pm
4:07 pm
5:21 pm
6:14 pm
6:42 pm
12:22 am
2:25 am
5:40 am
8:51 am
1:07 pm
2:21 pm
3:14 pm
3:42 pm

24 TUESDAY
2:18 am
3:33 am
7:33 am
12:46 am
5:43 am
8:14 am
9:25 pm
8:41 pm
9:18 pm
12:33 am
4:33 am
8:27 am
5:44 am
6:25 pm

25 WEDNESDAY
3:46 am
5:53 am
6:15 am
9:53 am
5:49 pm
12:46 am
2:53 am
3:15 am
11:09 am
2:49 pm
10:57

26 THURSDAY
1:57 am
7:10 am
10:27 am
11:10 am
7:22 pm
11:33 pm
4:10 am
7:27 am
8:10 am
4:22 pm
8:33 pm
9:25 pm
10:09 pm
3:24 pm
8:23 pm
10:52 pm
1:31 am
2:29 pm

27 FRIDAY
12:25 am
1:09 am
4:06 am
4:28 am
8:53 am
12:17 pm
1:40 pm
2:06 pm
7:56 pm
11:48 pm
1:06 am
1:28 am
5:53 am
9:17 am
9:26 am
10:40 am
11:06 am
4:56 pm
8:48 pm

28 SATURDAY
7:07 am
7:20 am
11:32 am
3:36 pm
4:58 pm
5:25 pm
4:07 am
4:20 am
8:32 am
12:36 pm
1:58 pm
2:25 pm

29 SUNDAY
12:45 am
2:08 am
4:40 pm
7:31 pm
11:24 pm
3:26 pm
4:42 pm
5:35 pm
10:29 pm
2:26 am
3:25 am
6:20 am
6:31 am
12:53 pm
4:59 pm
8:07 pm
9:45 pm
11:18 pm
2:18 am
3:33 am
4:40 am
7:31 am
11:24 am
1:42 pm
2:35 pm
7:29 pm
11:26 pm

30 MONDAY
12:18 am
3:33 am
5:53 am
6:15 am
9:53 am
5:49 pm
2:08 am
4:47 am
2:53 am
3:15 am
6:53 am
11:21 am
1:47 pm
4:31 pm
8:24 pm
12:26 am
1:42 am
5:07 pm

Eastern Standard Time in bold type
Pacific Standard Time in medium type

NOVEMBER 1998

☽ Last Aspect / ☽ Ingress

☽ Last Aspect day	EST / hr:m / PST	asp	☽ Ingress sign day	EST / hr:m / PST
1	5:59 am 2:59 am	⚹ ♆	♈ 1	6:27 am 3:27 am
3	5:28 am 2:28 am	△ ♃	♉ 3	6:12 am 3:12 am
5	4:29 am 1:29 am	△ ♂	♊ 5	5:11 am 2:11 am
7	4:01 am 1:01 am	△ ♀	♋ 7	5:39 am 2:39 am
9	8:52 am 5:52 am	☌ ♅	♌ 9	9:33 am 6:33 am
11	3:06 pm 12:06 pm	□ ♆	♍ 11	5:38 pm 2:38 pm
14	4:22 am 1:22 am	☍ ♃	♎ 14	4:58 am 1:58 am
16	5:11 pm 2:11 pm	☍ ♂	♏ 16	5:42 pm 2:42 pm
19	5:49 am 2:49 am	☌ ♀	♐ 19	6:13 am 3:13 am
21	1:52 pm 10:52 am	△ ♅	♑ 21	5:46 pm 2:46 pm

☽ Last Aspect / ☽ Ingress

☽ Last Aspect day	EST / hr:m / PST	asp	☽ Ingress sign day	EST / hr:m / PST
24	3:33 am 12:33 am	☌ ♆	♒ 24	3:43 am 12:43 am
26	7:10 am 4:10 am	△ ♃	♓ 26	11:14 am 8:14 am
27	7:56 am 4:56 pm	⚹ ♂	♈ 28	5:34 pm 2:34 pm
30	12:53 pm 9:53 am	⚹ ♀	♉ 30	4:52 pm 1:52 pm

☽ Phases & Eclipses

phase	EST / hr:m / PST
Full Moon	3 9:18 pm
Full Moon	4:12-18 am
4th Quarter	10 7:29 pm 4:29 pm
New Moon	18 11:27 pm 8:27 pm
2nd Quarter	26 7:22 am 4:22 am

Planet Ingress

	day	EST / hr:m / PST
☿ ♐	1	11:03 am 8:03 am
☉ ♐	17	4:06 pm 1:06 pm
☿ ♏	22	7:34 am 3:34 am
♂ ♎	27	5:10 am 2:10 am
♀ ♒	27	8:09 am 5:09 am

Planetary Motion

		day	EST / hr:m / PST
☿ D		12	10:58 pm 7:58 pm
⚷ D		13	7:33 am 4:33 am
♇ R.		21	6:40 am 3:40 am

EPHEMERIS CALCULATED FOR 12 MIDNIGHT GREENWICH MEAN TIME. ALL OTHER DATA AND FACING ASPECTARIAN PAGE IN **EASTERN STANDARD TIME (BOLD)** AND PACIFIC STANDARD TIME (REGULAR).

DECEMBER 1998

1 TUESDAY
2:21 am
12:55 am
2:36 am
5:36 am
4:25 am
7:25 am
5:13 am
8:13 am
7:51 am
10:24 am
4:03 pm
6:52 pm
7:45 pm
9:18 pm
10:43 pm
9:06 pm
9:40 pm

2 WEDNESDAY
2:46 am
4:53 am
9:41 am
12:25 pm
3:24 pm
4:42 pm
9:30 pm
1:43 am
4:32 am
9:22 am
11:09 am
4:21 pm
8:52 pm
11:53 pm

3 THURSDAY
2:09 am
3:26 am
5:14 am
7:50 am
10:20 am
3:56 pm
7:29 pm
10:31 pm
1:38 am
5:48 am
6:23 am
9:18 am
7:12 pm
8:10 pm

4 FRIDAY
1:13 am
3:47 am
7:47 am
12:08 pm
2:35 pm
4:46 pm
9:33 pm
11:32 pm
6:54 am
10:35 am
1:46 pm
6:33 pm
8:32 pm

5 SATURDAY
3:55 am
5:36 am
7:25 am
8:25 am
7:51 am
10:24 am

6 SUNDAY
12:05 am
4:43 am
7:32 am
12:22 pm
2:09 pm
11:52 pm
4:53 am
6:41 am
9:25 am
12:24 pm
1:42 pm
6:30 pm
10:09 pm

7 MONDAY
2:53 am
4:38 am
8:48 am
9:23 am
12:18 pm
12:10 pm
3:51 am
5:18 am
10:22 am
6:49 pm
6:49 pm
8:02 pm
1:38 am
5:48 am
6:23 am
9:18 am

8 TUESDAY
3:51 am
5:18 am
10:22 am
6:49 pm
6:49 pm
8:02 pm
12:51 am
2:18 am
7:22 am
3:49 pm
3:49 pm
5:02 pm
10:57 pm

9 WEDNESDAY
1:57 am
4:25 am
6:52 am
9:00 am
2:22 pm
12:51 am
2:18 am
7:22 am
3:49 pm
3:49 pm
5:02 pm
10:57 pm

10 THURSDAY
5:09 am
8:18 am
7:27 am
12:54 pm
2:22 pm
2:46 pm
8:08 pm
4:27 pm
9:54 pm
11:22 pm
11:46 pm
2:09 pm
5:18 pm

11 FRIDAY
5:24 am
5:54 am
11:31 am
1:22 pm
2:10 pm
2:23 pm
6:44 pm
9:02 pm
2:24 am
2:50 am
8:31 am
9:29 am
10:22 am
11:10 am
11:23 am
3:44 pm
6:02 pm

12 SATURDAY
4:13 am
4:32 am
7:51 am
11:58 am
7:10 pm
8:23 pm
1:13 am
1:32 am
4:51 am
8:58 am
4:10 pm
5:03 pm
5:23 pm

13 SUNDAY
3:17 am
4:05 am
6:51 am
6:11 am
6:28 pm
11:43 pm
12:17 am
1:05 am
3:31 am
5:37 am
3:11 pm
3:28 pm
8:43 pm
10:13 pm

14 MONDAY
1:13 am
6:20 am
8:03 am
5:29 pm
7:50 pm
8:50 pm
12:51 am
4:29 am
11:37 am
3:50 pm
4:15 pm
5:03 pm
5:50 pm

15 TUESDAY
9:43 am
10:24 am
4:33 pm
6:30 pm
8:05 pm
9:31 pm
6:43 am
7:24 am
1:33 pm
5:05 pm
9:53 pm

16 WEDNESDAY
12:53 am
6:39 am
7:42 am
1:52 pm
5:46 pm
8:14 pm
3:39 am
4:42 am
10:52 am
2:46 pm
5:14 pm
11:40 pm

17 THURSDAY
2:40 am
5:53 am
9:11 am
10:44 am
11:51 pm
1:53 am
7:21 am
7:46 am
7:48 am
2:19 am
3:41 am
8:51 am
11:54 am

18 FRIDAY
4:45 am
7:43 am
9:10 am
10:28 am
5:42 pm
5:50 pm
7:15 pm
7:33 pm
1:45 am
4:43 am
6:19 am
7:28 am
2:42 pm
2:50 pm
4:33 pm
10:07 pm

19 SATURDAY
3:57 am
11:37 am
4:41 am
6:50 am
7:42 am
7:56 pm
7:58 pm
11:47 pm
12:52 am
8:37 am
8:50 am
10:52 am
1:41 pm
3:50 pm
4:42 pm
4:56 pm
4:58 pm
8:47 pm

20 SUNDAY
9:30 am
4:37 pm
6:23 am
9:34 am
11:27 am
11:47 am
7:36 pm
3:23 pm
5:39 pm
8:27 pm
1:27 pm
4:36 pm

21 MONDAY
6:59 am
7:03 am
3:18 am
5:36 am
5:36 am
10:35 am
12:29 pm
12:18 am
2:36 am
7:16 am
9:25 am
10:29 am
10:41 am
10:42 am

22 TUESDAY
1:29 am
1:41 am
1:42 am
4:53 am
10:21 am
10:46 am
10:48 am
2:19 am
9:41 am
11:51 pm
1:53 am
7:21 am
7:46 am
7:48 am
3:41 am
7:44 am
7:27 pm

23 WEDNESDAY
2:54 am
4:23 am
4:37 am
10:56 am
1:42 pm
2:24 pm
6:10 pm
7:01 pm
8:24 pm
1:23 am
1:37 am
7:56 am
10:42 am
11:24 am
3:10 pm
4:01 pm
5:24 pm

24 THURSDAY
8:43 am
11:50 am
1:52 pm
2:00 pm
10:54 am
12:52 pm
8:50 am
8:37 am
1:41 am
3:50 pm
4:28 pm
7:54 pm
10:46 pm

25 FRIDAY
1:46 am
6:23 am
8:39 am
11:27 am
11:47 am
7:36 pm
3:23 pm
5:39 pm
8:27 pm
1:27 pm
4:36 pm

26 SATURDAY
5:46 am
5:26 am
7:48 am
11:28 am
1:31 pm
10:34 pm
2:46 am
5:26 am
8:48 am
10:29 am
1:31 pm
8:27 pm
10:34 pm
8:33 pm
8:40 pm

27 SUNDAY
1:34 am
6:29 am
7:58 am
10:33 am
12:04 pm
4:03 pm
7:42 pm
11:09 pm
3:29 am
4:58 am
7:33 am
1:03 pm
4:42 pm
8:09 pm
11:08 pm
11:38 pm

28 MONDAY
2:08 am
2:38 am
11:06 am
12:19 pm
4:01 pm
4:38 pm
6:59 pm
8:06 am
9:19 am
1:01 pm
1:38 pm
3:59 pm

29 TUESDAY
4:22 am
5:20 am
6:29 am
9:05 am
12:43 pm
2:22 pm
6:37 pm
9:07 pm
1:22 pm
2:20 pm
3:29 pm
6:05 pm
9:43 pm
10:28 pm
1:37 pm
3:37 pm
6:07 pm
9:52 pm
11:59 pm

30 WEDNESDAY
12:52 pm
2:59 pm
4:00 pm
3:45 pm
5:01 pm
3:23 pm
5:39 pm
8:27 pm
1:27 pm
4:36 pm
1:00 pm
12:45 pm
2:01 pm

31 THURSDAY
7:54 am
5:18 am
10:43 am
12:21 pm
2:01 pm
2:02 pm
2:50 pm
7:46 pm
8:28 pm
9:58 pm
11:06 pm
5:08 pm
6:48 pm
8:06 pm
4:54 am
7:43 am
9:21 am
11:01 am
11:02 am
11:50 pm
4:46 pm
5:28 pm
6:58 pm
2:08 pm
3:48 pm
5:06 pm

Eastern Standard Time in bold type
Pacific Standard Time in medium type

DECEMBER 1998

☽ Last Aspect day	EST / hr:mn / PST	asp	☽ Ingress sign day	EST / hr:mn / PST
1	**10:43 pm** 7:43 pm	✶ ♃	♊ 2	**4:30 pm** 1:30 pm
4	**12:08 pm** 9:08 am	✶ ♄	♋ 4	**4:28 pm** 1:28 pm
6	**2:09 pm** 11:09 am	□ ♄	♌ 6	**6:56 pm** 3:56 pm
8	5:02 pm	△ ♄	♍ 8	10:22 pm
8	**8:02 pm**	△ ♄	♍ 9	**1:22 am**
11	**11:31 am** 8:31 am	□ ♀	♎ 11	**11:44 am** 8:44 am
13	3:11 pm	☍ ♄	♏ 13	9:17 pm
13	**6:11 pm**	☍ ♄	♏ 14	**12:17 am**
15	**4:33 pm** 1:33 pm	△ ♃	♐ 16	**12:47 pm** 9:47 am
18	**5:50 pm** 2:50 pm	△ ♄	♑ 18	**11:55 pm** 8:55 pm
21	**3:18 am** 12:18 am	□ ♄	♒ 21	**9:17 am** 6:17 am
23	**10:56 am** 7:56 am	✶ ♄	♓ 23	**4:45 pm** 1:45 pm
25	**6:23 am** 3:23 am	☌ ♃	♈ 25	**10:04 pm** 7:04 pm
27	4:42 pm	☌ ♄	♉ 27	10:05 pm
27	**7:42 pm**	☌ ♄	♉ 28	**1:05 am**
29	11:22 am	△ ♀	♊ 29	11:22 pm
29	**2:22 pm**	△ ♀	♊ 30	**2:22 am**
31	**9:58 pm** 6:58 pm	✶ ♄	♋ 1/1	**3:16 am** 12:16 am

☽ Phases & Eclipses

phase	day	EST / hr:mn / PST
Full Moon	3	**10:20 am** 7:20 am
4th Quarter	10	**12:54 pm** 9:54 am
New Moon	18	**5:42 pm** 2:42 pm
2nd Quarter	26	**5:46 am** 2:46 am

Planet Ingress

	day	EST / hr:mn / PST
♀ ♑	11	**1:33 pm** 10:33 am
☉ ♑	21	**8:56 pm** 5:56 pm

Planetary Motion

	day	EST / hr:mn / PST
☿ D	10	10:24 pm
☿ D	11	**1:24 am**
⚶ ℞	19	**9:31 pm** 6:31 pm
♄ D	29	**10:14 am** 7:14 am

DATE		SID.TIME	SUN	MOON	NODE	MERCURY	VENUS	MARS	JUPITER	SATURN	URANUS	NEPTUNE	PLUTO	CERES	PALLAS	JUNO	VESTA	CHIRON
T	1	4:38:36	08 ♐ 34	01 ♉ 19	25 ♌ ℞ 39	10 ♐ ℞ 07	16 ♐ 29	02 ♎ 00	18 ♓ 41	27 ♈ ℞ 30	09 ♒ 35	00 ♒ 05	07 ♐ 57	06 ♊ ℞ 00	14 ♓ 26	15 ♏ 59	21 ♌ 09	25 ♏ 29
W	2	4:42:32	09 35	16 24	25 29	08 44	17 44	02 33	18 45	27 27	09 37	00 06	07 59	05 46	14 33	16 19	21 16	25 37
T	3	4:46:29	10 36	01 ♊ 35	25 19	07 22	18 59	03 06	18 48	27 24	09 39	00 08	08 01	05 32	14 40	16 39	21 24	25 44
F	4	4:50:25	11 37	16 41	25 08	06 05	20 14	03 40	18 52	27 22	09 42	00 09	08 04	05 18	14 47	16 59	21 31	25 52
S	5	4:54:22	12 37	01 ♋ 33	24 58	04 54	21 30	04 13	18 57	27 19	09 44	00 11	08 06	05 04	14 54	17 19	21 37	26 00
S	6	4:58:19	13 38	16 02	24 50	03 51	22 45	04 46	19 01	27 17	09 46	00 13	08 08	04 50	15 02	17 39	21 43	26 08
M	7	5:02:15	14 39	00 ♌ 02	24 44	02 58	24 00	05 18	19 06	27 14	09 48	00 14	08 11	04 36	15 10	17 58	21 49	26 15
T	8	5:06:12	15 40	13 33	24 40	02 16	25 16	05 51	19 10	27 12	09 51	00 16	08 13	04 23	15 18	18 18	21 54	26 23
W	9	5:10:08	16 41	26 36	24 39	01 46	26 31	06 24	19 15	27 09	09 53	00 18	08 15	04 09	15 27	18 38	21 59	26 31
T	10	5:14:05	17 42	09 ♍ 15	24 D 38	01 27	27 46	06 56	19 21	27 07	09 56	00 20	08 18	03 56	15 36	18 57	22 04	26 38
F	11	5:18:01	18 43	21 34	24 ℞ 38	01 D 19	29 02	07 29	19 26	27 05	09 58	00 22	08 20	03 43	15 45	19 17	22 08	26 46
S	12	5:21:58	19 44	03 ♎ 38	24 37	01 21	00 ♑ 17	08 01	19 31	27 03	10 01	00 23	08 22	03 30	15 54	19 36	22 12	26 53
S	13	5:25:54	20 45	15 33	24 34	01 33	01 32	08 33	19 37	27 01	10 03	00 25	08 25	03 17	16 04	19 55	22 15	27 01
M	14	5:29:51	21 46	27 24	24 29	01 54	02 48	09 06	19 43	27 00	10 06	00 27	08 27	03 05	16 14	20 15	22 18	27 08
T	15	5:33:48	22 47	09 ♏ 14	24 21	02 23	04 03	09 38	19 49	26 58	10 08	00 29	08 29	02 53	16 24	20 34	22 21	27 16
W	16	5:37:44	23 48	21 08	24 11	02 59	05 18	10 10	19 55	26 56	10 11	00 31	08 32	02 41	16 35	20 53	22 23	27 23
T	17	5:41:41	24 49	03 ♐ 07	24 00	03 42	06 34	10 41	20 02	26 55	10 14	00 33	08 34	02 29	16 46	21 12	22 24	27 31
F	18	5:45:37	25 50	15 13	23 48	04 30	07 49	11 13	20 08	26 54	10 16	00 35	08 36	02 17	16 57	21 31	22 25	27 38
S	19	5:49:34	26 51	27 28	23 38	05 23	09 04	11 45	20 15	26 52	10 19	00 37	08 38	02 06	17 08	21 50	22 26	27 45
S	20	5:53:30	27 52	09 ♑ 53	23 29	06 21	10 20	12 16	20 22	26 51	10 22	00 39	08 41	01 55	17 20	22 09	22 ℞ 26	27 52
M	21	5:57:27	28 53	22 27	23 22	07 23	11 35	12 47	20 29	26 50	10 25	00 41	08 43	01 45	17 32	22 28	22 26	28 00
T	22	6:01:24	29 55	05 ♒ 11	23 18	08 28	12 50	13 19	20 36	26 49	10 27	00 43	08 45	01 35	17 44	22 47	22 26	28 07
W	23	6:05:20	00 ♑ 56	18 06	23 17	09 36	14 06	13 50	20 43	26 49	10 30	00 45	08 47	01 25	17 56	23 06	22 25	28 14
T	24	6:09:17	01 57	01 ♓ 14	23 D 17	10 46	15 21	14 21	20 51	26 48	10 33	00 47	08 50	01 15	18 09	23 24	22 23	28 21
F	25	6:13:13	02 58	14 36	23 18	11 59	16 36	14 51	20 58	26 47	10 36	00 49	08 52	01 06	18 22	23 43	22 21	28 28
S	26	6:17:10	03 59	28 14	23 ℞ 19	13 15	17 52	15 22	21 06	26 47	10 39	00 51	08 54	00 57	18 35	24 01	22 18	28 35
S	27	6:21:06	05 00	12 ♈ 09	23 18	14 31	19 07	15 53	21 14	26 46	10 42	00 53	08 56	00 48	18 48	24 20	22 16	28 42
M	28	6:25:03	06 01	26 21	23 16	15 50	20 22	16 23	21 22	26 46	10 45	00 55	08 58	00 40	19 02	24 38	22 12	28 49
T	29	6:28:59	07 02	10 ♉ 49	23 12	17 10	21 37	16 53	21 31	26 D 46	10 48	00 57	09 00	00 32	19 16	24 56	22 08	28 56
W	30	6:32:56	08 04	25 28	23 07	18 31	22 53	17 23	21 39	26 46	10 51	00 59	09 03	00 25	19 30	25 14	22 04	29 02
T	31	6:36:53	09 05	10 ♊ 14	23 00	19 53	24 08	17 53	21 48	26 46	10 54	01 01	09 05	00 18	19 44	25 32	21 59	29 09

EPHEMERIS CALCULATED FOR 12 MIDNIGHT GREENWICH MEAN TIME. ALL OTHER DATA AND FACING ASPECTARIAN PAGE IN **EASTERN STANDARD TIME (BOLD)** AND PACIFIC STANDARD TIME (REGULAR).

JANUARY 1999

1 FRIDAY
2:06 am
3:30 am
5:07 am
5:07 am
7:51 am
4:08 pm
6:21 pm
9:27 pm
9:44 pm
9:50 pm

2 SATURDAY
2:39 am
4:06 am
7:47 am
3:43 pm
4:15 pm
7:28 pm
7:40 pm
8:31 pm
9:01 pm
11:31 pm
11:35 pm

3 SUNDAY
2:43 am
3:18 am
3:30 am
6:07 am
3:03 pm
3:41 pm
6:26 pm
7:06 pm
7:55 pm
11:06 pm
11:24 pm

4 MONDAY
12:01 am
2:35 am
4:43 am
6:23 am

5 TUESDAY
4:59 am
5:36 am
5:51 am
9:32 am
10:57 am
4:51 pm
6:21 pm
9:27 pm
9:44 pm
1:19 pm

6 WEDNESDAY
12:18 am
12:30 am
3:07 am
10:43 am
12:03 pm
12:41 pm
3:06 pm
4:55 pm
7:28 pm
8:00 pm

7 THURSDAY
3:18 am
6:07 am
3:03 pm
3:41 pm
6:59 pm
9:27 pm
11:24 pm

8 FRIDAY
12:27 am
1:21 am
5:43 am
3:24 pm
4:46 pm
6:56 pm
7:37 pm
8:31 pm

9 SATURDAY
5:05 am
5:14 am
6:23 am
9:21 am
1:16 am
4:10 pm
5:03 pm
6:22 pm

10 SUNDAY
1:32 am
6:55 am
8:22 am
10:40 am
7:40 pm
9:23 pm
10:23 pm
11:57 pm

11 MONDAY
12:23 am
1:23 am
2:57 am
7:08 am
8:51 am

12 TUESDAY
1:04 am
1:12 am
3:40 am
6:15 am
7:53 am
8:10 am
6:59 pm
9:27 pm
11:24 pm

13 WEDNESDAY
1:21 am
5:43 am
3:24 pm
4:46 pm
6:56 pm
7:41 pm
8:31 pm

14 THURSDAY
11:56 am
2:15 pm
4:02 pm
7:14 pm
8:15 pm
8:42 pm

15 FRIDAY
1:43 pm
6:13 pm
7:29 pm
10:34 pm
11:12 pm

16 SATURDAY
1:54 am
6:05 am
11:10 am
12:16 pm
3:58 pm
8:36 pm

17 SUNDAY
5:47 am
6:15 am
9:09 am
10:47 am
11:19 am
2:59 pm
5:25 pm
6:02 pm
7:19 pm

18 MONDAY
12:56 am
3:56 am
9:59 am
2:06 pm

19 TUESDAY
1:36 am
2:11 am
2:57 am
7:53 am
8:59 am
1:54 am
1:59 pm
2:38 pm
3:04 pm
4:55 pm
5:39 pm

20 WEDNESDAY
12:49 am
1:51 am
2:30 am
3:17 pm
8:05 pm
8:04 pm
10:42 pm

21 THURSDAY
7:25 am
12:19 pm
2:30 pm
3:17 pm
7:35 pm
8:05 pm
10:42 pm

22 FRIDAY
12:20 am
2:28 am
5:51 am
6:39 am
6:54 am
6:57 am
8:21 pm

23 SATURDAY
12:28 am
3:09 pm
9:09 pm
11:55 pm

24 SUNDAY
12:21 am
12:52 am
12:55 am
2:25 am
5:26 am
6:07 am
9:34 am
10:11 am
10:59 am
2:16 pm
2:16 pm
11:35 pm

25 MONDAY
3:44 am
7:57 am
9:39 am
12:30 pm
1:21 pm

26 TUESDAY
3:19 am
12:43 am
4:04 am
4:42 am
5:15 am
8:57 am
9:34 am
10:00 am
10:52 am
12:26 pm
12:54 pm
2:28 pm
8:41 pm

27 WEDNESDAY
2:08 am
10:28 am
6:23 am
10:25 am
10:27 am
2:04 pm

28 THURSDAY
5:11 am
6:27 am
2:40 am
7:52 am

29 FRIDAY
8:17 am
11:40 am
1:30 pm
3:31 pm
5:51 pm
7:17 pm

30 SATURDAY
3:08 am
4:50 am
9:16 am
3:57 pm

31 SUNDAY
6:03 am
8:47 am
11:07 am
1:31 pm
5:37 pm
7:15 pm
8:44 pm
10:15 pm
10:11 pm

5:17 am
8:40 am
9:01 am
10:30 am
12:12 pm
2:51 pm
4:17 pm

12:08 am
1:50 am
6:16 am
9:04 am
12:57 pm
11:25 pm

12:16 pm
1:54 pm
7:22 am
9:44 am
8:17 pm
3:22 pm
3:53 pm
4:04 pm
5:26 pm
7:15 pm

3:03 am
5:47 am
8:07 am
10:31 am
4:15 pm
5:44 pm
7:11 pm

Eastern Standard Time in **bold type**
Pacific Standard Time in medium type

JANUARY 1999

☽ Last Aspect day	EST / hr:mn / PST		asp	☽ Ingress sign	day	EST / hr:mn / PST	
31	**9:58 pm**	6:58 pm	✶ ♄	♋	1	**3:16 am**	12:16 am
2		11:35 pm	☍ ♀	♌	3	**5:31 am**	2:31 am
3	**2:35 am**		☍ ♀	♌	3	**5:31 am**	2:31 am
5	**6:31 am**	3:31 am	△ ☿	♍	5	**10:49 am**	7:49 am
7	**6:07 am**	3:07 am	☍ ♃	♎	7	**7:53 pm**	4:53 pm
9		10:32 pm	☍ ♄	♏	10	**7:48 am**	4:48 am
10	**1:32 am**		☍ ♄	♏	10	**7:48 am**	4:48 am
12	**7:53 am**	4:53 am	△ ♃	♐	12	**8:23 pm**	5:23 pm
14		10:43 pm	△ ♄	♑	15	**7:29 am**	4:29 am
15	**1:43 am**		△ ♄	♑	15	**7:29 am**	4:29 am

☽ Last Aspect day	EST / hr:mn / PST		asp	☽ Ingress sign	day	EST / hr:mn / PST	
17	**10:49 am**	7:49 am	□ ♄	♒	17	**4:12 pm**	1:12 pm
19	**5:44 pm**	2:44 pm	△ ♂	♓	19	**10:41 pm**	7:41 pm
21	**7:35 pm**	4:35 pm	☌ ♃	♈	22	**3:26 am**	2:26 am
24	**5:26 am**	2:26 am	☍ ♂	♉	24	**6:53 am**	3:53 am
26	**4:44 am**	1:44 am	□ ♀	♊	26	**9:30 am**	6:30 am
28	**7:52 am**	4:52 am	✶ ♄	♋	28	**11:57 am**	8:57 am
30	**11:17 am**	8:17 am	□ ♄	♌	30	**3:16 pm**	12:16 pm

☽ Phases & Eclipses phase	day	EST / hr:mn / PST	
Full Moon	1	**9:50 pm**	6:50 pm
4th Quarter	9	**9:21 am**	6:21 am
New Moon	17	**10:47 am**	7:47 am
2nd Quarter	24	**2:16 pm**	11:16 am
Full Moon	31	**11:07 am**	8:07 am
●	31	11° ♌ 20'	

Planet Ingress		day	EST / hr:mn / PST	
⚳	♊	2	**3:44 pm**	12:44 pm
♀	♒	4	**11:25 am**	8:25 am
☿	♑	6	**9:03 pm**	6:03 pm
⚷	♐	7	**3:16 pm**	12:16 pm
⚵	♐	15	**7:12 am**	4:12 am
☉	♒	20	**7:38 am**	4:38 am
☿	♒	26	**4:32 am**	1:32 am
♂	♏	26	**6:59 am**	3:59 am
♀	♓	28	**11:16 am**	8:16 am
⚳	♊	30	**12:55 pm**	9:55 am

Planetary Motion		day	EST / hr:mn / PST	
⚳	D	16	**10:32 am**	7:32 am

DATE		SID.TIME	SUN	MOON	NODE	MERCURY	VENUS	MARS	JUPITER	SATURN	URANUS	NEPTUNE	PLUTO	CERES	PALLAS	JUNO	VESTA	CHIRON
F	1	6:40:49	10 ♑ 06	24 ♊ 58	22 ♌ ℞ 53	21 ♐ 16	25 ♑ 23	18 ♎ 23	21 ♓ 56	26 ♈ 46	10 ♒ 57	01 ♒ 04	09 ♐ 07	00 ♊ ℞ 11	19 ♓ 58	25 ♏ 50	21 ♌ ℞ 54	29 ♏ 16
S	2	6:44:46	11 07	09 ♋ 32	22 47	22 40	26 38	18 53	22 05	26 47	11 01	01 06	09 09	00 05	20 13	26 08	21 48	29 23
S	3	6:48:42	12 08	23 50	22 41	24 05	27 53	19 22	22 14	26 47	11 04	01 08	09 11	29 ♉ 59	20 28	26 26	21 42	29 29
M	4	6:52:39	13 09	07 ♌ 47	22 38	25 31	29 09	19 51	22 23	26 48	11 07	01 10	09 13	29 54	20 43	26 44	21 35	29 36
T	5	6:56:35	14 10	21 19	22 D 36	26 58	00 ♒ 24	20 21	22 33	26 48	11 10	01 12	09 15	29 49	20 58	27 01	21 28	29 42
W	6	7:00:32	15 12	04 ♍ 25	22 36	28 25	01 39	20 50	22 42	26 49	11 13	01 14	09 17	29 44	21 13	27 19	21 21	29 48
T	7	7:04:28	16 13	17 09	22 37	29 52	02 54	21 18	22 52	26 50	11 17	01 17	09 19	29 40	21 29	27 36	21 13	29 55
F	8	7:08:25	17 14	29 33	22 38	01 ♑ 21	04 09	21 47	23 01	26 51	11 20	01 19	09 21	29 36	21 45	27 54	21 04	00 ♐ 01
S	9	7:12:22	18 15	11 ♎ 42	22 ℞ 40	02 50	05 24	22 15	23 11	26 52	11 23	01 21	09 23	29 33	22 01	28 11	20 56	00 07
S	10	7:16:18	19 16	23 39	22 40	04 19	06 39	22 44	23 21	26 53	11 26	01 23	09 25	29 30	22 17	28 28	20 46	00 13
M	11	7:20:15	20 17	05 ♏ 32	22 39	05 49	07 55	23 12	23 31	26 55	11 30	01 26	09 27	29 27	22 34	28 45	20 37	00 19
T	12	7:24:11	21 18	17 23	22 36	07 20	09 10	23 40	23 41	26 56	11 33	01 28	09 29	29 25	22 50	29 02	20 27	00 25
W	13	7:28:08	22 20	29 19	22 32	08 51	10 25	24 07	23 51	26 57	11 36	01 30	09 31	29 23	23 07	29 18	20 16	00 31
T	14	7:32:04	23 21	11 ♐ 21	22 27	10 22	11 40	24 35	24 02	26 59	11 40	01 32	09 32	29 22	23 24	29 35	20 05	00 37
F	15	7:36:01	24 22	23 34	22 22	11 54	12 55	25 02	24 12	27 01	11 43	01 35	09 34	29 21	23 41	29 52	19 54	00 43
S	16	7:39:57	25 23	05 ♑ 59	22 18	13 27	14 10	25 29	24 23	27 03	11 46	01 37	09 36	29 21	23 58	00 ♐ 08	19 42	00 49
S	17	7:43:54	26 24	18 38	22 14	15 00	15 25	25 56	24 34	27 05	11 50	01 39	09 38	29 D 20	24 16	00 24	19 30	00 54
M	18	7:47:51	27 25	01 ♒ 31	22 12	16 33	16 40	26 23	24 44	27 07	11 53	01 41	09 40	29 21	24 34	00 41	19 18	01 00
T	19	7:51:47	28 26	14 37	22 D 11	18 07	17 55	26 49	24 55	27 09	11 57	01 44	09 41	29 22	24 51	00 57	19 05	01 05
W	20	7:55:44	29 27	27 57	22 11	19 42	19 10	27 16	25 07	27 11	12 00	01 46	09 43	29 23	25 09	01 12	18 52	01 11
T	21	7:59:40	00 ♒ 28	11 ♓ 27	22 12	21 17	20 25	27 42	25 18	27 14	12 04	01 48	09 45	29 24	25 28	01 28	18 38	01 16
F	22	8:03:37	01 30	25 09	22 14	22 52	21 40	28 07	25 29	27 16	12 07	01 51	09 46	29 26	25 46	01 44	18 25	01 21
S	23	8:07:33	02 31	09 ♈ 01	22 15	24 29	22 55	28 33	25 40	27 19	12 11	01 53	09 48	29 29	26 04	01 59	18 11	01 27
S	24	8:11:30	03 32	23 01	22 ℞ 16	26 06	24 10	28 58	25 52	27 21	12 14	01 55	09 49	29 31	26 23	02 15	17 56	01 32
M	25	8:15:26	04 33	07 ♉ 09	22 16	27 43	25 25	29 23	26 03	27 24	12 17	01 57	09 51	29 35	26 42	02 30	17 42	01 37
T	26	8:19:23	05 34	21 23	22 15	29 21	26 40	29 48	26 15	27 27	12 21	02 00	09 53	29 38	27 01	02 45	17 27	01 42
W	27	8:23:20	06 35	05 ♊ 40	22 13	01 ♒ 00	27 54	00 ♏ 12	26 27	27 30	12 24	02 02	09 54	29 42	27 20	03 00	17 12	01 46
T	28	8:27:16	07 36	19 57	22 11	02 39	29 09	00 36	26 39	27 33	12 28	02 04	09 56	29 46	27 39	03 15	16 57	01 51
F	29	8:31:13	08 37	04 ♋ 10	22 09	04 19	00 ♓ 24	01 00	26 51	27 36	12 31	02 06	09 57	29 51	27 58	03 30	16 42	01 56
S	30	8:35:09	09 38	18 15	22 07	05 59	01 39	01 24	27 03	27 40	12 35	02 09	09 58	29 56	28 18	03 44	16 27	02 00
S	31	8:39:06	10 38	02 ♌ 09	22 05	07 41	02 54	01 47	27 15	27 43	12 38	02 11	10 00	00 ♊ 02	28 38	03 58	16 11	02 05

EPHEMERIS CALCULATED FOR 12 MIDNIGHT GREENWICH MEAN TIME. ALL OTHER DATA AND FACING ASPECTARIAN PAGE IN **EASTERN STANDARD TIME (BOLD)** AND PACIFIC STANDARD TIME (REGULAR).

FEBRUARY 1999

1 MONDAY
4:11 am
4:18 am
4:40 am
7:20 am
8:59 am
9:03 pm
1:11 am
1:18 am
1:40 am
4:20 am
5:59 am
6:03 pm
9:44 pm
9:46 pm
10:29 pm

2 TUESDAY
12:44 am
12:46 am
1:29 am
4:56 am
7:42 am
3:09 pm
3:43 pm
7:04 pm
8:17 pm
8:28 pm
10:10 pm
1:56 am
4:42 am
12:09 pm
12:43 pm
4:04 am
5:17 pm
5:28 pm
7:10 pm
9:59 pm
10:40 pm

3 WEDNESDAY
12:59 am
1:40 am
9:20 pm
10:02 pm
10:18 pm
10:59 pm
11:57 pm

4 THURSDAY
12:20 am
1:02 am
1:18 am
1:50 am
5:07 am
5:53 am
9:29 am
9:35 am
11:48 am
2:47 pm
2:07 am
2:53 am
4:29 am
6:35 am
8:48 am
11:47 am

5 FRIDAY
11:03 pm
9:36 pm
8:03 pm
12:36 am
6:11 am
1:09 pm
3:47 pm
3:11 am
6:38 am
10:09 am
11:32 am
12:47 pm

6 SATURDAY
12:59 am
12:22 am
1:23 pm
5:45 pm
6:03 pm
9:01 pm
9:16 pm
9:22 am
10:23 am
2:45 pm
3:03 pm
6:01 pm
6:16 pm

7 SUNDAY
1:05 am
3:28 am
12:34 am
6:31 pm
8:26 pm
12:28 am
9:34 am
2:52 pm
3:31 pm
5:26 pm
9:25 pm

8 MONDAY
12:25 am
6:58 am
8:24 am
2:39 pm
3:58 am
11:36 am
11:39 am
10:15 pm

9 TUESDAY
1:15 am
3:01 am
4:01 am
5:24 am
9:45 am
10:08 am
3:24 pm
5:06 pm
12:01 am
1:39 am
4:34 am
5:56 am
6:45 am
7:08 am
12:24 pm
2:06 pm
10:08 pm

10 WEDNESDAY
1:08 am
7:12 am
1:15 pm
7:03 pm
4:12 am
4:30 am
10:10 am
4:03 pm
9:35 pm

11 THURSDAY
12:35 am
11:13 am
12:59 pm
1:15 pm
2:49 pm
3:40 pm
7:13 pm
9:17 pm
9:33 pm
9:45 pm
8:13 am
9:59 am
11:49 am
12:40 pm
4:13 pm
6:17 pm
6:33 pm
6:45 pm

12 FRIDAY
4:07 am
5:56 am
5:10 am
9:07 am
11:56 am
4:46 pm
5:55 pm
1:07 am
2:56 am
2:10 am
6:07 am
8:56 am
1:46 pm
2:55 pm

13 SATURDAY
5:37 am
10:34 am
3:06 pm
9:54 pm
10:32 pm
2:37 am
7:34 am
12:06 pm
6:54 pm
7:32 pm
10:27 pm
10:39 pm

14 SUNDAY
1:27 am
1:39 am
4:34 am
5:56 am
6:28 am
7:13 am
7:37 am
10:39 pm
1:35 pm
2:06 pm
7:42 pm
1:34 am
2:56 am
3:28 am
4:13 am
4:37 am
7:39 am
10:36 pm
11:06 pm
4:42 pm

15 MONDAY
1:32 am
5:51 pm
2:51 am
10:40 pm

16 TUESDAY
1:40 am
4:42 am
8:01 am
10:49 am
11:33 am
12:06 pm
1:34 pm
2:26 pm
7:51 pm
7:54 pm
8:46 pm
1:42 am
5:01 am
7:49 am
8:33 am
9:06 am
9:41 am
10:34 am
11:26 am
4:51 pm
4:54 pm
5:46 pm
9:34 pm
11:55 pm

17 WEDNESDAY
12:34 am
2:55 am
3:26 am
6:18 am
10:13 pm
12:26 am
3:18 am
7:13 pm
10:59 pm
11:42 pm

18 THURSDAY
1:59 am
2:42 am
8:30 am
9:13 am
12:14 pm
2:49 pm
2:58 pm
3:03 pm
3:32 pm
6:59 pm
11:37 pm
11:55 pm
5:30 am
6:13 am
9:14 am
11:49 am
11:58 am
12:03 pm
12:32 pm
3:59 pm
8:37 pm
8:55 pm

19 FRIDAY
3:27 am
3:33 am
4:58 am
7:14 am
12:27 pm
12:33 pm
1:58 pm
4:14 pm

20 SATURDAY
9:18 am
6:18 pm
9:13 pm
12:13 pm
9:55 am
11:12 am
2:58 am
5:25 am
5:25 am
5:52 am
6:01 am
10:38 am
6:55 am
8:12 am
11:58 am
12:23 pm
12:25 pm
2:25 pm
2:52 pm
3:01 pm
7:38 pm
10:49 pm
11:32 pm

21 SUNDAY
1:49 am
3:08 am
5:32 am
6:47 am
11:46 am
4:36 pm
8:44 pm
12:08 pm
2:52 pm
3:27 pm
3:47 pm
8:46 pm
1:36 pm
5:44 pm

22 MONDAY
5:44 am
10:40 am
1:54 pm
6:10 pm
7:59 pm
9:05 pm
9:43 pm
2:44 am
7:40 am
10:54 am
2:05 pm
3:10 pm
4:59 pm
5:37 pm
6:05 pm
6:43 pm
11:31 pm

23 TUESDAY
2:31 am
5:43 am
6:37 am
8:18 am
8:32 am
2:41 pm
2:48 pm
2:43 am
3:37 am
5:18 am
5:32 am
11:41 am
11:48 am
11:22 pm

24 WEDNESDAY
2:22 am
3:23 am
10:49 am
5:28 pm
10:51 pm
11:29 pm
12:23 pm
7:49 pm
2:28 pm
7:51 pm
8:29 pm
9:08 pm
9:13 pm
10:18 pm
10:23 pm

25 THURSDAY
12:08 am
12:13 am
1:18 am
1:23 am
5:09 am
9:55 am
11:06 am
11:13 am
12:14 pm
6:43 pm
2:09 am
4:29 am
6:55 am
8:06 am
8:13 am
9:14 am
11:32 am
3:43 pm

26 FRIDAY
1:15 am
7:26 am
10:24 pm
10:15 am
4:26 pm
7:24 pm

27 SATURDAY
4:22 am
4:30 am
5:01 am
7:02 am
7:21 am
11:32 am
2:03 pm
2:16 pm
2:23 pm
3:35 pm
3:37 pm
5:04 pm
5:26 pm
1:22 am
1:30 am
2:01 am
4:02 am
4:21 am
8:32 am
11:16 am
11:16 am
11:23 am
12:35 pm
12:37 pm
2:04 pm
2:26 pm

28 SUNDAY
12:18 am
3:43 am
9:13 pm
12:18 am
12:57 am
6:13 am

3:04 pm
6:26 pm
12:04 pm
3:26 pm
10:31 pm
11:13 pm
11:24 pm
11:43 pm

Eastern Standard Time in bold type
Pacific Standard Time in medium type

FEBRUARY 1999

☽ Last Aspect day	EST	hr:mn / PST	asp	☽ Ingress sign	day	EST	hr:mn / PST
1	**4:40 pm**	1:40 pm	△ ♄	♍	1	**8:37 pm**	5:37 pm
3		10:18 pm	☍ ♃	♎	4	**4:55 am**	1:55 am
4	**1:18 am**		☍ ♃	♎	4	**4:55 am**	1:55 am
6	**12:22 pm**	9:22 am	☍ ♄	♏	6	**4:07 pm**	1:07 pm
9	**3:01 am**	12:01 am	△ ♃	♐	9	**4:38 am**	1:38 am
11	**3:40 pm**	12:40 pm	□ ♃	♑	11	**4:10 pm**	1:10 pm
13	**10:32 pm**	7:32 pm	□ ♄	♒	13		9:57 pm
13	**10:32 pm**	7:32 pm	□ ♄	♒	14	**12:57 am**	
16	**4:42 am**	1:42 am	✶ ♄	♓	16	**6:40 am**	3:40 am
17		11:42 pm	☌ ♀	♈	18	**10:07 am**	7:07 am
18	**2:42 am**		☌ ♀	♈	18	**10:07 am**	7:07 am
20	**11:12 am**	8:12 am	☌ ♄	♉	20	**12:29 pm**	9:29 am
21	**4:36 pm**	1:36 pm	✶ ☿	♊	22	**2:54 pm**	11:54 am
24	**5:28 pm**	2:28 pm	✶ ♄	♋	24	**6:09 pm**	3:09 pm
26	**10:24 pm**	7:24 pm	□ ♄	♌	26	**10:44 pm**	7:44 pm
27		9:18 pm	☍ ♅	♍	1	**5:05 am**	2:05 am
28	**12:18 am**		☍ ♅	♍	1	**5:05 am**	2:05 am

☽ Phases & Eclipses phase	day	EST	hr:mn / PST
4th Quarter	8	**6:58 am**	3:58 am
New Moon	15		10:40 pm
New Moon	16	**1:40 am**	
●	16	27° ♒ 08'	
2nd Quarter	22	**9:43 pm**	6:43 pm

Planet Ingress		day	EST	hr:mn / PST
♀	♈	3	**9:53 pm**	6:53 pm
♃	♈	12	**8:21 pm**	5:21 pm
☿	♓	12	**10:27 am**	7:27 am
☉	♓	18	**9:47 pm**	6:47 pm
♀	♈	21	**3:49 pm**	12:49 pm
♄	♉	28	**8:29 pm**	5:29 pm

Planetary Motion	day	EST	hr:mn / PST

DATE		SID.TIME	SUN	MOON	NODE	MERCURY	VENUS	MARS	JUPITER	SATURN	URANUS	NEPTUNE	PLUTO	CERES	PALLAS	JUNO	VESTA	CHIRON
M	1	8:43:02	11 ♒ 39	15 ♌ 47	22 ♌ D 04	09 ♒ 23	04 ♓ 08	02 ♏ 11	27 ♓ 27	27 ♈ 47	12 ♒ 42	02 ♒ 13	10 ♐ 01	00 ♊ 07	28 ♓ 57	04 ♐ 13	15 ♌ ℞ 55	02 ♐ 09
T	2	8:46:59	12 40	29 07	22 04	11 05	05 23	02 33	27 39	27 50	12 45	02 16	10 03	00 13	29 17	04 27	15 40	02 14
W	3	8:50:55	13 41	12 ♍ 08	22 04	12 49	06 38	02 56	27 52	27 54	12 49	02 18	10 04	00 20	29 37	04 41	15 24	02 18
T	4	8:54:52	14 42	24 50	22 05	14 33	07 52	03 18	28 04	27 58	12 52	02 20	10 05	00 27	29 58	04 54	15 08	02 22
F	5	8:58:49	15 43	07 ♎ 15	22 06	16 17	09 07	03 40	28 16	28 02	12 56	02 22	10 06	00 34	00 ♈ 18	05 08	14 52	02 26
S	6	9:02:45	16 44	19 26	22 07	18 03	10 21	04 01	28 29	28 06	12 59	02 24	10 08	00 42	00 38	05 21	14 36	02 30
S	7	9:06:42	17 44	01 ♏ 27	22 07	19 49	11 36	04 23	28 42	28 10	13 03	02 27	10 09	00 49	00 59	05 34	14 20	02 34
M	8	9:10:38	18 45	13 21	22 07	21 36	12 50	04 43	28 54	28 14	13 06	02 29	10 10	00 58	01 20	05 48	14 04	02 38
T	9	9:14:35	19 46	25 13	22 ℞ 08	23 24	14 05	05 04	29 07	28 18	13 10	02 31	10 11	01 06	01 41	06 00	13 48	02 42
W	10	9:18:31	20 47	07 ♐ 09	22 08	25 12	15 19	05 24	29 20	28 22	13 13	02 33	10 12	01 15	02 01	06 13	13 32	02 45
T	11	9:22:28	21 47	19 12	22 D 08	27 00	16 34	05 44	29 33	28 27	13 17	02 35	10 13	01 24	02 23	06 26	13 17	02 49
F	12	9:26:24	22 48	01 ♑ 27	22 08	28 49	17 48	06 03	29 46	28 31	13 20	02 38	10 14	01 34	02 44	06 38	13 01	02 52
S	13	9:30:21	23 49	13 58	22 08	00 ♓ 39	19 02	06 22	29 59	28 36	13 24	02 40	10 15	01 44	03 05	06 50	12 46	02 55
S	14	9:34:18	24 49	26 46	22 09	02 29	20 17	06 41	00 ♈ 12	28 40	13 27	02 42	10 16	01 54	03 27	07 02	12 30	02 59
M	15	9:38:14	25 50	09 ♒ 54	22 09	04 19	21 31	06 59	00 26	28 45	13 31	02 44	10 17	02 04	03 48	07 14	12 15	03 02
T	16	9:42:11	26 51	23 21	22 ℞ 10	06 09	22 45	07 17	00 39	28 50	13 34	02 46	10 18	02 15	04 10	07 25	12 00	03 05
W	17	9:46:07	27 51	07 ♓ 06	22 10	07 59	23 59	07 35	00 52	28 55	13 38	02 48	10 19	02 26	04 32	07 37	11 46	03 08
T	18	9:50:04	28 52	21 05	22 09	09 48	25 14	07 51	01 06	29 00	13 41	02 50	10 20	02 37	04 54	07 48	11 31	03 10
F	19	9:54:00	29 52	05 ♈ 16	22 09	11 37	26 28	08 08	01 19	29 05	13 44	02 53	10 21	02 49	05 16	07 59	11 17	03 13
S	20	9:57:57	00 ♓ 53	19 33	22 08	13 25	27 42	08 24	01 33	29 10	13 48	02 55	10 21	03 01	05 38	08 09	11 03	03 16
S	21	10:01:53	01 54	03 ♉ 53	22 07	15 12	28 56	08 40	01 46	29 15	13 51	02 57	10 22	03 13	06 00	08 20	10 49	03 18
M	22	10:05:50	02 54	18 12	22 06	16 57	00 ♈ 10	08 55	02 00	29 21	13 54	02 59	10 23	03 26	06 22	08 30	10 36	03 20
T	23	10:09:47	03 54	02 ♊ 26	22 D 05	18 40	01 24	09 10	02 13	29 26	13 58	03 01	10 24	03 38	06 45	08 40	10 23	03 23
W	24	10:13:43	04 55	16 32	22 05	20 20	02 38	09 24	02 27	29 31	14 01	03 03	10 24	03 51	07 07	08 50	10 10	03 25
T	25	10:17:40	05 55	00 ♋ 30	22 05	21 57	03 51	09 37	02 41	29 37	14 04	03 05	10 25	04 05	07 30	09 00	09 58	03 27
F	26	10:21:36	06 56	14 17	22 06	23 31	05 05	09 51	02 55	29 43	14 08	03 07	10 25	04 18	07 53	09 09	09 46	03 29
S	27	10:25:33	07 56	27 54	22 06	25 00	06 19	10 03	03 08	29 48	14 11	03 09	10 26	04 32	08 16	09 18	09 34	03 31
S	28	10:29:29	08 56	11 ♌ 19	22 ℞ 07	26 25	07 33	10 15	03 22	29 54	14 14	03 11	10 26	04 46	08 38	09 27	09 23	03 33

EPHEMERIS CALCULATED FOR 12 MIDNIGHT GREENWICH MEAN TIME. ALL OTHER DATA AND FACING ASPECTARIAN PAGE IN **EASTERN STANDARD TIME (BOLD)** AND PACIFIC STANDARD TIME (REGULAR).

MARCH 1999

1 MONDAY

☽ ⚻ ☿	**1:31 am**	
♀ ☌ ☿	**2:13 am**	
♀ △ ⚶	**2:24 am**	
☿ △ ⚶	**2:43 am**	
☽ △ ♄	**5:08 am**	2:08 am
☉ □ ♇	**7:04 am**	4:04 am
☉ △ ♂	**9:50 am**	6:50 am
☽ ⚻ ♆	**11:03 am**	8:03 am
☽ □ ⚷	**11:43 am**	8:43 am
☽ ⚻ ♃	**12:03 pm**	9:03 am
♀ △ ⚵	**1:13 pm**	10:13 am
☽ □ ⚳	**2:42 pm**	11:42 am
☽ ⚺ ⚶	**9:48 pm**	6:48 pm
☽ ⚻ ☿	**10:40 pm**	7:40 pm
☽ □ ⚵	**11:12 pm**	8:12 pm
☽ ⚻ ♀		9:08 pm
☽ □ ♇		9:30 pm
☽ ⚹ ♂		9:56 pm
☽ ☍ ☉		10:59 pm

2 TUESDAY

☽ ⚻ ♀	**12:08 am**	
☽ □ ♇	**12:30 am**	
☽ ⚹ ♂	**12:56 am**	
☽ ☍ ☉	**1:59 am**	
♀ △ ♇	**3:59 am**	12:59 am
☽ ⚻ ♅	**7:51 am**	4:51 am
♀ ⚻ ♂	**9:36 am**	6:36 am
☿ ⚺ ♄	**10:34 pm**	7:34 pm
♀ △ ⚵		11:12 pm

3 WEDNESDAY

♀ △ ⚵	**2:12 am**	
☽ ⚻ ♄	**2:06 pm**	11:06 am
☽ ☍ ☿	**3:18 pm**	12:18 pm
☽ △ ♆	**7:57 pm**	4:57 pm
☽ ⚹ ⚷	**8:36 pm**	5:36 pm
☽ ☍ ♃	**9:56 pm**	6:56 pm
☽ △ ⚳		9:46 pm

4 THURSDAY

☽ △ ⚳	**12:46 am**	
☽ ⚹ ⚶	**6:16 am**	3:16 am
☽ ⚹ ⚵	**9:05 am**	6:05 am
☽ ☍ ♀	**9:46 am**	6:46 am
☽ ⚹ ♇	**9:51 am**	6:51 am
☽ ⚺ ♂	**11:03 am**	8:03 am

♇ △ ☿	**12:30 pm**	9:30 am
☽ ☍ ♀	**3:47 pm**	12:47 pm
☽ ⚻ ☉	**4:27 pm**	1:27 pm
☽ △ ♅	**5:44 pm**	2:44 pm

5 FRIDAY

☉ ⚺ ♅	**8:50 am**	5:50 am
♀ ⚹ ♅	**12:04 pm**	9:04 am
☽ ☍ ♄		10:25 pm
♀ ⚺ ☉		10:56 pm

6 SATURDAY

☽ ☍ ♄	**1:25 am**	
♀ ⚺ ☉	**1:56 am**	
☽ ⚻ ☿	**6:11 am**	3:11 am
☽ □ ♆	**7:08 am**	4:08 am
☽ ⚺ ⚷	**7:45 am**	4:45 am
☽ ⚻ ♃	**10:13 am**	7:13 am
☽ ⚻ ⚳	**1:16 pm**	10:16 am
☽ □ ⚶	**4:57 pm**	1:57 pm
☽ ⚺ ⚵	**9:11 pm**	6:11 pm
☽ ⚺ ♇	**9:23 pm**	6:23 pm
☽ ⚻ ♀	**11:17 pm**	8:17 pm
☽ ☌ ♂	**11:18 pm**	8:18 pm
♂ ⚻ ♀		9:05 pm

7 SUNDAY

♂ ⚻ ♀	**12:05 am**	
☽ □ ♅	**5:44 am**	2:44 am
☿ ⚹ ♆	**5:47 am**	2:47 am
☽ △ ☉	**9:38 am**	6:38 am
☽ ⚻ ♀	**10:18 am**	7:18 am
♇ ☌ ⚵	**5:02 pm**	2:02 pm
☿ △ ⚷		10:17 pm

8 MONDAY

☿ △ ⚷	**1:17 am**	
☽ ⚻ ♄	**2:22 pm**	11:22 am
☽ ⚹ ♆	**7:46 pm**	4:46 pm
☽ ☌ ⚷	**8:19 pm**	5:19 pm
☽ △ ☿	**8:43 pm**	5:43 pm
☽ △ ♃	**11:57 pm**	8:57 pm

9 TUESDAY

☽ ☍ ⚳	**3:11 am**	12:11 am
☽ △ ⚶	**4:52 am**	1:52 am
☽ ☌ ♇	**9:57 am**	6:57 am
☽ ☌ ⚵	**10:20 am**	7:20 am
☽ ⚺ ♂	**12:28 pm**	9:28 am

Eastern Standard Time in bold type

Pacific Standard Time in medium type

☽ △ ♀	**1:56 pm**	10:56 am
☽ ⚹ ♅	**6:33 pm**	3:33 pm

10 WEDNESDAY

☽ □ ☉	**3:41 am**	12:41 am
☽ △ ♀	**5:41 am**	2:41 am
☽ △ ♄		11:58 pm

11 THURSDAY

☽ △ ♄	**2:58 am**	
⚳ ⚹ ⚶	**7:40 am**	4:40 am
☽ ⚺ ♆	**7:51 am**	4:51 am
☽ ⚺ ⚷	**8:17 am**	5:17 am
☽ □ ☿	**8:41 am**	5:41 am
☽ □ ♃	**12:57 pm**	9:57 am
☽ ⚻ ⚶	**4:00 pm**	1:00 pm
☽ ⚻ ⚳	**4:16 pm**	1:16 pm
☽ ⚺ ♇	**9:27 pm**	6:27 pm
☽ ⚺ ⚵	**10:17 pm**	7:17 pm
☽ ⚹ ♂		9:17 pm

12 FRIDAY

☽ ⚹ ♂	**12:17 am**	
☽ □ ♀	**3:14 am**	12:14 am
☿ △ ⚷	**4:36 am**	1:36 am
☽ ⚺ ♅	**5:55 am**	2:55 am
☿ ⚹ ♆	**6:29 pm**	3:29 pm
☽ ⚹ ☉	**7:28 pm**	4:28 pm
☽ □ ♀	**10:33 pm**	7:33 pm

13 SATURDAY

☽ □ ♄	**12:59 pm**	9:59 am
☽ ⚹ ☿	**4:26 pm**	1:26 pm
☽ ☌ ♆	**5:12 pm**	2:12 pm
☽ ⚹ ⚷	**5:31 pm**	2:31 pm
☽ ⚹ ♃	**10:56 pm**	7:56 pm
☽ ☍ ⚶		9:22 pm
☽ △ ⚳		11:15 pm

14 SUNDAY

☽ ☍ ⚶	**12:22 am**	
☽ △ ⚳	**2:15 am**	
☽ ⚹ ♇	**5:51 am**	2:51 am
☽ ⚹ ⚵	**7:01 am**	4:01 am
☽ □ ♂	**8:46 am**	5:46 am
☽ ⚹ ♀	**1:01 pm**	10:01 am
☽ ☌ ♅	**1:59 pm**	10:59 am

15 MONDAY

☽ ⚺ ☉	**6:47 am**	3:47 am
☽ ⚹ ♀	**10:40 am**	7:40 am
☽ ⚹ ♄	**7:13 pm**	4:13 pm
☽ ⚺ ☿	**7:47 pm**	4:47 pm

☽ ⚺ ♆	**10:50 pm**	7:50 pm
☽ □ ⚷	**11:02 pm**	8:02 pm
♅ ⚹ ♀		9:57 pm

16 TUESDAY

♅ ⚹ ♀	**12:57 am**	
☽ ⚺ ♃	**5:01 am**	2:01 am
☿ ⚺ ♄	**5:03 am**	2:03 am
☽ ⚻ ⚶	**5:10 am**	2:10 am
☽ □ ⚳	**8:18 am**	5:18 am
☽ □ ♇	**10:33 am**	7:33 am
♃ △ ⚶	**11:53 am**	8:53 am
☽ □ ⚵	**11:57 am**	8:57 am
☽ △ ♂	**1:26 pm**	10:26 am
☽ ⚺ ♅	**6:22 pm**	3:22 pm
☽ ⚺ ♀	**6:50 pm**	3:50 pm

17 WEDNESDAY

☽ ☌ ☉	**1:48 pm**	10:48 am
☽ ⚺ ♀	**6:20 pm**	3:20 pm
☽ ☌ ☿	**7:44 pm**	4:44 pm
☽ ⚺ ♄	**10:11 pm**	7:11 pm
☽ ⚹ ♆		10:19 pm
☽ △ ⚷		10:25 pm

18 THURSDAY

☽ ⚹ ♆	**1:19 am**	
☽ △ ⚷	**1:25 am**	
☿ ⚺ ♀	**4:44 am**	1:44 am
☽ △ ⚶	**7:06 am**	4:06 am
☽ ☌ ♃	**7:58 am**	4:58 am
☽ ⚹ ⚳	**11:19 am**	8:19 am
☽ △ ♇	**12:26 pm**	9:26 am
☽ △ ⚵	**2:00 pm**	11:00 am
☽ ⚻ ♂	**3:14 pm**	12:14 pm
☽ ⚹ ♅	**8:07 pm**	5:07 pm
☽ ☌ ♀	**9:49 pm**	6:49 pm

19 FRIDAY

☿ ☌ ☉	**2:14 pm**	11:14 am
☽ ⚺ ☿	**5:52 pm**	2:52 pm
☽ ⚺ ☉	**6:22 pm**	3:22 pm
♆ ⚹ ⚷	**7:43 pm**	4:43 pm
♀ ☌ ♄	**9:05 pm**	6:05 pm
☽ ☌ ♄	**11:26 pm**	8:26 pm
☽ ☌ ♀	**11:38 pm**	8:38 pm
☽ □ ♆		11:14 pm
☽ ⚻ ⚷		11:14 pm

20 SATURDAY

☽ □ ♆	**2:14 am**	
☽ ⚻ ⚷	**2:14 am**	

☽ □ ⚶	**7:44 am**	4:44 am
☽ ⚺ ♃	**9:32 am**	6:32 am
☽ ⚺ ⚳	**1:04 pm**	10:04 am
☽ ⚻ ♇	**1:09 pm**	10:09 am
☽ ⚻ ⚵	**2:55 pm**	11:55 am
☽ ☍ ♂	**3:54 pm**	12:54 pm
♇ ☍ ⚳	**4:54 pm**	1:54 pm
☽ □ ♅	**8:59 pm**	5:59 pm
☽ ⚺ ♀	**11:57 pm**	8:57 pm

21 SUNDAY

♀ ⚻ ⚷	**7:16 am**	4:16 am
♀ □ ♆	**8:15 am**	5:15 am
☽ ⚹ ☿	**3:52 pm**	12:52 pm
☽ ⚹ ☉	**10:52 pm**	7:52 pm
☽ ⚺ ♄		9:50 pm

22 MONDAY

☽ ⚺ ♄	**12:50 am**	
☽ ☍ ⚷	**3:15 am**	12:15 am
☽ △ ♆	**3:23 am**	12:23 am
☽ ⚺ ♀	**5:05 am**	2:05 am
☽ ⚹ ⚶	**8:52 am**	5:52 am
☽ ⚹ ♃	**11:37 am**	8:37 am
☽ ☍ ♇	**2:28 pm**	11:28 am
☽ ☌ ⚳	**3:30 pm**	12:30 pm
☽ ☍ ⚵	**4:28 pm**	1:28 pm
☽ ⚻ ♂	**5:10 pm**	2:10 pm
☽ △ ♅	**10:43 pm**	7:43 pm

23 TUESDAY

☽ ⚹ ♀	**3:06 am**	12:06 am
☉ ⚺ ♄	**7:07 am**	4:07 am
☽ □ ☿	**3:11 pm**	12:11 pm
♀ □ ⚶		11:07 pm

24 WEDNESDAY

♀ □ ⚶	**2:07 am**	
☽ ⚹ ♄	**3:53 am**	12:53 am
☽ □ ☉	**5:18 am**	2:18 am
☽ ⚻ ⚷	**5:57 am**	2:57 am
☽ ⚻ ♆	**6:13 am**	3:13 am
☽ ⚺ ⚶	**11:50 am**	8:50 am
☽ ⚹ ♀	**12:45 pm**	9:45 am
☉ △ ⚷	**2:10 pm**	11:10 am
☽ □ ♃	**3:38 pm**	12:38 pm
⚳ ☍ ⚵	**5:22 pm**	2:22 pm
☽ ⚻ ♇	**5:42 pm**	2:42 pm
☉ ⚹ ♆	**6:20 pm**	3:20 pm
☽ ⚻ ⚵	**7:56 pm**	4:56 pm
☽ ⚺ ⚳	**7:59 pm**	4:59 pm

☽ △ ♂	**8:17 pm**	5:17 pm
☽ ⚻ ♅		11:30 pm

25 THURSDAY

☽ ⚻ ♅	**2:30 am**	
☽ □ ♀	**8:35 am**	5:35 am
☽ △ ☿	**4:46 pm**	1:46 pm

26 FRIDAY

♀ ⚺ ♃	**5:26 am**	2:26 am
☽ □ ♄	**9:24 am**	6:24 am
☽ △ ⚷	**10:59 am**	7:59 am
☽ ☍ ♆	**11:26 am**	8:26 am
☽ △ ☉	**2:41 pm**	11:41 am
☽ ☌ ⚶	**5:17 pm**	2:17 pm
♂ ⚻ ⚳	**7:27 pm**	4:27 pm
♀ ⚻ ♇	**9:03 pm**	6:03 pm
☽ △ ♃	**10:13 pm**	7:13 pm
☽ △ ♇	**11:21 pm**	8:21 pm
☽ □ ♀	**11:34 pm**	8:34 pm
☽ □ ♂		10:41 pm
☽ △ ⚵		10:49 pm

27 SATURDAY

☽ □ ♂	**1:41 am**	
☽ △ ⚵	**1:49 am**	
☽ ⚹ ⚳	**3:08 am**	12:08 am
☽ ☍ ♅	**8:46 am**	5:46 am
☽ △ ♀	**4:46 pm**	1:46 pm
♀ ☍ ♂	**8:53 pm**	5:53 pm
☽ ⚻ ☿	**9:03 pm**	6:03 pm
♀ ⚻ ⚵		9:24 pm
☉ △ ⚶		11:07 pm

28 SUNDAY

♀ ⚻ ⚵	**12:24 am**	
☉ △ ⚶	**2:07 am**	
☽ △ ♄	**5:20 pm**	2:20 pm
☽ □ ⚷	**6:23 pm**	3:23 pm
☽ ⚻ ♆	**7:01 pm**	4:01 pm
☽ ⚺ ⚶		10:08 pm

29 MONDAY

☽ ⚺ ⚶	**1:08 am**	
☽ ⚻ ☉	**3:01 am**	12:01 am
♀ ⚺ ⚳	**3:39 am**	12:39 am
☽ ⚻ ♃	**7:14 am**	4:14 am
☽ □ ♇	**7:16 am**	4:16 am
♃ △ ♇	**8:54 am**	5:54 am
☽ ⚹ ♂	**9:12 am**	6:12 am
☽ □ ⚵	**9:56 am**	6:56 am
☽ □ ⚳	**12:44 pm**	9:44 am

☽ △ ♀	**1:25 pm**	10:25 am
☽ ⚻ ♅	**5:16 pm**	2:16 pm

30 TUESDAY

☽ ⚻ ♀	**3:22 am**	12:22 am
☽ ☍ ☿	**4:03 am**	1:03 am
☿ ⚺ ♀	**3:58 pm**	12:58 pm

31 WEDNESDAY

☽ ⚻ ♄	**3:20 am**	12:20 am
☽ ⚹ ⚷	**3:45 am**	12:45 am
☽ △ ♆	**4:37 am**	1:37 am
♀ □ ♅	**7:13 am**	4:13 am
☉ △ ♇	**8:58 am**	5:58 am
☽ ⚹ ⚶	**11:04 am**	8:04 am
☽ ⚹ ♇	**5:07 pm**	2:07 pm
☽ ☍ ☉	**5:50 pm**	2:50 pm
☽ ☍ ♃	**6:17 pm**	3:17 pm
☽ ⚺ ♂	**6:25 pm**	3:25 pm
☽ ⚹ ⚵	**7:54 pm**	4:54 pm
♂ ⚻ ♃	**10:22 pm**	7:22 pm
☉ ⚻ ♂		9:10 pm
☽ △ ⚳		9:25 pm
☉ ☌ ♃		10:10 pm

MARCH 1999

☽ Last Aspect

day	EST / hr:mn / PST	asp
1	1:59 am	☌♀
4	5:44 am 2:44 am	△♅
4	5:44 am 2:44 am	
7	9:38 am 6:38 am	✶♀
10	5:41 am 2:41 am	△♄
10	5:41 am 2:41 am	
12	10:33 am 7:33 am	△♀
15	10:40 am 7:40 am	✶♆
17	1:48 pm 10:48 am	☌☉

☽ Ingress

sign	day	EST / hr:mn / PST
≈	3	1:34 pm 10:34 am
≈	3	1:34 pm 10:34 am
♓	5	2:44 pm
		9:23 am
♈	8	6:23 am
♉	10	12:47 pm 9:47 am
♊	13	1:54 am 9:54 am
♋	15	7:32 am
♌	15	4:31 pm 1:31 pm
♍	17	7:13 pm 4:13 pm

☽ Last Aspect

day	EST / hr:mn / PST	asp
18	8:07 pm 5:07 pm	✶♅
21	3:52 pm 12:52 pm	□♀
23	11:11 pm	△♃
25	4:46 pm 1:46 pm	✶♂
27	8:46 am 5:46 am	△♄
30	4:03 am 1:03 am	✶♀

☽ Ingress

sign	day	EST / hr:mn / PST
♎	19	8:09 pm 5:09 pm
♏	21	9:05 pm 6:09 pm
♐	23	11:33 pm 8:33 pm
♑	25	4:22 am 1:22 am
♒	27	11:35 am 8:35 am
♓	30	8:50 pm 5:50 pm

⟩ Phases & Eclipses

phase	day	EST / hr:mn / PST
Full Moon	2	1:59 am 10:59 pm
Full Moon	2	1:59 am
4th Quarter	10	3:41 pm 12:41 pm
New Moon	17	1:48 pm 10:48 am
2nd Quarter	24	5:18 am 2:18 am
Full Moon	31	5:50 pm 2:50 pm

Planet Ingress

	day	EST / hr:mn / PST
☿ ≈	2	5:50 pm 2:50 pm
♀ ♓	17	4:23 am 1:23 am
☿ ♓	18	3:41 pm 12:41 pm
♀ ♈	20	4:59 am 1:59 am
☉ ♈	20	8:46 pm 5:46 pm

Planetary Motion

	day	EST / hr:mn / PST
☿ R	10	4:07 am 1:07 am
♀ R	13	10:56 am 7:56 am
♇ R	15	5:19 pm 2:19 pm
♂ R	18	8:40 am 5:40 am
♃ D	23	11:51 pm 8:51 pm
♆ R	30	1:58 pm 10:58 am

EPHEMERIS CALCULATED FOR 12 MIDNIGHT GREENWICH MEAN TIME. ALL OTHER DATA AND FACING ASPECTARIAN PAGE IN **EASTERN STANDARD TIME (BOLD)** AND PACIFIC STANDARD TIME (REGULAR).

APRIL 1999

1 THURSDAY

☉⚻♂	12:10 am	
☽△⚳	12:25 am	
☉☌♃	1:10 am	
☽△♅	3:39 am	12:39 am
☽⚻♀	5:47 am	2:47 am
♄⚻⚷	1:20 pm	10:20 am
☽⚻☿	1:45 pm	10:45 am
☽☍♀	3:59 pm	12:59 pm
☉△⚵	7:15 pm	4:15 pm

2 FRIDAY

☽⚺⚷	2:47 pm	11:47 am
☽☍♄	3:06 pm	12:06 pm
☽□♆	3:54 pm	12:54 pm
☽□⚶	10:45 pm	7:45 pm

3 SATURDAY

☽⚺♇	4:34 am	1:34 am
☽☌♂	5:04 am	2:04 am
☽⚻♃	7:04 am	4:04 am
☽⚺⚵	7:25 am	4:25 am
☽⚻☉	10:43 am	7:43 am
☽⚻⚳	1:51 pm	10:51 am
☽□♅	3:36 pm	12:36 pm
♃△⚵	11:07 pm	8:07 pm
☽☍♀		9:15 pm
☽△☿		11:01 pm

4 SUNDAY

☽☍♀	12:15 am	
☽△☿	2:01 am	
☽⚻♀	6:16 am	3:16 am
♂⚺♇	11:04 am	8:04 am
☿⚹♀	9:29 pm	6:29 pm

5 MONDAY

☽☌⚷	3:02 am	12:02 am
☽⚻♄	4:09 am	1:09 am
☽⚹♆	4:26 am	1:26 am
☽△⚶	11:41 am	8:41 am
☽⚺♂	4:33 pm	1:33 pm
☽☌♇	5:05 pm	2:05 pm
☉⚹⚳	7:11 pm	4:11 pm
☽☌⚵	7:52 pm	4:52 pm
☽△♃	8:54 pm	5:54 pm
☉⚹♅	11:56 pm	8:56 pm

6 TUESDAY

☽☍⚳	4:16 am	1:16 am
☽⚹♅	4:25 am	1:25 am
☽△☉	4:48 am	1:48 am
♅△⚳	9:40 am	6:40 am
♄□♆	10:07 am	7:07 am
☽□☿	4:07 pm	1:07 pm
☽⚻♀	7:35 pm	4:35 pm
☽△♀	9:11 pm	6:11 pm

7 WEDNESDAY

☽⚺⚷	3:16 pm	12:16 pm
☽⚺♆	4:55 pm	1:55 pm
☽△♄	5:11 pm	2:11 pm
☿⚺♀	8:12 pm	5:12 pm
☽⚻⚶		9:28 pm

8 THURSDAY

☽⚻⚶	12:28 am	
☽⚹♂	3:32 am	12:32 am
☽⚺♇	5:10 am	2:10 am
☽⚺⚵	7:45 am	4:45 am
☽□♃	10:11 am	7:11 am
☽⚺♅	4:26 pm	1:26 pm
☽⚻⚳	5:53 pm	2:53 pm
☽□☉	9:51 pm	6:51 pm

9 FRIDAY

☽⚹☿	5:58 am	2:58 am
☽□♀	10:35 am	7:35 am
☽△♀	1:06 pm	10:06 am
☽⚹⚷		10:31 pm

10 SATURDAY

☽⚹⚷	1:31 am	
☽☌♆	3:19 am	12:19 am
☽□♄	4:06 am	1:06 am
☽☍⚶	10:56 am	7:56 am
☽□♂	12:06 pm	9:06 am
☽⚹♇	2:46 pm	11:46 am
☽⚹⚵	5:01 pm	2:01 pm
☽⚹♃	8:38 pm	5:38 pm
☽☌♅		10:34 pm

11 SUNDAY

☽☌♅	1:34 am	
☽△⚳	4:22 am	1:22 am
☽⚹☉	11:02 am	8:02 am
☽⚺☿	4:59 pm	1:59 pm
☽⚹♀	8:16 pm	5:16 pm
♂□⚶	11:19 pm	8:19 pm
☽□♀		11:02 pm

12 MONDAY

☽□♀	2:02 am	
☽□⚷	8:05 am	5:05 am
☽⚺♆	9:59 am	6:59 am
☽⚹♄	11:09 am	8:09 am
☽△♂	4:57 pm	1:57 pm
☽⚻⚶	5:31 pm	2:31 pm
☽□♇	8:29 pm	5:29 pm
☽□⚵	10:22 pm	7:22 pm
☽⚺♃		11:54 pm

13 TUESDAY

☽⚺♃	2:54 am	
☽⚺♅	6:40 am	3:40 am
☽□⚳	10:31 am	7:31 am
☽⚺☉	7:10 pm	4:10 pm
☽☌☿	11:53 pm	8:53 pm
☽⚺♀		10:31 pm

14 WEDNESDAY

☽⚺♀	1:31 am	
☽⚹♀	9:45 am	6:45 am
☽△⚷	10:44 am	7:44 am
☽⚹♆	12:43 pm	9:43 am
☽⚺♄	2:12 pm	11:12 am
☽⚻♂	6:09 pm	3:09 pm
☽△⚶	8:14 pm	5:14 pm
♀☍⚷	9:39 pm	6:39 pm
☽△♇	10:28 pm	7:28 pm
☽△⚵		9:01 pm

15 THURSDAY

☽△⚵	12:01 am	
☽☌♃	5:22 am	2:22 am
☽⚹♅	8:12 am	5:12 am
☽⚹⚳	12:58 pm	9:58 am
♀△♆	11:20 pm	8:20 pm
☽☌☉	11:22 pm	8:22 pm
☿⚺♀		9:22 pm

16 FRIDAY

☿⚺♀	12:22 am	
☽☌♀	3:30 am	12:30 am
☽⚺☿	3:37 am	12:37 am
☽⚻⚷	10:45 am	7:45 am
☽□♆	12:52 pm	9:52 am
☽⚺♀	1:59 pm	10:59 am
☽☌♄	2:40 pm	11:40 am
☽☍♂	5:04 pm	2:04 pm
☽□⚶	8:37 pm	5:37 pm
☽⚻♇	10:14 pm	7:14 pm
☽⚻⚵	11:32 pm	8:32 pm
♀⚺♄	11:54 pm	8:54 pm

17 SATURDAY

☽⚺♃	5:49 am	2:49 am
☽□♅	7:56 am	4:56 am
☽⚺⚳	1:44 pm	10:44 am
♀⚻♂	9:39 pm	6:39 pm
☽⚺☉		11:11 pm

18 SUNDAY

☽⚺☉	2:11 am	
☽⚺♀	4:28 am	1:28 am
☽⚹☿	6:36 am	3:36 am
☽☍⚷	10:09 am	7:09 am
☽△♆	12:29 pm	9:29 am
☽⚺♄	2:42 pm	11:42 am
☽⚻♂	3:38 pm	12:38 pm
☽☌♀	5:37 pm	2:37 pm
☽⚹⚶	8:54 pm	5:54 pm
☽☍♇	9:55 pm	6:55 pm
☽☍⚵	10:59 pm	7:59 pm

19 MONDAY

☽⚹♃	6:32 am	3:32 am
☽△♅	8:00 am	5:00 am
☽☌⚳	3:09 pm	12:09 pm
♂☍♄	8:45 pm	5:45 pm

20 TUESDAY

☿△⚷	4:38 am	1:38 am
☽⚹☉	6:22 am	3:22 am
☽⚹♀	6:48 am	3:48 am
☽⚻⚷	10:59 am	7:59 am
☽□☿	11:35 am	8:35 am
☽⚻♆	1:40 pm	10:40 am
☽△♂	3:44 pm	12:44 pm
☽⚹♄	4:23 pm	1:23 pm
☉☌♀	5:37 pm	2:37 pm
♀⚹⚶	6:57 pm	3:57 pm
☽⚺⚶	11:07 pm	8:07 pm
☽⚺♀	11:26 pm	8:26 pm
☽⚻♇	11:30 pm	8:30 pm
♀☍♇		9:05 pm
☽⚻⚵		9:17 pm

21 WEDNESDAY

♀☍♇	12:05 am	
☽⚻⚵	12:17 am	
♀☍⚵	8:50 am	5:50 am
☽□♃	9:32 am	6:32 am
☽⚻♅	10:19 am	7:19 am
☿⚹♆	12:52 pm	9:52 am
☽⚺⚳	7:14 pm	4:14 pm
♇△⚶	11:35 pm	8:35 pm
☿⚻♂		11:31 pm

22 THURSDAY

☿⚻♂	2:31 am	
☽□♀	12:15 pm	9:15 am
☽□☉	2:02 pm	11:02 am
☽△⚷	2:43 pm	11:43 am
☽☍♆	5:49 pm	2:49 pm
☽□♂	6:36 pm	3:36 pm
☽△☿	8:44 pm	5:44 pm
☽□♄	9:12 pm	6:12 pm
☉⚻⚷	10:53 pm	7:53 pm
☿⚺♄		11:08 pm
⚵△⚶		11:49 pm

23 FRIDAY

☿⚺♄	2:08 am	
⚵△⚶	2:49 am	
☽△♇	4:11 am	1:11 am
☽△⚵	4:37 am	1:37 am
☽☌⚶	4:40 am	1:40 am
☽⚹♀	9:17 am	6:17 am
♃⚹♅	11:55 am	8:55 am
☽☍♅	3:54 pm	12:54 pm
☽△♃	3:58 pm	12:58 pm
♂□♆	10:12 pm	7:12 pm
☽⚹⚳		11:55 pm

24 SATURDAY

☽⚹⚳	2:55 am	
☉☍♂	12:37 pm	9:37 am
☉□♆	6:17 pm	3:17 pm
☽△♀	9:23 pm	6:23 pm
☽□⚷	9:42 pm	6:42 pm
☽⚹♂		9:29 pm
☽⚻♆		10:16 pm
☽△☉		10:51 pm

25 SUNDAY

☽⚹♂	12:29 am	
☽⚻♆	1:16 am	
☽△☉	1:51 am	
☽△♄	5:22 am	2:22 am
♀⚻⚷	5:32 am	2:32 am
♇☌⚵	7:08 am	4:08 am
☽⚻☿	10:43 am	7:43 am
☽□⚵	12:03 pm	9:03 am
☽□♇	12:05 pm	9:05 am
☽⚺⚶	1:38 pm	10:38 am
☿△⚵	9:56 pm	6:56 pm
☿△♇	11:13 pm	8:13 pm
☽□♀	11:15 pm	8:15 pm
☽⚻♅		9:35 pm
☽⚻♃		10:39 pm

26 MONDAY

☽⚻♅	12:35 am	
☽⚻♃	1:39 am	
☽□⚳	1:51 pm	10:51 am
♀△♅	1:55 pm	10:55 am
☿△⚶	5:50 pm	2:50 pm
♂☍♀	10:10 pm	7:10 pm

27 TUESDAY

☉☌♄	6:04 am	3:04 am
♀⚹♃	7:18 am	4:18 am
☽⚹⚷	7:18 am	4:18 am
☽⚺♂	8:44 am	5:44 am
☽⚻♀	9:29 am	6:29 am
☽△♆	11:18 am	8:18 am
☽⚻♄	4:09 pm	1:09 pm
☽⚻☉	4:55 pm	1:55 pm
☽⚹⚵	9:44 pm	6:44 pm
☽⚹♇	10:22 pm	7:22 pm
☽⚹⚶		10:09 pm

28 WEDNESDAY

☽⚹⚶	1:09 am	
☽☍☿	4:38 am	1:38 am
☽△♅	11:27 am	8:27 am
☽☍♃	1:37 pm	10:37 am
☽△♀	4:08 pm	1:08 pm
☽△⚳		11:56 pm

29 THURSDAY

☽△⚳	2:56 am	
♆□♀	10:44 am	7:44 am
♂⚺⚷	5:41 pm	2:41 pm
☽☌♂	6:30 pm	3:30 pm
☽⚺⚷	6:31 pm	3:31 pm
☉⚻⚵	9:40 pm	6:40 pm
☽□♆	10:56 pm	7:56 pm
☽☍♀	11:25 pm	8:25 pm

30 FRIDAY

☽☍♄	4:30 am	1:30 am
☽⚺⚵	8:46 am	5:46 am
☽☍☉	9:55 am	6:55 am
☽⚺♇	10:05 am	7:05 am
☉⚻♇	11:57 am	8:57 am
☿⚹♅	1:07 pm	10:07 am
☽□⚶	2:13 pm	11:13 am
☽□♅	11:35 pm	8:35 pm
☽⚻☿		10:06 pm
☽⚻♃		11:53 pm

Eastern Standard Time in bold type
Pacific Standard Time in medium type

APRIL 1999

☽ Last Aspect

day	EST / hr:mn / PST	asp
1	**3:39 am** 12:39 am	△ ♄
3	11:01 am	△ ♀
4	**2:01 am**	△ ♂
6	**4:07 pm** 1:07 pm	□ ♀
9	**1:06 pm** 10:06 am	△ ♀
11	11:02 am	□ ♃
12	**2:02 am**	□ ♂
13	**11:53 pm** 8:53 pm	□ ♀
15	**11:22 pm** 8:22 pm	△ ⊙
17	**7:56 am** 4:56 am	□ ☽

☽ Ingress

sign day	EST / hr:mn / PST
♏ 2	**7:49 am** 4:49 am
✗ 4	12:39 am
✗ 4	**8:08 pm** 5:08 pm
♑ 7	**8:08 pm** 5:08 pm
≈ 9	**8:39 pm** 5:39 pm
≈ 11	**7:24 am** 4:24 pm
✗ 11	11:35 pm
♈ 14	**2:35 am**
♉ 14	**5:46 am** 2:46 am
♊ 16	**6:07 am** 3:07 am
♋ 18	**5:39 pm** 2:39 pm

☽ Last Aspect

day	EST / hr:mn / PST	asp
20	**6:22 am** 3:22 am	✗ ⊙
21	**9:32 am** 6:32 am	□ ♀
23	**3:58 am** 12:58 am	△ ♀
25	**11:15 pm** 8:15 pm	△ ♀
25	**11:15 pm** 8:15 pm	□ ♀
28	**4:08 pm** 1:08 pm	△ ♀
31	**11:35 pm** 8:35 pm	□ ♀

☽ Ingress

sign day	EST / hr:mn / PST
♌ 20	**6:28 am** 3:28 am
♍ 22	**10:06 am** 7:06 am
♎ 24	**5:05 pm** 2:05 pm
♏ 26	11:47 pm
♏ 27	**2:47 am**
✗ 29	**2:13 pm** 11:13 am
♑ 1	11:36 pm
♑ 2	**2:36 am**

☽ Phases & Eclipses

phase	day	EST / hr:mn / PST
4th Quarter	8	**9:51 pm** 6:51 pm
New Moon	15	**11:22 pm** 8:22 pm
2nd Quarter	22	**2:02 pm** 11:02 am
Full Moon	30	**9:55 am** 6:55 am

Planet Ingress

	day	EST / hr:mn / PST
♀ ♊	12	**8:17 am** 5:17 am
♂ ♈	17	**5:09 pm** 2:09 pm
♀ ♈	19	**8:12 pm** 5:12 pm
⊙ ♉	20	**7:46 am** 4:46 am

Planetary Motion

	day	EST / hr:mn / PST
♃ D	2	**4:15 am** 1:15 am

Ephemeris Table

DATE	SID.TIME	SUN	MOON	NODE	MERCURY	VENUS	MARS	JUPITER	SATURN	URANUS	NEPTUNE	PLUTO	CERES	PALLAS	JUNO	VESTA	CHIRON
T 1	12:35:39	10 ♈ 49	11 ♎ 22	20 ♏ 26	20 ♓ 04	16 ♓ 19	11 ♏ 04	11 ♈ 01	03 ♉ 26	15 ≈ 45	04 ≈ 01	10 ✗ 24	14 ♊ 03	21 ♏ 39	11 ✗ 50	07 ♌ 20	03 ♏ 32
F 2	12:39:35	11 49	23 33	20 20	20 54	17 29	10 52	11 11	03 33	15 48	04 02	10 24	14 22	22 56	11 49	07 49	03 31
S 3	12:43:32	12 47	05 ♏ 36	20 20	21 53	18 42	10 42	11 11	03 41	15 52	04 03	10 23	14 43	22 56	11 48	07 07	03 29
S 4	12:47:29	13 46	17 33	20 34	23 20	19 54	10 30	11 11	03 48	15 52	04 03	10 22	14 56	23 56	11 47	07 32	03 27
M 5	12:51:25	14 45	29 26	20 34	24 49	21 07	10 18	11 59	03 56	15 54	04 04	10 22	15 11	23 27	11 46	08 37	03 25
T 6	12:55:22	15 44	11 ✗ 18	19 44	26 19	22 20	10 09	11 13	04 01	15 57	04 05	10 21	15 27	23 48	11 45	09 43	03 23
W 7	12:59:18	16 43	23 13	20 18	27 49	23 32	09 50	11 28	04 05	16 01	04 06	10 20	15 45	24 01	11 44	09 49	03 21
T 8	13:03:15	17 41	05 ♑ 11	20 13	29 20	24 45	09 41	11 12	04 08	16 05	04 07	10 19	16 06	24 24	11 43	09 55	03 19
F 9	13:07:11	18 40	17 12	20 11	00 ♈ 53	25 58	09 24	11 14	04 11	16 08	04 08	10 19	16 24	24 48	11 42	09 02	03 17
S 10	13:11:08	19 39	29 18	20 04	02 26	27 10	09 10	11 15	04 32	16 11	04 09	10 18	16 48	24 53	11 41	09 08	03 16
S 11	13:15:04	20 37	11 ≈ 34	20 39	04 01	28 23	09 00	11 13	04 33	16 16	04 10	10 17	17 12	25 59	11 29	09 16	03 14
M 12	13:19:01	21 36	23 56	20 20	05 41	29 36	08 45	11 17	04 47	16 19	04 11	10 16	17 31	25 52	11 25	09 24	03 12
T 13	13:22:58	22 35	06 ♓ 33	20 20	07 23	00 ♉ 49	08 32	11 18	04 55	16 22	04 12	10 15	17 51	25 45	11 21	09 32	03 10
W 14	13:26:54	23 34	19 18	20 03	09 07	02 01	08 14	11 17	05 02	16 25	04 13	10 14	18 14	26 42	11 17	09 40	03 08
T 15	13:30:51	24 32	02 ♈ 17	20 01	10 53	03 14	08 08	11 15	05 05	16 28	04 14	10 13	18 32	27 00	11 14	09 48	03 06
F 16	13:34:47	25 31	15 32	20 08	12 41	04 27	07 56	11 14	05 11	16 31	04 15	10 12	18 57	27 27	11 08	09 50	03 04
S 17	13:38:44	26 30	29 00	19 52	14 32	05 40	07 43	11 13	05 19	16 33	04 16	10 11	19 22	27 38	11 01	09 09	03 02
S 18	13:42:40	27 28	12 ♉ 45	19 18	16 24	06 52	07 32	11 12	05 24	16 30	04 17	10 10	19 55	29 58	10 55	09 19	03 01
M 19	13:46:37	28 27	26 43	20 30	18 17	08 05	07 21	11 11	05 31	16 30	04 18	10 09	20 19	29 49	10 49	09 26	02 59
T 20	13:50:33	29 26	10 ♊ 55	20 28	20 11	09 18	07 09	11 10	05 48	16 42	04 19	10 08	20 43	00 ♐ 42	10 43	09 33	02 57
W 21	13:54:30	00 ♉ 25	25 18	20 07	22 05	10 31	07 04	11 17	05 57	16 45	04 20	10 07	21 08	00 27	10 36	09 40	02 55
T 22	13:58:27	01 23	09 ♋ 49	19 53	23 58	11 44	06 53	11 16	06 09	16 48	04 21	10 06	21 33	00 57	10 30	09 48	02 53
F 23	14:02:23	02 22	24 23	20 00	25 51	12 57	06 45	11 18	06 23	16 51	04 22	10 05	21 57	00 59	10 21	09 55	02 52
S 24	14:06:20	03 21	08 ♌ 54	19 42	27 41	14 10	06 38	11 19	06 33	16 54	04 23	10 04	22 37	01 47	10 13	09 03	02 50
S 25	14:10:16	04 19	23 18	20 46	29 28	15 22	06 32	11 46	06 46	16 57	04 24	10 03	23 41	02 11	09 57	09 10	02 48
M 26	14:14:13	05 18	07 ♍ 29	20 37	01 ♉ 11	16 35	06 29	11 14	06 57	16 48	04 25	10 02	23 09	02 04	09 49	09 17	02 46
T 27	14:18:09	06 16	21 23	20 17	02 48	17 48	06 27	11 17	06 57	16 48	04 26	10 01	23 48	02 02	09 41	09 24	02 44
W 28	14:22:06	07 15	04 ♎ 56	19 18	04 20	19 01	06 27	11 18	07 09	16 57	04 27	10 00	23 50	03 36	09 30	09 32	02 42
T 29	14:26:02	08 13	18 09	19 16	05 43	20 14	06 27	11 43	07 21	16 59	04 28	09 59	24 37	03 08	09 30	09 46	02 13
F 30	14:29:59	09 12	02 ♏ 28	18 30	06 58	21 28	06 28	11 57	07 07	07 05	04 21	09 55	24 37	03 04	09 09	09 46	02 09

EPHEMERIS CALCULATED FOR 12 MIDNIGHT GREENWICH MEAN TIME. ALL OTHER DATA AND FACING ASPECTARIAN PAGE IN **EASTERN STANDARD TIME (BOLD)** AND PACIFIC STANDARD TIME (REGULAR).

MAY 1999

Eastern Standard Time in **bold type**
Pacific Standard Time in medium type

1 SATURDAY
1:06 am
2:53 am
10:36 am
4:59 pm 7:36 am
5:14 pm 1:59 pm
2:14 pm

2 SUNDAY
5:06 am 2:06 am
8:37 am 3:37 am
11:26 am 8:26 am
5:41 pm 2:41 pm
8:28 pm 5:28 pm
10:32 pm 7:32 pm

3 MONDAY
3:52 am 12:52 am
4:04 am 1:04 am
7:09 am 4:09 am
12:17 pm 9:17 am
1:43 pm
11:01 pm 8:01 pm

4 TUESDAY
5:37 am 2:37 am
7:55 am 4:55 am
3:55 pm 12:55 pm
6:50 pm 3:50 pm
11:58 pm 8:58 pm

5 WEDNESDAY
5:16 am 2:16 am
6:48 am 3:48 am
10:49 am 7:49 am
5:42 pm 2:42 pm
6:01 pm 3:01 pm
9:27 pm 6:27 pm
9:32 pm

6 THURSDAY
12:32 am
5:58 am 2:58 am
8:26 am 5:26 am
9:36 pm 6:36 pm
11:24 pm 8:24 pm
10:45 pm

7 FRIDAY
1:45 am
5:51 am 2:51 am
6:55 am 3:29 am
8:52 am 5:52 am
11:06 am 8:06 am
12:24 pm 9:24 am
5:59 pm 2:59 pm
6:17 pm 3:17 pm
6:29 pm 3:29 pm
7:53 pm 4:53 pm
9:25 pm 6:25 pm

8 SATURDAY
1:51 am
2:23 am
7:40 am 4:40 am
4:49 pm 1:49 pm
9:35 pm

9 SUNDAY
12:35 am
9:01 am 6:01 am
12:16 pm 9:16 am
1:28 pm 10:28 am
1:57 pm 10:57 am
6:50 pm 3:50 pm
11:52 pm 8:52 pm

10 MONDAY
12:48 am
2:24 am
4:03 am 1:03 am
4:41 am 1:41 am
8:08 am 5:08 am
10:51 pm 7:51 pm
11:41 pm 11:07 pm

11 TUESDAY
2:07 am
2:41 am
2:12 am
2:41 am
6:07 am 3:07 am
10:20 pm 8:13 pm
11:13 pm 11:22 pm

12 WEDNESDAY
2:22 am
3:43 am 12:43 am
6:22 am 3:22 am
7:57 am 4:57 am
9:10 am 6:10 am
11:47 am 8:47 am
5:05 pm 2:05 pm
7:39 pm 4:39 pm
11:30 pm

13 THURSDAY
2:30 am
4:26 am 1:26 am
10:37 am 7:37 am
12:59 pm 9:59 am
5:10 pm 2:10 pm
6:49 pm 3:49 pm
8:13 pm 5:13 pm
11:52 pm 8:52 pm
11:51 pm

14 FRIDAY
2:51 am
3:29 am 12:29 am
7:04 am 4:04 am
8:06 am 5:06 am
10:15 am 7:15 am
10:53 am 7:53 am
5:52 pm 2:52 pm
7:54 pm 4:54 pm
11:44 pm

15 SATURDAY
2:44 am
7:06 am 4:06 am
11:27 am 8:27 am
2:38 pm

16 SUNDAY
1:55 am
5:34 am 2:34 am
6:31 am 3:31 am
7:04 am 4:04 am
11:26 am 8:26 am
4:00 pm 1:00 pm
5:55 pm 2:55 pm
6:33 pm 3:33 pm
8:24 pm 5:24 pm
11:11 pm
11:38 pm

17 MONDAY
2:11 am
3:38 am 12:38 am
8:28 am 5:28 am
9:39 am 6:39 am
10:05 pm 7:05 pm
10:42 pm 9:45 pm
10:06 pm

18 TUESDAY
12:45 am
3:06 am 12:06 am
5:06 am 2:06 am
6:34 am 3:34 am
7:42 am 4:42 am
9:45 pm
10:06 pm

19 WEDNESDAY
12:40 am
10:32 am 1:32 am
2:52 pm 7:54 am
6:54 pm 3:54 pm
10:15 pm 7:15 pm

20 THURSDAY
1:07 pm 10:07 am
11:54 am
5:24 am 2:24 am
10:42 am 7:02 am
10:38 am 7:30 am
5:08 pm 2:08 pm
6:47 pm 3:47 pm
11:10 pm 8:10 pm
9:52 pm

21 FRIDAY
12:52 pm
10:04 am 7:04 am
3:15 pm 12:15 pm
4:07 pm 1:07 pm
8:19 pm 6:19 pm
9:19 pm
9:35 pm

22 SATURDAY
12:19 am
12:35 am
4:58 am 1:58 am
6:02 am 3:02 am
7:16 am 5:16 am
8:18 am 5:18 am
8:45 am 5:45 am
11:38 pm 8:55 pm
2:55 pm

23 SUNDAY
4:25 am 1:25 am
5:37 am 2:37 am
6:55 am 3:55 am
10:13 am 7:13 am
7:30 pm 4:30 pm
7:47 pm 4:47 pm
8:51 pm 5:51 pm
9:07 pm 6:07 pm
8:16 pm

24 MONDAY
4:22 am 1:22 am
9:15 am 6:15 am
11:59 am 8:59 am
2:45 pm 11:45 am
6:54 pm 3:54 pm
4:58 pm 1:58 pm

25 TUESDAY
2:45 am
4:41 am 1:41 am
1:22 am 10:22 am
1:36 pm 10:36 am
1:52 pm 10:52 am
3:12 pm 12:12 pm
5:29 pm 2:29 pm
5:33 pm 2:33 pm
5:38 pm 2:38 pm
9:12 pm 6:12 pm
9:58 pm 6:58 pm
10:46 pm 7:46 pm
10:36 pm

26 WEDNESDAY
1:36 am
7:46 am 4:46 am
9:56 am 6:56 am
11:10 am 8:10 am
8:31 pm 5:31 pm

27 THURSDAY
3:40 am 12:40 am
5:38 am 2:38 am
5:39 am 2:39 am
7:39 am 4:39 am
7:45 am 4:45 am
1:09 pm 10:09 am
2:38 pm 11:38 am
5:21 pm 2:21 pm
9:08 pm 6:08 pm

28 FRIDAY
5:54 am 2:54 am
8:19 am 5:19 am
12:54 pm 9:54 am
1:04 pm 10:04 am
4:08 pm 1:17 pm
9:17 pm 6:17 pm
9:54 pm 6:54 pm

29 SATURDAY
8:41 am 5:41 am
3:07 pm 12:07 pm
5:10 pm 2:10 pm
10:27 pm 7:27 pm
11:17 pm 8:17 pm

30 SUNDAY
1:40 pm 10:40 am
3:06 pm 12:06 pm
6:35 pm 3:35 pm
6:22 pm
3:22 pm
6:28 pm 3:28 pm
7:04 pm 4:04 pm
11:29 pm 8:29 pm

31 MONDAY
3:19 am 12:19 am
6:52 am 3:52 am
8:28 am 5:28 am
10:07 am 7:07 am
10:26 am 7:26 am
10:54 am 7:54 am
5:00 pm 2:00 pm
8:48 pm 5:48 pm
11:26 pm

MAY 1999

☽ Last Aspect day	EST / hr:mn / PST		asp	☽ Ingress sign day	EST / hr:mn / PST	
30	**11:35 pm**	8:35 pm	□♅	♐ 1		11:36 pm
30	**11:35 pm**	8:35 pm	□♅	♐ 2	**2:36 am**	
4	**5:37 am**	2:37 am	☍♀	♑ 4	**3:12 pm**	12:12 pm
6		10:45 pm	□♂	♒ 6		11:40 pm
7	**1:45 am**		□♂	♒ 7	**2:40 am**	
9	**9:01 am**	6:01 am	△♂	♓ 9	**11:16 am**	8:16 am
10	**10:51 pm**	7:51 pm	✶☉	♈ 11	**3:54 pm**	12:54 pm
13	**12:59 pm**	9:59 am	☍♂	♉ 13	**4:57 pm**	1:57 pm
15	**7:06 am**	4:06 am	☌☉	♊ 15	**4:08 pm**	1:08 pm
17	**10:05 am**	7:05 am	△♂	♋ 17	**3:40 pm**	12:40 pm

☽ Last Aspect day	EST / hr:mn / PST		asp	☽ Ingress sign day	EST / hr:mn / PST	
19	**2:52 pm**	11:52 am	✶☉	♌ 19	**5:38 pm**	2:38 pm
21	**3:15 pm**	12:15 pm	✶♂	♍ 21	**11:16 pm**	8:16 pm
23	**5:37 am**	2:37 am	✶♀	♎ 24	**8:29 am**	5:29 am
26	**9:56 am**	6:56 am	☌♂	♏ 26	**8:05 pm**	5:05 pm
28	**4:08 pm**	1:08 pm	△♀	♐ 29	**8:37 am**	5:37 am
31	**10:54 am**	7:54 am	△♃	♑ 31	**9:06 pm**	6:06 pm

☽ Phases & Eclipses phase	day	EST / hr:mn / PST	
4th Quarter	8	**12:28 pm**	9:28 am
New Moon	15	**7:06 am**	4:06 am
2nd Quarter	21		9:35 pm
2nd Quarter	22	**12:35 am**	
Full Moon	29		10:40 pm
Full Moon	30	**1:40 am**	

Planet Ingress	day	EST / hr:mn / PST	
♂ ♎	5	**4:32 pm**	1:32 pm
♀ ♋	8	**11:28 am**	8:28 am
⚳ ♋	13	**8:56 am**	5:56 am
☉ ♊	21	**6:52 am**	3:52 am
☿ ♊	23	**4:22 pm**	1:22 pm
⚷ ♐	29	**6:54 pm**	3:54 pm

Planetary Motion	day	EST / hr:mn / PST	
♆ ℞	6	**1:33 pm**	10:33 am
♅ ℞	21	**1:43 pm**	10:43 am

DATE		SID.TIME	SUN	MOON	NODE	MERCURY	VENUS	MARS	JUPITER	SATURN	URANUS	NEPTUNE	PLUTO	CERES	PALLAS	JUNO	VESTA	CHIRON
S	1	14:33:56	10 ♉ 11	14 ♏ 20	18 ☊℞ 16	16 ♈ 59	21 ♊ 20	01 ♏℞ 46	18 ♈ 11	07 ♉ 12	16 ♒ 37	04 ♒ 22	09 ♐℞ 54	25 ♊ 00	04 ♉ 58	09 ♐℞ 11	12 ♌ 00	02 ♐℞ 05
S	2	14:37:52	11 09	26 14	18 02	18 31	22 29	01 23	18 25	07 20	16 38	04 22	09 53	25 23	05 26	09 01	12 15	02 01
M	3	14:41:49	12 07	08 ♐ 06	17 49	20 06	23 37	01 02	18 39	07 28	16 39	04 22	09 51	25 47	05 53	08 51	12 30	01 57
T	4	14:45:45	13 06	19 59	17 39	21 42	24 44	00 40	18 52	07 35	16 40	04 22	09 50	26 10	06 21	08 40	12 45	01 53
W	5	14:49:42	14 04	01 ♑ 54	17 31	23 20	25 52	00 19	19 06	07 43	16 40	04 22	09 48	26 34	06 49	08 30	13 00	01 49
T	6	14:53:38	15 02	13 54	17 27	25 00	27 00	29 ♎ 58	19 20	07 51	16 41	04 22	09 47	26 58	07 17	08 19	13 16	01 45
F	7	14:57:35	16 00	26 04	17 25	26 42	28 07	29 37	19 34	07 58	16 42	04 ℞ 22	09 46	27 22	07 45	08 07	13 32	01 40
S	8	15:01:31	16 58	08 ♒ 28	17 D 25	28 26	29 14	29 17	19 47	08 06	16 43	04 22	09 44	27 45	08 13	07 56	13 48	01 36
S	9	15:05:28	17 56	21 10	17 ℞ 25	00 ♉ 12	00 ♋ 21	28 58	20 01	08 13	16 43	04 22	09 43	28 09	08 40	07 44	14 04	01 32
M	10	15:09:25	18 54	04 ♓ 16	17 25	01 59	01 28	28 38	20 15	08 21	16 44	04 22	09 41	28 33	09 09	07 32	14 21	01 28
T	11	15:13:21	19 52	17 49	17 23	03 49	02 34	28 20	20 28	08 29	16 45	04 22	09 40	28 57	09 37	07 20	14 38	01 23
W	12	15:17:18	20 50	01 ♈ 51	17 18	05 40	03 41	28 02	20 42	08 36	16 45	04 22	09 38	29 22	10 05	07 08	14 55	01 19
T	13	15:21:14	21 48	16 22	17 11	07 34	04 47	27 44	20 55	08 44	16 46	04 22	09 37	29 46	10 33	06 56	15 12	01 15
F	14	15:25:11	22 46	01 ♉ 17	17 02	09 29	05 53	27 27	21 09	08 51	16 46	04 21	09 35	00 ♋ 10	11 01	06 43	15 30	01 10
S	15	15:29:07	23 44	16 30	16 52	11 26	06 59	27 11	21 22	08 59	16 46	04 21	09 34	00 35	11 30	06 31	15 48	01 06
S	16	15:33:04	24 42	01 ♊ 50	16 41	13 25	08 05	26 55	21 35	09 06	16 47	04 21	09 32	00 59	11 58	06 18	16 06	01 02
M	17	15:37:00	25 40	17 04	16 32	15 26	09 10	26 41	21 48	09 14	16 47	04 20	09 30	01 23	12 26	06 05	16 24	00 57
T	18	15:40:57	26 38	02 ♋ 03	16 24	17 29	10 16	26 26	22 02	09 21	16 47	04 20	09 29	01 48	12 55	05 52	16 43	00 53
W	19	15:44:54	27 35	16 39	16 18	19 33	11 21	26 13	22 15	09 29	16 47	04 20	09 27	02 13	13 23	05 39	17 01	00 48
T	20	15:48:50	28 33	00 ♌ 48	16 15	21 39	12 26	26 00	22 28	09 36	16 48	04 19	09 26	02 37	13 52	05 25	17 20	00 44
F	21	15:52:47	29 31	14 28	16 D 13	23 46	13 30	25 49	22 41	09 43	16 48	04 19	09 24	03 02	14 21	05 12	17 40	00 40
S	22	15:56:43	00 ♊ 29	27 42	16 ℞ 13	25 54	14 35	25 37	22 54	09 51	16 ℞ 48	04 18	09 22	03 27	14 49	04 59	17 59	00 35
S	23	16:00:40	01 26	10 ♍ 32	16 13	28 04	15 39	25 27	23 07	09 58	16 48	04 18	09 21	03 52	15 18	04 45	18 19	00 31
M	24	16:04:36	02 24	23 04	16 11	00 ♊ 14	16 43	25 18	23 19	10 05	16 47	04 17	09 19	04 17	15 47	04 32	18 38	00 26
T	25	16:08:33	03 22	05 ♎ 21	16 08	02 26	17 46	25 09	23 32	10 13	16 47	04 17	09 18	04 42	16 16	04 18	18 58	00 22
W	26	16:12:29	04 19	17 28	16 01	04 37	18 50	25 01	23 45	10 20	16 47	04 16	09 16	05 07	16 45	04 05	19 18	00 17
T	27	16:16:26	05 17	29 28	15 52	06 49	19 53	24 54	23 58	10 27	16 47	04 16	09 14	05 32	17 13	03 51	19 39	00 13
F	28	16:20:23	06 15	11 ♏ 23	15 40	09 01	20 55	24 48	24 10	10 34	16 47	04 15	09 13	05 57	17 42	03 38	19 59	00 09
S	29	16:24:19	07 12	23 16	15 28	11 12	21 58	24 42	24 23	10 42	16 46	04 14	09 11	06 22	18 11	03 24	20 20	00 04
S	30	16:28:16	08 10	05 ♐ 08	15 15	13 23	23 00	24 38	24 35	10 49	16 46	04 14	09 09	06 47	18 41	03 11	20 41	00 ♐ 00
M	31	16:32:12	09 07	17 02	15 03	15 33	24 02	24 34	24 47	10 56	16 46	04 13	09 08	07 12	19 10	02 57	21 02	29 ♏ 56

EPHEMERIS CALCULATED FOR 12 MIDNIGHT GREENWICH MEAN TIME. ALL OTHER DATA AND FACING ASPECTARIAN PAGE IN **EASTERN STANDARD TIME (BOLD)** AND PACIFIC STANDARD TIME (REGULAR).

JUNE 1999

1 TUESDAY

☽ ⚺ ⚵	**2:26 am**	
☽ ⚺ ♆	**5:30 am**	2:30 am
☽ ☍ ⚳	**12:59 pm**	9:59 am
☽ ⚺ ♇	**3:15 pm**	12:15 pm
☽ ⚻ ☉	**7:11 pm**	4:11 pm
☽ △ ♄	**7:25 pm**	4:25 pm
☉ ⚺ ♄	**10:27 pm**	7:27 pm
☿ ⚺ ♀	**11:42 pm**	8:42 pm

2 WEDNESDAY

☽ ⚺ ♅	**6:30 am**	3:30 am
☽ △ ♀	**1:59 pm**	10:59 am
☽ ⚻ ☿	**4:16 pm**	1:16 pm
☽ ⚻ ⚶	**5:02 pm**	2:02 pm
☿ ✶ ⚶	**9:35 pm**	6:35 pm
☽ □ ♂	**9:44 pm**	6:44 pm
☽ □ ♃	**11:40 pm**	8:40 pm

3 THURSDAY

☽ ☍ ♀	**3:39 am**	12:39 am
☽ ✶ ⚷	**7:59 am**	4:59 am
☽ ✶ ⚵	**12:46 pm**	9:46 am
☽ ☌ ♆	**4:45 pm**	1:45 pm
☿ △ ♂		9:29 pm
♇ ⚻ ⚳		10:34 pm
☽ ✶ ♇		11:09 pm
☽ ⚻ ⚳		11:10 pm

4 FRIDAY

☿ △ ♂	**12:29 am**	
♇ ⚻ ⚳	**1:34 am**	
☽ ✶ ♇	**2:09 am**	
☽ ⚻ ⚳	**2:10 am**	
☽ □ ♄	**6:51 am**	3:51 am
☽ △ ☉	**10:59 am**	7:59 am
☿ ✶ ♃	**4:07 pm**	1:07 pm
☽ ☌ ♅	**4:57 pm**	1:57 pm
☽ □ ♀		11:32 pm

5 SATURDAY

☽ □ ♀	**2:32 am**	
☽ ☍ ⚶	**4:50 am**	1:50 am
♀ △ ⚷	**5:25 am**	2:25 am
☽ △ ♂	**7:38 am**	4:38 am
☽ ✶ ♃	**10:23 am**	7:23 am
☽ △ ☿	**1:27 pm**	10:27 am
☽ □ ⚷	**5:06 pm**	2:06 pm
☽ ⚻ ♀	**6:09 pm**	3:09 pm
☽ □ ⚵	**9:02 pm**	6:02 pm
☽ ⚺ ♆		10:41 pm

6 SUNDAY

☽ ⚺ ♆	**1:41 am**	
☽ □ ♇	**10:33 am**	7:33 am
☽ △ ⚳	**12:34 pm**	9:34 am
☿ ⚻ ⚷	**12:35 pm**	9:35 am
☽ ✶ ♄	**3:36 pm**	12:36 pm
☽ □ ☉	**11:21 pm**	8:21 pm
☽ ⚺ ♅		9:34 pm
♀ △ ⚵		10:31 pm

7 MONDAY

☽ ⚺ ♅	**12:34 am**	
♀ △ ⚵	**1:31 am**	
☿ ⚻ ⚵	**11:14 am**	8:14 am
☽ ✶ ♀	**11:43 am**	8:43 am
☽ ⚻ ⚶	**1:20 pm**	10:20 am
☽ ⚻ ♂	**2:33 pm**	11:33 am
☉ △ ♅	**4:14 pm**	1:14 pm
☽ ⚺ ♃	**5:48 pm**	2:48 pm
☽ △ ⚷	**11:01 pm**	8:01 pm
☿ ⚺ ♀	**11:49 pm**	8:49 pm
☽ △ ⚵		11:09 pm

8 TUESDAY

☽ △ ⚵	**2:09 am**	
☽ △ ♀	**4:26 am**	1:26 am
☽ □ ☿	**4:47 am**	1:47 am
☽ ✶ ♆	**7:15 am**	4:15 am
☽ △ ♇	**3:29 pm**	12:29 pm
☽ □ ⚳	**7:08 pm**	4:08 pm
☽ ⚺ ♄	**8:44 pm**	5:44 pm
☿ ⚻ ♆	**10:51 pm**	7:51 pm

9 WEDNESDAY

☽ ✶ ♅	**4:38 am**	1:38 am
☽ ✶ ☉	**7:17 am**	4:17 am
♂ ✶ ⚶	**4:52 pm**	1:52 pm
☽ ⚺ ♀	**4:54 pm**	1:54 pm
☽ ☍ ♂	**5:57 pm**	2:57 pm
☽ △ ⚶	**5:59 pm**	2:59 pm
♀ ☍ ♆	**7:51 pm**	4:51 pm
☽ ☌ ♃	**9:28 pm**	6:28 pm
☽ ⚻ ⚷		10:27 pm

10 THURSDAY

☽ ⚻ ⚷	**1:27 am**	
☽ ⚻ ⚵	**3:55 am**	12:55 am
☽ □ ♆	**9:21 am**	6:21 am
☽ □ ♀	**10:19 am**	7:19 am
☽ ✶ ☿	**2:15 pm**	11:15 am
☽ ⚻ ♇	**5:05 pm**	2:05 pm
☽ ✶ ⚳	**10:05 pm**	7:05 pm
☽ ☌ ♄	**10:30 pm**	7:30 pm

11 FRIDAY

☽ □ ♅	**5:35 am**	2:35 am
♂ ⚻ ♀	**5:45 am**	2:45 am
☽ ⚺ ☉	**11:28 am**	8:28 am
☿ ⚻ ♇	**1:44 pm**	10:44 am
♄ ✶ ⚳	**5:43 pm**	2:43 pm
☽ ⚻ ♂	**6:38 pm**	3:38 pm
☽ ☌ ♀	**6:59 pm**	3:59 pm
☽ □ ⚶	**7:38 pm**	4:38 pm
☽ ⚺ ♃	**10:21 pm**	7:21 pm
☽ ☍ ⚷		10:22 pm

12 SATURDAY

☽ ☍ ⚷	**1:22 am**	
☽ ☍ ⚵	**3:20 am**	12:20 am
☽ △ ♆	**9:10 am**	6:10 am
☽ ✶ ♀	**1:22 pm**	10:22 am
☽ ☍ ♇	**4:40 pm**	1:40 pm
☽ ⚺ ☿	**8:10 pm**	5:10 pm
☽ ⚺ ♄	**10:25 pm**	7:25 pm
☽ ⚺ ⚳	**11:02 pm**	8:02 pm

13 SUNDAY

☽ △ ♅	**4:59 am**	1:59 am
☽ ☌ ☉	**2:03 pm**	11:03 am
☿ ✶ ♄	**5:47 pm**	2:47 pm
☽ △ ♂	**6:22 pm**	3:22 pm
☽ ⚺ ♀	**7:59 pm**	4:59 pm
☽ ✶ ⚶	**8:16 pm**	5:16 pm
☽ ✶ ♃	**10:20 pm**	7:20 pm
☽ ⚻ ⚷		9:35 pm
☽ ⚻ ⚵		11:09 pm

14 MONDAY

☽ ⚻ ⚷	**12:35 am**	
☽ ⚻ ⚵	**2:09 am**	
☿ ☌ ⚳	**6:30 am**	3:30 am
☽ ⚻ ♆	**8:37 am**	5:37 am
☽ ⚺ ♀	**4:08 pm**	1:08 pm
☽ ⚻ ♇	**4:13 pm**	1:13 pm
♀ △ ♇	**5:30 pm**	2:30 pm
☽ ✶ ♄	**10:32 pm**	7:32 pm
☽ ☌ ⚳		9:16 pm
☽ ☌ ☿		10:52 pm

15 TUESDAY

☽ ☌ ⚳	**12:16 am**	
☽ ☌ ☿	**1:52 am**	
☽ ⚻ ♅	**4:54 am**	1:54 am
♀ □ ⚶	**10:17 am**	7:17 am
☽ ⚺ ☉	**5:47 pm**	2:47 pm
☽ □ ♂	**7:19 pm**	4:19 pm
☽ ⚺ ⚶	**10:12 pm**	7:12 pm
☽ ✶ ♀	**10:18 pm**	7:18 pm
☽ □ ♃	**11:39 pm**	8:39 pm
☽ △ ⚷		10:10 pm
☽ △ ⚵		11:24 pm

16 WEDNESDAY

☽ △ ⚷	**1:10 am**	
☽ △ ⚵	**2:24 am**	
☿ ⚻ ♅	**5:58 am**	2:58 am
☽ ☍ ♆	**9:46 am**	6:46 am
☽ △ ♇	**5:48 pm**	2:48 pm
☽ ☌ ♀	**9:18 pm**	6:18 pm
☉ △ ♂	**9:22 pm**	6:22 pm
☽ □ ♄		9:59 pm

17 THURSDAY

☽ □ ♄	**12:59 am**	
☽ ⚺ ⚳	**4:03 am**	1:03 am
☽ ☍ ♅	**7:19 am**	4:19 am
☽ ⚺ ☿	**10:31 am**	7:31 am
☽ ✶ ♂	**11:26 pm**	8:26 pm
☽ ✶ ☉		10:05 pm

18 FRIDAY

☽ ✶ ☉	**1:05 am**	
☽ ☌ ⚶	**3:29 am**	12:29 am
☽ □ ♀	**4:01 am**	1:01 am
☽ △ ♃	**4:10 am**	1:10 am
☽ □ ⚷	**4:52 am**	1:52 am
☽ □ ⚵	**5:45 am**	2:45 am
♃ ⚺ ♀	**10:12 am**	7:12 am
☽ ⚻ ♆	**2:16 pm**	11:16 am
☽ □ ♇	**10:53 pm**	7:53 pm
♀ ☍ ⚷		9:37 pm

19 SATURDAY

♀ ☍ ⚷	**12:37 am**	
☽ ⚺ ♀	**6:46 am**	3:46 am
☽ △ ♄	**7:10 am**	4:10 am
☽ ✶ ⚳	**11:55 am**	8:55 am
♀ □ ♄	**1:22 pm**	10:22 am
☽ ⚻ ♅	**1:27 pm**	10:27 am
♀ ☍ ⚵	**2:50 pm**	11:50 am
♃ △ ⚶	**7:35 pm**	4:35 pm
⚶ □ ⚷	**8:09 pm**	5:09 pm
♃ ⚻ ⚷	**8:43 pm**	5:43 pm
☽ ✶ ☿	**11:58 pm**	8:58 pm

20 SUNDAY

☉ ⚻ ⚷	**3:28 am**	12:28 am
☉ ✶ ♃	**5:29 am**	2:29 am
☽ ⚺ ♂	**7:41 am**	4:41 am
⚵ □ ⚶	**9:05 am**	6:05 am
☉ ⚻ ⚵	**9:16 am**	6:16 am
☉ ✶ ⚶	**9:33 am**	6:33 am
☽ ✶ ⚷	**12:26 pm**	9:26 am
☽ ⚻ ♃	**12:43 pm**	9:43 am
☽ ✶ ⚵	**12:52 pm**	9:52 am
☽ ⚺ ⚶	**1:03 pm**	10:03 am
☽ □ ☉	**1:13 pm**	10:13 am
☽ △ ♀	**2:06 pm**	11:06 am
♃ ⚻ ⚵	**6:10 pm**	3:10 pm
☽ △ ♆	**10:38 pm**	7:38 pm

21 MONDAY

♅ ⚻ ⚳	**7:02 am**	4:02 am
☽ ✶ ♇	**7:47 am**	4:47 am
☉ ⚺ ♀	**12:43 pm**	9:43 am
☽ ⚻ ♄	**5:11 pm**	2:11 pm
☽ ✶ ♀	**8:44 pm**	5:44 pm
☽ △ ♅	**11:14 pm**	8:14 pm
☽ □ ⚳	**11:52 pm**	8:52 pm

22 TUESDAY

♂ ⚺ ⚵	**3:01 pm**	12:01 pm
⚵ ☌ ⚷	**5:14 pm**	2:14 pm
☽ □ ☿	**5:37 pm**	2:37 pm
☽ ☌ ♂	**7:31 pm**	4:31 pm
☽ ⚺ ⚵	**11:07 pm**	8:07 pm
☽ ⚺ ⚷	**11:10 pm**	8:10 pm
☽ ☍ ♃		9:36 pm
☽ ✶ ⚶		11:09 pm

23 WEDNESDAY

☽ ☍ ♃	**12:36 am**	
☽ ✶ ⚶	**2:09 am**	
☽ ⚻ ♀	**3:47 am**	12:47 am
☽ △ ☉	**5:22 am**	2:22 am
♀ ☍ ♅	**7:15 am**	4:15 am
☽ □ ♆	**9:56 am**	6:56 am
☿ □ ♂	**3:52 pm**	12:52 pm
☽ ⚺ ♇	**7:24 pm**	4:24 pm

24 THURSDAY

☽ ☍ ♄	**5:41 am**	2:41 am
☽ □ ♅	**11:15 am**	8:15 am
☽ □ ♀	**1:27 pm**	10:27 am
☽ △ ⚳	**2:19 pm**	11:19 am
☿ △ ⚵	**6:47 pm**	3:47 pm
☿ △ ⚷	**10:49 pm**	7:49 pm
♂ ⚺ ⚵	**11:35 pm**	8:35 pm

25 FRIDAY

☽ ⚺ ♂	**9:14 am**	6:14 am
☽ ☌ ⚵	**10:54 am**	7:54 am
☽ ☌ ⚷	**11:26 am**	8:26 am
☽ △ ☿	**12:50 pm**	9:50 am
☉ ⚻ ♆	**1:23 pm**	10:23 am
☽ ⚻ ♃	**2:00 pm**	11:00 am
♀ ⚺ ⚳	**2:51 pm**	11:51 am
☽ □ ⚶	**4:53 pm**	1:53 pm
☽ ☍ ♀	**7:02 pm**	4:02 pm
☽ ✶ ♆	**10:26 pm**	7:26 pm
☽ ⚻ ☉	**11:15 pm**	8:15 pm

26 SATURDAY

☿ □ ♃	**3:22 am**	12:22 am
☽ ☌ ♇	**7:55 am**	4:55 am
☽ ⚻ ♄	**6:48 pm**	3:48 pm
☽ ✶ ♅	**11:43 pm**	8:43 pm

27 SUNDAY

☽ ⚻ ⚳	**5:12 am**	2:12 am
☽ △ ♀	**6:30 am**	3:30 am
☽ ⚺ ⚵	**10:37 pm**	7:37 pm
☽ ✶ ♂	**10:59 pm**	7:59 pm
☽ ⚺ ⚷	**11:35 pm**	8:35 pm

28 MONDAY

☽ △ ♃	**3:11 am**	12:11 am
☽ ⚻ ☿	**6:59 am**	3:59 am
☽ △ ⚶	**7:22 am**	4:22 am
☽ ⚻ ♀	**9:58 am**	6:58 am
☽ ⚺ ♆	**10:34 am**	7:34 am
☿ ⚺ ⚶	**2:38 pm**	11:38 am
☽ ☍ ☉	**4:38 pm**	1:38 pm
☽ ⚺ ♇	**7:53 pm**	4:53 pm
♆ △ ♀	**11:23 pm**	8:23 pm

29 TUESDAY

☽ △ ♄	**7:09 am**	4:09 am
☽ ⚺ ♅	**11:22 am**	8:22 am
☽ ☍ ⚳	**7:06 pm**	4:06 pm
☽ ⚻ ♀	**10:13 pm**	7:13 pm

30 WEDNESDAY

☿ ☍ ♆	**4:13 am**	1:13 am
☉ ⚻ ♇	**8:54 am**	5:54 am
☽ ✶ ⚵	**9:17 am**	6:17 am
☽ ✶ ⚷	**10:35 am**	7:35 am
☽ □ ♂	**11:37 am**	8:37 am
☽ □ ♃	**3:05 pm**	12:05 pm
☽ ⚻ ⚶	**8:27 pm**	5:27 pm
☽ ☌ ♆	**9:23 pm**	6:23 pm
☽ ☍ ☿	**10:41 pm**	7:41 pm
☽ △ ♀	**11:26 pm**	8:26 pm

Eastern Standard Time in bold type
Pacific Standard Time in medium type

JUNE 1999

Last Aspect / Ingress

	Last Aspect				Ingress		
day	EST / hr:mn / PST	asp		sign day	EST / hr:mn / PST		
3	3:39 am 12:39 am	☐ ♀		⊗ 16	3:07 am 12:07 am		
5	1:27 pm 10:27 am	△ ♃		♍ 18	7:18 am 4:18 am		
6	11:21 pm 8:21 pm	☐ ⊙		⚍ 20	3:10 pm 12:10 pm		
6	11:21 pm 8:21 pm			♏ 23	2:18 am		
9	9:28 pm 6:28 pm	♂ ♃		⚻ 25	2:51 pm 11:51 am		
9	9:28 pm 6:28 pm			♐ 25	12:50 pm 9:50 am		
11	5:35 am 2:35 am	☐ ♄		♑ 28	3:22 am		
11	5:35 am 2:35 am			⚌ 28	3:11 am 12:11 am		
13	10:20 pm 7:20 pm	☐ ✹ ♀		♒ 30	2:20 pm 11:20 am		
13	10:20 pm 7:20 pm			30	3:12 pm 12:12 pm		

Phases & Eclipses

phase	day	EST / hr:mn / PST	
4th Quarter	6	11:21 pm 8:21 pm	
New Moon	13	2:03 pm 11:03 am	
2nd Quarter	20	1:13 pm 10:13 am	
Full Moon	28	4:38 pm 1:38 pm	

Planet Ingress

	day	EST / hr:mn / PST	
♀ ⟋	5	4:25 pm 1:25 pm	
♀ ♐	6	7:18 am 4:18 am	
♀ ✗	13	7:58 am 4:58 am	
♀ ⟋	21	2:49 am 11:49 am	
⊙ ⚍	21	2:49 am 11:49 am	
☿ ⚋	23	6:22 am 3:22 am	
♀ ⚌	26	10:39 am 7:39 am	
♀ ⚍	28	4:27 am 1:27 am	

Planetary Motion

	day	EST / hr:mn / PST	
♂ D	3	10:12 pm	
♂ D	4	1:12 am	

EPHEMERIS CALCULATED FOR 12 MIDNIGHT GREENWICH MEAN TIME. ALL OTHER DATA AND FACING ASPECTARIAN PAGE IN **EASTERN STANDARD TIME (BOLD)** AND PACIFIC STANDARD TIME (REGULAR).

JULY 1999

1 THURSDAY

☽ ⚹ ♇	**6:26 am**	3:26 am
☽ ⚻ ☉	**8:16 am**	5:16 am
☽ □ ♄	**5:55 pm**	2:55 pm
☽ ☌ ♅	**9:26 pm**	6:26 pm
♆ ⚻ ⚶	**10:14 pm**	7:14 pm

2 FRIDAY

☿ ⚹ ♀	**6:22 am**	3:22 am
☽ ⚻ ⚳	**7:07 am**	4:07 am
☽ ☍ ♀	**11:39 am**	8:39 am
☽ □ ⚵	**6:13 pm**	3:13 pm
☽ □ ⚷	**7:47 pm**	4:47 pm
☽ △ ♂	**10:22 pm**	7:22 pm
☽ ⚹ ♃		9:59 pm

3 SATURDAY

☽ ⚹ ♃	**12:59 am**	
☽ ⚺ ♆	**6:15 am**	3:15 am
☽ ☍ ⚶	**7:25 am**	4:25 am
☽ □ ♀	**10:41 am**	7:41 am
☽ ⚻ ☿	**11:09 am**	8:09 am
☽ □ ♇	**2:58 pm**	11:58 am
☽ △ ☉	**9:16 pm**	6:16 pm
☽ ⚹ ♄		11:26 pm

4 SUNDAY

☽ ⚹ ♄	**2:26 am**	
☽ ⚺ ♅	**5:17 am**	2:17 am
☽ △ ⚳	**4:34 pm**	1:34 pm
☽ ⚻ ♀	**10:05 pm**	7:05 pm
☽ △ ⚵		9:51 pm
☽ △ ⚷		11:36 pm

5 MONDAY

☽ △ ⚵	**12:51 am**	
☽ △ ⚷	**2:36 am**	
☽ ⚻ ♂	**6:33 am**	3:33 am
☽ ⚺ ♃	**8:18 am**	5:18 am
☽ ⚹ ♆	**12:37 pm**	9:37 am
☽ ⚻ ⚶	**3:35 pm**	12:35 pm
☽ ⚹ ♀	**7:02 pm**	4:02 pm
☽ △ ☿	**7:51 pm**	4:51 pm
☽ △ ♇	**8:54 pm**	5:54 pm

6 TUESDAY

☽ □ ☉	**6:57 am**	3:57 am
☽ ⚺ ♄	**8:12 am**	5:12 am
☽ ⚹ ♅	**10:27 am**	7:27 am
☽ □ ⚳	**10:59 pm**	7:59 pm
♀ □ ⚵	**11:25 pm**	8:25 pm
☿ △ ♇		9:25 pm
☉ ⚹ ♄		11:48 pm

7 WEDNESDAY

☿ △ ♇	**12:25 am**	
☉ ⚹ ♄	**2:48 am**	
☽ ⚻ ⚵	**4:49 am**	1:49 am
☽ △ ♀	**5:07 am**	2:07 am
☽ ⚻ ⚷	**6:39 am**	3:39 am
☽ ☍ ♂	**11:50 am**	8:50 am
☽ ☌ ♃	**12:43 pm**	9:43 am
☽ □ ♆	**4:13 pm**	1:13 pm
♇ ☍ ♀	**7:11 pm**	4:11 pm
☽ △ ⚶	**8:44 pm**	5:44 pm
☽ ⚻ ♇		9:06 pm
☽ ⚺ ♀		9:18 pm
☽ □ ☿		9:49 pm

8 THURSDAY

☽ ⚻ ♇	**12:06 am**	
☽ ⚺ ♀	**12:18 am**	
☽ □ ☿	**12:49 am**	
☉ ⚻ ♅	**8:17 am**	5:17 am
☽ ☌ ♄	**11:14 am**	8:14 am
☽ □ ♅	**12:59 pm**	9:59 am
☽ ⚹ ☉	**1:19 pm**	10:19 am
♀ □ ⚷	**1:53 pm**	10:53 am
☽ ⚹ ⚳		11:38 pm

9 FRIDAY

☽ ⚹ ⚳	**2:38 am**	
☽ ☍ ⚵	**6:24 am**	3:24 am
☽ ☍ ⚷	**8:19 am**	5:19 am
☽ □ ♀	**9:09 am**	6:09 am
☿ ⚹ ♀	**12:32 pm**	9:32 am
☽ ⚻ ♂	**2:38 pm**	11:38 am
☽ ⚺ ♃	**2:44 pm**	11:44 am
☽ △ ♆	**5:33 pm**	2:33 pm
♂ ☍ ♃	**8:22 pm**	5:22 pm
☽ □ ⚶	**11:29 pm**	8:29 pm
☽ ☍ ♇		10:12 pm
☽ ⚹ ☿		11:56 pm

10 SATURDAY

☽ ☍ ♇	**1:12 am**	
☽ ⚹ ☿	**2:56 am**	
☽ ☌ ♀	**3:13 am**	12:13 am
☽ ⚺ ♄	**12:22 pm**	9:22 am
☽ △ ♅	**1:41 pm**	10:41 am
☽ ⚺ ☉	**5:28 pm**	2:28 pm

11 SUNDAY

☽ ⚺ ⚳	**4:41 am**	1:41 am
☽ ⚻ ⚵	**6:42 am**	3:42 am
☽ ⚻ ⚷	**8:42 am**	5:42 am
☽ ⚹ ♀	**11:37 am**	8:37 am
☽ ⚹ ♃	**3:36 pm**	12:36 pm
☽ △ ♂	**4:20 pm**	1:20 pm
☽ ⚻ ♆	**5:53 pm**	2:53 pm
☽ ⚹ ⚶		10:23 pm
☽ ⚻ ♇		10:33 pm

12 MONDAY

☽ ⚹ ⚶	**1:23 am**	
☽ ⚻ ♇	**1:33 am**	
☽ ⚺ ☿	**3:47 am**	12:47 am
☽ ⚺ ♀	**5:23 am**	2:23 am
♇ □ ⚶	**6:57 am**	3:57 am
☽ ⚹ ♄	**1:07 pm**	10:07 am
☽ ⚻ ♅	**2:04 pm**	11:04 am
☽ ☌ ☉	**9:24 pm**	6:24 pm

13 TUESDAY

☽ ☌ ⚳	**6:59 am**	3:59 am
☽ △ ⚵	**7:21 am**	4:21 am
☽ △ ⚷	**9:29 am**	6:29 am
☽ ⚺ ♀	**2:27 pm**	11:27 am
☽ □ ♃	**5:06 pm**	2:06 pm
⚳ △ ⚵	**5:50 pm**	2:50 pm
☽ □ ♂	**6:47 pm**	3:47 pm
☽ ☍ ♆	**6:56 pm**	3:56 pm
♂ □ ♆	**11:52 pm**	8:52 pm
☽ △ ♇		11:55 pm

14 WEDNESDAY

☽ △ ♇	**2:55 am**	
☽ ⚺ ⚶	**4:23 am**	1:23 am
☽ ☌ ☿	**5:10 am**	2:10 am
☽ ⚹ ♀	**8:50 am**	5:50 am
☽ □ ♄	**3:18 pm**	12:18 pm
☽ ☍ ♅	**3:54 pm**	12:54 pm
☿ ⚺ ⚶	**11:33 pm**	8:33 pm

15 THURSDAY

☽ ⚺ ☉	**3:26 am**	12:26 am
☽ □ ⚵	**10:03 am**	7:03 am
☽ ⚺ ⚳	**11:31 am**	8:31 am
☽ □ ⚷	**12:23 pm**	9:23 am
☽ ☌ ♀	**7:38 pm**	4:38 pm
☽ △ ♃	**9:01 pm**	6:01 pm
☽ ⚻ ♆	**10:24 pm**	7:24 pm
☽ ⚹ ♂	**11:55 pm**	8:55 pm

16 FRIDAY

☽ □ ♇	**6:55 am**	3:55 am
☽ ⚺ ☿	**8:37 am**	5:37 am
☽ ☌ ⚶	**10:21 am**	7:21 am
⚳ △ ⚷	**12:55 pm**	9:55 am
☽ □ ♀	**3:26 pm**	12:26 pm
☽ △ ♄	**8:30 pm**	5:30 pm
☽ ⚻ ♅	**8:43 pm**	5:43 pm

17 SATURDAY

☽ ⚹ ☉	**1:28 pm**	10:28 am
☽ ⚹ ⚵	**4:09 pm**	1:09 pm
☽ ⚹ ⚷	**6:41 pm**	3:41 pm
☽ ⚹ ⚳	**7:48 pm**	4:48 pm
♄ □ ♅	**10:58 pm**	7:58 pm

18 SUNDAY

☽ ⚺ ♀	**4:26 am**	1:26 am
☽ ⚻ ♃	**4:31 am**	1:31 am
☽ △ ♆	**5:22 am**	2:22 am
♀ △ ♃	**8:06 am**	5:06 am
☽ ⚺ ♂	**9:01 am**	6:01 am
☽ ⚹ ♇	**2:31 pm**	11:31 am
☽ ⚹ ☿	**2:49 pm**	11:49 am
☽ ⚺ ⚶	**8:21 pm**	5:21 pm
☿ △ ♇	**11:32 pm**	8:32 pm
☉ △ ⚵		9:50 pm
☽ △ ♀		11:08 pm

19 MONDAY

☉ △ ⚵	**12:50 am**	
☽ △ ♀	**2:08 am**	
☽ △ ♅	**5:08 am**	2:08 am
☽ ⚻ ♄	**5:24 am**	2:24 am
♀ ⚻ ♆	**9:26 am**	6:26 am
☽ ⚺ ⚵		10:51 pm

20 TUESDAY

☽ ⚺ ⚵	**1:51 am**	
☽ □ ☉	**4:01 am**	1:01 am
☽ ⚺ ⚷	**4:32 am**	1:32 am
☽ □ ⚳	**8:00 am**	5:00 am
☉ △ ⚷	**10:33 am**	7:33 am
☽ ☍ ♃	**3:31 pm**	12:31 pm
☽ □ ♆	**3:44 pm**	12:44 pm
☽ ⚹ ♀	**4:41 pm**	1:41 pm
☽ ☌ ♂	**9:54 pm**	6:54 pm
☽ □ ☿	**11:20 pm**	8:20 pm
☽ ⚺ ♇		10:23 pm

21 WEDNESDAY

☽ ⚺ ♇	**1:23 am**	
☽ ⚹ ⚶	**9:53 am**	6:53 am
♃ □ ♆	**10:55 am**	7:55 am
☿ □ ♂	**3:07 pm**	12:07 pm
☽ ⚻ ♀	**4:16 pm**	1:16 pm
☽ □ ♅	**4:29 pm**	1:29 pm
☽ ☍ ♄	**5:16 pm**	2:16 pm
♅ △ ♀	**8:54 pm**	5:54 pm

22 THURSDAY

☽ ☌ ⚵	**1:59 pm**	10:59 am
☽ ☌ ⚷	**4:41 pm**	1:41 pm
♄ ⚺ ♀	**6:22 pm**	3:22 pm
☽ △ ☉	**9:28 pm**	6:28 pm
☽ △ ⚳	**10:39 pm**	7:39 pm

23 FRIDAY

☽ ⚹ ♆	**3:59 am**	12:59 am
☽ ⚻ ♃	**4:27 am**	1:27 am
☽ □ ♀	**6:34 am**	3:34 am
☽ △ ☿	**8:44 am**	5:44 am
☽ ⚺ ♂	**12:46 pm**	9:46 am
☽ ☌ ♇	**1:49 pm**	10:49 am
☉ ☌ ⚳	**11:45 pm**	8:45 pm
☽ □ ⚶		9:52 pm

24 SATURDAY

☽ □ ⚶	**12:52 am**	
☽ ⚹ ♅	**4:52 am**	1:52 am
☽ ⚻ ♄	**6:10 am**	3:10 am
☽ ☍ ♀	**7:37 am**	4:37 am
☿ ⚺ ♀	**12:34 pm**	9:34 am
♂ ⚺ ♇	**3:22 pm**	12:22 pm
☽ ⚺ ⚵		11:28 pm

25 SUNDAY

☽ ⚺ ⚵	**2:28 am**	
☽ ⚺ ⚷	**5:03 am**	2:03 am
☽ ⚻ ⚳	**1:17 pm**	10:17 am
☽ ⚻ ☉	**2:59 pm**	11:59 am
☽ ⚺ ♆	**4:06 pm**	1:06 pm
☽ △ ♃	**5:10 pm**	2:10 pm
☽ ⚻ ☿	**5:35 pm**	2:35 pm
☽ △ ♀	**7:44 pm**	4:44 pm
☿ □ ♃	**11:44 pm**	8:44 pm
☽ ⚺ ♇		10:48 pm

26 MONDAY

☽ ⚺ ♇	**1:48 am**	
☽ ⚹ ♂	**3:13 am**	12:13 am
☉ ☍ ♆	**4:32 am**	1:32 am
☿ ☌ ☉	**10:48 am**	7:48 am
☽ △ ⚶	**2:58 pm**	11:58 am
☽ ⚺ ♅	**4:21 pm**	1:21 pm
☽ △ ♄	**6:06 pm**	3:06 pm
☿ ☍ ♆	**7:49 pm**	4:49 pm
☉ □ ♃	**9:06 pm**	6:06 pm
☽ ⚻ ♀	**9:51 pm**	6:51 pm

27 TUESDAY

☿ ☌ ⚳	**12:54 pm**	9:54 am
☽ ⚹ ⚵	**1:36 pm**	10:36 am
☽ ⚹ ⚷	**3:58 pm**	12:58 pm
♅ ⚻ ⚶		9:52 pm
☽ ☍ ☿		9:59 pm
☽ ☍ ⚳		11:07 pm
☽ ☌ ♆		11:32 pm

28 WEDNESDAY

♅ ⚻ ⚶	**12:52 am**	
☽ ☍ ☿	**12:59 am**	
☽ ☍ ⚳	**2:07 am**	
☽ ☌ ♆	**2:32 am**	
☽ □ ♃	**4:06 am**	1:06 am
☽ ☍ ☉	**6:25 am**	3:25 am
☽ ⚻ ♀	**6:39 am**	3:39 am
♀ ⚺ ☉	**9:38 am**	6:38 am
☽ ⚹ ♇	**11:57 am**	8:57 am
♆ ☍ ⚳	**1:06 pm**	10:06 am
☽ □ ♂	**3:39 pm**	12:39 pm
☽ ☌ ♅		10:50 pm
☽ ⚻ ⚶		11:52 pm

29 THURSDAY

☽ ☌ ♅	**1:50 am**	
☽ ⚻ ⚶	**2:52 am**	
☽ □ ♄	**3:56 am**	12:56 am
☽ △ ♀	**9:45 am**	6:45 am
☽ □ ⚵	**10:35 pm**	7:35 pm
☽ □ ⚷		9:42 pm

30 FRIDAY

☽ □ ⚷	**12:42 am**	
☽ ⚻ ☿	**6:44 am**	3:44 am
☽ ⚺ ♆	**10:44 am**	7:44 am
♄ △ ⚶	**12:09 pm**	9:09 am
☽ ⚻ ⚳	**12:27 pm**	9:27 am
☽ ⚹ ♃	**12:44 pm**	9:44 am
☽ ☍ ♀	**2:53 pm**	11:53 am
☽ ⚻ ☉	**7:00 pm**	4:00 pm
☽ □ ♇	**7:51 pm**	4:51 pm
♃ □ ⚳	**10:20 pm**	7:20 pm
☽ △ ♂		10:37 pm

31 SATURDAY

☽ △ ♂	**1:37 am**	
☉ △ ♇	**6:28 am**	3:28 am
☽ ⚺ ♅	**9:04 am**	6:04 am
☽ ⚹ ♄	**11:28 am**	8:28 am
☽ ☍ ⚶	**12:14 pm**	9:14 am
☽ □ ♀	**7:05 pm**	4:05 pm

Eastern Standard Time in bold type
Pacific Standard Time in medium type

JULY 1999

☽ Last Aspect / ☽ Ingress

☽ Last Aspect			☽ Ingress		
day	EST / hr:mn / PST	asp	sign day	EST / hr:mn / PST	
2	10:22 pm 7:22 pm	♂♀	⬥ ♓ 3	11:35 pm 8:35 pm	
	11:26 pm	⚹♄	⬥ ♓ 3	6:22 am 3:22 am	
3	2:26 am	⚹♄	↑ ♉ 5	6:22 am 3:22 am	
5	5:07 am 2:07 am	△♀	↑ ♉ 5	6:22 am 3:22 am	
7	10:22 am 7:22 am	□♀	☿ ♊ 7	10:22 am 7:22 am	
9	9:09 am 6:09 am	⚹♀	☐ ♋ 9	11:59 am 8:59 am	
11	11:37 am 8:37 am	△⊙	♌ 11	1:25 pm 10:25 am	
12	9:24 pm 6:24 pm	♂⊙	♍ 13	3:54 pm 12:54 pm	
14	3:54 pm 12:54 pm	⚹♀	♎ 15	4:39 pm 1:39 pm	
17	1:28 pm 10:28 am	□⊙	♏ 17	11:19 pm 8:19 pm	
20	4:01 am 1:01 am	□⊙	♐ 20	9:30 am 6:30 am	

☽ Last Aspect / ☽ Ingress (cont.)

day	EST / hr:mn / PST	asp	sign day	EST / hr:mn / PST	
22	9:28 pm 6:28 pm	△⊙	♑ 22	9:49 pm 6:49 pm	
24	4:52 am 1:52 am	⚹♀	♒ 25	10:09 am 7:09 am	
26	6:06 pm 3:06 pm	⚹♀	♓ 27	8:55 pm 5:55 pm	
29	3:56 am 12:56 am	⚹♀	♈ 30	5:27 am 2:27 am	

☽ Phases & Eclipses

phase	day	EST / hr:mn / PST	
4th Quarter	6	6:57 am 3:57 am	
New Moon	12	9:24 pm 6:24 pm	
2nd Quarter	20	4:01 am 1:01 am	
Full Moon	28	6:25 am 3:25 am	
	28	4° ♒ 58′	

Planet Ingress

	day	EST / hr:mn / PST	
♀ ♏	4	11:00 pm 8:00 pm	
♀ ♍	12	9:24 pm 6:24 pm	
♀ ♌	21	1:01 pm 9:40 am	
☿ ♌	21	10:44 am	
⊙ ♌	22	12:40 am	
☿ ♋	31	1:44 pm 1:44 am	

Planetary Motion

		day	EST / hr:mn / PST	
♀ R	12	6:26 pm 3:26 pm	
⚹♀ ♀	21	9:48 pm	
⚹♀ ♄	22	12:48 am	
☿ D	28	2:30 pm 11:30 am	
♀ R	29	8:41 pm 5:41 pm	

Ephemeris Table

DATE	SID. TIME	SUN	MOON	NODE	MERCURY	VENUS	MARS	JUPITER	SATURN	URANUS	NEPTUNE	PLUTO	CERES	PALLAS	JUNO	VESTA	CHIRON
1 Th	18:34:25	08 ♋ 44	02 ♒ 24	13 ♌ R 13	04 ♋ 11	24 ♋ 23	28 ♎ 42	00 ♉ 24	14 ♉ 13	16 ♒ R 11	03 ♒ R 38	08 ♐ R 20	20 ⬥ 35	04 ♌ 13	27 ♈ R 36	03 ♒ 52	27 ♏ 27
2 F	18:38:22	09 41	14 44	13 13	04 11	25 38	29 29	00 00	14 24	16 09	03 37	08 19	21 01	04 55	27 27	03 59	27 27
3 Sa	18:42:19	10 39	27	13 13	05 45	26 52	29	00 18	14	16 07	03 35	08 18	21 28	05	27 08	03	27 58
4 Su	18:46:15	11	10 ♓ 28	15	06	28	29 35	01 37	14	34	03	16	02	54	27	24	27 56
5 M	18:50:12	12 33	23 39	17	07	00 ♌ 07	00 ♏ 57	01 09	14	35	03 32	08 16	22 27	06	26 50	04 50	27 54
6 Tu	18:54:08	13 30	07 ♈ 09	13 R	08	01 18	01 37	01 18	14	33	03 31	16	22 54	39	26	05 16	27 52
7 W	18:58:05	14 28	20 58	13	08 06	02 26	01 58	01 52	14 45	31	03 29	08 15	23 20	40	26 32	05 42	27 49
8 Th	19:02:01	15 25	05 ♉ 05	13	09	03 31	02 20	01 20	55	29	03 28	14	47	07	26	06	27 47
9 F	19:05:58	16 23	19 29	13	09 08	04 34	02 34	01 34	55	27	03	13	24 13	42	26	06 34	27 45
10 Sa	19:09:54	17 20	04 ♊ 08	13	09 11	05 34	03 17	01	05	14	03 26	12	40	08 00	26	07 00	27 43
11 Su	19:13:51	18	19	16	09 R	06 31	03	02	05 50	15 52	03	08 11	25 07	07	26	07 26	42
12 M	19:17:48	19 14	03 ♋ 55	14	09 04	07	04 22	02	06	50	03	08 11	25 33	44	26	07 52	42
13 Tu	19:21:44	20 11	18	15	09	08 21	04 46	02	06	48	03 23	08 10	26 00	46	26	08 18	39
14 W	19:25:41	21 08	02 ♌ 54	12	08 59	09 09	05 11	02 50	06	46	03 22	08 09	27	47	26	08 44	37
15 Th	19:29:37	22 06	17	21	08 52	09 52	05 37	02	08	44	03	08	27	48	26 18	09 10	35
16 F	19:33:34	23 03	00 ♍ 36	20	08 43	10 30	06 03	03	08	42	03	08	27	50	26 14	09 36	34
17 Sa	19:37:30	24 00	14 43	19	08	11 03	06 29	03 31	09	39	03 14	08	28	50	26	10 02	33
18 Su	19:41:27	24 57	27	19	08	11 30	06 56	03 31	36	37	03	08 07	28 44	17	26 10	10	32
19 M	19:45:23	25 55	10 ♎ 40	13 R	08	11 52	07 24	03	40	35	03 11	08 06	29 10	17	26 09	10 54	31
20 Tu	19:49:20	26 52	23 22	13	07 22	12 08	07 52	03 46	44	33	03 09	08 05	29	18	08	11 20	30
21 W	19:53:16	27 49	05 ♏ 47	12	07	12 18	08 22	03 55	48	31	03 08	08 05	00 ♌ 03	18	26	11 46	29
22 Th	19:57:13	28 46	17 59	12	06	12 R	08 52	04 08	52	28	03 06	08 04	00 27	19	26 07	12 12	28
23 F	20:01:10	29 43	00 ♐ 03	12	06	12	09 22	04	56	26	03 04	08 03	00 59	19	07	12 38	28
24 Sa	20:05:06	00 ♌ 41	11	12	05	12	09 54	04 31	00	24	03 03	08 03	00 47	20	26 D	13 04	27
25 Su	20:09:03	01 38	23	13	05	12	10 26	04 59	54	22	03 01	08 02	54	20	26	13 44	27
26 M	20:12:59	02 35	05 ♑ 55	12	05	11 41	10 59	05	54	19	02 59	08 01	53	31	26	14 12	26
27 Tu	20:16:56	03 32	17 55	13	05	11 18	11 33	05 38	38	14	02 58	08 01	53	33	26	14 39	26
28 W	20:20:52	04 30	00 ♒ 04	13 D	04	10 48	12 08	05	44	17	02 56	08 01	52	34	26	15 07	26
29 Th	20:24:49	05 27	12 18	12	04	10 18	12 43	06 18	48	12	02 54	08 00	51	35	26	15 35	26
30 F	20:28:46	06 24	24	12	04	09	13 20	06	53	10	02 53	08 00	50	36	26	16 03	D 26
31 Sa	20:32:42	07 22	07 ♓ 01	12	00	09 24	13 R	06 52	08	08	02 51	07 58	50	20	26	16 31	25

EPHEMERIS CALCULATED FOR 12 MIDNIGHT GREENWICH MEAN TIME. ALL OTHER DATA AND FACING ASPECTARIAN PAGE IN EASTERN STANDARD TIME (BOLD) AND PACIFIC STANDARD TIME (REGULAR).

AUGUST 1999

1 SUNDAY

☽△⚵	**5:22 am**	2:22 am
☽△⚷	**7:14 am**	4:14 am
☽△☿	**11:03 am**	8:03 am
☽⚹♆	**4:45 pm**	1:45 pm
☽⚺♃	**7:05 pm**	4:05 pm
☽△⚳	**8:21 pm**	5:21 pm
☽⚻♀	**8:33 pm**	5:33 pm
♀⚺⚳		10:23 pm
☽△♇		10:36 pm

2 MONDAY

♀⚺⚳	**1:23 am**	
☽△♇	**1:36 am**	
☽△☉	**4:52 am**	1:52 am
☽⚻♂	**9:13 am**	6:13 am
☽⚹♅	**2:13 pm**	11:13 am
☽⚺♄	**4:52 pm**	1:52 pm
☽⚻⚶	**7:17 pm**	4:17 pm
☽⚹⚴		11:07 pm

3 TUESDAY

☽⚹⚴	**2:07 am**	
☽⚻⚵	**10:10 am**	7:10 am
☽⚻⚷	**11:46 am**	8:46 am
☽□☿	**2:12 pm**	11:12 am
☽□♆	**8:50 pm**	5:50 pm
☽☌♃	**11:28 pm**	8:28 pm
☽△♀		9:02 pm
☽□⚳		11:08 pm

4 WEDNESDAY

☽△♀	**12:02 am**	
☽□⚳	**2:08 am**	
☽⚻♇	**5:28 am**	2:28 am
☽□☉	**12:26 pm**	9:26 am
☽☍♂	**2:50 pm**	11:50 am
☽□♅	**5:35 pm**	2:35 pm
☽☌♄	**8:28 pm**	5:28 pm
☽△⚶		9:24 pm

5 THURSDAY

☽△⚶	**12:24 am**	
⚴△♃	**3:50 am**	12:50 am
☽⚺⚴	**7:14 am**	4:14 am
☽☍⚵	**1:22 pm**	10:22 am
☽☍⚷	**2:44 pm**	11:44 am
☽⚹☿	**4:35 pm**	1:35 pm
☽△♆	**11:26 pm**	8:26 pm
☽□♀		10:49 pm
☽⚺♃		11:19 pm

6 FRIDAY

☽□♀	**1:49 am**	
☽⚺♃	**2:19 am**	
☽⚹⚳	**6:20 am**	3:20 am
☽☍♇	**7:57 am**	4:57 am
☽⚹☉	**6:23 pm**	3:23 pm
☽⚻♂	**7:03 pm**	4:03 pm
☽△♅	**7:43 pm**	4:43 pm
☽⚺♄	**10:50 pm**	7:50 pm

7 SATURDAY

☽□⚶	**4:16 am**	1:16 am
☽☌⚴	**11:11 am**	8:11 am
♂□♅	**11:54 am**	8:54 am
☉☍♅	**1:38 pm**	10:38 am
☽⚻⚵	**3:37 pm**	12:37 pm
☉□♂	**3:56 pm**	12:56 pm
☽⚻⚷	**4:45 pm**	1:45 pm
☽⚺☿	**6:50 pm**	3:50 pm
☽⚻♆		10:14 pm
☽⚹♀		11:37 pm

8 SUNDAY

☽⚻♆	**1:14 am**	
☽⚹♀	**2:37 am**	
☽⚹♃	**4:24 am**	1:24 am
♇△⚳	**9:19 am**	6:19 am
☽⚻♇	**9:46 am**	6:46 am
☽⚺⚳	**9:47 am**	6:47 am
☽⚻♅	**9:25 pm**	6:25 pm
☽△♂	**10:48 pm**	7:48 pm
☽⚺☉	**11:47 pm**	8:47 pm
☽⚹♄		9:49 pm

9 MONDAY

☽⚹♄	**12:49 am**	
☽⚹⚶	**7:51 am**	4:51 am
☽⚺⚴	**3:01 pm**	12:01 pm
☉□♄	**3:51 pm**	12:51 pm
☽△⚵	**5:55 pm**	2:55 pm
☽△⚷	**6:49 pm**	3:49 pm
☽☌☿	**10:01 pm**	7:01 pm

10 TUESDAY

☽☍♆	**3:16 am**	12:16 am
☽⚺♀	**3:24 am**	12:24 am
☽□♃	**6:45 am**	3:45 am
⚴⚻♆	**7:56 am**	4:56 am
☽△♇	**12:02 pm**	9:02 am
☽☌⚳	**1:43 pm**	10:43 am
☽☍♅	**11:50 pm**	8:50 pm

11 WEDNESDAY

☽□♂	**3:27 am**	12:27 am
☽□♄	**3:36 am**	12:36 am
☽☌☉	**6:09 am**	3:09 am
♂☍♄	**7:28 am**	4:28 am
☽⚺⚶	**12:33 pm**	9:33 am
☽⚹⚴	**8:11 pm**	5:11 pm
☽□⚵	**9:31 pm**	6:31 pm
☽□⚷	**10:10 pm**	7:10 pm

12 THURSDAY

☽⚺☿	**3:40 am**	12:40 am
☽☌♀	**5:20 am**	2:20 am
☽⚻♆	**6:47 am**	3:47 am
☽△♃	**10:41 am**	7:41 am
☽□♇	**4:02 pm**	1:02 pm
☽⚺⚳	**7:36 pm**	4:36 pm
☿⚺♀	**10:31 pm**	7:31 pm

13 FRIDAY

☽⚻♅	**4:16 am**	1:16 am
☽△♄	**8:30 am**	5:30 am
☽⚹♂	**10:31 am**	7:31 am
☽⚺☉	**3:12 pm**	12:12 pm
♀⚻⚵	**3:47 pm**	12:47 pm
☽☌⚶	**7:50 pm**	4:50 pm
♀⚻⚷		11:36 pm

14 SATURDAY

♀⚻⚷	**2:36 am**	
☽⚹⚵	**3:45 am**	12:45 am
☽⚹⚷	**4:05 am**	1:05 am
☽□⚴	**4:08 am**	1:08 am
☿☍♆	**6:20 am**	3:20 am
☽⚺♀	**9:26 am**	6:26 am
☽△♆	**12:59 pm**	9:59 am
☽⚹☿	**1:32 pm**	10:32 am
☽⚻♃	**5:23 pm**	2:23 pm
☽⚹♇	**10:53 pm**	7:53 pm

15 SUNDAY

☽⚹⚳	**4:41 am**	1:41 am
☽△♅	**11:42 am**	8:42 am
☽⚻♄	**4:29 pm**	1:29 pm
☽⚺♂	**9:08 pm**	6:08 pm

16 MONDAY

☽⚹☉	**4:11 am**	1:11 am
⚵☌⚷	**5:06 am**	2:06 am
☽⚺⚶	**6:40 am**	3:40 am
☿□♃	**1:07 pm**	10:07 am
☽⚺⚷	**1:14 pm**	**10:14 am**
☽⚺⚵	**1:18 pm**	10:18 am
☽△⚴	**3:43 pm**	12:43 pm
☽⚹♀	**4:12 pm**	1:12 pm
♀⚹⚴	**9:17 pm**	6:17 pm
☽□♆	**10:24 pm**	7:24 pm

17 TUESDAY

☽☍♃	**3:18 am**	12:18 am
☽□☿	**4:49 am**	1:49 am
☽⚺♇	**8:56 am**	5:56 am
☽□⚳	**5:18 pm**	2:18 pm
☽□♅	**10:12 pm**	7:12 pm

18 WEDNESDAY

☽☍♄	**3:30 am**	12:30 am
☽☌♂	**11:12 am**	8:12 am
♀□⚵	**4:17 pm**	1:17 pm
☉⚺⚶	**6:13 pm**	3:13 pm
☿△♇	**6:59 pm**	3:59 pm
☽⚹⚶	**8:41 pm**	5:41 pm
☽□☉	**8:48 pm**	5:48 pm
♀□⚷		9:52 pm
☽□♀		10:07 pm
☽☌⚷		10:07 pm
☽☌⚵		10:40 pm

19 THURSDAY

♀□⚷	**12:52 am**	
☽□♀	**1:07 am**	
☽☌⚷	**1:07 am**	
☽☌⚵	**1:40 am**	
☽⚻⚴	**6:17 am**	3:17 am
☽⚹♆	**10:16 am**	7:16 am
☽⚻♃	**3:31 pm**	12:31 pm
☽☌♇	**9:10 pm**	6:10 pm
☽△☿		9:46 pm

20 FRIDAY

☽△☿	**12:46 am**	
♀☌☉	**6:58 am**	3:58 am
☽△⚳	**8:03 am**	5:03 am
☽⚹♅	**10:27 am**	7:27 am
☽⚻♄	**4:06 pm**	1:06 pm
♀⚺⚶	**10:40 pm**	7:40 pm
☽⚺♂		11:50 pm

21 SATURDAY

☽⚺♂	**2:50 am**	
☉□⚷	**4:22 am**	1:22 am
☽△♀	**10:38 am**	7:38 am
☽□⚶	**11:47 am**	8:47 am
☽⚺⚷	**1:49 pm**	10:49 am
☽△☉	**2:36 pm**	11:36 am
☽⚺⚵	**2:53 pm**	11:53 am
☉□⚵	**6:36 pm**	3:36 pm
☽☍⚴	**9:30 pm**	6:30 pm
☽⚺♆	**10:33 pm**	7:33 pm

22 SUNDAY

☽△♃	**3:55 am**	12:55 am
☽⚺♇	**9:24 am**	6:24 am
♅☍⚳	**6:58 pm**	3:58 pm
♆⚻♀	**8:32 pm**	5:32 pm
☽⚻☿	**9:59 pm**	6:59 pm
☽⚺♅	**10:10 pm**	7:10 pm
☽⚻⚳	**10:18 pm**	7:18 pm
☿☍♅	**11:22 pm**	8:22 pm
☿☌⚳		10:05 pm

23 MONDAY

☿☌⚳	**1:05 am**	
☽△♄	**3:55 am**	12:55 am
☽⚹♂	**5:13 pm**	2:13 pm
⚶⚹⚷	**5:50 pm**	2:50 pm
☽⚻♀	**6:58 pm**	3:58 pm
☽⚹⚷		10:00 pm
☽△⚶		10:16 pm
☽⚹⚵		11:33 pm

24 TUESDAY

☽⚹⚷	**1:00 am**	
☽△⚶	**1:16 am**	
☽⚹⚵	**2:33 am**	
☽⚻☉	**6:29 am**	3:29 am
☽☌♆	**9:05 am**	6:05 am
☽⚻⚴	**10:44 am**	7:44 am
♀□♂	**12:23 pm**	9:23 am
☽□♃	**2:20 pm**	11:20 am
☿□♄	**3:55 pm**	12:55 pm
☽⚹♇	**7:34 pm**	4:34 pm

25 WEDNESDAY

☽☌♅	**7:33 am**	4:33 am
☽☍⚳	**9:55 am**	6:55 am
☽□♄	**1:13 pm**	10:13 am
☉⚻♆	**3:33 pm**	12:33 pm
☽☍☿	**4:41 pm**	1:41 pm
⚵⚹⚶		9:17 pm
☽☍♀		10:04 pm

26 THURSDAY

⚵⚹⚶	**12:17 am**	
☽☍♀	**1:04 am**	
☽□♂	**4:31 am**	1:31 am
☽□⚷	**9:24 am**	6:24 am
☽□⚵	**11:21 am**	8:21 am
☽⚻⚶	**11:38 am**	8:38 am
☽⚺♆	**4:46 pm**	1:46 pm
☽☍☉	**6:48 pm**	3:48 pm
☽△⚴	**8:44 pm**	5:44 pm
☽⚹♃	**9:51 pm**	6:51 pm
☽□♇		11:50 pm

27 FRIDAY

☽□♇	**2:50 am**	
☽⚺♅	**2:04 pm**	11:04 am
☿☌♀	**3:42 pm**	12:42 pm
☽⚻⚳	**6:20 pm**	3:20 pm
☽⚹♄	**7:38 pm**	4:38 pm
♃⚹⚴		9:26 pm

28 SATURDAY

♃⚹⚴	**12:26 am**	
☽⚻♀	**4:52 am**	1:52 am
☽⚻☿	**7:35 am**	4:35 am
☉△♃	**12:25 pm**	9:25 am
☽△♂	**12:41 pm**	9:41 am
☽△⚷	**3:03 pm**	12:03 pm
☽△⚵	**5:24 pm**	2:24 pm
☽☍⚶	**6:59 pm**	3:59 pm
☽⚹♆	**9:50 pm**	6:50 pm
☽⚺♃		11:45 pm
☉⚹⚴		11:53 pm

29 SUNDAY

☽⚺♃	**2:45 am**	
☉⚹⚴	**2:53 am**	
☽□⚴	**3:49 am**	12:49 am
☽⚻☉	**3:51 am**	12:51 am
☽△♇	**7:37 am**	4:37 am
♄□⚳	**10:05 am**	7:05 am
☽⚹♅	**6:17 pm**	3:17 pm
☽⚺♄	**11:48 pm**	8:48 pm
☽△⚳		9:15 pm

30 MONDAY

☽△⚳	**12:15 am**	
☽△♀	**7:02 am**	4:02 am
☿□♂	**10:01 am**	7:01 am
☿□⚷	**1:46 pm**	10:46 am
☽⚻♂	**6:42 pm**	3:42 pm
☽⚻⚷	**6:51 pm**	3:51 pm
☽△☿	**7:39 pm**	4:39 pm
☽⚻⚵	**9:35 pm**	6:35 pm
♂☌⚷	**10:41 pm**	7:41 pm
☽⚻⚶		9:23 pm
☽□♆		10:12 pm

31 TUESDAY

☽⚻⚶	**12:23 am**	
☽□♆	**1:12 am**	
☽☌♃	**6:02 am**	3:02 am
☽⚹⚴	**9:05 am**	6:05 am
☉□♇	**10:21 am**	7:21 am
☽⚻♇	**10:52 am**	7:52 am
☿□⚵	**10:52 am**	7:52 am
☽△☉	**10:55 am**	7:55 am
☽□♅	**9:12 pm**	6:12 pm
♆△⚶	**10:52 pm**	7:52 pm
☽☌♄		11:46 pm

Eastern Standard Time in bold type
Pacific Standard Time in medium type

AUGUST 1999

☽ Last Aspect day	EST / hr:mn / PST	asp	☽ Ingress sign day	EST / hr:mn / PST
1	**11:03 am** 8:03 am	△☿	♈ 1	**11:47 am** 8:47 am
3	**2:12 pm** 11:12 am	□☿	♉ 3	**4:08 pm** 1:08 pm
5	**4:35 pm** 1:35 pm	✶☿	♊ 5	**6:57 pm** 3:57 pm
6	**7:43 pm** 4:43 pm	△♅	♋ 7	**8:52 pm** 5:52 pm
9	**10:01 pm** 7:01 pm	☌☿	♌ 9	**10:55 pm** 7:55 pm
11	**6:09 am** 3:09 am	☌☉	♍ 11	11:22 pm
11	**6:09 am** 3:09 am	☌☉	♍ 12	**2:22 am**
13	**10:31 am** 7:31 am	✶♂	♎ 14	**8:25 am** 5:25 am
16	**4:12 pm** 1:12 pm	✶♀	♏ 16	**5:41 pm** 2:41 pm
18	10:07 pm	□♀	♐ 19	**5:32 am** 2:32 am
19	**1:07 am**	□♀	♐ 19	**5:32 am** 2:32 am
21	**2:36 pm** 11:36 am	△☉	♑ 21	**5:59 pm** 2:59 pm
23	**5:13 pm** 2:13 pm	✶♂	♒ 23	**4:49 am** 1:49 am
26	**4:31 am** 1:31 am	□♂	♓ 26	**12:49 pm** 9:49 am
28	**12:41 pm** 9:41 am	△♂	♈ 28	**6:09 pm** 3:09 pm
30	**7:39 pm** 4:39 pm	△☿	♉ 30	**9:40 pm** 6:40 pm

☽ Phases & Eclipses phase	day	EST / hr:mn / PST
4th Quarter	4	**12:26 pm** 9:26 am
●	11	18° ♌ 21'
New Moon	11	**6:09 am** 3:09 am
2nd Quarter	18	**8:48 pm** 5:48 pm
Full Moon	26	**6:48 pm** 3:48 pm

Planet Ingress	day	EST / hr:mn / PST
☿ ♌	10	**11:25 pm** 8:25 pm
♀ ♌	15	**9:11 am** 6:11 am
⚴ ♋	18	**1:22 pm** 10:22 am
☉ ♍	23	**8:51 am** 5:51 am
⚶ ♎	27	**7:14 pm** 4:14 pm
⚵ ♐	30	**4:15 am** 1:15 am
☿ ♍	31	**10:15 am** 7:15 am

Planetary Motion	day	EST / hr:mn / PST
☿ D	5	**10:20 pm** 7:20 pm
♇ D	18	**5:59 pm** 2:59 pm
♃ R	24	**8:46 pm** 5:46 pm
♄ R	29	**7:09 pm** 4:09 pm

DATE		SID.TIME	SUN	MOON	NODE	MERCURY	VENUS	MARS	JUPITER	SATURN	URANUS	NEPTUNE	PLUTO	CERES	PALLAS	JUNO	VESTA	CHIRON
S	1	20:36:39	08 ♌ 19	20 ♓ 37	12 ♌ 58	29 ♋ R 54	05 ♍ R 03	11 ♏ 21	04 ♉ 03	16 ♉ 27	15 ♒ R 05	02 ♋ R 49	07 ♐ R 50	04 ♌ 22	20 ♊ 39	26 ♏ 22	16 ♍ 59	27 ♏ 26
M	2	20:40:35	09 17	04 ♈ 05	12 58	29 27	04 58	11 52	04 07	16 30	15 03	02 48	07 49	04 49	21 11	26 26	17 27	27 27
T	3	20:44:32	10 14	17 46	12 R 58	29 06	04 50	12 22	04 12	16 33	15 00	02 46	07 48	05 16	21 42	26 29	17 55	27 27
W	4	20:48:28	11 11	01 ♉ 40	12 58	28 49	04 39	12 53	04 16	16 35	14 58	02 45	07 48	05 42	22 14	26 33	18 23	27 28
T	5	20:52:25	12 09	15 46	12 58	28 39	04 26	13 24	04 20	16 38	14 56	02 43	07 47	06 09	22 45	26 37	18 52	27 28
F	6	20:56:21	13 06	00 ♊ 02	12 D 58	28 D 35	04 11	13 55	04 23	16 40	14 53	02 41	07 47	06 36	23 17	26 41	19 20	27 29
S	7	21:00:18	14 04	14 25	12 57	28 37	03 54	14 27	04 27	16 43	14 51	02 40	07 47	07 03	23 48	26 46	19 48	27 30
S	8	21:04:15	15 01	28 52	12 57	28 46	03 34	14 59	04 30	16 45	14 48	02 38	07 46	07 30	24 20	26 51	20 17	27 31
M	9	21:08:11	15 59	13 ♋ 19	12 57	29 02	03 12	15 31	04 34	16 47	14 46	02 37	07 46	07 57	24 52	26 56	20 46	27 32
T	10	21:12:08	16 56	27 40	12 57	29 25	02 48	16 03	04 37	16 50	14 44	02 35	07 46	08 24	25 23	27 01	21 14	27 33
W	11	21:16:04	17 54	11 ♌ 51	12 R 57	29 54	02 22	16 36	04 40	16 52	14 41	02 34	07 45	08 51	25 55	27 07	21 43	27 35
T	12	21:20:01	18 52	25 47	12 56	00 ♌ 30	01 54	17 09	04 42	16 54	14 39	02 32	07 45	09 18	26 26	27 13	22 12	27 36
F	13	21:23:57	19 49	09 ♍ 25	12 55	01 13	01 24	17 42	04 45	16 55	14 36	02 30	07 45	09 44	26 58	27 20	22 40	27 37
S	14	21:27:54	20 47	22 43	12 54	02 03	00 53	18 15	04 47	16 57	14 34	02 29	07 45	10 11	27 30	27 26	23 09	27 39
S	15	21:31:50	21 44	05 ♎ 41	12 52	02 59	00 20	18 49	04 49	16 59	14 32	02 27	07 44	10 38	28 01	27 33	23 38	27 41
M	16	21:35:47	22 42	18 19	12 51	04 01	29 ♌ 46	19 22	04 51	17 00	14 29	02 26	07 44	11 05	28 33	27 40	24 07	27 42
T	17	21:39:44	23 40	00 ♏ 40	12 49	05 10	29 11	19 56	04 53	17 02	14 27	02 24	07 44	11 32	29 04	27 47	24 36	27 44
W	18	21:43:40	24 37	12 48	12 48	06 24	28 35	20 31	04 54	17 03	14 25	02 23	07 44	11 59	29 36	27 55	25 06	27 46
T	19	21:47:37	25 35	24 47	12 D 48	07 44	27 58	21 05	04 56	17 04	14 22	02 21	07 D 44	12 26	00 ♋ 07	28 03	25 35	27 48
F	20	21:51:33	26 33	06 ♐ 40	12 49	09 10	27 21	21 40	04 57	17 05	14 20	02 20	07 44	12 53	00 39	28 11	26 04	27 50
S	21	21:55:30	27 31	18 33	12 50	10 40	26 43	22 15	04 58	17 06	14 18	02 19	07 44	13 19	01 11	28 19	26 33	27 53
S	22	21:59:26	28 28	00 ♑ 30	12 52	12 15	26 06	22 50	04 58	17 07	14 15	02 17	07 44	13 46	01 42	28 28	27 03	27 55
M	23	22:03:23	29 26	12 36	12 54	13 54	25 29	23 25	04 59	17 08	14 13	02 16	07 44	14 13	02 14	28 37	27 32	27 58
T	24	22:07:19	00 ♍ 24	24 54	12 56	15 37	24 53	24 01	04 59	17 09	14 11	02 14	07 45	14 40	02 45	28 46	28 01	28 00
W	25	22:11:16	01 22	07 ♒ 27	12 R 58	17 23	24 17	24 37	04 59	17 09	14 09	02 13	07 45	15 07	03 17	28 55	28 31	28 03
T	26	22:15:13	02 20	20 17	12 58	19 12	23 43	25 13	04 R 59	17 10	14 06	02 12	07 45	15 34	03 48	29 05	29 00	28 05
F	27	22:19:09	03 17	03 ♓ 24	12 57	21 04	23 09	25 49	04 59	17 10	14 04	02 10	07 45	16 00	04 20	29 15	29 30	28 08
S	28	22:23:06	04 15	16 49	12 55	22 57	22 37	26 25	04 58	17 11	14 02	02 09	07 46	16 27	04 51	29 25	30 00	28 11
S	29	22:27:02	05 13	00 ♈ 29	12 53	24 52	22 07	27 02	04 58	17 11	14 00	02 08	07 46	16 54	05 23	29 35	00 ♎ 29	28 14
M	30	22:30:59	06 11	14 23	12 49	26 48	21 38	27 38	04 57	17 11	13 58	02 06	07 46	17 21	05 54	29 45	00 59	28 17
T	31	22:34:55	07 09	28 26	12 46	28 45	21 11	28 15	04 56	17 R 11	13 55	02 05	07 47	17 48	06 25	29 56	01 29	28 20

EPHEMERIS CALCULATED FOR 12 MIDNIGHT GREENWICH MEAN TIME. ALL OTHER DATA AND FACING ASPECTARIAN PAGE IN **EASTERN STANDARD TIME (BOLD)** AND PACIFIC STANDARD TIME (REGULAR).

SEPTEMBER 1999

1 WEDNESDAY

☽ ☌ ♄	**2:46 am**	
☽ □ ⚳	**4:52 am**	1:52 am
☽ □ ♀	**8:29 am**	5:29 am
☿ ⚻ ♆	**11:20 am**	8:20 am
☿ ⚺ ⚶	**3:44 pm**	12:44 pm
☽ ☍ ⚷	**9:49 pm**	6:49 pm
☽ ☍ ♂	**11:46 pm**	8:46 pm
☽ ☍ ⚵		9:59 pm

2 THURSDAY

☽ ☍ ⚵	**12:59 am**	
☽ △ ♆	**3:51 am**	12:51 am
☽ △ ⚶	**4:57 am**	1:57 am
☽ □ ☿	**6:32 am**	3:32 am
☽ ⚺ ♃	**8:38 am**	5:38 am
♇ ⚻ ⚴	**10:05 am**	7:05 am
☽ ☍ ♇	**1:35 pm**	10:35 am
☽ ⚺ ⚴	**1:43 pm**	10:43 am
☽ □ ☉	**5:18 pm**	2:18 pm
☿ △ ♃	**9:37 pm**	6:37 pm
☽ △ ♅	**11:44 pm**	8:44 pm

3 FRIDAY

☽ ⚺ ♄	**5:25 am**	2:25 am
☽ ⚹ ⚳	**9:11 am**	6:11 am
☽ ⚹ ♀	**9:59 am**	6:59 am
♂ ☌ ⚵	**3:11 pm**	12:11 pm
☽ ⚻ ⚷		9:46 pm
♀ ☌ ⚳		10:29 pm

4 SATURDAY

☽ ⚻ ⚷	**12:46 am**	
♀ ☌ ⚳	**1:29 am**	
☽ ⚻ ⚵	**4:26 am**	1:26 am
☽ ⚻ ♂	**4:52 am**	1:52 am
☽ ⚻ ♆	**6:33 am**	3:33 am
☽ □ ⚶	**9:35 am**	6:35 am
☿ □ ♇	**9:57 am**	6:57 am
☽ ⚹ ♃	**11:20 am**	8:20 am
☽ ⚻ ♇	**4:27 pm**	1:27 pm
☽ ⚹ ☿	**5:30 pm**	2:30 pm
☽ ☌ ⚴	**6:31 pm**	3:31 pm
☽ ⚹ ☉	**11:56 pm**	8:56 pm
☽ ⚻ ♅		11:34 pm

5 SUNDAY

☽ ⚻ ♅	**2:34 am**	
☿ ⚹ ⚴	**3:08 am**	12:08 am
☽ ⚹ ♄	**8:23 am**	5:23 am
☽ ⚺ ♀	**12:10 pm**	9:10 am
☽ ⚺ ⚳	**1:55 pm**	10:55 am
♂ ⚹ ♆	**5:31 pm**	2:31 pm

6 MONDAY

☽ △ ⚷	**4:16 am**	1:16 am
♃ ⚻ ⚶	**7:02 am**	4:02 am
☽ △ ⚵	**8:32 am**	5:32 am
☽ ☍ ♆	**9:52 am**	6:52 am
☽ △ ♂	**10:40 am**	7:40 am
☉ ⚻ ♅	**12:50 pm**	9:50 am
☽ □ ♃	**2:39 pm**	11:39 am
☽ ⚹ ⚶	**2:57 pm**	11:57 am
☽ △ ♇	**8:03 pm**	5:03 pm
☽ ⚺ ⚴		9:08 pm

7 TUESDAY

☽ ⚺ ⚴	**12:08 am**	
☽ ⚺ ☿	**5:29 am**	2:29 am
☽ ☍ ♅	**6:13 am**	3:13 am
☽ ⚺ ☉	**7:35 am**	4:35 am
☿ ⚻ ♅	**10:36 am**	7:36 am
☽ □ ♄	**12:14 pm**	9:14 am
☽ ☌ ♀	**3:31 pm**	12:31 pm
☽ ☌ ⚳	**7:42 pm**	4:42 pm

8 WEDNESDAY

☽ □ ⚷	**8:56 am**	5:56 am
☿ ☌ ☉	**9:58 am**	6:58 am
☽ □ ⚵	**1:52 pm**	10:52 am
☽ ⚻ ♆	**2:21 pm**	11:21 am
☽ □ ♂	**5:52 pm**	2:52 pm
☽ △ ♃	**7:10 pm**	4:10 pm
☽ ⚺ ⚶	**9:43 pm**	6:43 pm
☽ □ ♇		9:58 pm

9 THURSDAY

☽ □ ♇	**12:58 am**	
☿ △ ♄	**5:51 am**	2:51 am
☽ ⚹ ⚴	**7:17 am**	4:17 am
☽ ⚻ ♅	**11:18 am**	8:18 am
☽ ☌ ☉	**5:03 pm**	2:03 pm
☽ △ ♄	**5:36 pm**	2:36 pm
♂ ⚻ ♃	**7:09 pm**	**4:09 pm**
♆ ⚹ ⚵	**7:18 pm**	4:18 pm
☽ ☌ ☿	**7:34 pm**	4:34 pm
☽ ⚺ ♀	**8:44 pm**	5:44 pm
☉ △ ♄		9:19 pm

10 FRIDAY

☉ △ ♄	**12:19 am**	
☽ ⚺ ⚳	**3:17 am**	12:17 am
☿ ⚺ ⚴	**3:43 am**	12:43 am
☽ ⚹ ⚷	**3:27 pm**	12:27 pm
☽ △ ♆	**8:45 pm**	5:45 pm
☽ ⚹ ⚵	**9:13 pm**	6:13 pm
☽ ⚻ ♃		10:38 pm

11 SATURDAY

☽ ⚻ ♃	**1:38 am**	
☽ ⚹ ♂	**3:23 am**	12:23 am
☽ ☌ ⚶	**6:45 am**	3:45 am
☽ ⚹ ♇	**7:58 am**	4:58 am
☽ □ ⚴	**4:50 pm**	1:50 pm
☽ △ ♅	**6:35 pm**	3:35 pm
♀ ⚺ ☉	**7:10 pm**	4:10 pm
☽ ⚻ ♄		10:13 pm

12 SUNDAY

☽ ⚻ ♄	**1:13 am**	
☽ ⚹ ♀	**4:38 am**	1:38 am
☽ ⚺ ☉	**5:24 am**	2:24 am
☽ ⚺ ☿	**1:02 pm**	10:02 am
☽ ⚹ ⚳	**1:31 pm**	10:31 am
♇ ⚹ ⚶	**2:04 pm**	11:04 am
☿ ⚺ ⚳	**5:17 pm**	2:17 pm
☽ ⚺ ⚷		9:34 pm

13 MONDAY

☽ ⚺ ⚷	**12:34 am**	
☽ □ ♆	**5:43 am**	2:43 am
☽ ⚺ ⚵	**7:19 am**	4:19 am
♅ ⚻ ⚴	**9:44 am**	6:44 am
☽ ☍ ♃	**10:38 am**	7:38 am
☽ ⚺ ♂	**3:58 pm**	12:58 pm
☽ ⚺ ♇	**5:37 pm**	2:37 pm
☽ ⚺ ⚶	**6:47 pm**	3:47 pm

14 TUESDAY

☽ □ ♅	**4:32 am**	1:32 am
☽ △ ⚴	**5:25 am**	2:25 am
☽ ☍ ♄	**11:30 am**	8:30 am
☽ □ ♀	**3:41 pm**	12:41 pm
☽ ⚹ ☉	**9:09 pm**	6:09 pm
♂ ☌ ♇	**11:20 pm**	8:20 pm
☽ □ ⚳		11:43 pm

15 WEDNESDAY

☽ □ ⚳	**2:43 am**	
☽ ⚹ ☿	**10:24 am**	7:24 am
☽ ☌ ⚷	**12:19 pm**	9:19 am
☽ ⚹ ♆	**5:12 pm**	2:12 pm
☽ ☌ ⚵	**8:05 pm**	5:05 pm
☽ ⚻ ♃	**10:01 pm**	7:01 pm
☿ ⚹ ⚷	**11:47 pm**	8:47 pm

16 THURSDAY

☽ ☌ ♇	**5:38 am**	2:38 am
☽ ☌ ♂	**7:23 am**	4:23 am
☽ ⚹ ⚶	**9:27 am**	6:27 am
☽ ⚹ ♅	**4:37 pm**	1:37 pm
☽ ⚻ ⚴	**8:22 pm**	5:22 pm
☽ ⚻ ♄	**11:43 pm**	8:43 pm

17 FRIDAY

☽ △ ♀	**5:07 am**	2:07 am
☿ △ ♆	**8:15 am**	5:15 am
☽ □ ☉	**3:06 pm**	12:06 pm
☽ △ ⚳	**5:38 pm**	2:38 pm
☽ ⚺ ⚷		10:21 pm

18 SATURDAY

☽ ⚺ ⚷	**1:21 am**	
☽ ⚺ ♆	**5:46 am**	2:46 am
☽ □ ☿	**9:27 am**	6:27 am
☽ ⚺ ⚵	**9:56 am**	6:56 am
☽ △ ♃	**10:16 am**	7:16 am
☿ ⚹ ⚵	**1:12 pm**	10:12 am
☿ ⚻ ♃	**2:52 pm**	11:52 am
☽ ⚺ ♇	**6:17 pm**	3:17 pm
♃ ⚻ ⚵	**10:39 pm**	7:39 pm
☽ ⚺ ♂	**11:28 pm**	8:28 pm
☽ □ ⚶		9:39 pm

19 SUNDAY

☽ □ ⚶	**12:39 am**	
♂ ⚹ ⚶	**4:07 am**	1:07 am
☽ ⚺ ♅	**4:54 am**	1:54 am
☽ ☍ ⚴	**11:20 am**	8:20 am
☽ △ ♄	**11:49 am**	8:49 am
☽ ⚻ ♀	**6:38 pm**	3:38 pm
☉ ⚺ ⚳	**9:13 pm**	6:13 pm
♄ ⚹ ⚴	**9:59 pm**	6:59 pm

20 MONDAY

☽ ⚻ ⚳	**7:34 am**	4:34 am
☽ △ ☉	**8:04 am**	5:04 am
☽ ⚹ ⚷	**1:11 pm**	10:11 am
☽ ☌ ♆	**4:59 pm**	1:59 pm
☽ □ ♃	**8:57 pm**	5:57 pm
☽ ⚹ ⚵	**10:10 pm**	7:10 pm
☿ ⚹ ♇		9:11 pm

21 TUESDAY

☿ ⚹ ♇	**12:11 am**	
☽ ⚹ ♇	**5:04 am**	2:04 am
☽ △ ☿	**5:48 am**	2:48 am
☽ ⚹ ♂	**1:10 pm**	10:10 am
☽ △ ⚶	**1:28 pm**	10:28 am
☽ ☌ ♅	**2:56 pm**	11:56 am
☽ □ ♄	**9:25 pm**	6:25 pm
☽ ⚻ ⚴	**11:29 pm**	8:29 pm

22 WEDNESDAY

☽ ☍ ♀	**5:38 am**	2:38 am
☽ ☍ ⚳	**6:07 pm**	3:07 pm
☽ ⚻ ☉	**9:10 pm**	6:10 pm
♂ ⚹ ♅	**9:31 pm**	6:31 pm
☽ □ ⚷	**9:47 pm**	6:47 pm
♅ △ ⚶		9:26 pm
☽ ⚺ ♆		9:56 pm

23 THURSDAY

♅ △ ⚶	**12:26 am**	
☽ ⚺ ♆	**12:56 am**	
☽ ⚹ ♃	**4:20 am**	1:20 am
☉ ⚹ ⚷	**6:27 am**	3:27 am
☽ □ ⚵	**6:54 am**	3:54 am
☽ □ ♇	**12:23 pm**	9:23 am
☽ ⚻ ☿	**8:39 pm**	5:39 pm
☽ ⚺ ♅	**9:27 pm**	6:27 pm
☽ ⚻ ⚶	**10:18 pm**	7:18 pm
☽ □ ♂	**10:44 pm**	7:44 pm

24 FRIDAY

☿ △ ♅	**3:10 am**	12:10 am
☽ ⚹ ♄	**3:27 am**	12:27 am
☽ △ ⚴	**7:35 am**	4:35 am
☽ ⚻ ♀	**1:01 pm**	10:01 am
☿ ☌ ⚶	**4:07 pm**	1:07 pm
☉ △ ♆	**11:51 pm**	8:51 pm
☽ ⚻ ⚳		9:45 pm
☿ ⚹ ♂		10:18 pm
☽ △ ⚷		11:50 pm

25 SATURDAY

☽ ⚻ ⚳	**12:45 am**	
☿ ⚹ ♂	**1:18 am**	
☽ △ ⚷	**2:50 am**	
☽ ⚹ ♆	**5:26 am**	2:26 am
☽ ☍ ☉	**5:51 am**	2:51 am
☽ ⚺ ♃	**8:20 am**	5:20 am
☽ △ ⚵	**12:03 pm**	9:03 am
☽ △ ♇	**4:21 pm**	1:21 pm
☽ ⚹ ♅		9:49 pm

26 SUNDAY

☽ ⚹ ♅	**12:49 am**	
☽ ☍ ⚶	**3:38 am**	12:38 am
☽ △ ♂	**4:42 am**	1:42 am
☿ ⚻ ♄	**4:48 am**	1:48 am
☽ ⚺ ♄	**6:28 am**	3:28 am
☽ ☍ ☿	**6:41 am**	3:41 am
♂ ⚹ ⚶	**6:51 am**	3:51 am
☽ □ ⚴	**12:24 pm**	9:24 am
☉ ⚻ ♃	**2:30 pm**	11:30 am
☽ △ ♀	**5:34 pm**	2:34 pm

27 MONDAY

☽ △ ⚳	**4:39 am**	1:39 am
☽ ⚻ ⚷	**5:25 am**	2:25 am
☽ □ ♆	**7:36 am**	4:36 am
☽ ☌ ♃	**10:06 am**	7:06 am
☽ ⚻ ☉	**11:40 am**	8:40 am
☽ ⚻ ⚵	**2:58 pm**	11:58 am
♂ ⚻ ♄	**3:26 pm**	12:26 pm
☽ ⚻ ♇	**6:20 pm**	3:20 pm
☽ □ ♅		11:30 pm

28 TUESDAY

☽ □ ♅	**2:30 am**	
☽ ⚻ ⚶	**7:09 am**	4:09 am
☽ ☌ ♄	**7:57 am**	4:57 am
☽ ⚻ ♂	**8:50 am**	5:50 am
⚳ □ ⚷	**1:07 pm**	10:07 am
☽ ⚻ ☿	**2:21 pm**	11:21 am
☽ ⚹ ⚴	**3:43 pm**	12:43 pm
☽ □ ♀	**9:01 pm**	6:01 pm

29 WEDNESDAY

♄ ⚻ ⚶	**3:48 am**	12:48 am
☽ ☍ ⚷	**7:15 am**	4:15 am
☽ □ ⚳	**7:41 am**	4:41 am
☿ □ ⚴	**8:30 am**	5:30 am
☽ △ ♆	**9:05 am**	6:05 am
☽ ⚺ ♃	**11:16 am**	8:16 am
☽ △ ☉	**4:48 pm**	1:48 pm
☽ ☍ ⚵	**5:26 pm**	2:26 pm
♂ ⚻ ♃	**6:40 pm**	3:40 pm
☽ ☍ ♇	**7:59 pm**	4:59 pm

30 THURSDAY

☽ △ ♅	**4:05 am**	1:05 am
☉ ⚹ ⚵	**5:19 am**	2:19 am
☽ ⚺ ♄	**9:30 am**	6:30 am
☽ △ ⚶	**10:44 am**	7:44 am
☽ ☍ ♂	**1:05 pm**	10:05 am
☽ ⚺ ⚴	**7:21 pm**	4:21 pm
☽ △ ☿	**10:13 pm**	7:13 pm
☽ ⚹ ♀		10:09 pm

Eastern Standard Time in bold type
Pacific Standard Time in medium type

SEPTEMBER 1999

☽ Last Aspect

day	EST / hr:mn / PST	asp
1	11:45 am 8:45 pm	☌♂
1	11:46 am 8:46 pm	☌♂
3	9:59 am 6:59 am	✶♄
5	5:23 am 2:23 am	☌♀
7	3:31 pm 12:31 pm	☍♀
9	7:34 pm 4:34 pm	☌♀
12	4:38 am 1:38 am	✶♀
12	4:38 am 1:38 am	✶♀
15	10:24 am 7:24 am	□♀
17	3:06 pm 12:06 pm	□☉

☽ Ingress

sign	day	EST / hr:mn / PST
♊	18	2:13 am
⊗	20	12:25 am
♌	3	3:10 am
♍	5	10:57 am
♎	7	4:34 pm
♏	10	5:16 pm
♐	13	2:09 am
♑	15	1:35 am
♒	17	11:13 am

☽ Last Aspect

day	EST / hr:mn / PST	asp
17	3:06 pm 12:06 pm	□☉
20	8:04 am 5:04 am	✶♄
22	5:38 am 2:38 am	□♄
24	3:27 am 12:27 am	△♄
26	5:34 am 2:34 am	△♀
28	9:01 pm 6:01 pm	✶♀
30		10:09 pm
1	1:09 am	

☽ Ingress

sign	day	EST / hr:mn / PST
♓	18	2:13 am
♈	20	9:51 pm 6:51 pm
♉	23	2:34 am
♊	25	2:34 am
⊗	27	4:52 pm 1:52 am
♌	29	6:21 am 3:21 am
♍	1	8:32 am 5:32 am

☽ Phases & Eclipses

phase	day	EST / hr:mn / PST
4th Quarter	2	5:18 pm 2:18 pm
New Moon	9	5:03 pm 2:03 pm
2nd Quarter	17	3:06 pm 12:06 pm
Full Moon	25	5:51 am 2:51 am

Planet Ingress

	day	EST / hr:mn / PST
♂ ♐	2	2:29 pm 11:29 am
♀ ♌	16	7:53 am 4:53 am
♀ ♍	23	6:31 am 3:31 am
♀ ♍	23	7:15 am 4:15 am
♀ ♍	27	11:20 am 8:20 am

Planetary Motion

	day	EST / hr:mn / PST
♀ D	10	7:25 am 4:25 pm

Main Ephemeris

DATE	SID.TIME	SUN	MOON	NODE	MERCURY	VENUS	MARS	JUPITER	SATURN	URANUS	NEPTUNE	PLUTO	CERES	PALLAS	JUNO	VESTA	CHIRON
W 1	22:38:52	08♍07	12♍35	12♋43℞	00♍43	20♋47	28♍52	04♉℞	17♉11	13♒53℞	02♒04℞	07♐47	18♌12	06♒57	07♐	01♎59	28♍24
T 2	22:42:48	09 06	26 47	12 D	41	20	01	04	17	13 10	03	07	19	28	00	02	27
F 3	22:46:45	10 04	11♎01	12	41	20	07	04	17	13	02	07	18	41	00	02	28
S 4	22:50:42	11 01	25 15	12	41	20	46	04	17	13	00	07	19	08	00	02	31
S 5	22:54:38	12 00	09♏58	12	42	19	00	04	17	12	59	07	20	59	01	03	38
M 6	22:58:35	12 58	23 23	12	43	19	22	04	17	12	58	07	28	33	04	03	42
T 7	23:02:31	13 56	07♐54	12	44	19	38	04	17	11	57	07	54	09	16	04	45
W 8	23:06:28	14 54	21 18	12℞	45	18	02	04	17	10	56	07	21	10	28	04	49
T 9	23:10:24	15 52	04♑34	12	14	18	55	04	17	09	55	07	21	11	41	05	53
F 10	23:14:21	16 51	17 41	12	18	18	12	04	17	07	53	07	22	11	53	05	57
S 11	23:18:17	17 49	00♒56	56	59	18	27	04	17	06	52	07	22	11	06	06	01
S 12	23:22:14	18 48	13 45	48	21	18	41	05	17	02	51	07	23	12	19	07	06
M 13	23:26:11	19 46	26 18	46	23	18	55	06	16	59	50	07	23	13	32	07	10
T 14	23:30:07	20 45	08♓37	44	03	18 D	09	07	16	57	49	07	24	13	46	08	14
W 15	23:34:04	21 43	20 43	43	05	19	31	08	16	56	48	07	24	14	59	08	19
T 16	23:38:00	22 41	02♈41	41	07	19	49	08	16	54	47	07	25	15	12	09	24
F 17	23:41:57	23 40	14 34	34	00	19	00	09	16	52	46	07	25	15	27	10	28
S 18	23:45:53	24 38	26 25	25	02	19	33	09	16	46	45	08	26	16	41	10	33
S 19	23:49:50	25 37	08♉17	37	02	20♋19	52	10	16	48	45	08	00♍	16	55	11	38
M 20	23:53:46	26 35	20 14	35	19	20	16	10	16	46	44	08	27	17	10	11	42
T 21	23:57:43	27 34	02♊21	47	16	21	41	11	16	43	43	08	27	17	24	12	47
W 22	00:01:39	28 32	14 40	12	14	21	46	11	16	41	42	08	09♍	18	54	13	52
T 23	00:05:36	29 31	27 15	28	12	22	10	12	16	38	41	08	28	18	03	13	57
F 24	00:09:33	00≏30	10⊗09	35	00	23	34	13	16	36	41	08	28	19	24	14	02
S 25	00:13:29	01 28	23 25	35	16	23	57	14	16	33	40	08	29	19	42	14	08
S 26	00:17:26	02 27	07♌00	37	53	23	12	14	16	33	40	08	29	20	39	15	13
M 27	00:21:22	03 25	20 57	35	22	24	36	15	16	27	39	08	01♍	20	55	15	18
T 28	00:25:19	04 24	05♍10	34	37	24	03	16	16	24	38	08	00	20	26	16	24
W 29	00:29:15	05 22	19 34	30	25	24	34	16	16	21	38	08	12	21	42	16	29
T 30	00:33:12	06 21	04♎03	23	22	24	57	17	16	18	39	08	13	21	43	16	35

EPHEMERIS CALCULATED FOR 12 MIDNIGHT GREENWICH MEAN TIME. ALL OTHER DATA AND FACING ASPECTARIAN PAGE IN **EASTERN STANDARD TIME (BOLD)** AND PACIFIC STANDARD TIME (REGULAR).

OCTOBER 1999

1 FRIDAY

2 SATURDAY

3 SUNDAY

4 MONDAY

5 TUESDAY

6 WEDNESDAY

7 THURSDAY

8 FRIDAY

9 SATURDAY

10 SUNDAY

11 MONDAY

12 TUESDAY

13 WEDNESDAY

14 THURSDAY

15 FRIDAY

16 SATURDAY

17 SUNDAY

18 MONDAY

19 TUESDAY

20 WEDNESDAY

21 THURSDAY

22 FRIDAY

23 SATURDAY

24 SUNDAY

25 MONDAY

26 TUESDAY

27 WEDNESDAY

28 THURSDAY

29 FRIDAY

30 SATURDAY

31 SUNDAY

Eastern Standard Time in bold type
Pacific Standard Time in medium type

OCTOBER 1999

☽ Last Aspect day	EST / hr:mn / PST	asp	☽ Ingress sign day	EST / hr:mn / PST
30	10:09 pm	✱ ♀	♋ 1	**8:32 am** 5:32 am
1	**1:09 am**	✱ ♀	♋ 1	**8:32 am** 5:32 am
3	**7:53 am** 4:53 am	□ ☿	♌ 3	**12:14 pm** 9:14 am
5	**3:15 pm** 12:15 pm	☌ ♀	♍ 5	**5:40 pm** 2:40 pm
7	**12:27 pm** 9:27 am	□ ♂	♎ 7	9:52 pm
7	**12:27 pm** 9:27 am	□ ♂	♎ 8	**12:52 am**
9	9:33 pm	✱ ♂	♏ 10	**10:01 am** 7:01 am
10	**12:33 am**	✱ ♂	♏ 10	**10:01 am** 7:01 am
11	**4:42 pm** 1:42 pm	☍ ♄	♐ 12	**9:18 pm** 6:18 pm
15	**7:49 am** 4:49 am	☌ ♂	♑ 15	**10:03 am** 7:0 am

☽ Last Aspect day	EST / hr:mn / PST	asp	☽ Ingress sign day	EST / hr:mn / PST
17	**9:59 am** 6:59 am	□ ☉	♒ 17	**10:17 pm** 7:17 pm
19	9:53 pm	△ ☉	♓ 20	**7:33 am** 4:33 am
20	**12:53 am**	△ ☉	♓ 20	**7:33 am** 4:33 am
21	**11:25 pm** 8:25 pm	△ ☿	♈ 22	**12:42 pm** 9:42 am
24	**2:05 pm** 11:05 am	☌ ♃	♉ 24	**2:26 pm** 11:26 am
26	**9:22 am** 6:22 am	☍ ☿	♊ 26	**2:34 pm** 11:34 am
28	**1:55 pm** 10:55 am	✱ ♃	♋ 28	**3:09 pm** 12:09 pm
30	**4:00 pm** 1:00 pm	□ ♃	♌ 30	**5:47 pm** 2:47 pm

☽ Phases & Eclipses phase	day	EST / hr:mn / PST
4th Quarter	1	**11:03 pm** 8:03 pm
New Moon	8	**6:34 am** 3:34 am
2nd Quarter	17	**9:59 am** 6:59 am
Full Moon	24	**4:03 pm** 1:03 pm
4th Quarter	31	**7:04 am** 4:04 am

Planet Ingress	day	EST / hr:mn / PST
☿ ♏	4	9:12 pm
☿ ♏	5	**12:12 am**
♀ ♍	7	**11:51 am** 8:51 am
♂ ♑	16	**8:35 pm** 5:35 pm
⚵ ♌	17	**1:56 pm** 10:56 am
♃ ♈	22	9:49 pm
♃ ♈	23	**12:49 am**
☉ ♏	23	**3:52 pm** 12:52 pm
♇ ♏	25	**5:07 am** 2:07 am
☿ ♐	30	**3:08 pm** 12:08 pm

Planetary Motion	day	EST / hr:mn / PST
♆ D	13	**5:01 pm** 2:01 pm
♅ D	22	**10:34 pm** 7:34 pm

DATE		SID.TIME	SUN	MOON	NODE	MERCURY	VENUS	MARS	JUPITER	SATURN	URANUS	NEPTUNE	PLUTO	CERES	PALLAS	JUNO	VESTA	CHIRON
F	1	0:37:08	07 ♎ 22	21 ♊ 59	11 ♌℞ 18	23 ♎ 42	25 ♌ 28	18 ♐ 38	02 ♉℞ 49	16 ♉℞ 18	13 ♒℞ 04	01 ♒℞ 38	08 ♐ 14	01 ♍ 26	22 ♋ 11	06 ♐ 58	17 ♎ 14	00 ♐ 40
S	2	0:41:05	08 21	06 ♋ 09	11 D 16	25 13	26 06	19 20	02 43	16 15	13 03	01 38	08 16	01 52	22 40	07 14	17 45	00 46
S	3	0:45:02	09 20	20 07	11 16	26 43	26 44	20 01	02 36	16 12	13 02	01 37	08 17	02 18	23 09	07 30	18 16	00 52
M	4	0:48:58	10 19	03 ♌ 51	11 ℞ 16	28 12	27 24	20 43	02 29	16 08	13 01	01 37	08 19	02 44	23 38	07 47	18 47	00 58
T	5	0:52:55	11 18	17 24	11 16	29 41	28 04	21 25	02 22	16 05	13 00	01 37	08 20	03 10	24 07	08 03	19 18	01 04
W	6	0:56:51	12 17	00 ♍ 44	11 14	01 ♏ 09	28 46	22 07	02 15	16 01	12 59	01 36	08 21	03 35	24 35	08 20	19 50	01 10
T	7	1:00:48	13 16	13 54	11 09	02 35	29 29	22 49	02 07	15 58	12 58	01 36	08 23	04 01	25 04	08 37	20 21	01 16
F	8	1:04:44	14 16	26 52	11 02	04 01	00 ♍ 13	23 32	02 00	15 54	12 58	01 36	08 25	04 27	25 32	08 54	20 52	01 22
S	9	1:08:41	15 15	09 ♎ 38	10 53	05 26	00 58	24 14	01 53	15 50	12 57	01 36	08 26	04 52	26 00	09 11	21 23	01 28
S	10	1:12:37	16 14	22 13	10 41	06 50	01 44	24 57	01 45	15 46	12 56	01 36	08 28	05 18	26 28	09 28	21 55	01 34
M	11	1:16:34	17 13	04 ♏ 37	10 28	08 13	02 31	25 39	01 38	15 43	12 55	01 35	08 29	05 43	26 56	09 45	22 26	01 40
T	12	1:20:31	18 13	16 49	10 16	09 35	03 19	26 22	01 30	15 39	12 55	01 35	08 31	06 09	27 24	10 03	22 57	01 46
W	13	1:24:27	19 12	28 51	10 05	10 56	04 07	27 05	01 22	15 35	12 54	01 35	08 33	06 34	27 51	10 20	23 29	01 53
T	14	1:28:24	20 12	10 ♐ 46	09 56	12 16	04 56	27 48	01 14	15 30	12 54	01 D 35	08 34	06 59	28 18	10 38	24 00	01 59
F	15	1:32:20	21 11	22 35	09 50	13 35	05 47	28 31	01 06	15 26	12 53	01 35	08 36	07 24	28 46	10 56	24 31	02 06
S	16	1:36:17	22 10	04 ♑ 25	09 47	14 52	06 37	29 14	00 58	15 22	12 53	01 35	08 38	07 50	29 12	11 13	25 03	02 12
S	17	1:40:13	23 10	16 18	09 D 46	16 08	07 29	29 57	00 50	15 18	12 53	01 35	08 40	08 15	29 39	11 31	25 34	02 19
M	18	1:44:10	24 09	28 20	09 ℞ 46	17 23	08 21	00 ♑ 40	00 42	15 14	12 52	01 36	08 41	08 40	00 ♌ 06	11 50	26 06	02 25
T	19	1:48:06	25 09	10 ♒ 37	09 47	18 36	09 15	01 24	00 34	15 09	12 52	01 36	08 43	09 05	00 32	12 08	26 37	02 32
W	20	1:52:03	26 09	23 15	09 46	19 47	10 08	02 07	00 26	15 05	12 52	01 36	08 45	09 30	00 58	12 26	27 09	02 38
T	21	1:56:00	27 08	06 ♓ 16	09 44	20 57	11 03	02 51	00 18	15 00	12 52	01 36	08 47	09 54	01 24	12 44	27 40	02 45
F	22	1:59:56	28 08	19 45	09 39	22 05	11 58	03 35	00 10	14 56	12 52	01 36	08 49	10 19	01 49	13 03	28 12	02 52
S	23	2:03:53	29 08	03 ♈ 42	09 31	23 10	12 53	04 18	00 02	14 51	12 D 52	01 37	08 51	10 44	02 15	13 21	28 43	02 59
S	24	2:07:49	00 ♏ 07	18 06	09 22	24 14	13 49	05 02	29 ♈ 54	14 47	12 52	01 37	08 53	11 08	02 40	13 40	29 15	03 05
M	25	2:11:46	01 07	02 ♉ 50	09 11	25 14	14 46	05 46	29 46	14 42	12 52	01 37	08 54	11 33	03 05	13 59	29 47	03 12
T	26	2:15:42	02 07	17 46	08 59	26 12	15 43	06 30	29 38	14 37	12 52	01 38	08 56	11 58	03 30	14 18	00 ♏ 18	03 19
W	27	2:19:39	03 07	02 ♊ 46	08 49	27 07	16 41	07 14	29 29	14 33	12 52	01 38	08 58	12 22	03 55	14 37	00 50	03 26
T	28	2:23:35	04 06	17 40	08 41	27 58	17 39	07 58	29 21	14 28	12 52	01 39	09 00	12 46	04 18	14 56	01 22	03 33
F	29	2:27:32	05 06	02 ♋ 20	08 35	28 45	18 38	08 42	29 13	14 23	12 53	01 39	09 02	13 10	04 42	15 15	01 53	03 40
S	30	2:31:28	06 06	16 41	08 31	29 28	19 37	09 27	29 05	14 19	12 53	01 40	09 04	13 35	05 06	15 34	02 25	03 47
S	31	2:35:25	07 06	00 ♌ 42	08 29	00 ♐ 06	20 37	10 11	28 57	14 14	12 53	01 40	09 06	13 59	05 29	15 54	02 57	03 54

EPHEMERIS CALCULATED FOR 12 MIDNIGHT GREENWICH MEAN TIME. ALL OTHER DATA AND FACING ASPECTARIAN PAGE IN **EASTERN STANDARD TIME (BOLD)** AND PACIFIC STANDARD TIME (REGULAR).

NOVEMBER 1999

	Eastern (bold)	Pacific (medium)
1 MONDAY	9:01 am	6:01 am
	8:36 am	5:36 pm
	8:43 am	5:43 pm
		10:17 pm
		11:12 pm
2 TUESDAY	1:17 am	
	2:12 am	
	3:22 am	12:22 am
	6:48 am	3:48 am
	6:55 am	3:55 am
	11:01 am	8:01 am
	4:00 pm	1:00 pm
	5:34 pm	2:34 pm
	10:07 pm	7:07 pm
	10:52 pm	7:52 pm
		9:50 pm
3 WEDNESDAY	12:50 am	
	3:20 am	12:20 am
	6:31 am	3:31 am
	11:23 am	8:23 am
	9:03 pm	6:03 pm
4 THURSDAY	3:53 am	12:53 am
	10:11 am	7:11 am
	10:12 am	7:12 am
	4:54 am	1:54 am
	5:16 pm	2:16 pm
	5:31 pm	2:31 pm
	9:00 pm	6:00 pm
	9:05 pm	6:05 pm
5 FRIDAY	12:39 am	
	7:03 am	4:03 am
	7:39 am	4:39 am
	9:16 am	6:16 am
	10:26 am	7:26 am
	2:05 pm	11:05 am
	2:43 pm	11:43 am
	5:05 pm	2:05 pm

	Eastern (bold)	Pacific (medium)
6 SATURDAY	8:52 am	5:52 am
	11:50 am	8:50 am
	1:01 pm	10:01 am
	7:37 pm	4:37 pm
	8:11 pm	5:11 pm
		9:18 pm
		11:08 pm
7 SUNDAY	12:18 am	
	6:18 am	3:18 am
	8:59 am	5:59 am
	11:11 am	8:11 am
	7:30 pm	4:30 pm
	10:53 pm	7:53 pm
		9:57 pm
		11:48 pm
8 MONDAY	12:57 am	
	2:48 am	
	5:35 am	2:35 am
	11:48 am	8:48 am
9 TUESDAY	4:31 am	1:31 am
	4:52 am	1:52 am
	4:55 am	1:55 am
	7:50 am	4:50 am
	8:56 am	5:56 am
	10:39 pm	7:39 pm
	11:20 pm	8:20 pm
10 WEDNESDAY	6:29 am	3:29 am
	7:15 am	4:15 am
	12:00 pm	9:00 am
	1:59 pm	10:59 am
	5:42 pm	2:42 pm
	5:18 pm	2:18 pm
	7:43 pm	4:43 pm
		9:38 pm
		11:30 pm

	Eastern (bold)	Pacific (medium)
11 THURSDAY	12:38 am	
	2:30 am	
	11:53 am	8:53 am
	1:28 pm	10:28 am
	7:09 pm	4:09 pm
	8:43 pm	5:43 pm
	11:45 pm	8:45 pm
12 FRIDAY	4:01 am	1:01 am
	6:25 am	3:25 am
	8:49 am	5:49 am
	12:28 pm	9:28 am
	1:18 pm	10:18 am
	7:33 pm	4:33 pm
	7:49 pm	4:49 pm
	8:42 pm	5:42 pm
13 SATURDAY	8:08 am	5:08 am
	10:25 am	7:25 am
	10:29 am	7:29 am
	11:20 am	8:20 am
	12:13 pm	9:13 am
	5:59 pm	2:59 pm
	8:49 pm	5:49 pm
		9:08 pm
14 SUNDAY	12:08 am	
	3:54 am	12:54 am
	4:41 am	1:41 am
	9:30 am	6:30 am
	5:11 pm	2:11 pm
	6:21 pm	3:21 pm
15 MONDAY	12:58 am	
	3:08 am	12:08 am
	3:48 am	12:48 am
	7:31 am	4:31 am
	7:44 am	4:44 am
	5:04 pm	2:04 pm
	9:37 pm	6:37 pm
	11:42 pm	8:42 pm
		10:49 pm
		11:11 pm

	Eastern (bold)	Pacific (medium)
16 TUESDAY	1:49 am	
	2:11 am	
	4:04 am	1:04 am
	4:19 am	1:19 am
	10:31 am	7:31 am
	7:57 pm	4:57 pm
	8:15 pm	5:15 pm
17 WEDNESDAY	3:41 am	12:41 am
	9:34 am	6:34 am
	10:35 am	7:35 am
	11:00 am	8:00 am
	1:43 pm	10:43 am
	3:29 pm	12:29 pm
	4:11 pm	1:11 pm
	4:49 pm	1:49 pm
	9:59 pm	6:59 pm
18 THURSDAY	5:01 am	2:01 am
	6:53 am	3:53 am
	7:14 am	4:14 am
	9:02 am	6:02 am
	12:50 pm	9:50 am
	4:04 pm	1:04 pm
	5:10 pm	2:10 pm
		10:59 pm
		11:22 pm
19 FRIDAY	1:59 am	
	2:22 am	
	5:34 am	2:34 am
	9:54 am	6:54 am
	3:55 pm	12:55 pm
	7:21 pm	4:21 pm
	7:41 pm	4:41 pm
	8:39 pm	5:39 pm
	9:37 pm	6:37 pm
	10:20 pm	7:20 pm
		9:48 pm
20 SATURDAY	12:48 am	
	5:16 am	2:16 am
	10:59 am	7:59 am
	12:10 pm	9:10 am
	1:46 pm	10:46 am
	6:51 pm	3:51 pm

	Eastern (bold)	Pacific (medium)
21 SUNDAY	7:42 pm	4:42 pm
	10:48 pm	7:48 pm
		9:41 pm
	12:41 am	
	4:41 am	1:41 am
	9:43 am	6:43 am
	12:05 pm	9:05 am
	1:34 pm	10:34 am
	5:26 pm	2:26 pm
	9:41 pm	6:41 pm
	10:45 pm	7:45 pm
		9:28 pm
		10:08 pm
22 MONDAY	12:28 am	
	1:08 am	
	1:40 pm	10:40 am
	3:09 pm	12:09 pm
	5:00 pm	2:00 pm
	7:25 pm	4:25 pm
	9:24 pm	6:24 pm
		11:04 pm
23 TUESDAY	2:04 am	
	4:26 am	1:26 am
	9:09 am	6:09 am
	11:57 am	8:57 am
	8:35 pm	5:35 pm
	9:25 pm	6:25 pm
	9:43 pm	6:43 pm
	10:06 pm	7:06 pm
		10:52 pm
		11:05 pm
24 WEDNESDAY	1:52 am	
	2:05 am	
	1:58 pm	10:58 am
	2:33 pm	11:33 am
	3:26 pm	12:26 pm
	6:21 pm	3:21 pm
	11:08 pm	8:08 pm

	Eastern (bold)	Pacific (medium)
25 THURSDAY	3:30 am	12:30 am
	3:48 am	12:48 am
	4:44 am	1:44 am
	11:48 am	8:48 am
	8:36 pm	5:36 pm
	9:54 pm	6:54 pm
	10:08 pm	7:08 pm
		10:47 pm
26 FRIDAY	1:47 am	
	3:43 am	12:43 am
	7:22 am	4:22 am
	3:29 pm	12:29 pm
	5:01 pm	2:01 pm
	6:35 pm	3:35 pm
		11:37 pm
27 SATURDAY	2:37 am	
	4:52 am	1:52 am
	9:32 am	6:32 am
	1:41 pm	10:41 am
	6:28 pm	3:28 pm
	9:42 pm	6:42 pm
		9:03 pm
		9:56 pm
28 SUNDAY	12:03 am	
	12:56 am	
	5:26 am	2:26 am
	8:10 am	5:10 am
	2:37 pm	11:37 am
	8:01 pm	5:01 pm
	9:42 pm	6:42 pm
	9:43 pm	6:43 pm
	9:58 pm	6:58 pm
	10:00 pm	7:00 pm
29 MONDAY	9:05 am	6:05 am
	9:45 am	6:45 am
	6:19 pm	3:19 pm
	11:40 pm	8:40 pm
		11:42 pm

	Eastern (bold)	Pacific (medium)
30 TUESDAY	2:42 am	
	3:25 am	12:25 am
	5:37 am	2:37 am
	7:10 am	4:10 am
	2:11 pm	11:11 am
	4:27 pm	1:27 pm
		11:22 pm

Eastern Standard Time in **bold type**
Pacific Standard Time in medium type

NOVEMBER 1999

Last Aspect / Ingress

☽ Last Aspect			☽ Ingress			
day	EST / hr:mn / PST		sign day	EST / hr:mn / PST		
1	8:43 pm 5:43 pm	⚹♂	♋ 2	11:07 am 8:07 am		
3	9:03 pm 6:03 pm	△♀	♌ 4	6:56 am 3:56 am		
6	1:01 am 10:01 am	△♄	♍ 6	4:45 pm 1:45 pm		
8	9:57 am	☌♂	♎ 8	4:15 am 1:15 am		
8 12:57 pm		△♃	♏ 11	4:15 am 1:15 am		
11 11:53 am 8:53 am	△♀	♐ 11	5:30 pm 2:00 pm			
13 9:08 pm		△♄	♑ 13	5:46 am 2:46 am		
14 12:08 am		⚹♀	♒ 16	5:46 am 2:46 am		
16 10:31 am 7:31 am	△♃	♓ 18	4:21 pm 1:21 pm			
18 4:04 pm 1:04 pm	△⊙	♈ 18	10:58 pm 7:58 pm			

Last Aspect / Ingress (2)

☽ Last Aspect			☽ Ingress			
day	EST / hr:mn / PST	asp	sign day	EST / hr:mn / PST		
20	7:42 pm 4:42 pm	♂♂	♉ 8	20	10:26 pm	
20	7:42 pm 4:42 pm	△♀	♊ 21	1:26 am		
22	9:24 pm 6:24 pm	△♃	♋ 22	10:14 pm		
22	9:24 pm 6:24 pm	□♄	♌ 23	1:14 am		
24	6:21 pm 3:21 pm	△♀	♍ 25	12:29 am	9:29 pm	
24	6:21 pm 3:21 pm	□♂	♎ 26		10:18 pm	
26	6:35 pm 3:35 pm	⚹♄	♏ 27	1:18 am		
26	6:35 pm 3:35 pm	△♀	♐ 29	5:11 am	2:11 am	
28	9:43 pm 6:43 pm	△⊙	♑ 12/1	2:29 pm	9:29 am	
30	2:11 am 11:11 am					

Phases & Eclipses

☽ phase	day	EST / hr:mn / PST	
New Moon	7	10:53 am	7:53 am
2nd Quarter	16	4:04 am	1:04 am
Full Moon	23	2:04 am	11:04 pm
4th Quarter	29	6:19 am	3:19 am

Planet Ingress

		day	EST / hr:mn / PST	
♀	≏	8	9:19 pm	6:19 pm
♀	♏	22	3:12 pm	12:12 pm
⊙	♐	22	1:25 pm	10:25 am
♂	≈	26	1:56 am	10:56 pm

Planetary Motion

		day	EST / hr:mn / PST	
♀	R	4	9:51 pm	6:51 pm
♀	D	24	10:53 am	7:53 am

Ephemeris Tables

DATE	SID.TIME	SUN	MOON	NODE	MERCURY	VENUS	MARS	JUPITER	SATURN	URANUS	NEPTUNE	PLUTO	CERES	PALLAS	JUNO	VESTA	CHIRON
M 1	2:39:22	08 ♏ 06	14 ♌ 23	08 ♋R 28	00 ♐ 38	21 ♎ 37	10 ♑ 56	28 ♈R 40	14 ♉R 06	12 ≈ 54	01 ≈ 41	09 ♐ 09	14 ♍ 08	05 ♌ 23	16 ♋R 13	28 ♏ 28	04 ♐ 02
T 2	2:43:18	09 06	27 44	28	01 01	22 37	38	28 40	04	12 54	01 41	09	15	06	16	11	04 04
W 3	2:47:15	10 07	11 ♍ 11	28	01 24	23 39	13 38	28 39	13 50	12 55	01 42	09 11	15	06 47	16 32	30	04 06
T 4	2:51:11	11 07	24 23	28	01 43	24 41	37	28 28	13 57	12 55	01 43	09 13	15	06	16 52	32	04 09
F 5	2:55:08	12 07	06 ≏ 20	20 08	01 58	25 42	58	28 26	13 50	12 56	01 43	09 15	16	07 00	17 12	34	04 16
S 6	2:59:04	13 07	18	49	02 08	26 40	39	28 11	13 45	12 57	01 44	09 17	16	07	17 31	35	04 20
S 7	3:03:01	14 07	00 ♏ 11	49	02 13 R	27 48	15 24	28	13 40	12 57	01 45	09 19	16 45	07	17 51	38	04 23
M 8	3:06:57	15 08	12 01	07	02 11 R	28 51	58	28	13 35	12 58	01 46	09 21	16	08 04	18 11	39 ♏	04 26
T 9	3:10:54	16 08	24 01	51	02 03 R	29 58	16 32	27 56	13 30	12 59	01 47	09 26	17	08 25	18 31	41	04 31
W 10	3:14:51	17 09	06 ♐ 03	20 00	01 48	01 ♏ 00	07	27 48	13 25	01 00	01 48	09 28	17	08 45	18 51	43	04 38
T 11	3:18:47	18 09	18	59	01 27	02 02	41	27 41	13 21	01 01	01 48	09 30	17 45	09 06	19 11	44	04 44
F 12	3:22:44	19 09	00 ♑ 59	47	01 01 R	03 04	17 34	27 32	13 16	01 02	01 49	09 32	18	09 27	19 31	46	04 50
S 13	3:26:40	20 12	18	47	00 34	04 06	25	27 27	13 11	01 03	01 50	09 34	18	09 48	19 52	48	04 56
S 14	3:30:37	21 09	24	38	00 09	05 07	18 09	27 20	13 08	06	01 04	01 51	09 37	19	10 09	20 12	50
M 15	3:34:33	22 11	06 ≈ 44	42	29 ♏ 45 D	06 08	44	27 13	13 03	04	01 05	01 52	09 39	19	10 31	20 32	52
T 16	3:38:30	23 13	18	41	29 24 R	07 08	19 21	27 00	12 59	59	01 06	01 54	09 43	20	10 52	20 53	54
W 17	3:42:26	24 14	00 ♓ 54	08	29 08	08 08	56	27	12 57	52	01 08	01 55	09 46	20	11 14	21 13	56
T 18	3:46:23	25 16	13	08	28 57	09 06	20 33	27	12 56	47	01 09	01 56	09 48	20	11 35	21 34	57
F 19	3:50:20	26 17	25	26	28 50 D	10 04	21 12	27	12 52	43	01 10	01 57	09 50	20	11 57	21 55	13 59
S 20	3:54:16	27 18	08 ♈ 14	09 47	28 50 R	10 59	49	27	12 50	38	01 12	01 58	09	21	12 19	22 15	14 01
S 21	3:58:13	28 20	21 20	26	28 54	11 54	22 27	26	12 48	33	01 13	01 59	09 53	21	12 40	22 36	14 03
M 22	4:02:09	29 21	04 ♉ 54	44	29 02	12 46	23 04	26	12 45	29	01 14	02 01	09 55	21 39	13 02	22 57	14 05
T 23	4:06:06	00 ♐ 23	18	50	29 14 R	13 36	44	26	12 43	24	01 16	02 02	09 57	21	13 24	23 18	14 44
W 24	4:10:02	01 24	02 ♊ 42	19	29 27	14 23	23	26	12 41	20	01 17	02 03	10 00	22	13 48	23 39	14 07
T 25	4:13:59	02 26	17	33	29 41	15 08	06	26	12 38	16	01 19	02 05	10 02	22	14 00	24 00	14 09
F 26	4:17:55	03 27	01 ♋ 57	05	29 58	15 49	48	26	12 36	14	01 20	02 06	10 04	22 48	14 21	24 21	14 48
S 27	4:21:52	04 29	16	04	00 ♐ 04	16 27	24 30	25	12 34	07	01 22	02 08	10 06	23	14 43	24 42	15
S 28	4:25:49	05 30	01 ♌ 02	26 R	18	17 01	25 13	25	12 32	05	01 24	02 09	10 08	23	52	25 04	17 48
M 29	4:29:45	06	16	24	35	17 31	58	25	12 30	03 58	01 26	02 10	10 11	23	13	25 25	18 50
T 30	4:33:42	07 18	00 ♍ 49	40	05 R	17 56	50	25 45	12 28	54	01 28	02 11	10 13	24	14	26 07	20 38

EPHEMERIS CALCULATED FOR 12 MIDNIGHT GREENWICH MEAN TIME. ALL OTHER DATA AND FACING ASPECTARIAN PAGE IN **EASTERN STANDARD TIME (BOLD)** AND PACIFIC STANDARD TIME (REGULAR).

DECEMBER 1999

1 WEDNESDAY
2:22 am
4:15 am — 1:15 pm
4:16 am — 1:16 pm
4:46 am — 1:45 pm
6:08 am — 3:08 pm
4:45 pm — 5:56 pm
8:56 pm — 7:30 pm
10:30 pm

2 THURSDAY
12:37 am
4:08 am
4:20 am
5:13 am
7:55 pm
2:27 am — 11:27 am
4:40 pm
6:37 pm — 3:37 pm

3 FRIDAY
3:56 am — 12:56 am
4:15 am — 1:15 am
5:10 am — 2:21 pm
11:13 am — 8:10 am
11:45 am — 10:03 am
1:45 pm — 10:45 am
3:38 pm — 12:38 pm
5:43 pm — 2:43 pm
6:04 pm — 3:04 pm
9:56 pm

4 SATURDAY
12:56 am
3:08 am — 12:08 am
11:50 am — 11:54 am
1:20 pm — 4:14 pm
8:45 pm — 6:31 pm
9:31 pm — 6:07 pm
10:07 pm
11:32 pm

5 SUNDAY
1:39 am
4:25 am — 1:25 am
6:26 am — 3:26 am
9:30 pm — 1:30 pm
— 8:41 pm
— 10:35 pm
— 11:14 pm
2:14 am

6 MONDAY
1:09 am
1:20 am — 2:01 am
5:01 am — 4:21 am
12:17 am — 9:17 am
3:15 pm — 12:15 pm

7 TUESDAY
12:38 am
12:45 am
2:43 am
4:43 am
4:49 am
6:31 am
11:12 am
12:32 pm
2:23 pm
3:37 pm

8 WEDNESDAY
6:53 am
9:53 am — 10:36 am
1:36 pm — 2:21 pm
5:21 pm — 4:25 pm
7:25 pm — 7:00 pm
10:00 pm

9 THURSDAY
1:12 am
4:12 am — 1:47 pm
4:44 am — 2:16 pm
4:47 am — 5:45 pm
8:45 pm — 6:31 pm
9:31 pm — 7:07 pm
10:07 pm

10 FRIDAY
12:18 am
3:18 am — 3:41 am
6:41 am — 9:09 am
12:09 pm — 1:23 pm
4:23 pm — 10:35 pm
11:41 pm — 11:14 pm

11 SATURDAY
1:25 am
12:35 am — 3:26 am
6:26 am — 8:17 am
11:17 am — 1:35 pm
2:53 pm — 3:34 pm
10:20 pm

12 SUNDAY
2:58 am
3:24 am — 12:49 pm
6:26 pm — 7:15 pm
10:15 pm — 10:19 pm
1:19 am — 12:47 pm
3:47 pm — 2:08 pm
5:08 pm — 4:09 pm
7:09 pm

13 MONDAY
5:42 am — 2:42 pm
1:46 pm — 10:46 am
3:56 pm — 12:56 pm
5:48 pm — 2:48 pm
10:41 pm — 7:41 pm
10:45 pm

14 TUESDAY
1:45 am — 1:18 am
4:18 am — 2:59 am
5:59 am — 5:42 am
8:42 am — 2:30 pm
5:30 pm — 4:41 pm
7:41 pm — 8:21 pm
8:21 pm — 8:52 pm
10:52 pm

15 WEDNESDAY
2:01 am
2:33 am — 12:15 pm
5:07 am — 2:07 pm
3:15 pm — 11:43 am
2:43 pm — 4:50 pm
7:50 pm — 7:29 pm
10:29 pm — 11:58 pm

16 THURSDAY
2:58 am — 5:12 am
8:12 am — 7:13 am
10:13 am — 8:22 am
11:22 am

17 FRIDAY
12:59 am
2:56 am — 3:24 am
3:49 am — 4:43 am
7:43 am — 8:15 am
11:15 am — 3:00 pm
6:00 pm — 4:08 pm
7:08 pm — 9:12 pm

18 SATURDAY
12:12 am
5:03 am — 2:03 am
9:34 am — 6:34 am
10:41 am — 7:41 am
12:27 pm — 9:27 am
4:19 pm — 1:19 pm
4:43 pm — 1:43 pm
11:52 pm — 8:52 pm

19 SUNDAY
4:27 am — 1:27 am
5:57 am — 2:57 am
7:53 am — 4:53 am
11:14 am — 8:14 am
1:29 pm — 10:29 am
2:43 pm — 11:43 am
5:46 pm — 2:46 pm

20 MONDAY
3:41 am — 1:41 am
9:53 am — 6:53 am
12:21 pm — 9:09 am
3:09 pm — 12:09 pm
2:05 pm
5:53 pm — 2:53 pm
5:54 pm — 3:34 pm

21 TUESDAY
4:57 am — 1:57 am
5:37 am — 2:37 am
6:08 am — 3:08 am
11:13 am — 8:13 am
1:03 pm — 10:03 am
1:05 pm — 10:17 am
1:17 pm — 3:29 pm
6:29 pm — 4:57 pm
7:57 pm

22 WEDNESDAY
4:03 am — 1:03 am
12:31 pm — 9:31 am
1:15 pm — 10:15 am
3:12 pm — 12:12 pm
4:22 pm — 1:22 pm
6:54 pm — 3:54 pm

23 THURSDAY
4:28 am — 1:28 am
4:38 am — 1:38 am
5:23 am — 2:23 am
9:32 am — 6:34 am
10:27 am — 7:27 am
10:32 am — 9:01 am
12:01 pm — 5:28 pm
8:28 pm — 6:07 pm
9:07 pm — 6:40 pm
9:40 pm — 6:48 pm
9:48 pm — 6:49 pm
9:49 pm

24 FRIDAY
3:31 am — 12:31 am
2:43 pm — 11:43 am
3:44 pm — 12:44 pm
3:49 pm — 12:49 pm
4:49 pm — 1:17 pm
5:21 pm — 2:21 pm
8:02 pm — 5:02 pm
— 9:01 pm

25 SATURDAY
12:01 am
4:49 am — 1:49 am
5:10 am — 2:10 am
5:51 am — 2:51 am
11:17 am — 1:30 pm
12:19 pm — 9:19 am
11:51 pm — 8:31 pm

26 SUNDAY
12:16 am
3:34 am — 12:34 am
5:07 am — 2:07 am
1:59 pm — 10:59 am
6:46 pm — 3:46 pm
6:56 pm — 4:04 pm
7:04 pm — 6:58 pm
9:58 pm — 7:04 pm
10:04 pm — 9:03 pm
— 10:04 pm

27 MONDAY
12:03 am
1:04 am — 1:16 pm
4:16 am — 4:57 pm
7:57 am — 5:53 pm
8:53 am — 6:18 pm
9:18 am — 12:10 pm
3:10 pm — 12:37 pm
3:37 pm — 6:39 pm
9:39 pm

28 TUESDAY
9:57 am — 6:57 pm
10:15 am — 7:15 pm
11:54 am — 8:54 pm
1:52 pm — 10:52 pm
3:01 pm — 12:01 am
3:15 pm — 12:15 pm
8:59 pm — 5:59 pm
— 9:59 pm
— 11:11 pm

29 WEDNESDAY
12:59 am
2:11 am — 12:19 pm
3:19 am — 5:08 am
9:05 am — 6:05 am
2:52 pm — 11:52 am
4:30 pm — 1:30 pm
4:35 pm — 1:35 pm
10:31 pm — 7:31 pm
10:56 pm — 7:56 pm

30 THURSDAY
3:59 am — 12:59 am
7:13 am — 4:13 am
10:35 am — 7:35 am
9:16 pm
10:51 pm

31 FRIDAY
5:02 am — 2:02 am
5:08 am — 2:08 am
8:31 am — 5:31 am
10:51 am — 7:51 am
1:04 pm — 10:04 am
3:44 pm — 12:44 pm
8:04 pm — 5:04 pm
— 9:35 pm
— 10:11 pm

Eastern Standard Time in bold type
Pacific Standard Time in medium type

DECEMBER 1999

☽ Last Aspect
	EST / hr:mn / PST	asp
30	2:11 am 11:11 am	⚹ ♀
2	6:04 pm 3:04 pm	♂ ♀
5	9:30 pm 6:30 pm	□ ♃
7	1:36 pm 10:36 am	△ ♀
10	11:14 am	⚹ ♄
11	2:14 am	
13	1:46 pm 10:46 am	△ ♃
15	7:50 pm 4:50 pm	□ ♀
18	5:03 am 2:03 am	△ ⊙
19	5:46 pm 2:46 pm	□ ♂

☽ Ingress
sign	day	EST / hr:mn / PST
♏	1	12:29 pm 9:29 am
♐	3	10:36 pm 7:36 pm
♑	6	10:28 am 7:28 am
♒	8	11:14 pm 8:14 pm
♓	11	11:59 am 8:59 am
♈	13	11:18 pm 8:18 pm
♉	16	7:30 am 4:30 am
♊	18	11:45 am 8:45 am
♋	20	12:39 pm 9:39 am

☽ Last Aspect
	EST / hr:mn / PST	asp
22	2:11 am 1:03 am	⚹ ♀
24	3:31 am 12:31 am	□ ♀
26	5:07 am 2:07 am	△ ♀
28	1:52 pm 10:52 am	⚹ ♀
30	10:35 am 7:35 am	△ ♂

☽ Ingress
sign	day	EST / hr:mn / PST
♌	22	11:52 am 2:32 pm
♍	24	11:32 am 8:32 am
♎	26	1:34 pm 10:34 am
♏	28	7:15 pm 4:15 pm
♏	30	4:37 am 1:37 am

☽ Phases & Eclipses
phase	day	EST / hr:mn / PST
New Moon	7	5:32 pm 2:32 pm
2nd Quarter	15	7:50 am 4:50 pm
Full Moon	22	12:31 pm 9:31 am
4th Quarter	29	9:05 am 6:05 am

Planet Ingress
	day	EST / hr:mn / PST
♀ ♏	5	5:41 am 2:41 am
⚹ ♒	10	2:09 pm 11:09 am
♂ ♒	10	9:09 pm 6:09 pm

Planet Ingress
	day	EST / hr:mn / PST
♀ ♎	2	5:32 pm 2:32 pm
☽ ♎	5		
⚹ ♐	15	
⊙ ♑	21	
♀ ♐	26	2:44 am 2:44 am
♀ ♐	30	11:54 am 8:54 am
♀ ♑	31	1:48 am 10:48 pm

Planetary Motion
	day	EST / hr:mn / PST
♃ R	15	5:56 pm 2:56 pm
♂ D	20	10:23 am 7:23 am

DATE	SID. TIME	SUN	MOON	NODE	MERCURY	VENUS	MARS	JUPITER	SATURN	URANUS	NEPTUNE	PLUTO	CERES	PALLAS	JUNO	VESTA	CHIRON
W 1	4:37:38	08 ✗ 42	20 ♍ 42	05 ♋ R 32	18 ♏ 16	24 ♎ 17	03 ♒ 37	25 ♈ R 26	11 ♉ R 50	13 ♒ 30	02 ♒ 02	10 ✗ 16	15 ♎ 12	24 ♎ 24	26 ♏ 28	19 ♑ R 14	07 ✗ 45
Th 2	4:41:35	09 43	03 ♎ 18	05 05	19 28	25 26	04 29	25 26	11 46	13 32	02 02	10 18	15 20	24 34	26 50	19 16	07 45
F 3	4:45:31	10 44	15 54	05 54	20 39	26 35	05 22	25 26	11 42	13 34	02 02	10 20	15 31	24 45	27 11	20 08	07 46
S 4	4:49:28	11 45	28 21	05 37	21 45	27 45	05 55	25 D 28	11 38	13 35	02 02	10 23	15 31	24 51	27 33	20 08	07 47
S 5	4:53:24	12 46	10 ♏ 18	05	23	28	06	25	11	13	02	10	15	24	27	21	08
M 6	4:57:21	13 48	22	04	24	01 ♏	07	25	11	13	02	10	15	25	28	21	08
T 7	5:01:18	14 49	04 ♐ 06	04	25	02	08	25	11	13	02	10	16	25	28	22	08
W 8	5:05:14	15 50	16	04	26	03	09	25	11	13	02	10	16	25	29	22	08
Th 9	5:09:11	16 51	28	04	27	05	10	25	11	13	02	10	16	25	29	23	08
F 10	5:13:07	17 53	10 ♑ 38	04	28	06	11	25	11	13	02	10	16	25	00 ♐	23	09
S 11	5:17:04	18 54	22	04	29	07	12	25	11	13	02	10	16	25	00	24	09
S 12	5:21:00	19	03 ♒	04	30	08	13	25	11	13	02	10	16	25	01	24	09
M 13	5:24:57	20	15	04	31	10	14	25	11	13	02	10	16	26	01	25	09
T 14	5:28:54	21	27	04	31	11	15	25	11	13	02	10	16	26	02	25	09
W 15	5:32:50	22	09 ♓	04	32	12	16	25	11	13	02	10	16	26	02	26	10
Th 16	5:36:47	23	21	04	33	14	17	25	10	13	02	10	15	26	03	27	10
F 17	5:40:43	24	03 ♈	04 R	33	15	18	25	10	13	03	10	15	26	04	27	10
S 18	5:44:40	25	16	04	33 R	16	19	25	10	13	03	10	15	26	04	28	10
S 19	5:48:36	26	28	04	37	18	20	25	10	14	03	11	15	27	05	28	10
M 20	5:52:33	27	11 ♉	04	30	19	21	25 D	10	14	03	11	15	27	05	29	10
T 21	5:56:29	28	24	04	28	20	22	25	10	14	03	11	15	27	06	29 ✗	11
W 22	6:00:26	29	08 ♊	04	27	22	23	25	10	14	03	11	15	27	06	00 ✗	11
Th 23	6:04:23	00 ♑	22	04	26	23	24	25	10	14	03	11	14	28	07	01	11
F 24	6:08:19	01	06 ♋	04	25	24	25	25	10	14	03	11	14	28	08	01	11
S 25	6:12:16	02	20	04 D	25	26	26	25	10	14	03	11	14	28	09	02	11
S 26	6:16:12	03	05 ♌	04	25 R	27	27	25	10	14	03	11	14	28	09	02	11
M 27	6:20:09	04	19	03	25	28	28	25	10	14	03	11	13	28	10	03	11
T 28	6:24:05	05	04 ♍	03 R	24	00 ✗	29	25	10	14	04	11	13	28	11	03	11
W 29	6:28:02	06	18	03	23	01	00 ♓	25	10	14	04	11	13	28	12	04	11
Th 30	6:31:58	07	02 ♎	03	22	03	01	25	11	14	04	11	13	28	12	04	11
F 31	6:35:55	08	16	03	21	04	02	25	11	14	04	11	13	28	13	05	11

LLEWELLYN COMPUTERIZED ASTROLOGICAL SERVICES

Llewellyn has been a leading authority in astrological chart readings for more than 30 years. We feature a wide variety of readings with the intent to satisfy the needs of any astrological enthusiast. **Be sure to give accurate and complete birth data on the following order form including exact time (A.M. or P.M.), date, year, city, county and country of birth. Note: Noon will be used as your birthtime if you don't provide an exact time. Check your birth certificate for this information! Llewellyn will not be responsible for mistakes from inaccurate information.**

Simple Natal Chart
Learn the locations of your midpoints and aspects, elements, and more. Discover your planets and house cusps, retrogrades, and other valuable data necessary to make a complete interpretation. Matrix Software programs and designs The Simple Natal Chart printout. **APS03-119 (2 pages)** $5.00

Personality Profile
Our most popular report! What makes you tick? This basic profile describes your "astrological self"—from your habits and outlook to your secret drives and inner needs! **APS03-503 (13 pages)** $20.00

Life Progression
As you progress through life, so does your horoscope. Discover what influences, challendges and opportunities await you in the next 12 months. This report forecasts your best bets for success in love, career, health and money. **Specify current residence. APS03-507 (15 pages)** $20.00

Compatibility Profile
What do the stars say about the two of you? Obtain startling revelations about the strengths, trouble spots and unique dynamics within your relationship. Send birth data for both persons. Indicate each person's gender and type of relationship (romance, business, etc.). **APS03-504 (18 pages)** $30.00

Personal Relationship Interpretation
What do you truly need and want from your relationships? Find out why certain people attract you and others leave you cold. Uncover your ideal partner in any kind of relationship—work, family, friends, or romantic.
APS03-506 .... $20.00

Ultimate Astro-Profile
Our most deluxe report is the closest thing to having your own personal astrologer! Your personal qualities and talents, drives and needs unfold in a 50-page booklet all about you! **APS03-505 (50 pages)** $40.00